Professional Guide to

Alcoholic Beverages

Robert A. Lipinski
Kathleen A. Lipinski

Van Nostrand Reinhold / NEW YORK

Library of Congress Catalog Card Number 88-5721
ISBN 0-442-25837-2

Printed in the United States of America

Designed by The Total Book

Van Nostrand Reinhold
115 Fifth Avenue
New York, New York 10003

Chapman & Hall
2-6 Boundary Row
London SE1 8HN, England

Thomas Nelson Australia
102 Dodds Street
South Melbourne, Victoria 3205, Australia

Nelson Canada
1120 Birchmount Road
Scarborough, Ontario M1K 5G4, Canada

16 15 14 13 12 11 10 9 8 7 6 5 4

Library of Congress Cataloging in Publication Data
Lipinski, Robert A.
  Professional guide to alcoholic beverages.

  Bibliography: p.
  Includes index.
  1. Alcoholic beverages. I. Lipinski, Kathleen A.
II. Title.
TP505.L56 1989   663'.1   88-5721
ISBN 0-442-25837-2

To our son, Johnnie:
May he always know the best.
And to our parents, for always giving us their best.

Contents

Foreword

Late in the 1970s, Banfi Vintners suffered a twinge of corporate conscience. We reviewed our societal role and found that we had been donating, year after year, to a growing list of good causes, national and local—and we still do—yet at that time we were doing nothing of direct benefit to the industry that had spawned our success. Our concern was not simply for the wine business itself but the whole hospitality trade. Obviously, some shifting of priorities was in order.

We addressed two questions: How could we wisely invest in the future development and progress of the hospitality field? And, equally important to us, how could we make that investment meaningful in human terms? The answer had to be found in the people who will shape the destiny of our trade in decades ahead. This led us to endow schools with hospitality-oriented curricula—such as Cornell's School of Hotel Administration, The Culinary Institute of America, Johnson & Wales College, and the University of Nevada (Las Vegas)—and to provide financial support for promising students at these and eight other schools through scholarships, fellowships, and grants-in-aid.

Our objectives are twofold: to help raise the standards of U.S. hotel and restaurant operations through a better and more widely informed executive staff, and to instill in these executives a knowledge of the fine wines of the world and an appreciation of what those wines truly are: a food that should be produced today from the healthiest of grapes under the most sanitary conditions achievable through advanced vinicultural technologies.

Of course, achievement of these goals depends upon how effectively the ideas are put forth by academia. Brilliant, colorful classroom lectures invariably inspire, but the backbone of solid education is still the textbook. Nothing registers a deeper, more permanent impression than the printed word.

Fortuitously, along come a couple of budding and well-qualified authors, Bob and Kathy Lipinski, whom we are pleased to find advancing goals identical to Banfi's through the convenience of a single definitive reference and textbook. I suspect that a library could be filled with the many excellent volumes published in recent years on hospitality management techniques, and hardly a day seems to pass when a new book on wine fails to achieve critical acclaim. But we were unaware, until now, of any scholars attempting to examine all facets of the hospitality business between the covers of a handy volume.

The Lipinskis can be credited with a literary feat: they have produced a solid technical work absent of the heavy, ponderous style of the normal textbook. The pages of *A Professional Guide to Alcoholic Beverages* are flavored with history, anecdotes, and no small amount of romance, especially in the treatment of the wines of the United States, Italy, and France. In easily readable language, the authors appeal to the widest possible audience: institutions of higher learning, their faculties and students, hotel food and beverage directors, restaurateurs, their chefs and barmen, even the casual reader seeking to learn a little more about wine and other alcoholic beverages.

In ancient Roman times, the orator and philosopher Cicero offered wise counsel: "Before beginning, prepare carefully." The Lipinskis took him seriously. Their presentation reflects years of study and experience, Bob's as a professor at the New York Institute of Technology, a winewriter, and, admittedly of amateur standing, a viticulturist and winemaker; and Kathy's as an educator in the medical science field. The hospitality business—and the alcoholic beverage trade, in particular—are indebted to them.

John Mariani, Jr.
Chairman and Chief Executive Officer
Banfi Vintners
Old Brookville, New York
and Montalcino
Tuscany, Italy

Preface

When we first thought of writing a book about alcoholic beverages, we assumed that countless texts already existed that were suitable for classroom instruction. After researching those that were currently available, however, we found that most of them amply covered bar service management, cost control, purchasing, and bartending, but that the beverages themselves were given only cursory coverage, and the material which was presented was often inaccurate or outdated. Books that did cover alcoholic beverages (distilled spirits, wines, and beers) gave little information about running a beverage facility. To learn about beverages, as well as about cost control and management of a beverage facility, it was necessary to buy two books. We have written this volume in an attempt to rectify that situation.

Our overall objective is to present comprehensive, in-depth information relative to running a facility to those people currently involved or planning to become involved in the alcoholic beverage industry. Individuals can become knowledgeable about beverage management through both controls and knowledge of the beverages.

The first part of the book discusses alcoholic beverages; the second half looks at the management or running of a facility. The reason for this format is simple: one cannot purchase, market, merchandise, or sell a product that one doesn't know, and the more one knows about the product, the easier the sale.

We have divided the book into 14 chapters, which can be adapted to most educational curricula encompassing 14 to 16 weeks of instruction. The remaining 2 weeks could utilize those chapters of specialized interest as well as the 6 appendixes. An instructor's manual is available from the publisher.

Acknowledgments

We would like to thank the many people, wineries, distilleries, breweries, public relations firms, and so on, who directly and indirectly contributed to making this book possible.

Among those who directly helped us are Carmel J. Tintle, vice president of public relations at Banfi Vintners; Paul Gillette, editor and publisher of *The Wine Investor*; Don Sebastiani, CEO, and Jim Knapp, director of communications, Sebastiani Vineyards, California; Jim Turley, New York Institute of Technology; Tom Bloom, director of Hospitality Management, California State Polytechnic University; Peter M. F. Sichel, H. Sichel Söhne, Inc.; Anne Luther, senior vice president, Moët-Hennessy; Michaela K. Rodeno, vice president of marketing and communications, Domaine Chandon; Donald K. Beaver, national retail sales department, and Bradley M. Coleman, national draft beer manager, Miller Brewing Company; Augusto Marchini, Italian Wine Center; Lucio Caputo, International Trade Center, Inc.; Rory P. Callahan, New York Bureau of the California Wine Institute; Carol Sullivan, German Wine Information Bureau; Brian Abbott, Bozell, Jacobs, Kenyon & Eckhardt; Linda Mann, Baron Philippe de Rothschild, Inc.; Edward L. Pohlman, Libbey Glass Company; Terry Yacona, Plastic Bottle Information Bureau; Scott L. Sunshine, Cognac Information Bureau; Hazel Carr, the Scotch Whisky Information Center; and Mary Lyons and Kathleen Talbert, Food & Wines from France.

We would also like to thank the following persons and companies: Francis X. Brown, dean, School of Hotel Administration and Culinary Arts, New York Institute of Technology; Angelo Papagni, Papagni Vineyards, California; Korbel California Champagne Cellars; Niki Singer, Niki Singer, Inc.; Jill Davis, winemaker, Buena Vista Vineyards, California; Karen Keehn, McDowell Vineyards, California; Marsha J. Palanci, director of public relations, Schieffelin & Somerset Co.; Joseph Seagram Sons & Co.; Sterling Vineyards, California; Simi Winery, California; Irving Smith "Smitty" Kogan, Champagne News & Information Bureau;

Weibel Winery, California; Fromm & Sichel, Inc.; *Impact Wine and Spirits Newsletter*; the National Restaurant Association; *Nation's Restaurant News*; Vlasic Pickles; Holiday Inn; and DISCUS (Distilled Spirits Council of the United States).

In addition, we would like to thank the following reviewers for their valuable contributions: Raymond A. Dault, Purdue University, Indianapolis, Indiana; Christopher C. Muller, Cornell University, Ithaca, New York; John M. Wolper, Mercyhurst College, Erie, Pennsylvania; Morton Hochstein; Karen MacNeil; Jack Miller; Robert Abrams, Jr., Penn Valley Community College, Kansas City, Missouri; John A. Lombardo, Lombardo's Restaurant, Kansas City, Missouri; and Robert Bennett, Delaware County Community College, Media, Pennsylvania.

A special thanks goes to our editor Cindy Zigmund for her patience and many well thought out and helpful suggestions. We would also like to thank Kate Scheinman of the The Total Book for all her help.

1

Grape Growing and Winemaking

This chapter discusses:

- The various types of grapevines and grape varieties grown throughout the world and the climatic conditions needed for growth.
- Grape growing.
- Methods of harvesting ripe grapes.
- The winemaking process.
- The aging of wines and barrel usage.
- Blending, bottling, and cork closures.

Grape growing and winemaking have been traced as far back as 8000 B.C., and although modern technology has presented wineries with the most sophisticated equipment and measuring devices, the basic methods of grape cultivation and winemaking remain largely unchanged.

Winemaking continues to be a fascinating art, tried by many but mastered by few. As modern technology expands, so does our knowledge of the intricacies involved in winemaking. We have come a long way since the days of uncontrolled fermentations producing mostly harsh, highly alcoholic, coarse wines, often resembling vinegar; but with all the modern advances we are really just scratching the surface of what is left to be known.

Grape Growing

The descriptive study, identification, and classification of grapevines is known as *ampelography*, from the Greek word *ampelidacedes*. The word

1

Vitis, which precedes the terms *vinifera, labrusca,* and *rotundifolia,* is Latin for vine. The earliest known variety of vine species, *Vitis sezannensis*, was probably growing some 60 million years ago.

Although there are more than 8,000 grape varieties in the world, most of them are not suitable for the production of fine wine, nor are their parent vine species highly regarded. For the production of fine wine, the most prominent grapevine species are *Vitis vinifera, Vitis labrusca,* and French-American hybrids.

Vitis Vinifera

Also referred to as the European or California grapevine species the *Vitis vinifera* grapevines produce the grapes whose names most consumers are familiar with. Some examples of *Vitis vinifera* grapes are given below.

White	*Red*
Aligoté	Alicante-Bouschet
Chardonnay	Barbera
Chenin Blanc	Cabernet Franc
Emerald Riesling	Cabernet Pfeffer
Flora	Cabernet Sauvignon
Folle Blanche	Carignane
French Colombard	Carmine
Gewürztraminer	Carnelian
Green Hungarian	Charbono
Grey Riesling	Centurion
Málaga	Gamay-Beaujolais
Melon de Bourgogne	Grenache
Müller-Thurgau	Grignolino
Muscadelle	Malbec
Muscat of Alexandria	Merlot
Muscat-Ottonel	Mission
Pinot Blanc	Napa Gamay
Pinot Gris	Nebbiolo
Sauvignon Blanc	Petite Sirah
Scheurebe	Petit Verdot
Sémillon	Pinot Meunier
Sylvaner	Pinot Noir

Thompson Seedless
Trebbiano
Ugni Blanc
White Riesling

Pinot St. George
Royalty
Rubired
Ruby Cabernet
Sangiovese
Tinta Madeira
Zinfandel

Vitis Labrusca

This grapevine species is often confused with Lambrusco (a semidry red wine from Emilia-Romagna, Italy), although it produces wines with an intense varietal, berrylike character. *Vitis labrusca* grapevines are native to the East Coast of the United States and have had their share of bad press; they produce wines that are often associated with being overly "grapy" or "foxy" (the latter is a name with no proved origin, although some wine makers feel that the name was given because foxes and deer enjoy eating the grapes). Some examples of *Vitis labrusca* grapes are listed below.

White	*Red*
Diamond	Agawam
Dutchess	Alexander
Elvira	Black Pearl
Missouri Riesling	Campbell's Early
Niagara	Catawba
Noah	Clinton
	Concord
	Cynthiana
	Delaware
	Diana
	Fredonia
	Iona
	Isabella
	Ives
	Lenoir

White	Red
	Pierce
	Steuben

French-American Hybrids

These are basically crossings between the European *Vitis vinifera* and the native *Vitis labrusca* vines. They were initially developed to combine the qualities of the *labrusca* and *vinifera* vines, as the latter were at that time believed not to be winter hardy. The following are some examples of French-American hybrids:

White	Red
Aurore	Baco Noir
Cayuga	Cascade
Melody	Chambourcin
Seyval Blanc	Chancellor
Verdelet	Chelois
Vidal Blanc	Colobel
Vignoles	de Chaunac
Villard Blanc	Delicatessen
	Landot
	Léon Millot
	Maréchal Foch
	Rosette
	Rougeon
	Vincent Noir

Heat and Sunshine

When a vintner decides on a grape variety to plant, many factors influence him: location, the soil and its composition, drainage, and the weather that will affect his crop and possibly bring it greatness. The most important criterion in the analysis, however, is *heat summation:* the geographic classification of regions in terms of heat degree days during the seven-month growing season.

In 1936, University of California (Davis) professor Albert Winkler decided that temperature was a basis for segregating the grape-producing areas of California into five climatic regions. For classification purposes, he used 50°F as a base temperature applied specifically to the seven-month grape-growing season from April 1 to October 31. (The base line is set at 50° because there is almost no shoot growth below this temperature). He then developed a formula for "heat summation" above this 50° base. Heat summation is defined as the mean temperature or average high and low, greater than 50°, from April 1 through October 31. The resulting figure is expressed as degree days.

For example, if the mean for a day is 70° (50° low and 90° high), the summation for the twenty-four-hour period is 20 degree days (70 − 50 = 20). If this condition occurred every day for a thirty-day month, the summation would be 600 degree days (20 degree days × 30 calendar days).

Based on this system, Winkler established five regions:

Region #1: (less than 2,500 degree days). The Rhine and Mosel regions of Germany; the Burgundy, Chablis, and Champagne regions of France; Switzerland and the southern part of Napa Valley, California.

Region #2: (2,501 to 3,000 degree days). Piedmont, Italy; Bordeaux France; Sonoma and the upper part of Napa Valley, California.

Region #3: (3,001 to 3,500 degree days). The Rhône Valley, France; Tuscany, Italy; and Livermore, California.

Region #4: (3,501 to 4,000 degree days). The Midi region of France; and much of Sicily, Italy; Greece; and central Spain.

Region #5: (4,001 or more degree days). Central Valley, California; North Africa (Morocco, Algeria); and southern Spain.

The heat summation regional designation is simply a method to separate each state/country into grape-growing regions of some similarity and to structure the separation based on total heat summation. It does not account for microclimate variations and does not mean a great deal in predicting the physiological response of the vines. It does correlate with distinct compositional changes in the fruit used for wine and quality differences in the wines.

California's climatic regions have been compared to the world's grape-growing areas:

Degree days

Mosel, Germany	1,700
Champagne, France	1,820
Santa Cruz, California	2,140
Upper Monterey, California	2,350
Bordeaux, France	2,390
Lower Monterey County, California	2,880
Asti, Italy	2,930
Sonoma, California	2,950
Ukiah, California (Mendocino County)	3,100
Oakville, California (Napa Valley)	3,100
Rhône, France	3,400
Douro Valley, Portugal	3,770
Jerez, Spain	4,190
Fresno, California	4,680

Source: 1980 Fromm & Sichel, Inc. Data Annual.

Grape Yield

The yield from an acre, or even a single grapevine, can vary greatly, depending on a number of factors, including: how much the vine has been pruned back, differences in pruning, the mixture of cultivars in the field, clones planted, soil structure, climatic conditions, fertilization, nutrition, spray treatments (figure 1-1), irrigation (figure 1-2), and rootstocks. If the viticulturist didn't prune the grapevines each and every year, they would grow uncontrollably, raising the yield considerably, but to the detriment of quality. Conversely, if the vines were pruned severely, the quality would be excellent but the yield would plummet and there would not be enough grapes to yield a profit for the winery. Viticulturists/winemakers prune for a balance somewhere between these two extremes of quantity and quality. A grapevine planted in 1842 at Carpintaria, California, was able to yield at full maturity (fifty-one years old) an unbelievable 8 tons of grapes in one year. This single grapevine, however, died in 1920.

As a rough determination of the tonnage of grapes and ultimately the gallonage of wine, winemakers weigh the grapes upon arrival from

Figure 1-1 Crop dusting by helicopter of Banfi vineyards..(Courtesy Banfi Vintners, Montalcino, Italy)

the vineyards. The average yield of grapes from an acre is approximately 2 to 4 tons. Each ton produces 135 to 170 gallons of juice. If the acre produced 3 tons and 150 gallons of juice were extracted from each ton, the winery would wind up with 450 gallons; 2,250 bottles (750 ml), or 187 cases of wine.

Grapes ripen in late summer and early autumn. The harvest period is different for each grape. For example, Chardonnay is usually harvested early and Cabernet last in the harvesting season. Prior to harvesting, the winemaker and viticulturist jointly decide what the correct sugar level of the grapes must be to produce a particular wine type. According to Zelma Long, vice president and winemaker at Simi Vineyards in California, grapes can accumulate sugar without a parallel in-

Figure 1-2 Overhead irrigation insures growth for young vines. (Courtesy California Wine Institute)

crease in flavor. Sugar content, expressed as degrees Brix (total soluble solids in grape juice, more than 90 percent of which are fermentable sugars), is easily measured. (Brix is an American term for measuring sugar in grapes, must, and wine.) Ripeness primarily means flavor and a proper balance between sugar, acid, and pH. Sugar is thus only one component of ripeness, but cannot alone define ripeness. In fact, we have no tests to measure ripeness or flavor, which is an essentially subjective, relative concept. Ripeness exists as a potential affected by individual vineyard characteristics and weather patterns.

To determine when the grapes are ready to be harvested, viticulturists test them numerous times in the field for sugar, acid, and pH levels. The instrument used to measure sugar level is called a *refractometer* (figure 1-3). It is a hand-held optical instrument that measures the amount of light bent as it passes through the juice, which can be viewed through an eye-piece. When the grapes reach the desired sugar/acid ratio, they are harvested.

To measure sugar content at the winery, a small sample of grapes are crushed and the liquid is strained and immediately placed into a graduated cylindrical tube where a hydrometer is placed into the tube

Figure 1-3 A grape grower checks ripe grapes for sugar content with a measuring instrument called a *refractometer*. (Courtesy California Wine Institute)

and allowed to bounce around freely until the weight of the displaced liquid equals the weight of the hydrometer and its movement ceases. The point where the hydrometer meets the surface of the grape juice is noted, and a reading of the hydrometer is taken.

Harvesting

For centuries the conventional method of harvesting grapes was by laborers who for days on end would go off into the vineyards, like a hoard of bees swarming down on the ripe grapes. With a sharp knife in hand (figure 1-4) they picked the grapes and placed them in "lug boxes," which held from 35 to 50 pounds. When filled, the boxes were dumped into large "gondolas" which transported the grapes to the winery for crushing or pressing (figure 1-5).

Figure 1-4 Most picking is done with stubby knives, but small shears are also used. (Courtesy California Wine Institute)

The mechanical harvester was first developed in the early 1950s by University of California at Sacramento agricultural engineer Lloyd Lamouria while working with viticulturist Albert Winkler. However, it wasn't until 1969 or 1970 that Mirassou Vineyards of San Jose, California, became the first winery to use the harvester on a commercial scale (figure 1-6). At that time only a handful of California winemakers actually believed that machine-harvested grapes were equal to hand-harvested grapes. During its infancy this machine had a number of obstacles to overcome: it was quite rough with the grapes, sometimes tearing them off the vines; the grapevines were not trained to accommodate mechanical harvesters; the space between rows was often times not sufficient for the harvesters; occasionally grapevines were pulled out of the ground; and, finally, some machines were unable to make a clean separation between fruit and leaves.

Figure 1-5 A harvest worker transfers a basket of grapes to a gondola which will carry the freshly picked grapes to a winery. (Courtesy California Wine Institute)

Mechanical Harvesting

Modern technology has dictated change in the vineyards. Mechanical harvesting has evolved into the preferred method of grape picking today. Among some of the advantages mechanical harvesting offers are greater efficiency in harvesting and increased control over grape quality.

A mechanical harvester is approximately 18 feet in length, 12 feet in width, and weighs about 18,000 pounds. The driver of this machine sits on the top and expertly guides this gentle giant through the vineyards, straddling each row of grapevines as the *pivotal pulsator* removes the ripe

11

Figure 1-6 A mechanical grape harvester stands in a vineyard where it is used to pick grapes of perfect ripeness to be made into wine. The grapes, which are crushed on board the harvester, are pumped into a tanker which moves alongside the harvester as it travels down vineyard rows. This immediate crushing assures that the fresh grape juice will arrive at the winery in the best possible condition. (Courtesy California Wine Institute)

grapes from the vines. As the harvester moves down the rows of vines, the pulsator or "trunk shaker" vigorously shakes the trunks on the vines, causing the grapes at the top of the vines to drop into the machine below. At the same time the curved tip of the four to six pivotal strikers, which consist of a double bank of flexible horizontal rods, reach up under the foliage canopy of the vine and strike the ends of the cordon, or cane, ejecting the fruit from the ends of the canes. The combination of the pulsator and pivotal strikers gives maximum efficiency in harvesting all of the ripe grapes on each vine.

As the grapes drop into the harvester they travel along a 15-inch-wide conveyor belt past suction blowers which expel any leaves that may have entered the machine along with the grapes. This minimizes possible green leaf off-flavors and bitterness, which characterized some of the earliest mechanical harvester experiments. The grapes then move up the conveyor to the top of the machine, where an extension of the conveyor carries them across the row to a gondola moving parallel to the harvester. The mechanical harvester picks an average of one acre of grapes (2 to 4 tons) per hour. The daily tonnage of grapes picked by one machine is equal to that of thirty manual laborers.

Another advantage of mechanical harvesters is that they can be used at any time of the day or night, twenty-four hours a day, enabling wineries to pick each grape variety at its optimum ripeness. To further ensure the highest quality of grapes, many wineries harvest them in the evening and early morning hours. During these periods of the day the grapes are cool and turgid. Cooler grapes are less susceptible to *polyphenolic browning* of the juice and the growth of "wild" yeasts and bacteria on the grapes and juice. By harvesting at night, a number of problems are overcome: there is little congestion of traffic on the roads to the winery; there are few if any bees or other insects; and the winery's refrigeration system doesn't use or demand much energy to quickly cool down the grapes because of the cool night air. White grapes, for example, will register temperatures of 50° to 60°F when harvested at night, compared to 60° to 80° during the day. Night harvesting also reduces the tendency of the grapes to juice before they reach the winery, and the cool night air diminishes color extraction in red grapes.

(*The Weibel Grapevine:* Fall 1982, San Jose, California)

Field Crushing

Around the same time (1969 to 1970) that Mirassou Vineyards first used mechanical harvesting they introduced the concept of field crushing. Grapes are crushed and sealed in a CO_2 atmosphere in tanks alongside the mechanical harvester, within minutes of picking. By conventional methods two to twenty hours may elapse between picking and crushing, during which oxidation can cause the loss of fresh flavor.

There are a number of different types of field crushing equipment used throughout the world. Cakebread Vineyards of Napa Valley, California uses the German-made Mortl system, which crushes the grapes in the field right after they are picked from the vines. The Mortl holds

5 tons of grapes and is pulled through the vineyard by a tractor. This process provides the ultimate in freshness preservation between the time the grapes are picked and the juice is processed.

Crushing/Destemming

After the harvested grapes are weighed and samples for analytical purposes are taken, they are dumped into a large hopper called a crusher/destemmer (figure 1-7), which cracks the berries, allowing the sugar-rich juice known as *free-run* to flow freely.

The second part of this simultaneous crushing/destemming operation removes the stems from the grapes by centrifugal force with the use of a large auger, which catches the stems, literally ripping off the berries. The stems exit at one side of the machine, while the berries and juice

Figure 1-7 Grapes are gently crushed, now on their way to becoming fine wine. (Courtesy California Wine Institute)

usually exit at the bottom. The stems, which are a good source of nitrogen, are loaded into trucks and dumped between the vineyard rows to decompose during the winter and be "disced" into the soil in the spring.

Winemaking

Alcohol

The percentage of alcohol contained in alcoholic beverages is critical, not only to health-conscious Americans but, perhaps more importantly, to the Treasury Department of the U.S. government. Table wine (7 percent to 14 percent alcohol) is taxed at one rate, while wine that is 14 percent to 20 percent alcohol is taxed at a higher rate.

As long as a wine's alcoholic content falls within the range of table wine, there is a fairly great latitude in labeling, with a permissible error of plus or minus 1.5 percent. A wine labeled 12.5 percent alcohol can have an actual range of from 11 percent to 14 percent. Even labels that give reasonably accurate-sounding figures are permitted the same margin of error. Generally, however, a label giving a figure of, for example, 13.3 percent will be accurate; and wineries must always submit an accurate analysis to the Bureau of Alcohol, Tobacco, and Firearms. In order not to let alcohol content interfere with consumers' appreciation of the wine, some wineries have begun to label their products table wine in lieu of indicating their alcohol percentage.

Chaptalization

In certain wine-producing countries of the world there is sometimes an insufficient amount of sugar present in the grapes at harvest to produce a stable wine. The finished wine would contain a very low alcohol level and would thus be unstable for travel and subject to bacterial infestation.

A limited amount of sugar, set by law, can be added to the *must* (unfermented grape juice) prior to fermentation when a lack of natural sugar exists. This is called *chaptalization*. This addition increases the sugar content of the must, producing a higher degree of alcohol. When the fermentation is complete, the wine is dry. The purpose of sugaring the must is only to raise the alcoholic content of the finished wine and has nothing at all to do with producing a wine with noticeable residual sugar.

Adding sugar to the must is permitted in most grape-growing countries north of the Alps (Austria, Germany, Luxembourg, and Switzerland) and in the northern regions of France, including Alsace, Bordeaux, Burgundy, and Loire. It is also practiced in New York state, but not in California or in Italy.

Fermentation

Fermentation, simply put, is the conversion of sugar contained in the grapes (by the action of yeast) into *ethyl alcohol* or *ethanol*. It was in 1789 that the famed French chemist Lavoisier made one of the first studies on the natural phenomena of fermentation; he was followed in 1810 by Monsieur Gay-Lussac who correctly devised the overall equation for fermentation. In 1857, Louis Pasteur began the first scientific study of fermentation in a town called Arbois, in the Jura region of France.

Gay-Lussac's formula for fermentation is:

$$C_6H_{12}O_6 = 2C_2H_5OH + 2CO_2$$
(sugar glucose)   (ethyl alcohol)   (carbon dioxide)

The equation describes the following process: yeast "eat" (metabolize) sugar and in the process create, in approximate equal proportions, alcohol and carbon dioxide gas (CO_2), with heat as a by-product. If yeast is added to a sugar-water mixture, fermentation would produce only alcohol and CO_2; but when grapes and yeast are put together the end product is wine.

(*Sebastiani Vineyards Newsletter* (February 1979), vol. 7, no. 2.)

Dry red wine. If a dry red wine is to be made, harvested grapes are immediately transferred into large stainless steel tanks, where they are lightly sprayed with sulfur dioxide to kill any microorganisms, "wild" yeast, and spoilage bacteria and make them virtually sterile. The winemaker determines what type of red wine is to be produced, based in part on the initial chemical analyses. Yeast is then added to the must. The culture of pure yeast (*Saccharomyces cerevisiae*) can slightly or dramatically impart aroma and flavor and contribute to the wine's clarity.

To ferment red wine, the temperature of the must is brought between 70° to 90°F. Above 90° there is a chance that the heat will kill the yeast; below 70° the yeast acts at a slower pace, extracting less pigments, flavonoids, and so on. At the 70° to 90° range the yeast quickly multiplies, and metabolization of the sugar, converting it to alcohol, is increased. During fermentation the grape skins rise to the surface of the tank or barrel due to the fact that pigments, flavonoids, tannins, and other compounds are being extracted, making the skins lighter than the must. When the skins reach the surface they harden, forming what is known as the "cap" or "hat." Several times a day this cap must be broken up to allow the carbon dioxide gasses to escape. It is also important for the skins to stay in contact with the fermenting juice, to aid extraction. To accomplish this the wine is pumped from the bottom of the tank over the cap of floating skins and seeds at the top of the tank three times a day. Some wineries, with the aid of long paddles or oars, break up the cap and stir the skins back into the juice (figure 1-8).

If the skins are allowed to rest for prolonged periods of time at the surface, volatile acids (spoilage bacteria) form which, if left unattended, could result in the transformation of the wine into vinegar. The other problem associated with volatile acidity is the large numbers of fruit flies (*Drosophila melanogaster*) that are drawn by the smell of vinegar. These

Figure 1-8 Punching down the wine skin "cap" during fermentation at Beaulieu Vineyards. (Courtesy Beaulieu Vineyards, Napa Valley, California)

17

fruit flies are carriers of vinegar bacteria and their numbers must be kept to a bare minimum.

The fermentation time for red wines is somewhere between five and seven days. The completion of fermentation is evident from a lack of movement ("bubbling") inside the tank. At this point the yeast has totally consumed the sugar, causing the fermentation to cease, with the yeast now dying off, settling to the bottom of the tank, and dissolving (called *autolysis*), forming what is commonly called the *lees*.

The red wine is then pumped directly into a wine press, which presses the remaining juice out of the skins until no more comes out when pressure is exerted. The highly compacted grape skin mass (consisting of skins, pulp, and pits) is called *pomace*, or the "cake." The pomace is, like the stems, a good source of nitrogen, and like them is loaded into trucks and dumped between the vineyard rows. Some wineries in Italy and France take the pomace to a distillery, where it is made into a high proof distillate called *grappa* (Italy) or *marc* (France).

The wine from the press is pumped into wooden barrels for aging (figures 1-9, 1-10). The exact number of months or years that the wine spends in wood is determined by the winemaker after carefully evaluating and weighing many factors.

Dry white wine. The process of making white wine is somewhat different. After going through the crusher/destemmer, the grapes immediately go to the press, which presses the juice from the skins, which are later discarded. Only the juice goes into the fermentation tank, where it is inoculated with a strain of yeast. For the production of white wine, the must is fermented at a lower temperature than for red wine—45° to 60°F, which retains the aromatic fragrances (esters and aldehydes) and subtle freshness of the grape. Because of the lower temperature the fermentation time for white wine is longer than for red: ten to fourteen days, and often longer. If the fermentation temperature should rise considerably—say above 70°F—the aromatic properties would be volatilized, in the same manner if you were to cook a sauce over a high flame on the stove. If the temperature during fermentation should drop considerably below 35°F, the yeasts become torpid, losing motion and vigor, and the conversion of sugar to alcohol almost ceases.

When fermentation is complete, the wine is allowed to settle, and is then pumped into a clean stainless steel tank or, in the case of chardonnay, into oak barrels, leaving behind the sediment.

Dry rosé or blush wines. Technically speaking, there is no such thing as a rosé grape, and rosés are not made by combining red and white

Figure 1-9 Large redwood aging tanks in a modern winery. (Courtesy California Wine Institute)

wines. To make a rosé, the initial procedure for making red wines is employed, but instead of the must fermenting for five to seven days, the juice stays in contact with the skins for only a matter of hours. The red pigmentation contained in the skins is not soluble in the juice, but dissolves in the presence of acidity and newly formed alcohol as it is produced during fermentation. After the desired degree of color has been reached, the juice is quickly separated from the skins, then allowed to finish fermenting. When fermentation is complete, the wine (like white wine) is put into stainless steel tanks for aging.

The red pigmentation material *(anthocyanins)* is on the inside of the grape skin, not in the pulp, which is clear. All but a few of the red grape varieties in the world yield white juice when crushed. (Some examples of red-juice grapes are Alicante-Bouschet, Royalty, and Rubired, from the United States; Primitivo, from Italy; and Gamay à jus rouge, from France.) Therefore, a rosé or even a white wine can be made from red

Figure 1-10 A room full of oak barrels used to age red wine in a winery. (Courtesy California Wine Institute)

grapes, providing that the contact of skin and must is minimal or non-existent. This is how the new wines such as White Zinfandel and "blush wines" are created. The champagne term *blanc de noirs* (white wine from red grapes) would also apply in this case.

Wines with residual sugar. For the production of semidry or sweet wines (usually white or rosé, rarely reds), the fermentation is stopped before all of the sugar is metabolized. This is generally accomplished by superchilling the fermenting must to a temperature of perhaps 26°F for several weeks. This not only stops any fermentation but also "cold stabilizes" the wine, helping to crystallize and remove any excess potassium bitartrate. The wine is then filtered through a sterile membrane filter (0.45 microns), which promotes biological stability by removing malolactic bacteria and spoilage organisms; at the same time the yeast is filtered out, eliminating the possibility for future refermentation. The wine is left to rest in stainless steel tanks until it is bottled.

The Aging of Wines

Allowing wines to age has been standard practice for countless centuries, and various methods of maturation (a subjective quality) have been tried. One unorthodox method was used by the Mont-Rouge Vineyards in Livermore, California. From approximately 1910 to 1920 grapes were grown in nearby vineyards and the wine produced was pumped into barrels and loaded on ships. The wine was then shipped to Liverpool, England and back to Livermore via the Cape of Good Hope. Once returned to the winery, the barrels were emptied and the wine bottled and sold. The rationale for this unusual journey was that the rocking motion of the ship would cause the wines to age faster. Actually, it was probably the heat at the equator and extreme temperature fluctuations that changed the wine.

Countless factors influence the aging of a wine: fermentation time; fermentation temperature; the pH and acidity of the juice; the type of yeast used for fermentation; the amount of time the juice stays in contact with the skins; the outside temperature during fermentation and aging; temperature fluctuations; humidity; vibrations; how often the wine is moved or racked; if periodic topping takes place; the amount of sulfur dioxide present in the wine; the geographic elevation; the size and age of the container; the type of material the container is made of; the condition of the cork (if bottle aged); aging time; whether or not the wine was ever racked, filtered, or fined; etc. What's more important, what kind of wine does the winemaker desire to produce as a final product, and when should it be consumed? Wine is living matter, subject to chemical changes that alter its life cycle; any of the above factors, can change its color, aroma, and taste.

The Aging Process

During the aging process, extraction occurs as the alcohol in the wine dissolves flavor-affecting chemicals present in the wooden barrels. The wine nearest the barrel wall becomes more dense from taking on the added weight of the extractables; this heavier liquid then falls away, causing circulation, which brings the lighter wine from the center of the barrel to the walls to pick up added extractable elements. The smaller the barrel, the more rapid the circulation and the extraction, and hence the more rapid the aging process.

Barrels. For the aging of most red, and also some white wines, the wooden barrel is essential. In fact, the wine barrel as we know it today was invented in Egypt sometime around 2800 B.C. Although most of the barrels used for wine (over 90 percent), are made of oak, other kinds of wood; such as redwood, spruce, Douglas fir, chestnut, sugar maple, yellow or sweet birch, white ash, beech, black cherry, sycamore, bald cypress, elm, and basswood are also suitable for barrel making. Trees that contain large "knots" are unsuitable for use in making barrels.

Making the barrels is a time-consuming task which is done completely by hand by experienced craftsmen known as *coopers*. The narrow strips of wood that will ultimately form the sides of the casks must be aged in the open air for at least four years before they can be curved into final form over open fires. Nails are never used, which ensures that the aging wine or spirit will come into contact with nothing but wood.

Wood aging versus stainless steel aging. The aging of a wine depends on two considerations: what the winemaker hopes to accomplish by aging (or non aging) the wine, and the general style and body of the wine.

One winery might produce fresh, fruity, light, "nouveau" wines while also producing more complex, heavier types. As a rule, barrel aging will compromise and actually deteriorate the lively, fresh, fruity character of white wines and of light, fresh reds, and the color, aroma, and taste of oak will be extracted by the wine. Therefore, barrel aging should be either totally avoided or allowed only for a minimal amount of time. Today most white and rosé table wines never see wooden barrels, but are fermented and aged in stainless steel containers. Consumers seem to enjoy the freshness of these wines, which makes them easier to drink. The only drawback when wines are not aged in wood and not fermented in contact with skins or stems is that they have a shorter shelf life.

There are some white wines, such as Chardonnay and occasionally Sauvignon Blanc, that might gain from an abbreviated period of time in wooden barrels. However, there are still two distinct schools of thought on the correct procedure for making Chardonnay wines. The first is more traditional for white wines, and involves fermenting the juice in stainless steel and aging it in a combination of stainless steel and oak barrels. The second method, known as *barrel fermentation* (used in Burgundy, France for decades), is now being used with more frequency in California. After crushing and pressing, the juice is settled overnight, yeasted, and moved to oak barrels for fermentation lasting one to two weeks. The new wine is simply left in the barrel—yeast, sediment, and all—for several months until it is judged ready to bottle, with the barrels topped periodically with wine from the same wine lot. The yeast contact seems to give an extra fullness to the wine. The barrel fermentation seasons the barrel, as the yeast precipitates in the barrel; and a harsh "overbarreled" taste is avoided. The most important aspect of this old method is the minimal handling of the wine, allowing the maximum translation of the fruit intensity of the grapes to the wine. This technique, rather than imposing a style on the wine, serves to mature the wine in the most gentle way while integrating the character of the oak barrel with the wine.

The more complex fuller-bodied wines (generally reds) need prolonged periods of time in barrels to soften the effect of their extended contact with the grape skins, pits (if they are crushed), and occasionally stems. Skins, pits, and stems all contain *tannin*, which gives red wine its astringency (or bitterness) and red color. All grapes, red and white, contain some degree of tannin, although in whites the level is generally lower. A grape that contains little tannin should be aged in smaller casks to absorb tannin from the wood, whereas harder or more tannic grapes should be aged in larger barrels to help precipitate the tannin.

The tannin contained in the skins, stems, and pits is "bitter" (or "hard") tannin, while the tannin extracted from wooden barrels is "soft." Tannins are natural antioxidants, and since oxygen is the great enemy of aging wine, tannins are responsible for extending the life of bottled wine. This is also why the barrel-fermented and oak-aged Chardonnay and Sauvignon Blanc will last longer in the bottle than ones otherwise produced.

Racking. Racking is a natural clarifying process that aids in settling suspended particles in the wine and removing them from contact with it—dead yeast cells, grape solids, bits of skin, and solidified dead matter. The wine is carefully drawn from one barrel, leaving behind the sediment, and put into a clean barrel where it will rest until the next racking. After racking, winemakers are careful to keep the barrels filled to the top with wine to eliminate oxidation; this is called *topping*. There is no set number of rackings that a wine must undergo. The frequency of rackings is dependent upon a multitude of factors such as: the growing season; the size of the grape berry; the degree to which it was crushed; the yeast used; the fermentation temperature; whether the wine was fermented on or off the skins; the duration of fermentation; the pH and acidity; etc. There are some drawbacks to excessive racking. Every time the wine is racked it is exposed to a considerable amount of oxygen, which is absorbed by the wine, and the level of sulfur dioxide (a natural antioxidant) drops dramatically. Some winemakers, however, feel that wines *should* be exposed to air during racking in order to help develop the wine's flavors.

Analysis while aging. While the wine is aging in wooden barrels, stainless steel tanks, or carboys or demijohns (five-gallon glass containers that are usually used to hold bottled spring or mineral water), periodic analyses of it are conducted. Tests are made to determine the levels of: alcohol (usually with an ebulliometer); pH; total acidity; residual sugar; volatile acidity; total phenolics; extracts; protein; trace elements; gasses, sulfur dioxide; hydrogen sulfide; and malolactic bacteria. Its specific gravity and heat and cold stability are also tested. The color of the wine is monitored, and a sensory evaluation is made.

It is easy to remove a sample of wine from stainless steel tanks, because they are generally fitted with spigots. With wooden barrels and glass carboys, other measures must be taken to withdraw a sample. In the United States a glass tube or pipette, called a "wine thief," is inserted into the barrel and a small sample is extracted (figure 1-11).

Filtering and Fining

The wide range of lovely colors of wine, whether shades of red or gold, as reflected in a long-stemmed glass, contribute to its appeal. Its beautiful brilliant hues are sometimes taken for granted, except by those involved in the winemaking process. To obtain the clarity that we are accustomed to, wines are filtered to remove all grape particles, which are not only unattractive but may also cause the wine to become unstable over a period of time. Solids in wine come from the grape skins, seeds, and pulp, tiny particles that become suspended in the liquid during fermentation. Filtration removes these suspended particles and helps to prevent bacteria fermentations and off-odors initiated by the presence of protein particles.

The process of "polishing" or clarifying a cloudy or hazy wine to brilliancy by removing suspended particles is known as *fining*. Most wineries use fining agents to help clarify wines by removing precipitates of excess pectin, peptides, iron compounds, or unstable protein, which are generally positively charged. Other wineries use these agents (which carry a negative charge) for the softening of excessive tannin levels in red wines and the removal of browning agents. There are many fining agents used throughout the world; among them are casein, bentonite,

Figure 1-11 Using a "wine thief," winemakers frequently taste wine aging in small oak barrels to assure that the wine will be bottled at its peak of flavor. (Courtesy California Wine Institute)

charcoal, colloidal silica, egg white, gelatin, isinglass, Sparkolloid, and (in ancient times) animal blood.

Blending

Some wines are bottled as "varietals" (reds as well as whites), with the name of the predominant grape variety stated on the label, while others (mostly reds) are bottled as "generic blends." Wines are blended for several reasons. In a given growing season, for instance, two red grapes might ripen completely, but one of the grapes may be deficient in natural acidity and the second grape have an excess of it. By blending together these two wines, the acid level will even out somewhat, producing a relatively smooth wine. Other factors, among which are the amount of sugar; the pH; flavonoids; anthocyanins (red pigmentation); and total phenolics (tannin) must be considered prior to the blending. Blending two or more wines together, either from the same or different years, creates a synergistic effect; the total is greater than the sum of its parts. In addition, with blending a consistent product can be produced year after year, which some winemakers call the "house style."

Bottling

When it is deemed that the wine has aged sufficiently, either in oak barrels or stainless steel containers, the final step is bottling. This includes the addition of labels, corks or screw tops, and a foil capsule; finally the bottles are packed in cardboard cases, ready to be shipped (figure 1-12). Some wineries will not ship their wines at this point but

Figure 1-12 Almaden's modern bottling line. (Courtesy Almaden Vineyards, Madera, California)

will "bottle age" them until it is determined that they are ready for consumption.

Corks

The use of corks as closures for wine and champagne bottles has been universal since the seventeenth century. Corks are occasionally used as stoppers for bottles of cordials and liqueurs, distilled spirits, or even beer. Cork, with its great elasticity—expands and contracts depending on temperature and atmospheric conditions—makes the perfect tight seal for the neck of a bottle.

Yet the ever-growing demand for high-quality corks has put considerable pressure on the two major cork-producing countries, Portugal and Spain (Sardinia, Italy also produces some cork) to increase production. Cork trees mature slowly; their outer bark, which is the cork, is harvested only when the tree reaches twenty-five years of age, and once every nine years thereafter. And it is only with the third harvest, when the tree is at least forty-three years old, that the cork is of a quality suitable for wine closures.

After the bark is cut from the tree, it is processed and cut into circular shapes of various lengths. There is a very strict grading system which categorizes the corks according to color, smell, texture, the age of the tree, the number of imperfections and fissures, its pliability, and so on. Most corks are 1.75 inches long and are graded by the number of holes in them (the less holes, the less chance for leakage). French Bordeaux wines traditionally use 2.25-inch corks which often must be able to withstand decades of aging. For obvious reasons, the finest corks command the highest prices.

As the demand for fine cork has been rising producers have been looking into other ways of satisfying it. One type of cork developed in 1925 (for which scraps of cork are glued together and then reformed into the shape of a cork) goes by several names: particle cork, composition cork, or agglomerated cork.

The life of a cork. Generally speaking, the finest corks have a peak life of about twenty-five years, after which time they slowly deteriorate and should be closely examined for possible leakage. Chateau Lafite-Rothschild of Bordeaux, France not only recorks every bottle of their wine when it reaches its twenty-fifth birthday, but on a yearly basis will send out an entourage around the world to recork, free of charge, any bottles of Lafite-Rothschild that have reached or passed their twenty-fifth year.

Problems with corks. Storage conditions present many problems for corks. Sustained high humidity causes corks to swell, and it is not uncommon to find them partially out of the bottle ("pumped") or even leaking when wine is kept in this type of environment. Conversely, when wines are stored in sustained low humidity, the corks will start to dry out, causing shrinkage and the eventual oxidation to the wine.

Perhaps the biggest problem associated with corks is extracting them from the bottle. In restaurants, countless bottles of wine are returned to the management because either the cork broke off with part of it remaining in the bottle's neck or an overly rough waiter found a way to push the cork into the bottle. Every time this happens the restaurant "eats" the bottle and loses a sale. Without proper training and retraining of waiters this can and does occur in most restaurants, regardless of their quality. The number of bottles of wine per year that are returned in restaurants for this reason is probably in excess of one million, which could easily mean more than five million dollars in lost revenues.

Wines destined to be consumed within three to five years need not be bottled in cork-finished bottles. For early consumption, modern screw-top closures would actually be superior to corks. In addition, restaurant storage space would be greatly increased, with vertical stacking of more than five cases being allowed.

Corks are said to "breathe." If this is true, which way do they breathe, in or out? If they "breathe" in, then there must be a vacuum system present inside the bottle for this to happen. If air is taken in, what does it displace—wine? If air is taken in, then the wine is actually becoming oxidized. If the reverse is true, and the cork is "breathing" out, what is causing it to do so? Wineries literally spend millions of dollars each and every year to ensure that their wines are in an oxygen-free environment. Why, then, would a winemaker want a cork that "breathes," thereby oxygenating his wine?

Why use a cork at all when one of the patent modern twist-off closures can do the job just as well and provide a reliable seal, which enables half-full bottles to be stood up in a refrigerator? Corked wine bottles seem to add something to the dining experience—prestige, romance, and a sense of Old World charm not present with screw-top bottles, which have a lowly image. (When has a waiter ever, after opening a bottle of wine in front of a customer, presented him the screw top to examine?) Corks are aesthetically pleasing, but they do occasionally give the wine a "corked" (mushroomlike) odor or taste which immediately detracts from the pleasures of wine.

Screw-top bottles have almost completely replaced corked bottles for distilled spirits, cordials, and beer. Screw-top bottles for wines and sparkling wines have actually been used for years on airlines and trains (with little departure from tradition, at least as seen by travelers) for their convenience and because they need not be stored horizontally.

Suggested Readings

Amerine, Maynard A. and Vernon L. Singleton. *Wine: An Introduction.* Berkeley: University of California Press, 2d ed., 1977.

Amerine, Maynard A., H. W. Berg, Ralph E. Kunkee, Cornelius S. Ough, Vernon L. Singleton, and Dinsmoor A. Webb. *Technology of Wine Making.* Westport, Conn. AVI, 4th ed., 1980.

Cattell, Hudson and Lee Miller. *The Wines of the East: The Hybrids.* Lancaster, Pa.: L & H Photojournalism, 1978.

Cattell, Hudson and Lee Miller. *The Wines of the East: The Vinifera.* Lancaster, Pa.: L & H Photojournalism, 1979.

Cattell, Hudson and Lee Miller. *The Wines of the East: Native American Grapes.* Lancaster, Pa.: L & H Photojournalism, 1980.

Galet, Pierre and Lucie T. Morton. *A Practical Ampelography: Grapevine Identification.* Ithaca, N.Y.: Cornell University Press, 1979.

Peynaud, Emile. *Knowing and Making Wine.* New York: John Wiley, 1984.

Vine, Richard P. *Commercial Winemaking: Processing and Controls.* Westport, Conn.: A.V.I., 1981.

Winkler, Albert J., J. A. Cook, W. M. Kliewer, and L. A. Lider. *General Viticulture.* Berkeley: University of California Press, 2d ed., 1974.

Periodicals

The Vinifera Wine Growers Journal. The Plains, Va.
Vineyard and Winery Management. Watkins Glen, N.Y.
Wines and Vines. San Francisco, Calif.

Discussion Topics and Questions

1. Although grape growing continues to be the primary job of a viticulturist, what decisions must be made jointly by the wine maker and viticulturist?

2. Viticulturists are constantly seeking the best grape variety for the soil and climate where they are located. What effect does this have on the number of wine types that can be produced by "selective" growing?

3. Has the mechanical age of pruning, harvesting, and field crushing narrowed the field of viticulture? Discuss hand versus mechanical harvesting.

4. Wine making has come a long way since Gay-Lussac and Louis Pasteur first analyzed fermentation. What major discoveries, if any, have been made since, relative to understanding how fermentation really works?

5. Has modern science and technology, with its shiny stainless steel tanks, ultramodern pumping and filtering equipment, research laboratories, and overhead catwalks eliminated the "romance" of winemaking?

6. Is "push-button" wine making the future of the wine industry, or will time-honored methods continue to be employed?

7. Will the ever-growing demand and dwindling supply of corks force wine drinkers to consume expensive bottles of wine with screw caps?

2

Wines of the United States

This chapter discusses:

- The federal wine laws applicable to U.S. wineries.
- California's wine-producing regions, and its most popular wineries.
- The history of New York State wines and its wine-producing regions.
- Other wine-producing states.

Since the repeal of Prohibition in 1933, the quality of wine produced in the United States, especially California, has risen so dramatically and to such a high level that winemakers in Europe are now seeking advice and technology from the United States. Today, more than forty states produce wine, mostly from grapes, although fruit wines flourish in some areas. The United States grows more types of grapes and produces more varieties of wine than any other country. The diversity of tastes and quality is staggering.

Wine Label Laws

Americans are rapidly surpassing their European counterparts in their eagerness to learn more about the wines they buy. As the U.S. wine industry has developed, matured, and perfected the delicate art of winemaking, it has been able to offer a choice of wines to suit every palate and pocketbook. As Americans have become more adventurous in their wine selections, they look to the label for information. What can the label tell the consumer? What makes one wine different from another? What is the dominant grape in the wine? Where it is grown?

Federal regulations are quite detailed, and the information they require winemakers to display on their labels is sufficient to assist the consumer in making a choice. The following labeling regulations became effective on January 1, 1983:

Vintage date. A vintage date on the label indicates that 95 percent or more of the wine is produced from grapes grown in that year. If a vintage date is shown on the label, an appellation of origin, other than a country, will be shown also.

Varietal designations. Varietal designations are the names of the dominant grapes used in the wine. Cabernet Sauvignon, Seyval, Riesling, Cayuga White, Pinot Noir, Baco Noir, Chancellor, and Chenin Blanc are examples of grape varieties. A varietal designation on the label requires an appellation of origin and means that at least 75 percent of that grape variety is used in the wine. Wines made from *Vitis labrusca* grapes—such as Concord—are an exception because of the grape's intense flavor. These wines must contain a minimum of 51 percent of that grape variety and it will be so stated on the label. If the label carries no percentage statement, the wine must contain at least 75 percent of the *labrusca* variety.

Wine labels are not required to bear a varietal designation. Other designations (red wine, white wine, table wine) are used to identify the wine without label information on the type of grape used or where it was grown. On California wine labels, designations such as "Chablis" or "Burgundy" indicate wines similar in name only to the wines originally made in geographic regions indicated by those names. Other notable examples of U.S.-produced "generic" wines are Sauterne, Rhine, Chianti, champagne, Tokay, Madeira, sherry, and port. There are no federal regulations that stipulate the grape varieties that American-produced "generic" wines may contain.

Some wines, such as Pommard (France) and Rüdesheimer (Germany), are designated with distinctive names that are permissible only on specific wines from a particular site or region within the country of origin.

Alcohol content. A statement of alcohol content in percentage by volume appears on most labels. As an alternative some bottlers prefer to label wine with an alcohol content between 7 and 14 percent as "table wine" or "light wine."

Appellation of origin. An appellation of origin means simply the name of the place in which the dominant grapes used in the wine are grown. It can be the name of a country, state, county, or geographical region known as a viticultural area. A country, state, or county appellation on the label means that at least 75 percent of the wine is produced from grapes grown there. If two or three states or counties are listed as an appellation of origin, 100 percent of the wine is made from grapes grown in those areas, and the label will indicate the percentage from each location.

Viticultural area. A U.S. viticultural area is a well-defined grape grow- ing region with soil, climate, history, and geographic features that set it apart from the surrounding areas and make it ideal for grape growing. A viticultural area appellation on the label indicates that 85 percent or more of the wine is produced from grapes grown in the particular area. On December 21, 1981, the Bureau of Alcohol, Tobacco, and Firearms granted a historic "single-vineyard appellation" to California's Guenoc Winery, in the Lake County district.

Estate bottling. When "estate bottled" appears on a label it means that 100 percent of the wine comes from grapes grown on land owned or controlled by a winery located in a particular viticultural area. Besides growing the grapes, that winery has also crushed, fermented, finished, aged, processed, and bottled the wine in one continuous operation.

California

California is the classic wine land. Its long, gentle, sunlit seasons nurture the world's great wine grapes. Its fabled vineyards and wineries combine tradition with modern science to produce wines for every taste, occasion, and pocketbook. Each wine possesses its own merits and characteristics.

Wine-Producing Regions

California is divided into wine-producing or viticultural areas whose numbers seem to be increasing on a monthly basis. The most important areas are:

North coast: Napa Valley, Sonoma County, Mendocino County, and Lake County.

North-central coast: Monterey County, Santa Clara, and Livermore.

South-central coast: San Luis Obispo and Santa Barbara.

Central Valley: San Joaquin Valley.

California's Wineries

Almaden Vineyards, established in 1852 in Madera, is the oldest winery in operation in the state. Almaden produces Cabernet Pfeffer, a wine named after the winemaker and vine breeder William Pfeffer, who came to northern California in the 1860s.

Almaden's unique jug bottle design (since 1966) was named as one of the twenty-five best-designed products in America by *Fortune* magazine (1977).

Today, Almaden Vineyards is owned by Grand Metropolitan, International Distillers and Vintners of London, who purchased it in 1987 from the National Distillers and Chemical Corporation.

Although the *Paul Masson Winery* of Saratoga claims that it was established in 1852, Paul Masson actually came to the state in 1878. Masson, who would later marry the daughter of Charles LeFranc, the owner of Almaden Vineyards, was a Frenchman born in Beaune, in the region of Burgundy. In 1942 Paul Masson Vineyards was purchased by Seagram's; early in 1987 it was sold to a group called Vintners International.

In 1857 the *Buena Vista Winery* of Sonoma County was established by Agoston Haraszthy, who once produced a wine from mission grapes which he called Lachryma Montis (Tears of the Mountain). It is now being revived by the winery, which is noted for its Cabernet Sauvignon, Pinot Noir, and an unusual wine called Spiceling, made from a blend of Gewürztraminer and Riesling. Today, Buena Vista is owned by the A. Racke company of West Germany.

The *Simi Winery* was established in 1876 by the brothers Giuseppe and Pietro Simi; since 1980 it has been owned by Moët-Hennessy of France. Simi produces some of California's finest wines, among them a Cabernet Sauvignon, Chardonnay, and Sauvignon Blanc.

In 1876 the brothers Jacob L. and Frederick Beringer from Mainz, Germany established the *Beringer Winery* in Napa Valley. Today Beringer, which is owned by the Nestle Company of Switzerland, produces a wide range of wines, among them a Cabernet Sauvignon, Chardonnay, Sauvignon Blanc, and Zinfandel. Also produced are proprietary wines; Barenblut (made from Pinot Noir and Grignolino grapes) and Traubengold.

In 1879 *Inglenook Vineyards* of Napa Valley was established by the Finnish captain Gustave Ferdinand Niebaum. Inglenook is quite famous for a number of wines, including a Cabernet Sauvignon and a full-bodied red wine labeled Charbono. Inglenook also bottles wines under the

Navalle label. Today Inglenook is part of the huge conglomerate owned by Grand Metropolitan of England.

In 1882 *Château Montelena Winery* of Calistoga was founded by Alfred L. Tubbs, a state senator. In the famous Paris competition held on May 24, 1976, California wines were tasted against their French counterparts, and a 1973 Château Montelena Chardonnay won the competition.

In 1883 Carl Heinrich Wente established the *Wente Brothers Winery* in Livermore. Wente specializes in white wines and also produces a sparkling wine. Among the whites are a Chardonnay, Sauvignon Blanc, Grey Riesling, Le Blanc de Blancs, and a semisweet wine, Château Wente, made in part with Sémillon grapes. Wente Brothers was the first winery to bottle Chardonnay (1934) and Sauvignon Blanc (1935) as separate varietals.

In 1900 *B.V.* (Beaulieu Vineyards; translated, it means "beautiful place") of Napa Valley was established by Georges de Latour, a native of the Périgord region of France who came to the United States in 1883. In 1938, Mr. de Latour traveled to Paris in search of a new enologist and hired a young man by the name of André Tchelistcheff. Today, Tchelistcheff is considered the dean of California winemakers. The vineyards are now owned by Grand Metropolitan of London.

B. V. produces a number of fine wines, including a Pinot Noir, Chardonnay, Sauvignon Blanc, and an interesting wine labeled Muscat de Frontignan. It was first made in 1922 and is now produced in a solera system dating back to the 1960s. This muscat grape, with its French heritage, produces a dessert wine of 18 percent alcohol with an intense muscat aroma and flavor.

B. V. Cabernet Sauvignon Georges de Latour Private Reserve, first produced in 1936, is considered to be the finest example of Cabernet Sauvignon made in California. Its reputation is so high that the 1970 vintage has become the favorite California red wine of President Ronald Reagan.

In 1904 the *Sebastiani Winery* of Sonoma County, originally known as the Sonoma Mission Vineyards, was established by Samuele Sebastiani. In 1972 Sebastiani Winery became the first to produce a Nouveau Gamay-Beaujolais. Among its many wines are two unusual but quite good ones; Eye of the Swan, a salmon-colored wine made from Pinot Noir grapes, and Rosa, an unusual name used for a pink-colored Gewürztraminer. Also produced is a sparkling wine, along with a Cabernet Sauvignon, Muscat Canelli, Chardonnay, and many others.

In 1906 the *Kenwood Winery* was established in Napa Valley by Julius Pagani. Kenwood Vineyards' 1975 Cabernet Sauvignon wine label by artist David Lance Goines was given an "X rating" by the Bureau of Alcohol, Tobacco, and Firearms for depicting on the label a nude woman sunbathing, which the government called "obscene and indecent."

The winery produces a Cabernet Sauvignon, Zinfandel, Pinot Noir, and Chardonnay.

In 1922 *Louis M. Martini Winery* of Napa Valley was established. The Martini Winery is a family-owned winery in its truest sense, for family members have been involved in every aspect of running the business for decades. In 1968 the winery became the first to bottle Merlot as a separate varietal. Among the many wines produced are a Cabernet Sauvignon, Merlot, Barbera, Pinot Noir, Moscato Amabile, Chardonnay, Folle Blanche, and two excellent sherries.

In 1933 the world-famous *Gallo Winery* of Modesto was established by Ernest and Julio Gallo. Gallo makes more than 30 percent of all wines produced in the United States. During the winery's expansion, the American Vineyards of Livingston was purchased, making the 130-million-gallon winery the largest in the world. In 1957 proprietary flavored aperitif wines labeled Thunderbird and Gypsy Rose made their debut; in 1960 Ripple followed; in 1964, Hearty Burgundy; in January 1968 Gallo bottled a cream sherry labeled Old Decanter. Since that time other wines such as Paisano, Night Train, Boone's Farm, Madria-Madria Sangria, Tyrolia, Spañada, Polo Brindisi, Carlo Rossi, and Bartles & Jaymes Wine Coolers have been produced.

Today Gallo, in addition to "jug" wines, produces an entire line of quite good varietal wines which first appeared in 1978 under the label of The Wine Cellars of Ernest & Julio Gallo.

In 1939 the *Freemark Abbey Winery* of Napa Valley was established. It is noted for producing Cabernet Sauvignon, "Bosche" and a late-harvested Riesling.

In 1953 *Stony Hill Vineyards* of St. Helena was established by Fred and Eleanor McCrea. The winery is noted for an exceptional Chardonnay, which is in very limited supply.

In 1956 *Hanzell Vineyards* of Sonoma County was established. The Hanzell name is derived from a combination of those of its founders: zell stands for James D. Zellerbach, then ambassador to Italy; his wife's name is Hana. The winery produces one of the finest Pinot Noirs in the state.

In 1960 *Chalone Vineyards* of Soledad was established; it is noted for its Pinot Noir and Chardonnay, both of which are produced in limited quantities.

In 1961 *Heitz Winery*, located in St. Helena, was established by Joseph and Alice Heitz. Heitz's Cabernet Sauvignon with the Martha's Vineyard designation (first produced in 1966), named after Martha May, a local grape grower, is considered one of California's finest.

In 1962 the *Ridge Winery*, originally known as the Montebello Winery, was founded in Montebello. In 1987 Ridge was purchased by Otsuka, a Japanese pharmaceutical company. Ridge is noted almost exclusively for red wines; an extremely full-bodied Cabernet Sauvignon, Petite Sirah, and Zinfandel.

In 1966 the *Robert Mondavi Winery* of Napa Valley was established. Today, Mondavi is considered one of the premier wineries in the country, producing a full line of varietal wines including Cabernet Sauvignon, Pinot Noir, Chardonnay, Fumé Blanc (Sauvignon Blanc), Chenin Blanc, and a line of proprietary blended wines simply labeled Robert Mondavi red, white, and rosé.

In 1981 at a California wine auction, Chuck Mara, a retailer in Syracuse, New York, paid $24,000—a record sum—for a case of 1979 red wine (later called Opus 1). The wine was jointly made by Robert Mondavi of Napa Valley and Baron Philippe de Rothschild of Bordeaux, France.

In 1964, *Sterling Vineyards* of Napa Valley, currently owned by Seagram's, was established. This chalk white, picturesque, monasterylike winery can be seen for miles on the right side of the road when traveling north at the upper end of Napa Valley. The only way most tourists can visit this beautiful winery is by means of a cable car. One of the interesting things about this winery is its instructive "self-guided" tours through the crushing and fermenting areas and the aging cellars. Its tasting room is on top of the winery, with a spectacular view of the valley.

Sterling is noted for its Cabernet Sauvignon, Merlot, Chardonnay, and Sauvignon Blanc.

In 1971 *Caymus Vineyards* of Rutherford was established by Charles Wagner. The winery is famous for its Cabernet Sauvignon, Zinfandel, and Riesling.

In 1972 *Clos du Val Winery* of Napa Valley was established by Bernard Portet. He is the son of Andre Portet, the technical advisor of Château Lafite-Rothschild of Bordeaux, France. This winery produces a Cabernet Sauvignon, Zinfandel, and Chardonnay.

In 1972 *Stag's Leap Wine Cellars* of Napa Valley was established by Warren and Barbara Winiarski. (Incidentally, this winery has no connection with Stags' Leap Vineyards, which is owned by Carl and Joanne Doumani.)

In the famous Paris taste-off held on May 24, 1976, California wines were tasted against their French counterparts, and a 1972 Stag's Leap Wine Cellars Cabernet Sauvignon won first prize.

In 1973 the *Angelo Papagni Winery* of Madera County in Central Valley was established by Angelo Papagni. Papagni Vineyards produces a number of red wines (Alicante-Bouschet, Barbera, and Charbono); white wines (Muscat of Alexandria and Moscato d'Angelo); a sweet sparkling Muscat wine (Spumante d'Angelo); and two sherries (Finest Hour dry and sweet).

In 1973 the *Château St. Jean Winery* was established in Sonoma County. It is owned by Suntory International of Japan. St. Jean specializes in white wines, with an emphasis on single-vineyard Chardonnays, late-harvested Rieslings, and a Gewürztraminer.

In 1973 the *Joseph Phelps Winery*, originally known as Stonebridge, of St. Helena was established. The winery is best known for its late-harvested Rieslings and Gewürztraminers, a German variety called Scheurebe, and Syrah, the true grape variety of the Rhône Valley in France.

In 1976 the *Jordan Winery* of Healdsburg was established by Tom and Sally Jordan. Jordan specializes in Chardonnay, Merlot, and Cabernet Sauvignon.

In 1976 the *Clos du Bois Winery* of Healdsburg was established by Frank Woods; it produces Cabernet Sauvignon, Johannisberg Riesling, and Chardonnay.

In 1978 film producer Francis Ford Coppola started his own vineyards (the Niebaum-Coppola Vineyards) in Napa Valley. He specializes in a Cabernet Sauvignon–Cabernet Franc blended wine in the French style.

Secondary Wine Labels

Many well-known California wineries sometimes bottle wine under a different or second label. Below is a list of well-known labels and their corresponding secondary labels.

Well-known label	Secondary label
Acacia Vineyards	Caviste
Beringer Winery	Los Hermanos or Napa Ridge

Bouchaine	Poplar Vineyards
Brander Vineyards	St. Carl
Burgess Cellars	Bell Canyon Cellars
Caymus Vineyards	Liberty School
Chalone Vineyards	Gavilan, Carmenet and Edna Valley Vineyards
Chamisal Vineyards	Corral de Piedra
Château Chevalier	Mountainside
Château Montelena	Silverado Cellars
Clos du Bois	River Oaks Vineyards
Clos du Val	Gran Val
Cuvaison Vineyards	Calistoga Vineyards
David Bruce Winery	Old Dog Winery
Davis Bynum Winery	River Bend Cellars
Fetzer Vineyards	Bel Arbors
Foppiano Winery	Riverside Farms or Fox Mountain
Girard Winery	Stephens
Giumarra Vineyards	Breckenridge Cellars
Grand Cru Vineyards	Foxhollow
Inglenook Vineyards	Navalle
Joseph Phelps Vineyards	Le Fleuron
Kendall-Jackson	Northstar Cellars
J. Lohr Winery	Jade Wine Company
Markham Vineyards	VinMark
Mark West Vineyards	Russian River Valley Vineyards
Martin Ray Vineyards	La Montana
Mill Creek Vineyards	Felta Springs and Claus Vineyards
Navarro Vineyards	Indian Creek
Roudon-Smith Vineyards	MacKenzie Creek
Sebastiani Vineyards	Vendange
Shafer Vineyards	Chase Creek
Smith & Hook	Deer Valley

Well-known label	Secondary label
Sonoma Vineyards	Windsor Vineyards
Spring Mountain Winery	Falcon Crest
Stag's Leap Wine Cellars	Hawk Crest
Stags' Leap Vineyards	Pedregal
Stevenot Winery	Calaveras Cellars
Story Vineyards	Consumnes River Vineyard
Stratford	Cantebury Cellars
V. Sattui Winery	Hibbard-Braden Estate
Weibel Champagne Cellars	Redwood Valley Cellars or Stanford or Château Napoleon

New York State

In New York State, the art of cultivating fine grapes and producing superior wines is steeped in a long and proud tradition.

The first settlers in North America discovered huge plantations of wild *labrusca* vines flourishing in the state's fertile valleys. Nurtured by a unique combination of sun, soil, and climate, these native vines were ripe with Concord, Delaware, and Niagara grapes. Farsighted wine grape growers and dedicated wine masters attentively cultured the rich native crop. Some growers crossed the native vines with the *vinifera* species to produce hybrid grapes.

In 1829 Reverend William Bostwick, an Episcopalian minister, planted the first cultivated vines (Catawba and Isabella) at the southern tip of Lake Keuka. Brotherhood Winery, established in 1839 in the Hudson River region, is the nation's oldest operating winery. Great Western Winery, which began operating on March 15, 1860 in Hammondsport as the Pleasant Valley Wine Company (adopting its present name in 1865), is the oldest winery in the Finger Lakes region, and became U.S. Bonded Winery No. 1. In 1987 Vintners International purchased Great Western from Seagram's.

In the years following Great Western, other wineries opened in the Finger Lakes region. Gold Seal Vineyards, opened in 1865, was known as the Urbana Wine Company until 1957. Owned since 1979 by Seagram's, it was sold in 1987 to Vintners International. Barry Wine Company, formerly known as the O-Neh-Da Vineyards, was established in 1872. The Taylor Wine Company which opened in 1880, had been owned by Seagram's since 1983, but was sold in 1987 to Vintners International. In 1888 a Swiss couple, John Jacob Widmer and his wife Lysette, established the Widmer Winery; and in 1907, Alexander Bolognesi and family started the Hudson Valley Winery.

The Canandaigua Winery (*Canandaigua* in the language of the Seneca Indian, means "the chosen place") was established in 1945. The winery produces a wine labeled Virginia Dare, the oldest brand name wine in the United States. In 1957 Mark Miller bought the Andrew Jackson Caywood Vineyards and renamed them Benmarl Vineyards, where the first "nouveau"-style wine on the East Coast was produced. In 1962 Vinifera Wine Cellars was established by Dr. Konstantin Frank, who produced a Johannisberg Riesling *Trockenbeerenauslese* in 1957, 1962, and 1971.

In 1970 Bully Hill Winery was founded in Hammondsport by Walter S. Taylor, who opened the first wine museum on his property. In 1973, Long Island saw its first vineyards, planted by Louisa and Alex Hargrave. In the same year, the Cascade Winery was established. But the real boom in New York wineries started with the Farm Winery Act of 1976, which essentially made it economically feasible to own and operate a winery producing fewer than 50,000 gallons per year.

Among the new wineries are:

Clinton Vineyards, established by Ben Feder in 1977.

Cascade Mountain Vineyards, established by Bill Wetmore in 1977.

Heron Hills Winery of Hammondsport, established by Peter Johnstone in 1977.

Glenora Winery, established in 1977, which also has the honor of having had a magnum of its 1980 Chardonnay auctioned off for $2,700, the highest sum ever paid for a bottle of New York State wine.

Wagner Vineyards, of Hammondsport, established by Bill Wagner in 1978.

Hermann J. Wiemer Vineyards, established in 1979.

West Park Wine Cellars, established in 1979.

Pindar Vineyards of Long Island, established in 1980.

Banfi Vintners, Nassau County's first commercial winery, established in 1982.

In recent years these wineries have launched many new products, including wine coolers.

The successful planting of *Vitis vinifera*, without crossing it with native grapes, was accomplished in New York by Dr. Konstantin Frank and Charles Fournier, who in 1961 produced New York's first Chardonnay wine.

New York State is the nation's second-largest producer of grapes and wines. There is a wine for every taste, with white, red, sparkling, and dessert wines and wine coolers produced from *Vitis labrusca*, French-American hybrids, and *Vitis vinifera* grapes. Wines that carry the New York State appellation, regardless of whether they are estate bottled, must have a minimum of 75 percent of their volume derived from grapes grown in New York State.

Wine-Producing Regions

The scenic Finger Lakes, Hudson Valley, Long Island, and Lake Erie–Chautauqua regions are the largest wine grape growing and winemaking areas in the state.

The Finger Lakes region. The clear deep waters of the Finger Lakes keep this region's climate temperate, and plentiful shale beds (similar to those in Champagne, France) help drain the soil. The slow-warming lakes retard spring growth, protecting it against the danger of frost, and keep the vines warmer on chilly fall nights. The Finger Lakes vineyards are located approximately 350 miles northwest of New York City along Lakes Canandaigua, Cayuga, Hemlock, Keuka, and Seneca.

The Hudson River region. The Hudson River region is one of the oldest wine-producing areas in North America, with a history that dates from the late 1500s, when immigrant French Huguenots planted grapes on Mohonk Mountain. When Henry Hudson sailed up the river in 1609, he found its banks covered with wild native Catawba and Concord grapes.

From that time wines have been made in the region from these native grapes. In the 1860s French-American hybrid vines were introduced to the area by viticulturist Andrew Jackson Caywood, who developed the Dutchess grape variety. In recent years, growing consumer interest in quality New York State wines has led to a resurgence in vineyard development in this region.

Long Island. Grapes were cultivated on Long Island in colonial times. "Moses the Frenchman" Fournier had extensive vineyards in Cutchogue in the early 1700s and no doubt grew *vinifera* with the help of the grafting expertise of the local Indians. Just after the American Revolution, the first governor of New York granted Paul Richards a monopoly on the sale of wines produced from his "Little Fief" on the island. Anyone planting grapes owed him a royalty.

In the 1800s William Robert Prince experimented extensively with many varieties of grapes in Flushing, Queens. He even offered a Zinfandel in his catalogue that was occasionally known as "Black St. Peter."

The North Fork strip of Long Island is ideally suited for winemaking and grape growing. The growing season is approximately 210 days a year (the same as in Bordeaux, France, and Napa Valley, California). It is the only wine-growing region in the world surrounded on three sides by water, which provides temperatures that rarely go below zero in the winter and a low humidity—the perfect combination for producing excellent wine grapes.

Erie-Chautauqua. Long hours of summer sun, well-drained gravel and shale soils, and the moderating influence of Lake Erie on the local climate combine to make the Erie-Chautauqua region one of the finest grape growing areas in the East.

Arkansas

The state of Arkansas has six bonded wineries in operation, a far cry from the 106 original wineries in existence during the early 1800s. Its best-known wineries are:

Wiederkehr Winery, located in Altus; established in 1880 by Johann Andreas Wiederkehr.

Post Winery, also located in Altus; established in 1880; owned by Mathew J. Post.

Hawaii

There is only one commercial winery in Hawaii, located on the beautiful island of Maui approximately 2,000 feet above sea level on part of a 22,000-acre ranch; its vines were first planted in 1974.

Tedeschi Winery, owned and operated by Emil and Joanne Tedeschi, produces an unusual wine made from pineapples and called Maui Blanc. It is produced in two versions, still and sparkling, using the *méthode champenoise* method. Tedeschi's first grape harvest was in 1977 when Carnelian grapes (a cross between Grenache, Cabernet Sauvignon, and Carignane) were picked with good results. Tedeschi has more than 20 acres planted so far and is experimenting with *Vitis vinifera* varieties, hoping someday to produce top-quality varietals.

Idaho

Although Idaho has seven working wineries, the most prominent is Ste. Chapelle Winery, founded in 1975 by Bill Broich. In 1978 Symms Vineyards merged with Ste. Chapelle Winery (then located in Emmett) and moved to Sunny Slope, 13 miles southwest of Caldwell. Today Ste. Chapelle produces a Cabernet Sauvignon, Chardonnay, Chenin Blanc, Gewürztraminer, Johannisberg Riesling, and Pinot Noir.

Illinois

As far back as 1880, when the U.S. Department of Agriculture published a special report on the progress of grape viticulture and wine production in the nation, Illinois was one of the wine-growing enterprises of the Midwest. Vineyards around the village of Nauvoo, on the Mississippi River, were first planted around 1845. Today wines are made from *Vitis labrusca* varieties such as Catawba, Concord, Ives, and Niagara, although French-American hybrids and *Vitis vinifera* varieties are also widely planted.

The Thompson Winery, founded in 1964 by John Thompson, is one of the leading producers of sparkling wines, two of which are Père Marquette and Père Hennepin. The Lynfred Winery, owned and operated by Lynn and Fred Koehler, is located in the flatlands west of O'Hare Field in Roselle. It was established in 1975, but didn't officially open its doors to the public until October 22, 1979. Within the past few years,

Lynfred Winery has captured a number of medals with bottles of *Vitis vinifera* wines.

Indiana

Indiana has seven bonded wineries; the best known are:

The Bloomington Winery, in Bloomington; established in 1983; owned by James and Susan Butler.

Château Thomas Winery, in Indianapolis; established in 1984; owned by Charles and Jill Thomas.

Huber Orchard Winery, in Borden; established in 1978; owned by Gerald and Carl Huber.

Maryland

Today there are twelve bonded wineries; the best known are:

Berrywine Plantations, in Mount Airy; established in 1971; owned by Jack and Lucille Aellen.

Boordy Vineyards, in Hydes; established in 1942 (Maryland's oldest); originally owned by Philip and Jocelyn Wagner, now owned by Robert Deford III. The first French-American hybrid varietal wine made in the United States was made in 1947 in the Boordy Vineyards by Philip Wagner.

Byrd Vineyards, in Myersville; established in 1976; owned by William and Sharon Byrd.

Montbray Cellars, in Westminster; established in 1966; owned by Dr. G. Hamilton and Phyllis Mowbray. In 1974 Montbray was the first United States winery to commercially produce an "ice wine," a Riesling; however, only seventy-five bottles were produced.

Michigan

Of the seventeen bonded wineries in operation, the best known are:

St. Julian Winery, in Paw Paw; the state's oldest winery; established by Mariano Meconi in 1921.

Tabor Hill Winery, in Buchanan; established in 1970; owned by David F. Upton.

Warner Vineyards, in Paw Paw; established in 1939; owned by James J. Warner.

New Jersey

There are fifteen wineries in New Jersey; the best known are:

The Renault Winery, in Egg Harbor City; established in 1864 by Louis Nicholas Renault, who came to the United States in 1855, representing the ancient champagne house of the Duke of Montebello at Reims. By 1870 Renault had introduced his New Jersey champagne and became the largest shipper of champagne (sparkling wine) in the United States. Renault is the third bonded winery to open in the United States, the first being the California-based Cucamonga Winery, and the second the Brotherhood Winery in New York State. The winery is owned by Joseph P. Milza.

The Gross Highland Winery, in Absecon; established in 1934 by John Gross; owned by Bernard d'Arcy.

Tewksbury Wine Cellars, in Lebanon; established in 1979; owned by Dr. Daniel F. Vernon.

Ohio

Ohio boasts over thirty-five bonded wineries bordering mostly along Lake Erie and in the Sandusky Island area. The most famous winery of Ohio is Meier's, established in Silverton in 1895 by John C. Meier. Today it is owned by Paramount Distillers.

Oregon

Prior to Prohibition, grape growing was sparse and haphazard, with little documentation on the type or variety of grapes grown and no information on the quality of wine produced. Following Prohibition, small wineries, often family owned, started to sprout, encouraging further planting and the start of Oregon's wine industry. Today there are more than forty-six bonded wineries, mostly situated in or near the Umpqua Valley in the western part of Oregon and in Willamette Valley in the north.

In the mid-1970s, Oregon winemakers drafted and lobbied into legislation consumer-oriented wine labeling regulations whose key provisions are:

A vintage date indicates that at least 95 percent of the grapes used are harvested during the year stated.

The name of a wine can be varietal (containing at least 90 percent of the grape variety used, with the exception of Cabernet Sauvignon, which is traditionally blended).

No Oregon-produced wine may be given a generic name—for example, Chablis, Burgundy, or Rhine.

The best-known wineries are:

Eyrie Vineyards, in Dundee; established in 1966 and the oldest *vinifera* vineyard and winery in the Willamette Valley; owned by David and Diana Lett.

The Knudsen-Erath Winery, in Dundee; established in 1972; owned by the Knudsen family.

The Tualatin Winery in Forest Grove; established by Bill Malkmus and Bill Fuller in 1973.

Other wineries are: Adelsheim Vineyards; Elk Cove Vineyards; Honeywood Winery (the state's oldest, dating back to 1934); and Oak Knoll Winery.

Pennsylvania

Grape growing and winemaking flourished during the 1800s and early 1900s. But with the coming of Prohibition after World War I the last of the state's existing wineries went out of business. Pennsylvania emerged from that era as a tightly controlled monopoly state. It was not until 1968, with the passage of the Limited Wine Act, that the modern period began. In recent years the changes have been dramatic. Wineries and vineyards continue to spring up across the state.

Today there are forty-three bonded wineries in existence; the best known are:

Bucks Country Winery, in New Hope; established in 1973 by Arthur and Marilyn Gerold.

The Chaddsford Winery, in Chadds Ford; established in 1982 by Eric and Lee Miller.

Presque Isle Wine Cellars, in North East; established in 1964 by Douglas and Marlene Moorhead.

Texas

There are eighteen bonded wineries in Texas; the best known are:

Fall Creek Vineyards, in Tow; established in 1979 by Hugo Edwin Auler.

Val Verde Vineyards, in Del Rio; the state's oldest winery, located right across the border from Mexico; established in 1883 by Francisco Qualia.

Llano Estacado Winery, in Lubbock; established in 1976.

La Buena Vida Winery (the good life), in Springtown; established in 1978 by Dr. Bobby G. Smith.

Virginia

The first glass wine bottle as we know it today was actually manufactured in 1608 in Jamestown, Virginia. The production of fine wines is not new to the Commonwealth. Over a century ago Virginia enjoyed an international reputation for producing good Bordeaux-style red wines. The inspiration then and now came from Virginia's original wine pioneer and "father of the American wine industry," Thomas Jefferson. He recognized that Virginia's climate and soils were very similar to those of the European wine regions and insisted that fine wine grapes could be grown there.

Today Thomas Jefferson's vision is borne out in vineyards that flourish from the Allegheny Mountains to Chesapeake Bay. The state can also claim four official viticultural areas: Monticello, Shenandoah Valley, Rocky Knob, and the North Fork of the Roanoke, with more on the way. There are thirty-two bonded wineries; the best known are:

Barboursville Winery, in Barboursville; originally owned by Governor James Barbour. The site is a registered Virginia historic landmark and includes the picturesque ruins of Barbour's mansion which was designed by Thomas Jefferson and burned on Christmas Day, 1884. The current winery was established in 1979 and is owned by Zonin Gambellara of Italy.

Ingleside Plantation Vineyards, in Oak Grove; established in 1980; owned by Carl F. Flemer.

Meredyth Winery, in Middleburg; established in 1975; owned by Archie M. Smith.

Washington

Washington is the second-largest producing state (after California) of *Vitis vinifera* grapes, with just over 9,000 acres under cultivation (figure 2-1). Most of the *vinifera* acreage is in the Columbia Valley in the south-central portion of the state. Its vineyards lie just north of the 46° latitude, which is the same as that of the Bordeaux and Burgundy regions of France. The vine growth pattern is also similar to that of the French regions because of the long summer days (averaging 17.4 hours of daylight in June) and crisp, cool nights.

This favorable combination in the annual growing cycle provides additional light for photosynthesis. Near harvest the sun's rays are less intense, causing warm days but very cool nights. This day/night temperature difference helps to produce balanced grapes—heavy in sugar but still high in natural acidity, with a distinctive varietal character. There is an added bonus to growing grapes in these conditions: Washington is free of phylloxera. This root louse can't seem to survive here, making the costly process of resistant root grafting totally unnecessary.

There are thirty-four bonded wineries in Washington, centering on the Columbia, Yakima, and Snake rivers in the east, Spokane to the northeast, and Seattle to the west. The best known are:

Château Ste. Michelle Winery (formerly known as the American Wine Growers Winery), in Woodinville; established in 1934; owned by the United States Tobacco Company. This is Washington's foremost producer of premium *(Vitis vinifera)* table wines. Growing from just over 6,000 cases in 1967 (first crush under the new name), it now produces approximately 9 to 10 million cases annually.

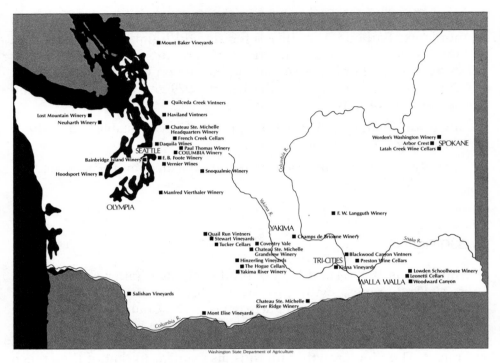

Figure 2-1 Washington State Wineries: 1984.

Arbor Crest Winery, in Spokane; established in 1982; owned by Harold and David Mielke.

Associated Vintners, Inc. (also known as the Columbia Winery), in Bellevue; established in 1962; owned by Dan Baty.

Preston Wine Cellars, in Pasco; established in 1976; owned by Bill and Joann Preston.

Quail Run Vintners, in Zillah; established in 1982; owned by Leon J. Willard.

Wisconsin

There are twelve bonded wineries in this state. The best known is the Wollersheim Winery, founded in 1857 as the Kehl Winery, by Peter Kehl. When the present owner, Robert Wollersheim, purchased the winery in 1972, the name was changed to Wollersheim.

Suggested Readings

Adams, Leon. *The Wines of America*. New York; McGraw-Hill, 3d ed., 1985.

Balzer, Robert Lawrence. *Wines of California*. New York; Harry N. Abrams, 1978.

Grossman, Harold J. *Grossman's Guide to Wines, Beers and Spirits*. New York; Scribner's, 7th ed., 1983.

Lichine, Alexis. *New Encyclopedia of Wines and Spirits*. New York; Alfred A. Knopf, 3d ed., 1981.

Mariani, John F. *The Dictionary of American Food and Drink*. New York; Ticknor and Fields, 1983.

Robards, Terry. *California Wine Label Album*. New York; Workman Publishing, 1986.

Tartt, Gene. *The Vineyard Almanac and Wine Gazetteer*. (Self-published from Saratoga, Cal.) 1984.

Discussion Topics and Questions

1. Compare and contrast the wine laws of the United States with those of France and Italy.

2. Does the 75 percent minimum for varietal designation limit winemakers' creativity in producing top-quality wines? Discuss, and cite examples.

3. Does the designation of viticultural areas in California help or confuse consumers? Why?

4. Although federal regulations govern the production of wine in the United States, Oregon has enacted more restrictive regulations for its state. What differences exist between Oregon's regulations and the federal regulations?

5. Which California wineries were the first to bottle specific grape varieties as single varietals?

6. New York State claims to be the second-largest wine-producing state in the United States. Washington State claims to be the second-largest grower of *Vitis vinifera* grapes in the United States. How is this possible?

7. How many states are major producers of fruit wines? Which are they? Identify the major fruits utilized.

3

Wines of Italy

This chapter discusses:

- Italy's comprehensive wine laws.
- Italy's DOC and DOCG designations.
- Generic, varietal, and proprietary wines.
- Italy's twenty wine-producing regions.

Italy is literally one vast vineyard, stretching from Piedmont in the north to Sicily in the south, encompassing more than three million acres of vineyards. Italy is divided into twenty wine-producing regions which are subdivided into almost one hundred provinces (figure 3-1).

Italy, the largest producer of wine in the world since 1974 (1.9 billion gallons in 1984), is also the world's largest wine consumer. In 1985, 24.5 gallons of wine per capita were consumed. Italy is also the largest exporter of wines into the United States (69 million gallons in 1985) and leads all other countries in the exportation of table wines into the United States (58.5 million gallons in 1985). Italy is the largest producer of vermouth in the world; the leading exporter of sparkling wines (7.4 million gallons in 1985); and the third-largest exporter of fortified wines to the United States (194,000 gallons in 1985).

Italy's Wine Laws

DOC Laws

On July 12, 1963, the president of the Republic of Italy, Antonio Segni, signed into law at the Palazzo del Quirinale (his official residence) the Italian wine laws known as the *Denominazione di Origine Controllata* (or

Figure 3-1 Italy's twenty wine-producing regions.

DOC laws), under Presidential Decree No. 930. On July 15, these laws were published in the *Gazzetta Ufficiale della Republica Italiana,* the official registry of the Italian government.

The basic aim of the wine law was to protect the name of origin and the sources of musts (unfermented grape juice) and wines, and to provide measures to prevent fraud and unfair competition. Figure 3-2 shows a comprehensive wine label that incorporates many of the DOC regulations.

These very comprehensive laws cover just about every phase of grape cultivation and wine production and provide strict controls at every step of the process. The following are some of the aspects of wine production that are regulated under these laws:

Area of production.

Type of soil.

Location of vineyard.

Type of grape variety used.

Pruning and cultivation techniques.

Allowable yields per acre (tonnage).

Allowable yield of juice per ton of grapes.

Minimum sugar levels.

Minimum acid and extract levels.

Methods of vinification.

Minimum aging requirements.

These laws are quite similar to those of France and Germany. One major exception is that the wines of Italy may not be chaptalized (sugar added to the must).

Every wine awarded a DOC designation has a set of rules and regulations that apply solely to that wine. A Chianti wine might therefore have completely different rules for production than a Bardolino. Currently there are more than 1,200 wines that have been granted DOC status.

DOCG

DOCG stands for *Denominazione di Origine Controllata e Garantita;* this designation is given to those wines that are considered to be of a higher quality than DOC wines and made under even stricter guidelines.

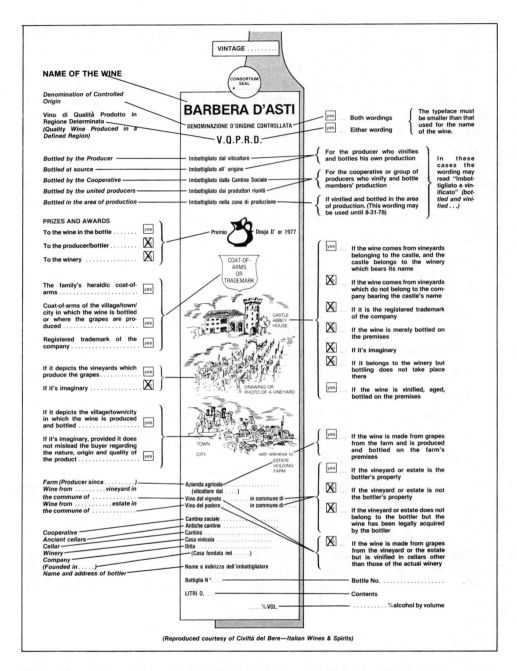

(Reproduced courtesy of Civiltà del Bere—Italian Wines & Spirits)

Figure 3-2 Comprehensive wine label. (Courtesy of *Italian Wines & Spirits Magazine*)

The upgrading of DOC to DOCG does not occur automatically, but only when a certain number of producers of a given DOC wine apply for the designation. In fact, such a choice on the part of the producers can bring about serious economic consequences.

DOC wines can be sold to the consumer in bulk, but DOCG wines must be bottled in containers not surpassing five liters in capacity. Their bottling must be guaranteed by a *state seal* applied to the bottle top. The seal is applied in such a way that it prevents removal of the wine from the bottle without breaking the seal.

Like DOC wines, all DOCG wines must undergo viticultural and enological controls established by Italian law as well as by their respective production regulations. In addition, DOCG wines must be submitted for an organoleptic evaluation before bottling by a panel of experts appointed by Italy's Ministry of Agriculture and Forestry. Each DOCG wine is tasted by a different panel composed of experts for that particular wine.

All DOC and DOCG wines undergo obligatory production controls by agricultural inspectors at harvest time; the controls cover maximum yields, minimum natural alcohol content, and so on. The wines are inspected by fraud prevention authority representatives who examine their chemical, physical, and organoleptic characteristics.

If a producer's wine does not pass the taste test, it is deprived of its DOCG status and declassified to ordinary table wine (*vino da tavola*). There is legislation before the ministry that would allow DOC wines to retain their classification if denied DOCG status, instead of being declassified to *vino da tavola*.

On July 1, 1980, Brunello di Montalcino was the first wine to be granted the DOCG status. Since that time, Vino Nobile di Montepulciano, Barolo, Barbaresco, and Chianti have also been granted the DOCG status. Applications for the status have been made and are pending for, among others, Albana di Romagna, a white wine.

There are some very good to excellent Italian wines that do not carry the DOC or DOCG designation, because they are either new blends or made from grapes that fall outside of the DOC region. Some examples are Tignanello, Sassicaia, and Riunite Lambrusco.

Generic, Varietal, and Proprietary Wines

Italy's wines are referred to as *generic* (named for their place of origin), *varietal* (named for the variety of grape from which they are made), and *proprietary* (producer named). Soave is a generic wine, Pinot Grigio a varietal wine, and Est! Est!! Est!!! a proprietary wine.

Two wines that often cause confusion are Vino Nobile di Montepulciano and Montepulciano d'Abruzzo. Vino Nobile di Montepulciano, a generic wine, is named for the town of Montepulciano in Tuscany. Montepulciano d'Abruzzo, a varietal wine, is named after the Montepulciano grape variety grown in Abruzzo as well as other regions. Some of Italy's most common proprietary wines are listed below.

Wine	*Translation*
Balestriere	Crossbow Archer
Barbacarlo	Uncle Charles
Buttafuoco	Spitfire
Corvo	Crow
Est! Est!! Est!!!	It is! It is!! It is!!!
Frecciarossa	Red Arrow
Inferno	Hell
Lacrima Christi	Tears of Christ
Lacrima d'Arno	Tears of the Arno River
Regaleali	Royal Land
Sangue di Giuda	The Blood of Judas
Scacciadiavoli	Drive the Devil Out
Settesoli	Seven Suns
Vino Santo	Wine of the Saints

Italy's Wine-Producing Regions

Abruzzo

Abruzzo is located just south of Latium in the south-central part of Italy off the Adriatic Sea. In this region there are only two grape varieties of importance: Trebbiano (a white grape) and Montepulciano (a red grape). These grape varieties produce the region's only DOC wines:

Trebbiano d'Abruzzo (white): minimum 11.5 percent alcohol; received DOC 6/28/72; best consumed young.

Montepulciano d'Abruzzo (red): minimum 12 percent alcohol; if aged a minimum of two years may be labeled *vecchio* (old); received DOC 5/24/68; produced in both rosé and red from a minimum of 85 percent Montepulciano grapes and a maximum of 15 percent Sangiovese grapes.

Montepulciano d'Abruzzo is often vinified in a very light, fresh style, similar to a Beaujolais, and should be consumed very young.

Apulia

Apulia stretches from the "spur" to the "heel" of the boot-shaped Italian peninsula. The southwestern shore of the region lies along the Ionian Sea, while its entire eastern shore lies along the Adriatic. Apulia is bordered by Molise to the north and Campania and Basilicata to the west. The region's climate is temperate and the country is mainly flat.

For years this region was considered by many to be incapable of producing quality table wines because of its intense heat and arid climate. The wines that were produced (mostly reds) were heavy, dark in color, highly alcoholic, and flat tasting (lacking acidity). Therefore, a good percentage of the wines were shipped north to Piedmont where they were blended with other varieties and used in the production of vermouth.

Within the last few years, however, modern technology has overtaken the region's vineyards, drastically lowering its total wine production. In place of the heavy alcoholic wines, today's vineyards produce lighter, fresher wines with surprisingly good acidity levels. The producers have sacrificed yield for quality and are now making some of Italy's best rosé wines.

Cabernet Franc and Malbec, Chardonnay, and Pinot Bianco are some of the nonlocal grape varieties that have been introduced in the area.

There are thirty-three wines that have gained DOC status; some of the better known ones are:

Castel del Monte Bianco (white): minimum 11.5 percent alcohol; received DOC 5/19/71; a blend of Pampanuto and other grape varieties; best consumed young.

Castel del Monte Rosato (rosé) (referred to as "Rivera"): minimum 11.5 percent alcohol; received DOC 5/19/71; a blend of Bombino Nero and other grape varieties; best consumed young.

Castel del Monte Rosso (red): minimum 12 percent alcohol; if 12.5 percent alcohol and aged three years, may be labeled *riserva;* received DOC 5/19/71; a blend of Bombino Nero and other grape varieties; best consumed at two to five years old, or if *riserva,* at six to eight years.

Although not a DOC wine, one of the finest wines of Apulia is Torre Quarto, produced in red, rosé, and white versions. The white is a blend of Bombino Bianco, Trebbiano, and Greco grape varieties. The red and rosé are blends of Malbec and Uva di Troia grapes and are best if consumed when five to seven years old.

Basilicata

Basilicata is a relatively small and unknown wine-producing region best known for its steep, rugged mountains, hot weather, and highly alcoholic red wines.

This inland region is the home of Monte Vulture (Vulture Mountain), a now extinct volcano, at whose base and on whose slopes grows the famous red Aglianico grape. Aglianico del Vulture is this region's only DOC wine:

Aglianico del Vulture (red): minimum 11.5 percent alcohol; if 12.5 percent alcohol and aged three years, may be labeled *vecchio;* if 12.5 percent alcohol and aged five years, may be labeled *riserva;* received DOC 2/18/71; best consumed at five to sevèn years old; if *vecchio,* at seven to nine years; if *riserva,* at ten to fifteen years.

According to legend, the Aglianico grape was brought to Italy by ancient Greek settlers around 800 B.C. Its name is a corruption of the ancient Greek vine *Ellenico* or *Hellenica.* Today the Aglianico grape is widely cultivated throughout much of southern Italy, especially in Basilicata and Campania.

Calabria

There are ten wines from this region that have gained DOC status; some of the better known are:

Cirò Bianco (white): minimum 12 percent alcohol; received DOC 4/2/69; a blend of Greco Bianco and Trebbiano Toscano; best consumed young.

Cirò Rosato (rosé): minimum 13.5 percent alcohol; received DOC 4/2/69; a blend of Gaglioppo, Trebbiano, and Greco Bianco grapes; best consumed young.

Cirò Rosso (red): minimum 13.5 percent alcohol; received DOC 4/2/69; if aged three years, may be labeled *riserva*; if produced in the heart of Cirò, may be labeled *classico*; a blend of Gaglioppo, Trebbiano, and Greco Bianco grapes; best consumed at four to six years old; if *riserva*, at seven to nine years.

Campania

When most people think of wines from southern Italy they immediately think of Naples. Actually, vineyards are not found in the city of Naples but in the outlying areas.

There are ten wines produced in this region that have gained DOC status; some of the better known are:

Taurasi (red): minimum 12 percent alcohol; received DOC 5/25/70; must be aged three years; if aged four years, may be labeled *riserva*; a blend of Aglianico, Piedirosso (red feet), and Sangiovese and/or Barbera grapes; has an unusually long life, sometimes lasting two decades; best consumed at seven to nine years old; if *riserva*, at ten to fifteen years.

Lacrima Christi del Vesuvio Bianco (white): minimum 11 percent alcohol; received DOC late in 1979; a blend of Coda di Volpe (fox's tail), Greco di Torre, and Biancolella grapes; best consumed young; also produced in a non-DOC semidry version. Lacrima Christi del Vesuvio Rosso (red); minimum 12 percent alcohol; best if consumed at three to eight years old.

Greco di Tufo (white): minimum 11.5 percent alcohol; a blend of Greco and Coda di Volpe grape varieties; best consumed at two to four years old.

Fiano di Avellino (white): minimum 11.5 percent alcohol; a blend of Fiano, Greco, Coda di Volpe, and Trebbiano Toscano grape varieties; best consumed at two to five years old.

There are many legends surrounding the Lacrima Christi (tears of Christ) wine. One is that the banished angel Lucifer broke off a piece of heaven and let it fall to earth. When the Lord saw the loss, he immediately began to weep, and with each tear another grapevine grew.

Emilia-Romagna

Emilia-Romagna is the home of Lambrusco, the city of Bologna (noted for its rich cuisine), prosciutto ham, and the operatic tenor Luciano Pavarotti.

Most Lambrusco produced here is non-DOC and is available in both a dry and semidry style. Lambrusco is typically *frizzante*, although a *spumante* version can be found. It can be red, white, or rosé and is best when consumed very young.

The best-selling wine in the United States is Riunite Lambrusco, of which more than eight million cases per year are sold. Other Lambrusco wines sold in the United States are Giacobazzi, Cella, and Zonin.

In Italy, local growers formed what is known as a *consorzio*, to help protect and promote their wines. These *consorzios* give member wineries special labels for attachment to the bottle's neck. Each neck label depicts a different scene, insignia, or emblem. The labels on Lambrusco, Albana di Romagna, and Sangiovese di Romagna wines, for instance, show a white cock and grapes on a red ground, or a man and woman treading grapes.

There are nineteen wines from this region that have gained DOC status; some of the better known are:

Lambrusco di Sorbara: minimum 11 percent alcohol; received DOC 5/1/70; a blend of Lambrusco di Sorbara and Lambrusco Salamino grapes.

Lambrusco Grasparossa di Castelvetro: minimum 10.5 percent alcohol; received DOC 5/1/70; a blend of Lambrusco Grasparossa and other grape varieties.

Lambrusco Reggiano: minimum 10.5 percent alcohol; received DOC 7/22/71; a blend of Lambruschi Marani, Salamino, Montericcio, Maestri, and other grape varieties.

Lambrusco Salamino di Santa Croce: minimum 11 percent alcohol; received DOC 5/1/70; a blend of Lambrusco Salamino and other grape varieties.

Albana di Romagna Secco (white): minimum 12 percent alcohol; also produced as a spumante; received DOC 7/21/67; 100 percent Albana grapes; best consumed young.

Sangiovese di Romagna (red): minimum 11 percent alcohol; received DOC 7/9/67; if 12 percent alcohol, from a specified area, may be labeled *superiore;* if aged two years, may be labeled *riserva;* 100 percent

Sangiovese grapes; best consumed at one to two years of age; *riserva*, at two to three years.

Trebbiano di Romagna (white): minimum 11.5 percent alcohol; received DOC 8/31/73; 100 percent Trebbiano grapes; best consumed young.

Gutturnio (red): minimum 12 percent alcohol; received DOC 7/9/67; produced in either a still or slightly *frizzante* version; a blend of Barbera and Bonarda grapes; best consumed young.

Friuli-Venezia-Giulia

One of the smallest of Italy's wine-producing regions, Friuli-Venezia-Giulia borders on Austria and Yugoslavia in the most northeastern region of Italy. Its terrain is predominantly rocky and hilly and the climate generally quite mild. Pordenone, Gorizia, and Udine are the important wine centers of this region.

There are six delimited zones within the Friuli region; from smallest to largest, they are: Latisana, Aquilea, Isonzo, Collio, Colli Orientali del Friuli, and Grave del Friuli. The four most important of these wine-producing zones are Grave del Friuli, Colli Orientali del Friuli, Collio, and Isonzo.

Grave del Friuli. This area produces seven wines, all of which were granted the DOC designation on July 20, 1970.

The white wines, which are all dry and 100 percent varietals, should be consumed young:

Pinot Bianco: minimum 11.5 percent alcohol.

Pinot Grigio: minimum 11 percent alcohol.

Tocai Friulano: minimum 11 percent alcohol.

Verduzzo Friulano: minimum 11 percent alcohol.

The red wines are all dry and 100 percent varietals:

Cabernet: minimum 11.5 percent alcohol; best consumed when two to four years old.

Merlot: minimum 11 percent alcohol; best consumed young.

Refosco: minimum 11 percent alcohol; best consumed young.

Colli Orientali del Friuli. This area produces twelve DOC wines, all of which received the designation on July 20, 1970. Some of the better known ones are listed below.

The white wines, which are all dry (except for Picolit) and 100 percent varietals, should be consumed young:

Tocai: minimum 12 percent alcohol; has a characteristically bitter taste.

Pinot Bianco: minimum 12 percent alcohol.

Pinot Grigio: minimum 12 percent alcohol.

Sauvignon Blanc: minimum 12 percent alcohol.

Riesling Renano: minimum 12 percent alcohol.

Verduzzo: minimum 12 percent alcohol.

Picolit: minimum 15 percent alcohol; if aged two years, may be labeled *riserva;* 100 percent Picolit grapes (technically known as Picolit Giallo).

Picolit vines thrived in Friuli during the late 1700s, and by the mid-nineteenth century produced the most prestigious wines of Italy, bottles of which graced the tables of royalty throughout England, France, Russia, and Austria.

Unfortunately, the vine in later years produced very few grapes, and was thought to have a genetic disease called *floral abortion.* Modern research conducted by Dr. Giovanni Cargnello at the Conegliano Institute, however, discovered that the Picolit grape variety is not self-pollinating because it is purely female and not, as is usual, hermaphroditic.

Picolit, a brightly golden-colored dessert wine, is produced in dry, semidry, and sweet versions (without the help of *Botrytis cinerea,* known as *muffa nobile,* or "noble rot"). The sweet version is made from dried grapes (called *passito*). Picolit commands extremely high prices; the dry and semidry types are best consumed when three to eight years old; the sweet version is best consumed when seven to twelve years old.

The red wines are all dry and 100 percent varietals:

Refosco dal Peduncolo Rosso: minimum 12 percent alcohol; received DOC 7/21/75; if aged two years, may be labeled *riserva;* best consumed when two to four years old; *riserva,* three to five years.

Merlot: minimum 12 percent alcohol; best consumed when two to five years old.

Cabernet: minimum 12 percent alcohol; if aged two years, may be labeled *riserva;* best consumed when five years old; *riserva,* at five to seven years old.

Pinot Nero (Noir): minimum 12 percent alcohol; if aged two years, may be labeled *riserva;* best consumed when two to four years old; *riserva,* at three to six years.

(Most Italian red wines labeled "Cabernet" are actually Cabernet Franc; if the wine is a Cabernet Sauvignon, both words will (and must) appear on the label.)

Collio. This area produces nine wines, all of which were granted the DOC designation on May 24, 1968. Some of the better known ones are listed below.

The white wines, which are all dry and 100 percent varietals, should be consumed young:

Pinot Bianco: minimum 12 percent alcohol.

Pinot Grigio: minimum 12.5 percent alcohol.

Riesling Italico: minimum 12 percent alcohol.

Tocai Friulano: minimum 12 percent alcohol.

Sauvignon Blanc: minimum 12.5 percent alcohol.

Traminer (or Gewürztraminer): minimum 12 percent alcohol.

The Pinot Grigio produced by Livio Felluga is called Ramato (which means copper colored), due to the fact that it is vinified in contact with the grape skins, causing greater depth of color and flavor.

The red wines are all dry 100 percent varietals, and are best consumed young:

Cabernet Franc: minimum 12 percent alcohol.

Merlot: minimum 12 percent alcohol.

Pinot Nero: minimum 12.5 percent alcohol.

Isonzo. The area of Isonzo produced ten wines, all granted the DOC designation on October 30, 1974. Some of the better known are listed below.

The white wines, which are all dry and 100 percent varietals, should be consumed young:

Malvasia Istriana: minimum 10.5 percent alcohol.

Pinot Bianco: minimum 11 percent alcohol.

Pinot Grigio: minimum 11 percent alcohol.

Riesling Renano: minimum 11 percent alcohol.

Tocai Friulano: minimum 10.5 percent alcohol.

Sauvignon Blanc: minimum 11 percent alcohol.

Traminer Aromatico (Gewürztraminer): minimum 11 percent alcohol.

Verduzzo Friulano: minimum 10.5 percent alcohol.

The red wines are all dry 100 percent varietals, and should be consumed young:

Cabernet (Franc or Sauvignon): minimum 11 percent alcohol.

Merlot: minimum 10.5 percent alcohol.

Latium

Latium (*Lazio*, in Italian), whose regional capital is Rome, is located in the central part of Italy. It is bordered in the north by Umbria and Tuscany; in the south by Molise and Campania; in the east by Abruzzo; and in the west by the Tyrrhenian Sea.

The production of wine in Latium is approximately 90 percent white (DOC), with the remaining 10 percent mostly devoted to non-DOC reds. Some of the best wines of this region are in fact not DOC wines, and are bottled under the name of Castelli Romani.

There are twenty-two wines produced in the region that have gained DOC status; some of the better known are:

Colli Albani (white): minimum 11.5 percent alcohol; received DOC 8/6/70; if 12.5 percent alcohol, may be labeled *superiore;* a blend of Malvasia, Trebbiano, and other grape varieties; best consumed young.

Est! Est!! Est!!! di Montefiascone (dry or semidry white): minimum 10.5 percent alcohol; received DOC 3/3/66; a blend of Trebbiano Toscano, Malvasia, and Rossetto grapes; best consumed young.

Frascati (dry and sweet white): 11.5 percent alcohol; received DOC 3/3/66; if 12 percent alcohol, may be labeled *superiore;* also produced as a spumante; a blend of Malvasia Bianca di Candia, Malvasia del Lazio, Greco, and Trebbiano Toscano, with small amounts of Bellone and Bonvino permitted; dry version labeled *secco* or *asciutto;* two sweet styles are made from grapes affected by the "noble rot"; the semisweet *amabile* or sweet *cannellino,* or *dolce;* dry best consumed young, and the sweeter at three to five years; well-known producers are Alfredo, Gotto d'Oro, and Fontana Candida.

Marino (white): minimum 11.5 percent alcohol; received DOC 8/6/70; if 12.5 percent alcohol, may be labeled *superiore;* also produced as a spumante; a blend of Malvasia Bianca, Trebbiano, and other grape varieties; best consumed young.

Trebbiano di Aprilia (white): minimum 11 percent alcohol; received DOC 5/13/66; a blend of Trebbiano Giallo and/or Toscano; best consumed young.

In the year 1110, Bavarian bishop Baron Johannes Fugger of Augsburg was traveling to Rome on a visit to the Vatican, under the instructions of Emperor Henry V. The nobleman, a connoisseur of good food and wine, sent his faithful servant Martino ahead to find suitable quarters for food, drink, and lodging. He was instructed to chalk the word *est* (*it is*) at the entrance of every inn where the wine was especially good, and *non est* (*it is not*) on all others. The servant was so enthusiastic about the wine of Montefiascone that he wrote "Est! Est!! Est!!!" on the door of a local inn. The baron agreed with his servant's choice, so much so in fact that he remained in Montefiascone.

Upon his death, the baron agreed to give all his money to the local church in exchange for a small favor. Each year, on the anniversary of his death in August, a barrel of Est! Est!! Est!!! was to be poured over his grave so he could once again savor that glorious wine. That tradition was carried on for centuries until Cardinal Barberigo, who became Montefiascone's bishop, thought it better to donate the wine to the poor rather than wasting it on the baron, who was dead.

The story is commemorated in this ancient town at the church of San Flaviano, where on a tombstone is this inscription, in Latin; translated, it reads:

> *It is, It is, It is,*
> *and though too much it is,*
> *my master Johannes Fugger,*
> *dead is.*

Liguria

Liguria, the second-smallest wine-producing (Val D'Aosta is the smallest) region in Italy, is located on the Italian Riviera. Only three of its wines have gained DOC status. The best known is:

Cinque Terre (a white wine named after the five communes in which it is produced): minimum 11 percent alcohol; received DOC 5/29/73; a blend of Bosco, Albarola, and Vermentino grape varieties; best consumed young.

Lombardy

The region of Lombardy, located in the center of northern Italy, borders on Switzerland to the north, Veneto and Trentino to the east, Emilia-Romagna to the south, and Piedmont to the west. Three of Italy's largest freshwater lakes—Maggiore, Como, and Garda—are in Lombardy. The Po, Italy's longest river, flows through this region's premier agricultural zone, the Po River Valley. Milan, Italy's industrial capital and second-largest city, next to Rome, is in Lombardy.

There are three major areas of wine production in Lombardy: Oltrepò Pavese, Valtellina, and Brescia, which includes the area south of Lake Iseo and the Lake Garda district. Two smaller areas of production also contribute to the regional output: the Colli Morenici Mantovani del Garda, the hills just south of Lake Garda in the province of Mantua; and the area north of Bergamo, in central Lombardy.

Oltrepò Pavese. Oltrepò Pavese was once part of Piedmont and is also referred to as "Vecchio Piemonte," or Old Piedmont. This area has for the past century been Milan's chief supplier of Barbera and Bonarda wines.

The Barbera and Bonarda (also known as Croatina) red grape varieties, the principal ones of the area, are cultivated exclusively in hillside vineyards. Increasing amounts of vineyard space, however, are being devoted to such white varieties as Riesling Italico, Riesling Renano, Moscato Bianco, Pinot Grigio, Chardonnay, and Müller-Thurgau. Pinot Nero and Uva Rara (both red) are also grown.

Ten DOC wines are produced in the Oltrepò Pavese; some of the better known are:

Barbacarlo (red): minimum 12 percent alcohol; received DOC 12/7/75; a blend of Barbera and Bonarda grapes; best consumed when three to six years old.

Buttafuoco (red): minimum 12 percent alcohol; received DOC 7/21/75; a blend of Barbera and Bonarda grapes; best consumed young.

Riesling (white): minimum 11 percent alcohol; also produced as a spumante; received DOC 8/6/70; a blend of Riesling Renano and/or Riesling Italico; best consumed young.

Sangue di Giuda (red): minimum 12 percent alcohol; received DOC 12/7/75; a blend of Barbera and Bonarda grapes; best consumed young.

Frecciarossa (brand name): a single-vineyard producer, Dr. Odero, bottles four different wines, all under the umbrella name Chateau Frecciarossa; two, La Vigne Blanche (dry) and Sillery (semidry), are white; Saint George is a rosé; Grand Cru is red.

Valtellina. Valtellina, situated in the Adda River Valley in the northern province of Sondrio, is one of the few places where the Nebbiolo grape thrives. This grape, a well-known Piedmont variety, is called Chiavennasca in Lombardy and has been grown there since the fifth century A.D. It is the principal variety of the area and is cultivated in the terraced vineyards that scale the steep, rugged north bank of the valley. Here the grapes receive optimum exposure to the sun, as well as all the other microclimatic conditions needed for them to flourish. Other varieties are also grown: Rossola, Brugnola, Pignola Valtellinese, Merlot, and Pinot Nero.

The area's two DOC wines, Valtellina and Valtellina Superiore, are produced from the Nebbiolo grape. The bottle label of a Valtellina Superiore will usually carry the name of the designated area where the wine was produced. DOC law recognizes only four such geographic subdistricts for Valtellina Superiore: Sassella, Grumello, Valgella, and Inferno.

Valtellina (red): minimum 11 percent alcohol; received DOC 8/11/68; must be aged one year; if 12 percent alcohol and aged two years, may be labeled *superiore*; if aged four years, may be labeled *riserva*; a blend of Chiavennasca, Merlot, Pinot Nero, Rossola, Pignola Valtellinese, and Brugnola grape varieties; best consumed when three to five years old.

Sfurzat (red): minimum 14.5 percent alcohol; produced from the same grapes as Valtellina, except that it is made from partly dried grapes that have been allowed to dry on racks from the harvest until December; must be aged three years; deep, vinous, and sometimes slightly reminiscent of port; best consumed when seven to twelve years old.

Grumello, Inferno, Sassella, and Valgella (reds): received DOC 8/11/68; all four are Valtellina Superiores, so they must be aged two years or more; if aged four years, may be labeled *riserva*; individual characteristics (color, bouquet, taste) of each wine are slightly different; best consumed when five to seven years old.

One of the finest producers of Valtellina Superiore is Nino Negri, who labels his wines Castel Chiuro and Castel Chiuro Riserva.

Brescia. Wine production in the province of Brescia can be divided roughly into three areas: the Lake Garda district, the hills of Lake Iseo in the DOC zone known as Franciacorta, and the hills around the provincial capital of Brescia.

Four DOC wines are made in this district: Lugana, Tocai di San Martino della Battaglia, Riviera del Garda Bresciano Chiaretto, and Riviera del Garda Bresciano Rosso.

Today many vines are cultivated in the Lake Garda district: Groppello, Barbera, Sangiovese, Marzemino, Nebbiolo, Cabernet Franc, Trebbiano, Tocai Friulano, Pinot, and Riesling.

Lugana (white): minimum 11.5 percent alcohol; received DOC 7/21/68; also produced as a spumante; a blend of Trebbiano di Lugana and other grape varieties; best consumed young.

Riviera del Garda Bresciano Chiaretto (rosé): minimum 11.5 percent alcohol; received DOC 7/21/67; a blend of Groppello, Sangiovese, Barbera, and Marzemino grape varieties; best consumed young.

The DOC appellation of Franciacorta applies to three wines produced in the hills south of Lake Iseo near the town of Cortefranca in central Lombardy: Franciacorta Pinot Spumante, Franciacorta Pinot Bianco, and Franciacorta Rosso. The vines grown in the area are Pinot Bianco, Chardonnay, Cabernet Franc, Barbera, Nebbiolo, and Pinot Nero.

Mantua. The province of Mantua, ruled by the noble Gonzaga family during the Middle Ages and the Renaissance, is also the home of the relatively new DOC zone, the Colli Morenici Mantovani del Garda. Three wines—a white, a rosé, and a red—carry this appellation.

Many vines are planted in the area, including Rossanella, Rondinella, Negrara, Sangiovese, Lambrusco, Merlot, Trebbiano Giallo, Trebbiano

Toscano, Trebbiano di Soave, Trebbiano del Mantovani, Pinot Bianco, Riesling Italico, and Tocai Friulano.

Marches

The region of Marches is located in the north-central part of Italy, with its entire east coast on the Adriatic Sea. It is bordered to the west by Umbria, to the south by Abruzzo, and to the north by Emilia-Romagna and Tuscany.

In parts of Marches and Abruzzo, the peasant growers make a wine that they call *vino cotto*. It is actually a cooked wine, where the liquid content is reduced to 40 percent of its original volume. Fresh juice is then added, allowed to ferment, and aged for two years, producing a heavy, sweet wine of 18 to 20 percent alcohol. Unfortunately its production has severely dwindled in recent years.

There are nine wines produced in this region that have gained DOC status; some of the better known are:

Verdicchio dei Castelli di Jesi (white): minimum 11.5 percent alcohol; received DOC 8/11/68; also produced as a spumante; a blend of Verdicchio, with the possible addition of Trebbiano Toscano and Malvasia Toscano; best consumed young.

Rosso Piceno (red): minimum 11.5 percent alcohol; received DOC 8/11/68; if 12 percent alcohol, may be labeled *superiore;* a blend of Sangiovese (60 percent) and Montepulciano (40 percent) grape varieties; best consumed young.

Rosso Conero (red): minimum 11.5 percent alcohol; received DOC 7/21/78; a blend of Montepulciano (85 percent) and Sangiovese grape varieties; best consumed young.

Verdicchio is occasionally bottled in the traditional "amphora-shaped" bottles that were used to bring wine from Greece to the Italian peninsula in ancient times. It is one of the oldest wine bottle shapes in the world, predating the Bordeaux bottle.

One of the most popular brands of Verdicchio in the United States is from the firm of Fazi-Battaglia, featuring a *cartiglio* or tiny scroll, giving information about the wine, attached to the neck of the bottle. The *consorzio's* neck label on bottles of Verdicchio depicts a heraldic lion.

Molise

Molise is Italy's youngest wine-producing region; originally it was part of Abruzzo, but a change in the laws of 1963 made it a separate region.

In 1983 these wines gained DOC status: Biferno Bianco, Biferno Rosso, Biferno Rosato, Pentro di Isernia Rosato, Pentro di Isernia Bianco, and Pentro di Isernia Rosso.

Piedmont

Piedmont is in northwestern Italy, bordered by France to the west and Switzerland to the north. The Ligurian Apennines and the Alps surround Piedmont to the south, west, and north.

The Nebbiolo grape. Piedmont has been producing good to excellent wines for well over a century and has used the most underrated wine grape in the world, the Nebbiolo. Originally called *Vitis vinifera Pedemontana* (the vine of Piedmont), the grape is referred to as *Nubiola, Nebiola, Nibiol,* and *Nebiolum* in documents dating back to the Middle Ages. Its present name and spelling, officially sanctioned in 1962, is derived from the word *nebbia* (fog). Some say that it was given this name because of the persistent fog found in the area of cultivation, while others believe that it alludes to the thick bloom that forms on the grape skins, making them look as if they were surrounded by tiny patches of fog.

In Vercelli and Novara, the Nebbiolo is called Spanna.

The Nebbiolo produces wines that are usually rough and tannic when young but with age evolve into wines of extraordinary power, depth, and complexity. When blended with other varieties, the Nebbiolo grape gives the resultant wine body and substance.

Cultivated only in certain parts of Piedmont and Lombardy, the Nebbiolo vine is extremely sensitive to microclimatic conditions. It is particularly affected by slight variations in soil conditions. These variations explain in part why separate DOC appellations have been granted to Nebbiolo wines (for example, Barolo and Barbaresco) produced in adjoining zones of production. Nebbiolo grapes require fairly warm summers and rather cool and damp autumns, particularly in late October and early November when the grapes reach maturity.

Another characteristic of Piedmont is the practice of growing different grape varieties on the same slope: for instance, Barbera will be planted to a certain altitude, followed progressively by varieties that require more sun, such as Dolcetto, Moscato, or Nebbiolo. This explains how one area can produce wines with different denominations: e.g., Nebbiolo d'Alba, Dolcetto d'Alba, and Barbera d'Alba.

Wine production. Piedmont produces the greatest number of superb red wines in Italy. Piedmont has more than thirty-nine DOC appellations, as well as two DOCG wines, Barolo (7/1/80) and Barbaresco (10/3/80). Grape varieties that mature early or have built-in resistance to the cold and damp Piedmont autumns tend to prevail in the region. Nebbiolo is the region's best-known grape variety, but Barbera is by far the most prolific; more than 50 percent of all acreage under vine in Piedmont is planted with this grape. The vines are generally cultivated on hillsides to give them optimum exposure to the light and warmth of the sun.

The production of both DOC and non-DOC wines is concentrated in the southern part of Piedmont in the provinces of Cuneo, Asti, and Alessandria. This area of exclusively hilly vineyards accounts for 90 percent of the total regional output. Other areas of production are the hills between the towns of Novara and Vercelli and the zone around the regional capital of Turin. As the fame of Piedmont's fine wine has spread throughout the world, exports abroad have increased accordingly.

Piedmont today. Winemakers in this area are beginning to use newer or lighter methods of vinification for a host of reasons. For some the concern is strictly economic; they are paying exorbitant interest on bank loans and need a quick turnover of wines to pay off their debts. Others feel that most wine drinkers today do not want to wait twenty-plus years for a bottle of wine to mature.

In years past the practice was to ferment red wines on the skins, allowing them to sit one or more months after zero Brix (sugar) was reached. The wine then picked up additional grape tannins (phenolics) and a concentration of flavor. This also necessitated several years of barrel aging, several years more of bottle aging, and then more years of cellar aging before the wines became drinkable. This method is being replaced, by some producers, by shorter skin contact time and less barrel aging. Some growers and producers are trying to force DOC authorities to cut the minimum aging (barrel) requirement because they feel that the traditional methods produce wines that are lacking fruit and are actually dried out before they become ready to drink.

Barolo. Barolo is frequently referred to as "il vino dei re e il re dei vini" (the wine of kings and the king of wines). This powerful, robust, tannic, full-bodied red wine requires considerable aging before it can be fully enjoyed.

The DOC for Barolo, which was granted on April 23, 1966, requires that Barolo with the DOC and DOCG designations be produced from 100 percent Nebbiolo grapes grown in the area centering around the town of Barolo in the Langhe Hills just southeast of Alba. Barolo is garnet red in color with orange highlights and an intense but delicate bouquet. Very dry and full-bodied, it has an austere taste that becomes velvety and harmonious with age. Barolo DOC must be aged a minimum of three years, two of which must be in wood, and have a minimum alcohol content of 13 percent. When aged four years it may be labeled *riserva* and at five years *riserva speciale*. Barolo DOCG, which differs somewhat in that it must be aged five years to qualify as a *riserva*, has no *riserva speciale* designation. This dry, full-bodied wine can be consumed when six to twenty years old.

The Barolo *consorzio* features on its neck label a golden lion or a helmeted head on a blue background, according to the particular district it comes from.

Barbaresco. Barbaresco is often referred to as Barolo's "younger brother" or the "queen of Piedmont's wines." While not quite as powerful Barbaresco does share Barolo's robust and austere qualities. It has only recently been granted the DOCG status, but its production has actually been subject to local government regulations since 1908. A quality control group was set up at that time which, among other things, established the precise boundaries of the Barbaresco production zone. These boundaries were officially recognized by the DOC law of 1963. The law states that Barbaresco DOC and DOCG must be produced from 100 percent Nebbiolo grapes grown in vineyards located in the towns of Barbaresco, Neive, Treiso, and Alba, all in the southern province of Cuneo. Barbaresco is garnet red with characteristically orange highlights, and has an intense bouquet reminiscent of violets; dry and full-bodied, it nevertheless exhibits a surprising gentleness. Barbaresco DOC must be aged for a minimum of two years, one of which must be in wood, and must have an alcohol content of no less than 12.5 percent. When aged three years, Barbaresco may be labeled *riserva*, and at four years *riserva speciale*. Barbaresco DOCG must be aged four years to qualify as a *riserva*. There is no *riserva speciale* designation for this appellation. This dry, full-bodied wine can be consumed when six to fifteen years old.

The Barbaresco *consorzio* features on its neck label the ancient tower of Barbaresco, in gold, on a blue background.

Gattinara. Gattinara's DOC, which was granted on July 9, 1967, states that Gattinara must be made from 90 percent Nebbiolo (known locally as Spanna), with up to 10 percent Bonarda grapes, grown exclusively within the territory known as Gattinara. It must attain a minimum of 12 percent alcohol and be aged four years (two in wood). This dry, full-bodied wine is best consumed when six to ten years old.

The Gattinara *consorzio* features on its neck label towers standing among the vineyards.

The Barbera grape and its wines. Barbera is Piedmont's most prolific grape variety, accounting for 50 percent of the region's total acreage. Barbera is a particularly vigorous, resilient vine with consistently abundant yields and an easy adaptability to a variety of growing conditions. It is widely planted throughout Italy, from Piedmont—where the climate is temperate and is said to produce the best Barbera wines—to Campania, Sicily, and Sardinia, where the Mediterranean climate produces wines with a different, distinctive style.

The Barbera d'Asti *consorzio* features on its neck label blue grapes superimposed on the old city's tall part-Roman, part-Medieval tower, in red.

Piemontese Barberas are generally full-bodied and slightly tannic, with a high natural amount of acidity; they are best enjoyed with food. Of the four DOC Barberas, Barbera d'Asti is the most full-bodied. These dry red wines are best consumed at four to six years of age:

Barbera d'Alba: minimum 11.5 percent alcohol; received DOC 5/27/70; aged one year minimum; if 12.5 percent alcohol and aged two years, may be labeled *superiore*; 100 percent Barbera grapes.

Barbera d'Asti: minimum 12 percent alcohol; received DOC 1/7/70; aged one year minimum; if 12.5 percent alcohol and aged two years, may be labeled *superiore*; 100 percent Barbera grapes.

Barbera dei Colli Tortonesi: minimum 12 percent alcohol; received DOC 10/9/73; if 12.5 percent alcohol and aged two years, may be labeled *superiore*; a blend of Barbera (85 percent minimum), and Freisa, and/or Bonarda grape varieties.

Barbera del Monferrato: minimum 12 percent alcohol; received DOC 1/9/70; if 12.5 percent alcohol and aged two years, may be labeled *superiore*; a blend of Barbera (85–90 percent), and Freisa, and/or Grignolino, and/or Dolcetto.

Dolcetto, Grignolino, and Freisa. Dolcetto, Grignolino, and Freisa are all dry red varietals produced in the northeastern part of Piedmont. Like all DOC varietals, the labels of these wines must indicate the specific area of production. The nature of the soil, exposure to sunlight, altitude, and other important factors account for discernible differences in wines produced from the same grape varieties grown in different areas. Dolcetto, Grignolino, and Freisa differ from the more famous Piemontese wines like Barolo in that they are lighter, are intended to be drunk young, and usually have a high level of acidity, and are occasionally quite sharp, almost to the point of being sour.

The name *Dolcetto* could be roughly translated to mean "little sweet one." The name, however, is misleading: Dolcetto is a dry red wine with a pleasing bitter aftertaste.

Dolcetto is produced in the Langhe Hills just south of the town of Alba. The Dolcetto vine is indigenous to the area and was subject to local government regulations as early as 1593. It is Piedmont's most widely planted vine after Barbera. Inherently a little weak, it is not an easy vine to cultivate; it requires much pruning and thrives only in the calcareous soil characteristic of the Langhe area.

It is considered the everyday wine of the locals, who drink it with most of their meals.

There are seven DOC Dolcettos; some of the better-known ones are:

Dolcetto d'Acqui: minimum 11.5 percent alcohol; received DOC 12/1/72; if 12.5 percent alcohol and aged one year, may be labeled *superiore;* 100 percent Dolcetto grapes; what may be the finest-quality Dolcetto d'Acqui available in the United States is that sold under the brand name Argusto.

Dolcetto d'Asti: minimum 11.5 percent alcohol; received DOC 6/10/74; if 12.5 percent alcohol and aged one year, may be labeled *superiore;* 100 percent Dolcetto grapes.

Dolcetto d'Alba: minimum 11.5 percent alcohol; received DOC 7/6/74; if 12.5 percent alcohol and aged one year, may be labeled *superiore;* 100 percent Dolcetto grapes.

The Grignolino vine is indigenous to the Asti area of southern Piedmont, and its presence there can be traced back to 1252. Small and inconsistent in yield, it is a difficult vine to tend and thrives only in certain types of light, sandy soil.

The relative scarcity of this dry, somewhat bitter wine has only served to enhance its desirability, elevating it to almost legendary status.

There are only two DOC zones of production for Grignolino; Alessandria and Asti, both in southern Piedmont. The name of one of these two places must appear on the label of every bottle of Grignolino DOC. The best-known Grignolino wine is:

Grignolino d'Asti: minimum 11 percent alcohol; received DOC 5/29/73; a blend of 90 percent Grignolino (minimum) and up to 10 percent Freisa grape varieties; best consumed young.

The Freisa grape produces two styles of wine: a dry and a slightly sweet one (*amabile*). The *amabile*, which is often *frizzante* (lightly effervescent), is the better known of the two and is considered an ideal accompaniment to desserts. The best-known Freisa wine is:

Freisa d'Asti: received DOC 9/1/72; minimum 11 percent alcohol; if 11.5 percent alcohol and aged for one year, may be labeled *superiore*; also made *frizzante*, and as a *spumante*; 100 percent Freisa grapes.

Freisa d'Asti features on its neck label black grapes superimposed on a yellow tower in Asti.

Nebbiolo d'Alba. This wine is produced from 100 percent Nebbiolo grapes grown in the sandy soil of the steep, rugged Roero Hills. Situated just north of the town of Alba in the southern province of Cuneo, this area is also close to Turin, which has traditionally been a major market for its wine.

Perhaps the softest of the Nebbiolo family of wines, Nebbiolo d'Alba requires less aging than Barolo and Barbaresco, and is not as costly. Classy and elegant, this ruby red wine has a delicate bouquet reminiscent of violets and raspberries, and a full, velvety, pleasantly bitter taste.

Nebbiolo d'Alba: received DOC 5/27/70; minimum 12 percent alcohol; must be aged for one year; dry, sweet, and *spumante* versions produced; the dry version is best consumed when three to six years old.

Other red wines. Several other well-known Piemontese wines are:

Brachetto d'Acqui: received DOC 8/13/69; minimum 11.5 percent alcohol; dry or *amabile spumante* versions produced; a blend of Brachetto (90 percent), Aleatico, and/or Moscato Nero grape varieties; best consumed young.

Carema: received DOC 7/9/67; minimum 12 percent alcohol; minimum four years aging (two in barrel); 100 percent Nebbiolo grapes; best consumed when six to ten years old.

Fara: received DOC 8/13/69; minimum 12 percent alcohol; minimum three years aging (two in barrel); a blend of Nebbiolo, Vespolina, and Bonarda Novarese grape varieties; best consumed when four to six years old.

Ghemme: received DOC 9/18/69; minimum 12 percent alcohol; minimum four years aging (three in barrel); a blend of Nebbiolo, Vespolina, and Bonarda Novarese grape varieties; best consumed when six to nine years old.

Moscato Bianco. Believed to have originated in the eastern basin of the Mediterranean, the Moscato Bianco grape is widely planted throughout Italy. The wine it produces is generally vinified to be sweet and is particularly renowned for its fragrant aroma. In some parts of Italy, most notably Sicily, Moscato Bianco grapes are partially dried, then pressed to produce an exquisite dessert wine called Moscato Passito. The Moscato Bianco vine has been an integral part of Piedmont's viticulture for centuries.

Moscato Bianco is the principal grape of several related Piedmontese DOC wines, including Moscato Naturale d'Asti, Moscato d'Asti, and Asti Spumante. Together these wines account for almost 50 percent of the total regional DOC production. Asti Spumante in particular enjoys a very fine reputation and is, in fact, Piedmont's most exported DOC wine. Moscato d'Asti, though not as well known, shares many of the same characteristics:

Moscato d'Asti (sweet): received DOC 7/9/67; minimum 10.5 percent alcohol; 100 percent Moscato Bianco grapes; best consumed very young.

The Moscato d'Asti *consorzio* features on its neck label a blue helmeted head on a gold background, or San Secundo, the patron saint of Asti, mounted in red, on a blue background.

Gavi or Cortese di Gavi. Cortese is the traditional white wine grape of Piedmont; it produces wines of particular refinement. Once widely cultivated throughout southern Piedmont, its area of production is now limited to the Colli Tortonesi, Monferrato, and Novi Ligure zones of Alessandria. An extremely resilient vine, it thrives in vineyards that have good exposure to the sun.

Gavi, or Cortese di Gavi (dry): received DOC 6/26/74; minimum 10.5 percent alcohol; 100 percent Cortese grapes; best consumed young; two top brand names available in the United States are Principessa Gavi and Granduca Cortese di Gavi.

Sardinia

Sardinia, the second-largest island in the Mediterranean, has been for centuries a little-known wine-producing region, even to most Italians from the mainland and Sicily. It is located across the Tyrrhenian Sea, just west of Rome. Its largest winery (actually, it is a wine cooperative) is Sella & Mosca, established about eighty years ago.

Viticulture in Sardinia has recently undergone tremendous changes thanks to extremely effective efforts on the part of regional authorities, cooperatives, and private producers. Sardinia's goal is to update production methods for the sixteen DOC wine varieties, as well as for the range of high-quality non-DOC wines.

Sardinia produces sixteen wines that have gained DOC status; some of the better-known ones are:

Cannonau di Sardegna (dry or sweet white): received DOC 7/21/72; minimum 13.5 percent alcohol; a blend of Cannonau and other grape varieties.

Vernaccia di Oristano (dry or sweet white): received DOC 8/11/71; minimum 15 percent alcohol; if 15.5 percent alcohol and aged three years, may be labeled *superiore;* if aged four years, may be labeled *riserva;* can also be produced as a *liquoroso;* 100 percent Vernaccia grapes; best consumed when two to six years old.

Sicily

Sicily is one of the world's oldest wine-making regions. The Greeks founded a colony in the eighth century B.C. on the eastern end of the island, and established commercial supremacy in the Mediterranean that was rivaled only by the Carthaginians.

Since the end of World War II, the Sicilian wine industry has seen an intensive modernization of the ancient traditional methods of viticulture and vinification.

The Regional Institute of Wines & Vines was founded in the 1950s to review and improve Sicily's wine industry. The result of the institute's research provided Sicily's growers and vintners with new guidelines which helped develop a modern, flourishing industry. Growers were advised to concentrate on planting specific grape varieties, giving preference to the native Catarratto, Grecanico, Grillo, and Damaschino, and experimenting with other varieties such as Trebbiano and Sangiovese, which appeared to thrive in the Sicilian soil.

The wineries and vinification methods were also carefully reviewed, and large sums of money invested to introduce the latest equipment. Rigorous quality control standards were imposed and the quality symbol of "Q" inscribed with "Regione Siciliana" (Sicilian Region) was adopted as Regional Law No. 14 in 1966. It was devised to indicate the most prestigious, genuine wines of distinctive quality, character, and elegance. The quality symbol is awarded by a committee of wine experts; its aim is to assure consumers that the wine is among the best that Sicily produces.

Some Sicilian wines tend to have a higher alcoholic content than is usual, due to the fact that they receive a great deal of sunshine throughout the year. The heat of the sun often bakes the grapes or causes them to become "sunburnt"; the effect is very noticeable in white wines. Direct sun causes a higher sugar content, darker color white wine (due to a high concentration of coloring matter in the skins), and a heaviness in taste. Wines produced from grapes with very high sugar levels also tend to be "flat," lacking a sufficient acid backbone supporting the high sugar and alcohol levels.

Credit must be given to the skills of the modern Sicilian winemakers who in spite of difficult working conditions have produced wines that display lightness of body, freshness of taste, and a good balance between fruit and acidity.

In a bold move to improve the visibility of Sicilian wines, the government is working on a plan that will reduce the number of labels from the current five hundred. This will help establish more standardization and aid in regional wine promotions.

There are sixteen Sicilian wines (three of which are Marsalas) that have gained DOC status; some of the better known are:

Alcamo or Bianco di Alcamo (white): received DOC 7/21/72; minimum 11.5 percent alcohol; a blend of Catarratto Bianco, Damaschino, Grecanico, and Trebbiano grape varieties; best consumed young.

Cerasuolo di Vittoria (red): received DOC 5/29/73; minimum 13 percent alcohol; a blend of Frappato, Calabrese, and other grape varieties; best consumed young.

Etna Bianco: received DOC 9/17/68; minimum 11.5 percent alcohol; if 12 percent alcohol, may be labeled *superiore*; a blend of Carricante, Catarratto, and other grape varieties; best consumed young.

Etna Rosato or Rosso: received DOC 9/17/68; minimum 12.5 percent alcohol; a blend of Nerello Mascalese and other grape varieties; both rosé and red are best consumed young.

There are some very good to excellent Sicilian wines that do not carry the DOC designation because they are either new blends or are made from grapes that are grown outside of the DOC districts of each region. Some notable wines are:

Corvo: founded on the estate of Edoardo Alliata di Villafranca, duke of Salaparuta, in 1824, in the small town of Casteldaccia; produces Rosso, Bianco, Colomba Platino (dry white), and Spumante Brut and Demi-Sec.

Regaleali: owned since 1835 by Count Giuseppe Tasca; produces four unique wines considered to be among the finest of Sicily—Bianco, Rosato, Rosso, and a specially aged (two years in wood, one year in glass) limited reserve called Rosso del Conte, which is 14 percent alcohol.

Segesta: originally called Egesta by the Greeks and renamed Segesta by the Romans; produced today by Diego Rallo (of Marsala fame) as a dry red or dry white wine.

Other non-DOC wines include: Bonifato, Canicatti, Donnafugata, Draceno, Drepano, Porto Palo, Saturno, Settesoli, Solunto, and Steri.

Trentino-Alto-Adige

Trentino-Alto-Adige, bordered by Austria and Switzerland, was part of the Austro-Hungarian Empire until it was annexed to Italy by the Treaty of Versailles after World War I.

Geographically and climatically, Trentino-Alto-Adige has all the requirements for producing top-quality wine. The region is roughly on the same latitude as Burgundy and northern Bordeaux, where France's finest wines are made. The high Alps create a natural wind block to protect the vines from the harsh, cold weather of central Europe. The Adige River, flowing south through the length of the region, has created a wide fertile valley whose center supports some of Italy's best fruit orchards, while vineyards terrace every inch of its slopes. The foothills of the Dolomites provide perfect altitudes and soil types for vine cultivation. In fact, the Adige River Valley has often been referred to as one big natural vineyard.

There are seventeen wines from this region that have gained DOC status; some of the better-known ones are listed below.

Dry red wines

Cabernet del Trentino: minimum 11 percent alcohol; (received DOC 8/4/71); must be aged a minimum of two years; if aged three years, may be labeled *riserva;* minimum 90 percent Cabernet Sauvignon and/ or Cabernet Franc grapes; best consumed when four to seven years old.

Marzemino del Trentino: 11 percent alcohol; (received DOC 8/4/71); must be aged a minimum one year; if aged two years, may be labeled *riserva;* minimum 90 percent Marzemino grapes; best consumed when three to five years old.

Merlot del Trentino: minimum 11 percent alcohol; (received DOC 8/4/71); must be aged a minimum of one year; minimum 90 percent Merlot grapes; best consumed young.

Caldaro or Lago di Caldaro: known as Kalterersee in Germany; minimum 10.5 percent alcohol; (received DOC 3/23/70); a blend of Schiava, Pinot Nero, Lagrein, and other grape varieties; best consumed when three to five years old.

Santa Maddalena: minimum 11.5 percent alcohol; (received DOC 8/11/71); a blend of Schiava and other grape varieties; best consumed when three to five years old.

Dry white wines

These wines should all be consumed young:

Pinot del Trentino: minimum 11 percent alcohol; (received DOC 8/4/71); also produced as a *spumante;* a blend of Pinot Bianco and/or Pinot Grigio grape varieties.

Riesling del Trentino: minimum 11 percent alcohol; (received DOC 8/4/71); minimum 90 percent Riesling grapes.

Traminer Aromatico (Gewürztraminer) del Trentino: minimum 12 percent alcohol; (received DOC 8/4/71); minimum 90 percent Traminer grapes.

Tuscany

Tuscany is the home of such great native red wines as Chianti, Brunello di Montalcino, and Vino Nobile di Montepulciano. With the influx of imported grape vines some new great red wines such as Tignanello, Cabreo di Biturica, Sassicaia, Cabernet Sauvignon, Cabernet Franc, Merlot, and others have appeared on the international wine scene. Some very fine white wines are also produced in Tuscany, including Vernaccia di San Gimignano, Galestro, Vin Santo, and some excellent new wines made from Pinot Grigio, Chardonnay, and Sauvignon Blanc grapes.

Banfi Vintners. The most adventurous viticultural endeavor ever undertaken in Italy was the development of 7,100 acres of virgin land into the most technologically advanced vineyard/winery in the world. The land, located in Montalcino, was originally primarily forests and pastures; it has since been planted with more than a million *vinifera* grapevines (figure 3-3). Since 1978 Banfi Vintners has been engaged in its biggest production venture ever; when completed, it will bring Banfi into the twenty-first century of technology and winemaking.

The winery occupies five acres and is equipped with computerized crushers, gleaming stainless steel fermentation tanks and the latest in refrigeration and filtering units (figures 3-4, 3-5). Beneath the facility, cathedral-like cellars house thousands of Troncais oak barrels to mellow Cabernet, Chardonnay and Chianti, and giant Slavonian oak barrels for the classic Brunello di Montalcino.

A medieval castle, dating back to the ninth century, towers above the estate at Montalcino and gives the Banfi vineyard an atmosphere of history and romance. The castle is undergoing restoration and will be converted into a resort. Located nearby will be a learning center to host wine symposia, and a laboratory and enological research facility which Banfi plans to donate to Cornell University (Ithaca, N.Y.). Scholarship students of viticulture and viniculture will study here under the tutelage of Dr. Ezio Rivella, president of the World Enological Society.

The company's goals are: to raise existing wine standards; to revive wines that were popular centuries ago but fell from favor because artisan production methods could not maintain continuity of quality and taste; and to create new wines.

Figure 3-3 Militarily precise rows of grapevines at Banfi vineyards. (Courtesy Banfi Vintners, Montalcino, Italy)

The wines of Tuscany. There are twenty-three wines produced in Tuscany that have gained DOC status; some of the better-known ones are listed below.

White wines

Moscadello di Montalcino: famous in ancient times, this was one of the most distinguished wines of Tuscany; slightly sparkling, straw colored, with an intense aromatic bouquet and the sweet and distinctive characteristic flavor of the Moscato grape; best consumed young.

Vernaccia di San Gimignano (dry): on March 3, 1966, became the first wine granted a DOC status; minimum 12 percent alcohol; if aged a minimum of one year, may be labeled *riserva*; the DOC stipulates

Figure 3-4 Banfi's state-of-the-art winery at Montalcino, Italy, Europe's most techno-logically advanced winery. (Courtesy Banfi Vintners, Montalcino, Italy)

that only Bordeaux-shaped bottles may be used; 100 percent Vernaccia di San Gimignano grapes; best consumed young.

The blue seal of the *consorzio* Vernaccia di San Gimignano shows a lion rampant on a crest.

Red wines

Brunello: received DOC 3/28/66; first wine to receive DOCG status, 7/1/80; minimum 12.5 percent alcohol; must be aged minimum of four years (from January 1, after harvest) in oak barrels; if aged five years, may be labeled *riserva;* 100 percent Sangiovese Grosso grapes (also called Brunello grapes).

Rosso di Montalcino (also called Rosso di Brunello or Rosso dei Vigneti di Brunello): received DOC 11/25/83; produced by the same vineyards as the world-famous Brunello di Montalcino; 100 percent Brunello grapes (also called Sangiovese Grosso); can be made from very young vines not considered mature enough for Brunello di Montalcino or a Brunello wine aged for a shorter period of time than required under DOC laws; full-bodied, fragrant; best consumed when four to six years old.

Figure 3-5 To capture the nuances of the *vinifera* grape, stainless steel tanks store wine at 0°c at Banfi vineyards. (Courtesy Banfi Vintners, Montalcino, Italy)

Brunello di Montalcino is a picturesque and very hilly section of Tuscany situated approximately twenty-five miles southeast of Siena and Chianti Classico, approximately 1,600 feet above sea level. It is bordered by the Orcia River to the south and the Ombrone River to the west.

In 1967 the producers of Brunello wines voluntarily formed a *consorzio* to establish a uniform price structure and quality control system (its seal is a southern European evergreen oak with hollylike leaves, on a green background). Brunello and Barolo are the longest-lived of all Italian wines. Most Brunello wines are best consumed when nine to twelve years old, and the *riservas* at twelve to fifteen years; if produced in great years, a life of twenty-five years is not uncommon for riservas.

Chianti. Chianti was originally known as Vermiglio in the latter part of the fourteenth century. While today's Chianti is red, documents of the fourteenth century call a local white wine Chianti. Baron Ricasoli, a descendant of Baron Bettino Ricasoli, has in his possession a document dated June 18, 1696, which is believed to be the certificate of origin for Chianti wine.

Geographically and historically Chianti is an area lying between Florence and Siena, encompassing the towns of Arezzo, Pistoia, and Pisa. In the heart of this area, in the hills between Florence and Siena, lie approximately 175,000 acres of land where Chianti Classico is made. The historic center of this area belonged to an ancient military league formed in 1270 called the Lega del Chianti. Although its primary purpose was the defense of both its land and people, it was probably the first organization in the world to establish a wine quality law.

In the eighteenth century, Chianti was produced from Sangiovese, Canaiolo, Mammolo, and Marzemino grapes. No mention was made of the Trebbiano or Malvasia grapes in connection with Chianti. These white grapes were vinified separately for a white style of Chianti. In 1835, Baron Bettino Ricasoli (1809–1880), prime minister of Italy, developed and defined the grape variety formula for Chianti; this consisted of a blend of Sangiovese, Canaiolo, and Malvasia grapes.

A technique (known as *governo toscano*) used in the production of Chianti during Ricasoli's time was to induce a secondary fermentation by the addition of 5 to 10 percent must, pressed from selected grapes partly dried on wicker frames known as *cannici* or *castelli*. This secondary fermentation took place immediately after the first racking of the wine before December 31. This process produced wines meant for early consumption. Most of the wines made by the *governo* technique were, and still are, bottled in squat bottles covered with straw, called *fiasci*.

When the DOC law for Chianti was drawn up and finally instituted on August 9, 1967 (Chianti was granted DOCG status on July 2, 1984), the producers decided not to register a white wine but asked to be allowed to include white grapes in the blend for red Chianti. Regulations (amended in 1984) specify that Chianti be made from four principal grapes: Sangiovese, Canaiolo Nero, Trebbiano, and Malvasia. These regulations, for the first time, permit winemakers to introduce up to 10 percent of nontraditional grape varieties into the Chianti blend, including Cabernet Sauvignon, Merlot, and others. Many people give credit to Piero Antinori for the introduction of this new blend, pioneered after his legendary red wine Tignanello, which contains no white grapes.

Since 1932 Chianti has been produced in an area encompassing five provinces: Arezzo, Florence, Pisa, Pistoia, and Siena, which are subdivided into seven areas. These are listed below, with descriptions of their *consorzios'* neck labels:

Chianti Classico: the label shows a black rooster or cock (in Italian, *gallo nero*); this was the crest of the thirteenth-century Chianti Defense League; first used on May 14, 1924.

Chianti Montalbano: the label shows the Tower of Montalbano.

Chianti Rufina: the label of this *consorzio* (founded in 1927) shows a *putto* (little boy) or cherub.

Chianti Colli Fiorentini (also known as Putto): the label of this *consorzio* (founded in 1927) shows the infant Bacchus, naked and entwined in a vine with clusters of purple grapes, a detail from Della Robbia's painting, *Hospital of the Innocents.*

Chianti Colli Senesi: the label depicts Romulus and Remus with the she-wolf.

Chianti Colli Aretini: the label shows a chimera.

Chianti Colline Pisane: the label shows a centaur or, more commonly, the Leaning Tower of Pisa.

Under both DOC and DOCG regulations, if a Chianti is aged for a minimum of three years and has attained an alcohol content of 12.5 percent, it may be labeled *riserva.* Chianti is best consumed when four to six years old; and Chianti riserva when eight to twelve years old and, if produced in a great year, when it is as much as twenty years old.

There are many producers of Chianti; among them are Antinori, Banfi Vintners, Ruffino, Nozzole, Brolio, Monsanto, Badia a Coltibuono, Castello di Gabbiano, Melini, Rocca della Macie, and Castellare.

Other DOC wines. *Vino Nobile di Montepulciano* is produced in a small area surrounding the town of Montepulciano, in the province of Siena. It was granted DOC status on July 12, 1966, and was raised to a DOCG wine on November 1, 1982. It must be aged a minimum of two years, and if aged three years it is entitled to be labeled *riserva;* at four years of age it may be labeled *riserva speciale.* It must have a minimum of 12.5 percent alcohol, and is a blend of Prugnolo Gentile (Sangiovese Grosso), Canaiolo Nero, Malvasia del Chianti, and several other grape varieties. This dry wine is best consumed when three to five years old; the *riserva* is best when six to eight years old. The Vino Nobile di Montepulciano *consorzio* features on its neck label a griffin rampant on a white background within a red circle.

There are some very good to excellent Tuscan wines that do not carry the DOC designation on their label because they are either new blends or are made from grapes grown outside of the DOC districts of each region. Several of these are described below.

Bianco Toscano is made from a small percentage of Malvasia and Trebbiano, the white grapes grown in Tuscany that are used in the production of Chianti and other red wines. Recently Chianti producers have begun using a higher proportion of black grapes in their wines, thereby increasing the percentage of white grapes available for other purposes. As a result, more and more producers are now vinifying the Trebbiano and Malvasia grapes to produce a fragrant, dry white table wine. The wine is usually labeled Bianco Toscano, or sold under a brand name; it is best consumed young.

Galestro was first produced by Villa Antinori, Ruffino, Ricasoli, and Frescobaldi in the late 1970s. The original idea was to find use for the Trebbiano grapes whose use in Chianti was on the decline. This delicate, light white wine takes its name from the ancient rocks of its native Tuscany. It owes its distinctive aroma to the presence of Trebbiano Toscano and, often, small amounts of Chardonnay, Vernaccia, Malvasia, and Pinot Bianco grapes.

Vin Santo, or Vino Santo, is produced in several regions of Italy, each claiming that theirs is the true area of origin. Vin Santo Toscano is made from the ripest Trebbiano and Malvasia grapes, which are tied together and either hung from the beams of a well-ventilated room or dried on wicker trays. This process results in the evaporation of a high percentage of the grapes' water content, at the same time increasing the percentage of sugar. The higher the sugar content of the grape, the higher the resulting alcoholic content and the richer the final product. For a sweet Vin Santo, the bunches are left to raisin for about two and a half months; for a Vin Santo that is semidry to dry, they are left about two months.

The grapes are crushed during the winter, and the must placed into small oak casks called *caratelli* which hold no more than one hectoliter (26.42 gallons). The same casks are used over and over again, and a small amount of the previous Vin Santo in the cask is always left inside to blend with the new must (this is similar to Sherry Solera production). The *caratelli* are filled to three-quarters capacity, closed with a cork bung, and placed in the winery's attic or a room exposed to heat, where the wine is left to ferment slowly for three years. Each winter fermentation is interrupted by the cold, but starts again in the spring. During fermentation carbon dioxide accumulates and creates high pressure that slows down the process. For this reason the barrels are stored directly under the roof of the winery, where the summer heat causes the wood of the top part of the barrel not in contact with the wine to contract, allowing air to enter and oxidation to occur. This gives Vin Santo its characteristic amber-brown color and contributes to the complexity of its aroma. Another characteristic of this special aging process is the development of a sort of "cooked" or *maderized* taste in the wine.

Vin Santo has an unmistakable tangy, nutty bouquet and taste, similar to that of an Amontillado sherry, Bual Madeira, or dry Marsala. Its alcoholic content is usually somewhere between 15 to 18 percent. The dry version is an excellent aperitif, served chilled from the refrigerator, while the sweeter Vin Santo is best enjoyed at room temperature after dinner. Vin Santo is best consumed when six to ten years old and often has a life of more than twenty years.

Other non-DOC wines are listed below.

Cabernet Sauvignon

Tavernelle, produced by Banfi Vintners.

Sassicaia, produced by the Tenuta San Guido estate.

Solaia, produced by Villa Antinori, is approximately 75 percent Cabernet Sauvignon and 25 percent Cabernet Franc grapes.

Cabernet Sauvignon/Sangiovese blends

Predicato di Biturica Cabreo Il Borgo, by Ruffino, is a blend of approximately 70 percent Sangiovese and 30 percent Cabernet Sauvignon grapes.

Tignanello, by Villa Antinori (first produced in 1971), is a blend of approximately 80 percent Sangiovese and 20 percent Cabernet Sauvignon grapes.

Chardonnay

Fontanelle, produced by Banfi Vintners.

Predicato del Muschios Cabreo La Pietra, produced by Ruffino.

Pinot Grigio

San Angelo, produced by Banfi Vintners.

Several wineries in Tuscany also make versions of a *"nouveau"* wine, called *vino novello*. Two of the main producers are Antinori, which makes San Giocondo, and Banfi Vintners, which makes Santa Costanza (from Brunello grapes).

Umbria

Italy's only landlocked region, Umbria is surrounded by Tuscany, Latium, and the Marches. It is known as the "green heart of Italy" because it lies in the center of the peninsula and is rich in woods and pastures. The hillsides and gentle inclines of the Umbrian landscape are carpeted with olive trees and vines; the region's major freshwater lake—Trasimeno, which gives its name to one of the area's three DOC wines—is surrounded by vineyards. The Tiber River flows from north to south through the eastern part of the region, creating the Upper Tiber Valley, a major viticultural zone of Umbria. Perugia, the region's capital city, stands on a hilltop just east of Lake Trasimeno. Other major cities of Umbria are Assisi, Spoleto, Todi, Gubbio, Norcia, Spello, and Montefalco. The smaller towns of Orvieto and Torgiano have lent their names to the two DOC wines of the region.

Umbria's major wine-producing areas include the Colli Altotiberini to the north; the Colli del Trasimeno to the west; Torgiano, near Assisi; and the well-known Orvieto zone in the southwest. Fourteen of their wines have gained DOC status: the better-known ones are described below.

Orvieto. Named for the city in southern Umbria, this wine is produced in the Paglia and Upper Tiber valleys as well as throughout the province of Terni. The Orvieto Classico area is in the heart of this DOC zone. This well-known white wine is made from 50 to 65 percent Procanico grapes (also known as Trebbiano Toscano) and 15 to 25 percent Verdello, with the rest a blend of Grechetto, Drupeggio, and Malvasia Toscano grapes. It is produced in both *secco* (dry) and *abboccato* (semisweet) styles.

Although not known well in the United States, Orvieto *abboccato* has been produced for centuries. Its golden color and delicate sweetness made it one of Italy's most esteemed wines during the Renaissance. Orvieto *abboccato* achieves its semisweet taste from grapes that have been attacked by *Botrytis cinerea*, a mold. Just as the grapes begin to become affected they are harvested and left to continue to develop the *Botrytis* in open trays.

After World War II, popular taste shifted to dry wines, and production of Orvieto *secco* was stepped up considerably, with many producers investing in expensive equipment and the best technology for making dry white wine.

Orvieto *secco*, a crisp straw-colored wine, is best consumed very young. It received its DOC on August 7, 1971, and must have a minimum of 12 percent alcohol.

In 1970, special emphasis was placed on upgrading the image of Orvieto by replacing its traditional squat bottles (called *pulcianelle* or *toscanelli*) with the more familiar Bordeaux-shaped green bottles.

The Orvieto Classico *consorzio* (formed in 1934) features on its neck label the cathedral of the town of Orvieto.

Torgiano. This wine is named after the town of Torgiano. The DOC (May 25, 1968) area in which it is produced is in the province of Perugia. The most famous winery is the Cantine Lungarotti. Lungarotti has also pioneered the growing of Cabernet Sauvignon and Chardonnay vines and is one of the finer producers of wines made from these grapes. Torgiano is produced in both white and red varieties:

> Torgiano Rosso (also known as Rubesco): minimum 12 percent alcohol; if aged three years, may be labeled *riserva*; a blend of 50 to 70 percent Sangiovese, 15 to 30 percent Canaiolo, 10 percent Trebbiano, and 10 percent Ciliegiolo and Montepulciano grapes; best consumed when two to six years old; *riserva* is best when six to twelve years old.

> Torgiano Bianco (also known as Torre di Giano): minimum 11.5 percent alcohol; a blend of 50 to 70 percent Trebbiano Toscano; 15 to 35 percent Grechetto, and up to 15 percent Malvasia Toscana, Malvasia di Candia, and Verdello grapes; best consumed young.

Veneto

Veneto takes its name from its capital, Venezia (Venice), once one of the most powerful coastal nations in history. There are three distinct Veneto wine zones: the Verona area, famous for Soave, Valpolicella, and Bardolino; the Euganean hills between Vicenza and Padova, where table wines are made; and the areas of Treviso and Conegliano, which lie approximately forty miles due north of Venice. The latter are best known for excellent varietal wines, especially Tocai, Merlot, and Cabernet.

Treviso. Treviso is one of the seven provinces that make up the region of Veneto; also known as the Marca Trevigiana, it borders on the Dolomite Mountains to the north; the region of Friuli-Venezia-Giulia to the east; the province of Venice, twenty-five miles to the south; and Padova to the west. The Piave River, one of Italy's most important waterways, flows south through the province to the Adriatic.

A wide range of both native and imported grape varieties are grown in the area. Sixty percent of the total wine production is red wines, and 40 percent white wines. Most of the wine produced in the province of Treviso comes from six grape varieties. Three are white: Prosecco, Verduzzo, and Tocai Italico; and three are red: Merlot, Cabernet, and Raboso. Other varieties grown are Verdiso, Pinot Bianco, Pinot Grigio, Pinot Nero, Riesling Italico, and Sauvignon Blanc. One of the most important of Treviso's DOC wines is:

Prosecco di Conegliano-Valdobbiadene (a *spumante*): received DOC 4/2/69; minimum 11 percent alcohol; if 11.5 percent alcohol, may be labeled *superiore*; 100 percent Prosecco grapes, best consumed young.

Verona. The picturesque town of Verona in northeast Italy is the setting of Shakespeare's *Romeo and Juliet.*

All of the following white wines are dry and should be consumed young:

Bianco di Custoza: received DOC 2/8/71; minimum 11 percent alcohol; also produced as a *spumante;* a blend of Trebbiano Toscano, Garganega, and other grape varieties.

Gambellara: received DOC 3/26/70; minimum 11 percent alcohol; if 11.5 percent alcohol, may be labeled *superiore*; a blend of Garganega and Trebbiano grapes.

Soave: received DOC 8/21/68; minimum 10.5 percent alcohol; if 11.5 percent alcohol, may be labeled *superiore*; if labeled *classico*, it must come from a strictly delimited area of production; a blend of Garganega and Trebbiano Toscano grapes.

Verduzzo del Piave: received DOC 6/11/71; minimum 11 percent alcohol; 100 percent Verduzzo grapes.

There is also a Recioto di Soave (14 percent alcohol), made from partially dried grapes. It is sweet to the taste, with overtones of pears, apricots, and bananas, and is best enjoyed after dinner.

These red wines are dry:

Bardolino: received DOC 5/28/68; minimum 10.5 percent alcohol; if 11.5 percent alcohol and aged one year, may be labeled *superiore;* a blend of Corvina Veronese, Rondinella, and other grape varieties; best consumed young.

Valpolicella: received DOC 8/21/68; minimum 11 percent alcohol; if 12 percent alcohol and aged one year, may be labeled *superiore;* a blend of Corvina, Rondinella, Molinara, and other grape varieties; best consumed young.

There is also a very light Bardolino, resembling a rosé, called Bardolino Chiaretto.

When one thinks of great Italian red wines, wines like Barolo, Barbaresco, Chianti Riserva, and Brunello di Montalcino all come to mind. But what about Amarone, that rich, mouth-filling wine that sends warmth and vigor to the body and taste buds? For some unknown reason Amarone is not mentioned in the same context as other great red wines.

According to Pierluigi Bolla (whose family owns Bolla wines), his grandfather actually developed Amarone for personal consumption prior to 1950, and gave it its name. It received such acclaim that his grandfather decided to bottle and sell it in limited quantities. He first put a label on Amarone with the 1950 vintage; it featured a self-portrait. Unfortunately, neither the label nor the name Amarone were ever registered, and the Kentucky producer of Old Grand Dad Bourbon forced Pierluigi Bolla to stop using his grandfather's portrait on Bolla labels, claiming that it was a trademark infringement.

The word *Amarone* comes from the Veronese dialect meaning bone dry almost to the point of bitterness. The grapes used are the same as those in Valpolicella: Corvina Veronese, Rondinella, Molinara, Rossignola, Negrara, Sangiovese, and Barbera. Amarone, however, unlike Valpolicella, is made exclusively from the best grapes, which are located at the top and outside perimeter of the clusters. The grapes used for Amarone are grown on three-foot-high trellises in the hills of Valpolicella that rise one to two thousand feet above sea level. The best grapes, which have received the most direct sunshine, are called *recie* or *orecchie* (ears); hence the name Recioto della Valpolicella Amarone (*recioto* is also a word from the old Veronese dialect of the area).

In the picking process 50 percent of the grapes are immediately rejected because they are not ripe enough. In addition, the bunches that are selected are those whose grapes are sufficiently spaced to allow air to circulate between them in the eventual drying process (this limits the formation of grey mold). These grapes, whose sugar levels are the highest because of the amount of sunlight they receive, are then arranged on flat drawers which easily fit into racks that allow a good circulation of air. It is very important that they be kept in a dry, cool, well-ventilated room. In years past, bamboo, wicker mats, or trellises were used to dry the grapes. Each mat is clearly marked with the day the grapes were picked and the part of the vineyard from which they originate. The grapes are cleaned and turned about every twenty days and are constantly inspected during the two-and-one-half- to three-month drying period. This drying period causes a 40 percent loss of juice, resulting in grapes low in juice but extremely high in sugar and varietal character. The best Amarones produced depend on the formation of *Botrytis cinerea*, which releases gluconic acid during the drying process. Enzymatic action also changes the properties (internally) of the acids and sugar balance. The dried grapes, which resemble shriveled raisins, are pressed just after Christmas and fermented slowly for approximately forty-five days with the skins and stems intact. The wine is aged for a minimum of eighteen months in wood, but it is not uncommon for Amarone to be aged for five years or more in barrels prior to bottling and further bottle aging.

The resultant wine is, not surprisingly, highly alcoholic: a minimum of 14 percent under DOC law. However, most Amarones are higher in alcohol, sometimes even 17 percent alcohol. When produced in the heart of the DOC production zone the wine may be labeled *classico*. Amarone received its DOC status on 8/21/68.

Amarone can be described as having a remarkably beautiful, darkish ruby red color, with a lush persistent bouquet—a moderately heavy, strong, concentrated, complex flavor of fruit, reminiscent of raisins, with considerable finesse; velvety rich, with a dry, spicy taste, and slightly bitter. The aftertaste is warming and quite dry, with sensations of rich spicy fruit. It is suitable for long aging (often decades), with some wines of the late 1950s and early 1960s still needing more years of maturing.

Amarone should be served at room temperature, and should be uncorked at least two to three hours before serving. It is best drunk during the cold months, but can be enjoyed year round when complimented with strong cheeses such as Gorgonzola or Asiago. Amarones are well suited to game (venison), roasts, stews, most red meats, and pasta dishes, especially those with large amounts of grated cheese and hot pepper.

The *consorzio* of Amarone features the Roman arena at Verona on its neck labels.

There are other *recioto* wines. Some are labeled Recioto della Valpolicella; Recioto della Valpolicella Spumante; Recioto della Valpolicella Liquoroso, or simply Recioto. Reciotos without the suffix Amarone are *amabile* (semisweet to sweet) and contain more than one percent residual sugar (the maximum that Amarone can have under DOC regulations). The *liquoroso* designation is for a very sweet dessert wine (with a minimum of 16 percent alcohol). There is also a *spumante*, which is also an *amabile* with a remarkable amount of body and finesse.

To produce an *amabile* or *spumante*, the fermentation is halted before all of the sugar is metabolized, and the wine is immediately filtered to eliminate the yeast. The *spumante* is made by inducing a secondary fermentation that creates effervescence (less of it, however, than in champagne).

The *consorzios* of Soave, Bardolino, and Valpolicella feature a Roman arena at Verona on their neck labels.

Some very fine producers of Veronese wines are Allegrini, Bertani, Bolla, Fabiano, Lamberti, Masi, Santa Sofia, Sartori, Tedeschi, and Tommasi.

Suggested Readings

Anderson, Burton. *Vino: The Wines & Winemakers of Italy*. Boston, Mass.: Little, Brown, 1980.

Dallas, Philip. *Italian Wines*. London: Faber and Faber, 2d ed. 1983.

Flower, Raymond. *Chianti: The Land, the People and the Wine*. New York: Universe Books, 1979.

Italian Wines & Spirits Magazine (Civiltà del Bere). Italy.

Ray, Cyril. *The Wines of Italy*. New York: Octupus, 1966.

Roncarati, Bruno. *Viva Vino: 200 + DOC + DOCG Wines & Wine Roads of Italy*. London: Wine and Spirit Publications, 1987.

Wasserman, Sheldon and Pauline Wasserman. *Italy's Noble Red Wines*. Piscataway, N.J.: New Century Publishers, 1985.

Discussion Topics and Questions

1. Although Italy's wine laws were only enacted in 1963, in many ways they are more restrictive than those of France. Discuss the major differences between these countries' laws.

2. Chaptalization is strictly prohibited in Italy, but in France and Germany it is utilized every year; why the difference?

3. In 1980, Brunello di Montalcino was granted its DOCG status. Does this higher designation really mean a better wine? Give reasons for your answer.

4. Italy's proprietary wine names seem to be somewhat comical. What is the origin of most of them?

5. On a map, identify each of Italy's twenty wine regions.

6. Which regions produce mostly white wines?

7. Which regions are experimenting with Cabernet Sauvignon, Chardonnay, and Sauvignon Blanc grape varieties?

4

Wines of France

This chapter discusses:

- The French *appellation contrôlée* wine laws.
- The major wine-producing regions.
- Alsace and its wines and wine laws.
- Bordeaux, and its status as producer of the world's greatest red wines.
- The wine classification of 1855.
- Sauternes.
- Burgundy's complex wine laws.
- Burgundy's village and vineyard names.
- The ever-popular wines from Beaujolais.
- The Rhône's rich red wines.

For many the wines of France evoke pictures of lush vineyards filled with ripe grapes, huge fermentation tanks, and rows of barrels filled with some of the world's finest wines—but this description fits every wine-producing country in the world. A formidable public relations campaign and excellent public image obviously enhance France's reputation as a great wine-producing country; but that reputation is solidly based on centuries of winemaking experience and the country's climate and soil, which are ideal for growing the world's great wine grapes.

French Wine Laws

On July 30, 1935, a French law established the Institut National des Appellations d'Origine (INAO) for wines and spirits, and decrees governing each wine appellation were laid down by the minister of agriculture.

Under the *appellation d'origine contrôlée* (AOC) wines and spirits must conform to certain conditions regarding area of production, root stocks, output per hectare (2.471 acres), minimum alcoholic strength, processes of cultivation, and winemaking (or distillation). Only wines meeting the specified requirements can be sold under the appellation, and shipments must be documented. Controls are provided for checking vintage returns, plantings within the delimited area, dressing the vine stock, output, and aging, and so on.

Conceived to guarantee the authenticity of wines released under an appellation, the AOC system is also a guarantee of taste and quality, ensuring that all wines from a delimited area will be similar, and will be different from those of other areas.

There are other designations under this system: the letters *VDQS* that appear on some wine labels were first used on December 18, 1949; they stand for *vins délimités de qualité supérieure*, denoting wines that are just slightly below the AOC designation in quality. Wines designated as *vins de pays*, simple regional country wines, are below VDQS wines in quality. *Vins ordinaires* include almost 70 percent of all French wines; these are not controlled by the government and are simple wines made locally for everyday consumption.

In 1936, a number of French wine districts were officially given their AOC designation. They were: Barsac (September 11); Sauternes (September 30); St. Émilion, St. Estèphe, St. Julien, and Pauillac (November 14); and Pomerol (December 8). On March 4, 1937, the wines of Graves were officially granted their AOC designation; on August 10, 1954, the designation was granted to the wines of Margaux.

Secondary Wine Labels

Many well-known French vineyards, wineries, and shippers sometimes bottle wine under a different or second label. The table below lists some well-known labels and their corresponding secondary labels.

Well-known label	Secondary label
Château Beychevelle	Amiral de Beychevelle
Albert Bichot	Paul Bouchard

Château Brane-Cantenac	Château Notton
Château Cos d'Estournel	Château de Marbuzet
Château Croizet-Bages	Enclos de Moncabon
Château de Glana	Moulin du Glana
Joseph Drouhin	Jaffelin
Château Durfort-Vivens	Domaine de Curebourse
Château Duhart-Milon Rothschild	Moulin de Duhart
Château LaGaffeliere	Château Roquefort
Château Gloria	Château Peymartin or Château Haut-Beychevelle Gloria
Château Gruaud-Larose	Sarget de Gruaud-Larose
Château Haut-Batailley	Tour 'Aspic
Château Haut-Brion	Château Bahans-Haut-Brion
Château Lagrange	Château St. Julien
Château Lafite-Rothschild	Carruades de Lafite (old label); Moulin des Carruades (new label)
Château La Mission-Haut-Brion	La Tour Haut-Brion
Château Lascombes	Château La Gombaude
Château Latour	Les Forts de Latour
Château La Tour-Blanche	Cru St. Marc
Château Leoville-Las-Cases	Clos de Marquis
Château Leoville-Poyferre	Château Moulin-Riche
Château Les Ormes-de-Pez	La Tour Haut-Vignoble or Château Moulin Joli

Well-known label	Secondary label
Château Lynch-Bages	Haut-Bages-Averous
Château Margaux	Pavillon Rouge
Moillard	Thomas Freres
Château Pichon-Lalande	Réserve de la Comtesse de Lalande
Château Prieure-Lichine	Château Clairefort (2d wine); Campion (3d wine)
Château Rieussec	Clos Labere
Château St.-Pierre	Château St. Louis du Bosq

Shippers Wines

Some of the finest wines in the world are the red and white wines of France's six wine-producing regions (figure 4-1), which are under the auspices of the AOC. These wines, because of their status, are also higher in price, and an intellegent purchase generally takes a basic knowledge of wine. There is, however, another possibility, and that is to choose what are known as French country wines—simple wines made for easy daily consumption, without all the fuss often associated with higher-priced wines. Some of the wines that are often used as "house" or "pouring" wines are:

B.&G.	Dourthe	Papillon	Rene Junot
Boucheron	French Rabbit	Partager	Valbon
Canteval	Le Jardinet	Père Patriarche	
Chantefleur	Musette	Remy Pannier	

France's Wine-Producing Regions

France is divided into six wine-producing regions:

Alsace: produces white and red dry wines.

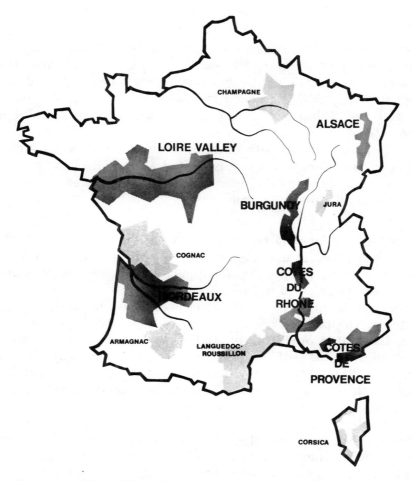

Figure 4-1 Map of France's major wine-producing regions.

Bordeaux: produces red and white dry wines, and also some sweet wines.

Burgundy: produces red and white dry wines.

Champagne: produces sparkling wines.

Loire Valley: produces white and rosé dry wines.

Rhône Valley: produces red, white, and rosé dry wines.

There are many other fine wine-producing areas in France, but they are too numerous to cover.

Alsace

This storybook region, which is dotted with picturesque villages, occupies a narrow strip of land between Strasbourg and Mulhouse. It is not more than a mile or two wide and about sixty miles long, with an area of approximately 30,000 acres. It is nestled between the Vosges Mountains and the Rhine River, just east of Champagne and Burgundy (figure 4-2).

Alsace produces one-fifth of all of France's white wines entitled to the AOC designation. Because it is located so far north there is generally insufficient sunshine to fully ripen the red grapes. Therefore, better than 90 percent of all wines are white.

Bottling and labeling regulations. A 1972 law requires all Alsatian wines to be bottled in tall, elegant "flute" bottles, and it is compulsory for wines sold under the Alsace appellation to have been bottled in Alsace, and not shipped in casks.

Labels on Alsatian wines usually indicate the grape variety used, and provide the shipper or grower's postal address. When the name of the vineyard is stated on the label, 100 percent of the grapes used must come from that vineyard. The labeling terms *réserve personnelle, cuvée,* or *réserve* indicate quality level: wines so designated are considered to be among the finest that a house produces. *Appellation contrôlée, grand cru,* and *crémant d'Alsace* may appear on labels.

In 1962 the wines of Alsace were given their *appellation contrôlée* designation. To help promote the wines of Alsace, a wine brotherhood, Confrérie Saint-Etienne, was formed in the fourteenth century. It still meets every year at the Château of Kientzheim near Colmar for a festival and special promotional meeting.

In 1975, wine legislation created the *grand cru* appellation in Alsace. For a vineyard to qualify as *grand cru,* it must demonstrate every year that its wines are of excellent quality and consistently show the personality of its soil and microclimate.

The *grand cru* appellation has been awarded to forty-seven vineyards at this time, but the list is not final. These vineyards are on the slopes with excellent drainage and exposure.

All wines must be tasted by an INAO panel each year before receiving the *grand cru* appellation. Sometimes the panel will decree that a wine not be released until it has been aged an additional year. The *grand cru* wines are at this time a very small percentage of Alsatian exports to the United States.

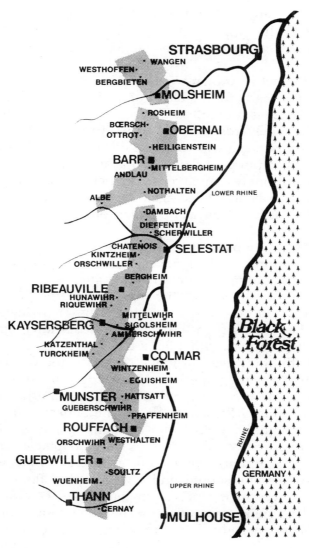

Figure 4-2 Map of Alsace.

The wines of Alsace. By longstanding tradition, the wines of Alsace have usually been named after a single grape variety. They are vinified completely dry (except for one percent of late harvest wines), unlike the majority of their German counterparts. Because of the abundance of fruit in many Alsatian wines, some mistakenly call them semisweet, confusing the fruit in a dry wine with the residual sugar found in a semisweet wine.

Alsace is the only major French wine region that identifies its wine by the name of the grape. AOC regulations for Alsace wine mandate that any wine called by the varietal name be made 100 percent from that grape.

Some of the better-known wines of Alsace are described below.

Edelzwicker is made from a blend of noble grape varieties.

Gewürztraminer is a quintessentially Alsatian wine. Twenty percent of the Alsatian vineyards are planted with this grape, and very few if any countries produce a wine of equal distinction. It is delicious, spicy, and fruity, with a pungent flavor and a highly perfumed and flowery bouquet that is strongly reminiscent of grapefruit. Gewürztraminer, once tasted, can always be identified again and again in a blind tasting—it is that distinctive. It is not always popular; one tends to either love it or hate it.

Muscat d'Alsace is planted in only 3 percent of Alsace's vineyards. The wine has an intense bouquet of sweet, ripe grapes, although the wine itself is dry with a delicate, lingering aftertaste.

Pinot Blanc (Clevner is the local name for Pinot Blanc) can also be found in Burgundy and northern Italy. The wine is more structured and fuller-bodied than the Sylvaner (see below), but is still very crisp, fresh, and supple, with a floral bouquet.

Riesling is the most elegant grape of Alsace and one of the world's most noble white wine grapes. In Alsace it is planted in 20 percent of the vineyards. The Riesling of Alsace is always the Johannisberg Riesling, the aristocrat of Rieslings. This is the perfect grape for northern climates. Although its yield is never high, it matures late and will continue to ripen in cool weather. A very adaptable vine, it can be found in various terrains, producing a different wine in each. In a Riesling of Alsace one should find a well-defined floral bouquet with fine steely nuances in the nose. On the palate there should be firm fruit, framed by good crisp acidity. The wine should fill the mouth, but not be heavy in body, and a combination of subtle flavors should linger.

Sylvaner is one of the most widely planted grape varieties in Alsace today, accounting for just over 20 percent of the vineyards. The wine is very crisp, fruity, and usually light. Sylvaner is often described as a wine for any time and purpose.

Pinot Gris, which is also called Tokay d'Alsace, is not to be confused with Hungarian Tokay; with that in mind the European Economic Community (EEC) has banned the use of the name Tokay in France. The vine, which accounts for only 5 percent of the production of Alsace, produces wines that are well-balanced and full-bodied. They can be fruity, but that sensation on the palate is followed by a luscious, slightly smoky, absolutely dry finish.

A small percentage of Pinot Noir is planted in Alsace. Traditionally it was used to produce a rosé wine called either Pinot Noir or Rosé d'Alsace. If the producer wishes, this grape can produce a more robust and typical Pinot Noir. The production of this type of wine is on the increase, and imports to the United States have risen dramatically, although it still contributes little to the total Alsace imports.

Cremant d'Alsace is an AOC sparkling wine made by the *méthode champenoise*. It is fresh, fruity, and appealing. Much Cremant d'Alsace is made from the Pinot Blanc grape, but some is made from Riesling, and the name of the grape variety is often added under the Cremant d'Alsace name.

Vendanges tardives and *récolte tardives* are late-harvested wines made from Riesling, Gewürztraminer, Pinot Gris, or Muscat grapes. In years of abundant sunshine the grapes are left to ripen on the vine, resulting in much higher levels of natural sugar. During vinification almost all of this sugar is fermented into alcohol, creating a wine that is rich, fills the mouth, and has an extraordinary depth of flavor. Wine laws passed in 1984 officially recognize the *vendanges tardives* classification. These laws established the minimum sugar level and allowable grape varieties and require that the wine be aged at least eighteen months before release.

Selection de grains nobles are even rarer and sweeter wines than the *vendanges tardives*. They were recognized as a classification in the wine laws of 1984 and are subject to the same restrictions as the *vendanges tardives*, with even higher minimum levels of natural sugar and alcohol. Only produced in truly great years from individually selected grapes affected by the "noble rot" (*Botrytis cinerea*), *selection de grains nobles* wines are pure nectar, highly concentrated, with a lingering flavor. Produced in very small quantities, these wines are very difficult to obtain in the United States.

Major producers of Alsatian wines

Aussay
Dopff "Au Moulin"
Dopff et Irion

F. Brucker

Gustave Lorentz

Hugel

Klipfel

Laugel

Léon Beyer

Muré-Clos St. Landelin

Pierre Sparr

Trimbach

Willm

Bordeaux

Bordeaux is known the world over for its incomparable red, equally fine dry white, and superb sweet white wines. Wine production in Bordeaux is far easier to learn about than Burgundy; its *châteaus* are larger, have been in the same hands for several generations, and are owned by fewer *vignerons*.

Appellation contrôlée wines. Bordeaux's production of AOC wines is approximately 75 percent reds and 25 percent whites. Bordeaux is the largest AOC wine-producing region, producing approximately 25 percent of all of France's AOC wines.

The more precise the designation on a Bordeaux label, the more distinguished the wine. If the wine is labeled *appellation Bordeaux contrôlée*, the wine is of the lowest standard permitted. The next higher designation would be *appellation Bordeaux supérieur contrôlée*; higher yet is a specific area designation, such as *appellation Médoc contrôlée*. The most specific designation short of a *château* name would be, for instance, *appellation Pauillac contrôlée*; this appears only on wines of the highest quality.

Bordeaux is divided into many districts, most of which are called *communes*. The four most important communes, which make up the Médoc district, are located on the west side of the Gironde River. The Médoc produces dry red wines, with only one exception, a white wine of Château Margaux. The communes from north to south are St. Estèphe, Pauillac, St. Julien, and Margaux. On the right bank of the Dordogne River are the districts St. Émilion and Pomerol, both of which produce only dry red wines. South of Médoc, along the Garonne River, in the capital of Bordeaux, lies the Graves district, where dry red and white wines are produced. Farther south is the district of Sauternes, noted for its extremely sweet white wines and a few dry white wines as well.

Only five grape varieties are permitted in the production of red wine in Bordeaux:

Cabernet Sauvignon: predominant variety in the Médoc, sometimes accounting for as much as 90 percent of a blend; known locally in Graves as Vidure.

Merlot: predominant variety in St. Émilion and, especially, Pomerol, sometimes accounting for as much as 90 percent of a blend.

Cabernet Franc: used in small amounts as a blending grape; known as Bouchet in St. Émilion and Pomerol and Breton in Touraine.

Malbec: used in small amounts as a blending grape; known as Pressac in St. Émilion; and as Cot, or Auxerrois in southwestern France.

Petit Verdot: used in small amounts as a blending grape.

Graves and Sauternes are the only districts in Bordeaux that produce white wines. Only three grape varieties are permitted: Sauvignon Blanc, Sémillon, and Muscadelle.

Médoc. This is the largest and most important wine district of Bordeaux, and possibly the greatest producer of red wines in the world.

Its four most important vineyards are Château Lafite-Rothschild; Château Mouton-Rothschild; Château Latour; and Château Margaux.

The famous 1855 classification. The classification of 1855 applies to the wines of the Médoc (with the exception of Château Haut-Brion, in Graves), and the wines of Sauternes and Barsac.

In the Médoc, the classification divides the sixty-two great vineyards into five categories, known as *crus* or "growths," according to their recognized quality in 1855, based on the prices obtainable for their wine at that time (a first-growth or *premier cru* vineyard, for instance, is of the highest quality, and a fifth-growth one or *cinquième cru* the lowest). The Bordeaux Wine Classification of April 18, 1855, was established under the sponsorship of Emperor Napoléon III, who wanted to showcase the classification at the 1855 Paris Exposition (World's Fair).

The 1855 classification has been in effect for so long partly because the soil content and climate, for instance, of any given vineyard have naturally not changed dramatically, and still, where they are good, have the same beneficial influence. However, some owners today produce far better-quality wines than they did in 1855, and their wines deserve to be elevated to a higher classification. Others, unfortunately, produce somewhat lower-quality wines that should be lowered or even declassified from the 1855 ratings.

In 1953, a classification of the wines of Graves was begun by the INAO, who completed the task in 1959. In 1954, the INAO laid down a classification for St. Émilion which divided the seventy-six great vineyards into two classes: *premier grand cru* and *grand cru* classe. The *premier grand cru* classe is subdivided into *a* and *b* classifications. Château Ausone and Cheval Blanc are the only two vineyards considered worthy of an *a* classification. Ten vineyards were classified as *b*. Provision was made in the decree for a revision of the classification every ten years—and in fact eight of the ten vineyards were given the *grand cru* status *a* in 1969.

The error of trying to grade vineyards first, second, third, etc., which tends to handicap certain wines, especially in a publicity-conscious age, was not made with the more recent Graves and St. Émilion classifications.

There is no official classification of the wines of the Pomerol Region, though Château Pétrus would undoubtedly rate *grand cru* status if 1855 standards were applied.

The following is a list of red wines as they were classified in 1855.

Chateau	Commune
First growth (premier cru)	
Château Lafite-Rothschild	Pauillac
Château Latour	Pauillac
Château Margaux	Margaux
Château Haut-Brion	Graves
Château Mouton-Rothschild	Pauillac
Second growth (deuxième cru)	
Château Cos d'Estournel	St. Estèphe
Château Rausan-Ségla	Margaux
Château Rauzan-Gassies	Margaux
Château Léoville-Las Cases	St. Julien

Château Léoville-Poyferré	St. Julien
Château Léoville-Barton	St. Julien
Château Durfort-Vivens	Margaux
Château Lascombes	Margaux
Château Gruaud-Larose	Margaux
Château Brane-Cantenac	Cantenac-Margaux
Château Pichon-Longueville	Pauillac
Château Pichon-Lalande	Pauillac
Château Ducru-Beaucaillou	St. Julien
Château Montrose	St. Estèphe

Third growth (troisième cru)

Château Kirwan	Cantenac-Margaux
Château d'Issan	Cantenac-Margaux
Château Lagrange	St. Julien
Château Langoa-Barton	St. Julien
Château Giscours	Labarde (Margaux)
Château Malescot-Saint-Exupéry	Margaux
Château Cantenac-Brown	Cantenac-Margaux
Château Boyd-Cantenac	Margaux
Château Palmer	Cantenac-Margaux
Château La Lagune	Ludon
Château Calon-Ségur	St. Estèphe
Château Ferrière	Margaux
Château Marquis-d'Alesme-Becker	Margaux

Fourth growth (quatrième cru)

Château Saint-Pierre-Sevaistre	St. Julien
Château Saint-Pierre-Bontemps	St. Julien
Château Talbot	St. Julien
Château Branaire-Ducru	St. Julien
Château Duhart-Milon-Rothschild	Pauillac
Château Pouget	Cantenac-Margaux
Château La Tour-Carnet	St. Laurent
Château Lafon-Rochet	St. Estèphe
Château Beychevelle	St. Julien

Fourth growth (quatrième cru) (continued)	
Château Prieuré-Lichine	Cantenac-Margaux
Château Marquis-de-Terme	Margaux

Fifth growth (cinquième cru)	
Château Pontet-Canet	Pauillac
Château Batailley	Pauillac
Château Haut-Batailley	Pauillac
Château Grand-Puy-Lacoste	Pauillac
Château Grand-Puy-Ducasse	Pauillac
Château Lynch-Bages	Pauillac
Château Lynch-Moussas	Pauillac
Château Dauzac	Labarde (Margaux)
Château Mouton-Baronne-Philippe	Pauillac
Château du Tertre	Arsac
Château Haut-Bages-Liberal	Pauillac
Château Pédesclaux	Pauillac
Château Belgrave	St. Laurent
Château Camensac	St. Laurent
Château Cos Labory	St. Estèphe
Château Clerc-Milon	Pauillac
Château Croizet-Bages	Pauillac
Château Cantemerle	Macau

The name Château Lafite-Rothschild evokes visions of grand *châteaus* and centuries-old winemaking methods; in fact this *château* produces one of the finest red wines in the world, and has a fascinating history.

In 1716, the Marquis Alexander de Ségur acquired Château Latour, Château Mouton-Rothschild, and Château Lafite-Rothschild through a marriage to Marie-Therese de Clauzel. In addition to these three properties, he also owned Château Calon-Ségur and Château Phélan-Ségur. Although he certainly didn't realize it at the time, he had taken possession of the finest three vineyards in the world. During the Revolution, however, the properties were split up and Ségur retained only Calon and Phélan. He is said to have been fond of saying, when talking about his empire, "I make wine at Lafite and Latour, but my heart is at Calon"; but one can be sure that his heart would skip more than a beat today if he saw the astronomical prices that these first-growth wines fetch.

It wasn't until 1787 that Lafite was vintage dated; in 1797 it was *château* or *estate* bottled for the first time. The 1795 vintage of Château Lafite-Rothschild was blended with Hermitage (a red wine from the Rhône Valley) to give it strength. It was almost standard practice to blend wines with those from the Rhône Valley or even Spain that contained high alcohol. The blended Lafite wine was labeled Lafite-Hermitaged.

On August 8, 1868, Baron James Rothschild purchased Lafite for a record three million dollars. By then the famous classification of 1855 had taken place and Lafite-Rothschild was unanimously voted a first-growth vineyard.

During the years 1885–1905, *château* bottling was not permitted because vines that had been devastated by the *Phylloxera* root louse had to be replanted.

At one time Lafite produced a white wine (the grapes were later uprooted) for the personal use of Baron Elie de Rothschild. The last vintage of this wine (1959) fetched $230 per bottle at auction in August 1978.

In 1962, Lafite's owners acquired Château Duhart-Milon, a fourth-growth vineyard producing a red Bordeaux, and later added Château Clarke, of Listrac, and Château La Cardonne, in the Bas-Médoc region.

Carruades de Lafite (last produced in 1966) was the so-called "second" wine of Lafite. It has now been replaced by Moulin des Carruades, formerly the "third" wine of Lafite.

Today the wines produced by Lafite, along with those of Château Mouton-Rothschild and Château Pétrus, command the highest prices of any red Bordeaux wine, often more than $100 per bottle.

An interesting aside to the Lafite-Rothschild story is that, in 1882, Baron Edmond de Rothschild (son of James) decided to give financial assistance to some Russian Jews in the development of winemaking in Palestine, where Israel's present winemaking industry originated. Carmel Vineyards is the result of the Rothschild family's financial and technological expertise and shrewd marketing strategies.

Chateau Mouton-Rothschild was in 1820 known as Chateau Brane-Mouton until Baron Nathaniel de Rothschild purchased it on May 11, 1853. Since 1853 Mouton-Rothschild has been owned by members of successive generations of Rothschilds; first Nathaniel, then James, Henri, and, since October 22, 1922, Philippe.

In 1924, Mouton was *château* bottled for the first time. It was with the 1934 vintage that Mouton's labels first mentioned the number of bottles produced in that year. The letters *RC* occasionally appear on labels, meaning that the wine is reserved for the *château* and normally not released to the public.

Baron Philippe signs his name on the bottle's label, which led one enterprising individual in Venezuela and another in Los Angeles to superimpose the signature onto a French bank check (these attempts failed miserably and led to their arrest). Baron Philippe uses a slightly different signature for business and personal matters. It is the letter *R* that makes the difference, and it is speculated that this was the reason why he changed his traditional signature on the label from "Philippe de Rothschild" to "Baron Philippe" in 1979.

One of the most fascinating aspects of Château Mouton-Rothschild bottles is the art work on the label. Every year Baron Philippe de Rothschild commissions a famous artist to design the upper portion of Mouton's label. The tradition began in 1927 for the 1924 label; but the practice did not become regular until 1945. It continues today. Some examples are shown in figure 4–3.

The world-renowned artists who design the labels are not paid in money; rather, they receive five cases of good years of Mouton, ready to drink when the design is delivered, and five cases of the vintage it was created for when the vintage is marketed.

These are the artists who have been commissioned to paint labels for Château Mouton-Rothschild:

1924	Jean Carlu	1966	Pierre Alechinsky
1945	Philippe Jullian	1967	César
1946	Jean Hugo	1968	Bona
1947	Jean Cocteau	1969	Joan Miró
1948	Marie Laurencin	1970	Marc Chagall
1949	Andre Dignimont	1971	Wassily Kandinsky
1950	Georges Arnulf	1972	Serge Poliakoff
1951	Marcel Vertès	1973	Pablo Picasso
1952	Léonor Fini	1974	Robert Motherwell
1953	No illustrated label	1975	Andy Warhol
1954	Jean Carzou	1976	Pierre Soulages
1955	Georges Braque	1977	Tribute to Her Majesty Queen Elizabeth (commemorative label)
1956	Pavel Tchelitchew		
1957	André Masson		
1958	Salvador Dali	1978	Jean-Paul Riopelle
1959	Richard Lippold	1979	Hisao Domoto
1960	Jacques Villon	1980	Hans Hartung
1961	Georges Mathieu	1981	Arman
1962	Matta	1982	John Huston

Figure 4-3 Mouton Rothschild labels. (Courtesy Baron Philippe de Rothschild, Inc.)

1963	Bernard Dufour	1983	Saul Steinberg
1964	Henry Moore	1984	Yaacov Agam
1965	Dorothea Tanning	1985	Paul Delvaux

(No label was commissioned in 1953 because both the wine and label in that year were dedicated to Mouton's first three Rothschild owners to commemorate its centenary.)

In 1933, Philippe de Rothschild acquired Château Mouton-d'Armail-hacq, a fifth-growth vineyard producing a red Bordeaux wine. In 1956 the name was changed to Château Mouton-Baron-Philippe, and in 1975 to Château Mouton-Baronne-Philippe. Finally, in 1979, Baron Philippe again changed the name to Château Mouton-Baronne-Pauline, to honor his late wife Pauline, who died in 1976.

In 1962 the world-famous wine library of Château Mouton-Rothschild first opened its doors to the public. In 1970 Baron Philippe purchased Château Clerc-Milon, a fifth-growth Pauillac vineyard. On June 22, 1973, Château Mouton-Rothschild was officially granted *grand cru* status by Monsieur Jacques Chirac, then France's minister of agriculture (later prime minister). Before this reclassification (from second- to first-growth status) Château Mouton-Rothschild had this world-famous slogan: "First I am not, Second I do not Deign to be, I am Mouton." In 1973 the slogan was changed to: "First I am; Second I was; Mouton does not change."

Today Mouton-Rothschild produces no "second" wine, but does produce a regional red, white, and rosé wine labeled Mouton-Cadet, which is produced in huge quantities. Before 1933 the wine was called Carruades de Mouton-Rothschild.

Château Latour is noted for extremely dark, hard, full-bodied wines that need decades of aging before becoming even remotely drinkable. It is one of the longest-lived wines in the world and, unfortunately, many people drink it before its time. Latour has the uncanny ability to produce good wines even in mediocre vintages (e.g., 1963, 1965, 1968, and 1974). Latour is generally blended with a high percentage of Cabernet Sauvignon, which gives it longevity.

The Latour label depicts an ancient tower which, according to records, was originally used to guard against pirates during the second half of the Hundred Years War. A lion is perched on top, ready to strike its enemies.

Since 1966, Château Latour has produced a "second" wine called Les Forts de Latour, made from younger vines. This wine features three towers on its label.

Château Margaux, originally known as Château Lamothe or Château La Motte, is the only classified wine that uses its commune name as its vineyard name.

In 1977 the Mentzelopoulos family, owners of a French supermarket chain, purchased Château Margaux from the Ginestet family, who for a long period, had been slowly bringing Château Margaux down in quality and reputation.

Although basically a red wine producer, Château Margaux has produced a very excellent and costly dry white wine since 1847. It is labeled Le Pavillon Blanc de Chateau Margaux, and is entitled to be sold under the appellation *Bordeaux Blanc Contrôlée*. Château Margaux produces a "second" red wine called Le Pavillon Rouge.

Graves. The most important vineyard in this district is Château Haut-Brion, the producer of one of the finest red wines in the world. Less well known is its superb white dry wine labeled Château Haut-Brion Blanc.

Although only one Graves wine (Château Haut-Brion) was classified in 1855, there are many fine vineyards in this district which, if classified today, would certainly rank quite high. Graves produces very good dry white wines from Sauvignon Blanc and Sémillon grapes; unfortunately they represent only about 5 percent of the total Graves production. The vineyards listed below are the best in Graves. They are mainly red wine vineyards; an asterisk indicates that the vineyard also produces white wine.

Château La Mission Haut-Brion

Château La Tour-Haut-Brion

Château Pape-Clément

Château Haut-Bailly

Domaine De Chevalier*

Château de Fieuzal*

Château Oliver*

Château Carbonnieux*

Château Chantegrive

Château Bouscaut*

Château Smith-Haut-Lafitte

Château La Tour-Martillac*

Château Malartic-Lagravière*

Château Laville-Haut-Brion (only makes white wine)

Château Couhins (only makes white wine)

Pomerol and St. Émilion. Although the wines of Pomerol were never officially classified, several of them would rank with the finest from Médoc.

Most Pomerols and St. Émilions (both make only red wines) are made with a predominance of the Merlot grape, which yields a softer wine than those made with a higher proportion of Cabernet Sauvignon grapes. This is not to say that Pomerols and St. Émilions lack staying power or aging ability; for the most part they mature slightly faster than their counterparts from the Médoc. The use of the Merlot grape in the production of Pomerols and St. Émilions is important: the Merlot ripens earlier than the Cabernet Sauvignon grape, and therefore often escapes early frosts or severe late fall weather while Cabernet Sauvignon grapes are still ripening on the vines. The 1967 vintage, for example, was only fair in the Médoc district because of early autumn rains, but was exceptional in Pomerol and St. Émilion.

Among the best vineyards in Pomerol are:

Château Pétrus	Château Nénin
Château Petit-Village	Château Gazin
Château Trotanoy	Château Lafleur
Château L'Évangile	Château La Fleur-Pétrus
Château Latour à Pomerol	Vieux Château-Certan

In St. Émilion some of the best vineyards are:

Château Cheval Blanc	Château Pavie
Château Ausone	Château Clos Fourtet
Château Beauséjour-Duffau	Château L'Angélus
Château Beauséjour-Fagout	Château Canon-La Gaffelière
Château Bel-Air	Château La Tour-Figeac
Château Canon	Château Trimoulet
Château Figeac	Château Monbousquet
Château La Gaffelière	Château Simard
Château La Magdelaine	

Incidentally, although almost all of the vineyards of the Médoc use

118

château in their names, in St. Émilion *clos* (enclosure or field) is used instead in some vineyard names, but the meaning is the same.

To help promote the wines of St. Émilion, John Lackland, on July 8, 1199, established the Jurade de Saint-Émilion, a wine brotherhood still in existence today.

Regional, proprietary, shippers, unclassified, and cru bourgeois wines. Although the wines classified in 1855 are the finest available from Bordeaux, they are also the most expensive and, for many, are not affordable. One could certainly not drink them every day; generally they are reserved for special occasions.

In addition to *château*-bottled wines, there are many wines that are bought, aged, bottled, and shipped by cooperatives and shippers under one of the names listed below. Careful shoppers look for these lower-priced shippers' wines, which are of good to excellent quality:

Alexis Lichine	Cruse
B.&G.	Ginestet
Calvet	J.P. Moueix
Cordier	Sichel

Some *proprietary wines* are Mouton-Cadet; Lacour Pavillon; Grand Marque; and Maitre d'Estournel.

Regional wines are simply labeled with the name of the commune or district that produces them: Médoc, St. Émilion, Graves, Bordeaux, and so on.

Some *unclassified* and *cru bourgeois* wines are:

Château Chasse-Spleen	Château Lanessan
Château Coufran	Château La Rose-Trintaudon
Château Fombrauge	Château Meyney
Château Fourcas-Hosten	Château de Pez
Château Gloria	Château Phélan-Ségur
Château Greysac	Château Trimoulet

Sauternes. Sauternes (which take their name from the Sauternes district where they are produced) are, along with the German *Trockenbeerenauslese*, the sweetest wines in the world and among the most expensive. It is produced from three white grape varieties: Sauvignon Blanc, Sémillon, and Muscadelle.

Sauternes are made by utilizing a mold called the "noble rot" (technically, *Botrytis cinerea*). This mold is present as spores at all times in most vineyards. Depending on the grape variety, the time of year, and climatic conditions it can greatly enhance or severely damage the grapes in a vineyard.

Ideally for the production of Sauternes, high humidity from an early rainfall or fog just before harvest time allows moisture to form on the surface of the fruit. If this is followed by dry, warm (60° to 70°F) air, the desired *Botrytis* growth can form in as little as eighteen hours. (If, on the other hand, the high humidity is followed by cold weather, and the skins crack, a deleterious infection will occur.) The fungus that forms on the moist grape skins is quite uneven in any given grape cluster and will often require multiple pickings, berry by berry, to obtain the maximum amount of berries.

The grapes that have been attacked by the "noble rot" are extremely overripe and must be hand picked individually after the ripeness has been determined. From each bunch of grapes the pickers might select one or two berries to use. The same vineyard might have to be picked over several times in order to obtain all the affected grapes. It is said that it takes one picker one full day to pick enough grapes to produce one bottle of Sauternes. Obviously, the result is an extremely high cost of production.

Botrytis is an ugly, hairy mold, gray or even pinkish brown in color. Affected berries resemble dessicated, cracked raisins, but do not have the caramelized taste of a raisin. Long threads resembling spikes penetrate the skins, allowing the spores to grow safely inside, protected by the biological barrier. There is no exposure of the pulp or juice to air.

The action of the *micellae* of the mold causes dehydration. Water is evaporated as sugar concentrations increase some 30 percent to 40 percent. Flavor, grape acids, grape essence, and aromatic compounds in the remaining juice are greatly magnified. Glycerine is produced in high levels, giving the wine a soft, almost oily tinge on the tongue and palate.

Wines made from these grapes are gold-amber in color with a distinctive honeylike, raisiny character. They are extremely sweet and have an unusually long bottle life, lasting easily ten to twenty years, and if from an excellent vintage as long as fifty years or more.

The five communes entitled to be called Sauternes are: Sauternes, Barsac, Preignac, Fargues, and Bommes. (Only wines from the commune of Barsac are entitled to the Barsac *appellation contrôlée*; however, a decree of 1936 gave this commune the right to the illustrious Sauternes appellation as well.) The Sauternes appellation requires a minimum alcoholic content of 13 percent; and, for some unknown reason, chaptalization is permitted.

To help promote the sweet wines of Sauternes, a wine brotherhood, the Commanderie du Bontemps de Sauternes et Barsac, was established and is active today.

The sweet wines of Sauternes and Barsac were among those ranked by the 1855 classification; the vineyards are listed below by classification:

Château	Commune
First "great" growth (grand premier cru)	
Château Y'Quem	Sauternes
First growth (premier cru)	
Château La Tour Blanche	Bommes
Château Lafaurie-Peyraguey	Bommes
Clos Haut-Peyraguey	Bommes
Château de Rayne-Vigneau	Bommes
Château Climens	Barsac
Château Guiraud	Sauternes
Château Coutet	Barsac
Château Rieussec	Fargues
Château Suduiraut	Preignac
Château Rabaud-Promis	Bommes
Château Sigalas-Rabaud	Bommes
Second growth (deuxième cru)	
Château Myrat	Barsac
Château Doisy-Daëne	Barsac
Château d'Arche	Sauternes
Château Broustet	Barsac
Château Doisy-Dubroca	Sauternes
Château Doisy-Védrines	Barsac
Château Caillou	Barsac
Château Filhot	Sauternes
Château Suau	Barsac
Château Nairac	Barsac
Château de Malle	Preignac
Château Lamothe	Sauternes
Château Romer	Fargues

Sauternes, because of its intense sweetness, is actually a dessert in itself and could be served alone, or with fruit. An excellent combination is to serve an ice-cold Sauternes with an extremely overripe Roquefort cheese (at room temperature), as dessert. Some producers recommend serving Sauternes throughout dinner, from the appetizer through the main course, finishing with dessert.

Burgundy

Burgundy's four wine-producing districts Saône-et-Loire, Côte d'Or, Rhône, and Yonne, are known around the world for the wines they produce.

Throughout its turbulent history Burgundy's boundaries contracted and expanded according to the fortunes of war. The French Revolution abruptly changed Burgundy's viticulture, as the large estates owned by the nobility and the church were seized and sold. Properties were broken up into small lots, and purchasers subdivided these lots into thousands of small patches which they sold to the peasants. Further fragmentation was continued by the French laws of inheritance, and now a comparatively small volume of wine is made by an enormous number of producers. Ownership of a Burgundian vineyard, no matter how minuscule, is a badge of prestige.

At the time when the land was divided (and subdivided) the unit of measurement was the *journal*, a *journal* being anywhere from 1/3 to 5/6 of an acre. This explains why there are often more than forty different individual owners of one vineyard.

Many of these small vineyards sell their grapes to shippers; others make their own wine or sell it in *hogsheads* (barrels holding approximately 60 gallons) to shippers who mature and then sell it. About 75 percent of the wine sold by shippers is made by small independent proprietors. No big shipper has the time to deal with a multitude of growers. Intermediaries known as *courtiers* (brokers), who work on commission, handle most of the sales of the small growers' wines to the shippers. They know what the shipper wants and try to match what is available to his or her needs.

A number of cooperatives have been formed to deal with the problems of the small producer. Twenty-nine cooperative wineries make 24 percent of the total wine production in Burgundy (24 percent is low compared to other French wine-producing areas). They are located in the areas of Beaujolais, Mâcon, and Chablis.

Approximately 80 percent of the Burgundy wine produced is red; most of it is from the Côte de Nuits. The other 20 percent is white, mostly from the Côte de Beaune.

Burgundy is the northernmost great red wine-producing region in the world, and is the easiest of France's wine-producing regions to understand in terms of the grape varieties permitted, under law, to be grown there. There are five: Pinot Noir for red wines; Chardonnay and Pinot Blanc for white wines (including Chablis); and Gamay for Beaujolais. Also grown is another white grape variety, Aligoté, predominantly used in the south, with its name usually appearing on the label (figure 4-4).

In 1951 the Confrérie des Vignerons de Saint-Vincent was formed; it is the wine brotherhood responsible for promoting the wines of Mâcon in southern Burgundy. A yearly celebration is held every January 22, on the birthday of Saint Vincent, Burgundy's patron saint.

Chablis. This grape-growing area takes its name from the charming village of Chablis, which is nestled by the side of the Serein River.

Chablis is seventy-five miles north of the Côte d'Or in Burgundy on a parallel that runs north of Seattle, Washington. Frost is always a danger in the northern climates, and the Serein River compounds the problem. When a frost arrives it sinks into the river bottom and hovers for days, searing the delicate vines on the river's banks.

Today Chablis is known the world over. The chalky soil gives it its clean taste, and fruitiness and a bouquet are contributed by the Chardonnay grape. It is an extremely dry, crisp wine with a refreshing acidity that compliments delicate fish, particularly oysters.

By law there are four Chablis: *grand cru, premier cru, chablis,* and *petit chablis. Grand cru* Chablis must have a minimum alcoholic content of 11 percent; *premier cru,* 10.5 percent; *chablis,* 10 percent; and *petit chablis,* 9.5 percent alcohol. Chaptalization is not only permitted but is practiced yearly, but only after the minimum alcoholic content is reached. Chablis received its AOC designation in 1938, which specifies that only the Chardonnay grape (known locally as Aubaine or Beaunois) may be used to produce Chablis.

The most elegant Chablis is the *grand cru.* There are seven varieties, all from one stretch of hillside at the end of the village:

Blanchots	Les Preuses
Bougros	Valmur
Grenouilles	Vaudésir
Les Clos	

123

HOW TO READ A WINE LABEL

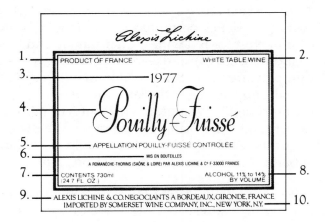

READING A BURGUNDY WINE LABEL

1. The wine is a product of France

2. The color of the wine

3. Vintage

4. It is either the name of the grape, vineyard or specific place-name where the vineyard is located.

5. Appellation (d'Origine) Contrôlée: controlled place-name of origin. These words represent certification that the wine comes from the regulated place-name indicated on the label.

6. "Mis en Bouteilles à" or "put in bottles at . . ." The name of the property where the wine was bottled.

7. The net contents of the bottle

8. The alcoholic percentage by volume

9. The name and address of the shipper

10. The name and address of the importer

At the other end of that same hill, and facing it across the narrow river, are the vineyards from which the *premier cru* Chablis is produced. Until much-needed changes in the law, in 1967, there were more than thirty vineyards entitled to be called *premier cru*. These have been narrowed down to eleven:

Beauroy	Melinots	Vaillons
Cote de Lechet	Montée-de-Tonnerre	Vaucoupin
Fourchaume	Montmains	Vosgros
Les Fourneaux	Monts de Milieu	

Simple *chablis* and the lightest wine, *petit chablis*, are produced from vineyards farther from the village. The latter is rarely exported to the United States.

Les Pilliers Chablisiens is the wine brotherhood responsible for promoting the wines of Chablis.

Some reputable producers and shippers of Chablis are:

Bacheroy-Josselin	Louis Jadot	A. Regnard & Fils
Albert Bichot	J. Moreau & Fils	Ropiteau Freres
Joseph Drouhin	Albert Pic & Fils	

The Côte d'Or. The Côte d'Or (Golden Slopes) is twenty-five to thirty miles long and only one mile wide at its widest point. The greatest vineyards in Burgundy are in this district, which is traditionally divided into two wine-producing areas: Côte de Nuits in the north; and Côte de Beaune in the south.

Soil content is one factor critical to the development of a wine's qualities. The soil of the Côte de Nuits is a mixture of clay, silica, and limestone; that of the Côte de Beaune is high in limestone, or its near relation, chalk.

By law, the red wines of the Côte d'Or are made exclusively from the Pinot Noir grape. The Pinot Noir seems to like warmth spread throughout the day, rather than cool mornings and hot afternoons.

The Côte de Nuits stretches for about twelve miles, from the town of Fixin in the north to Nuits-Saint-Georges in the south. There are twenty-nine *appellation contrôlée* wines produced in this region. Only three white wines are entitled to the *appellation contrôlée* designation in the Côte de Nuits: Musigny Blanc; Nuits-Saint-Georges Blanc; and Clos Blanc de Vougeot.

All of the *grand cru* and the most important *premier cru* wines of this area are listed below, under the names of the communes that produce them.

Fixin	
Grand cru	*Premier cru*
None	Les Hervelets
	Clos de la Perrière
	Clos du Chapitre
	Les Meix-Bas
	Clos Napoléon
	Les Arvelets

Gevrey-Chambertin	
Chambertin	Clos-Saint-Jacques
Ruchottes-Chambertin	Les Varoilles
Clos de Bèze	
Charmes-Chambertin	
Chapelle-Chambertin	
Griotte-Chambertin	
Latricières-Chambertin	
Mazis-Chambertin	
Mazoyères-Chambertin	

Morey-Saint-Denis	
Clos de Tart	Clos des Lambrays
Clos Saint-Denis	Le Clos-des-Ormes
Clos de la Roche	Monts-Luisants
Bonnes Mares (Part)	

Vosne-Romanée	
Les Richebourg	Les Suchots
La Romanée	Les Malconsorts
La Romanée-Conti	La Chaume
La Tâche	La Grand Rue
La Romanée Saint-Vivant	Les Beaux-Monts

Flagey-Échézeaux	
Les Échézeaux	None
Les Grands-Échézeaux	

Chambolle-Musigny	
Les Musigny	Les Charmes
Les Bonnes Mares (Part)	Les Amoureuses

Vougeot	
Clos de Vougeot	Clos Blanc de Vougeot
	Les Cras

Nuits-Saint-Georges	
None	Les Saint-Georges
	Les Cailles
	Les Porets
	Les Vaucrains
	Les Pruliers

The southern half of the Côte d'Or, the Côte de Beaune, extends approximately fifteen miles, from Nuits-Saint-Georges in the north to Santenay in the south. It is wider, longer, and has nearly twice the amount of land of its northern neighbor. The city of Beaune, during the early Middle Ages, was wealthy and important; the ring of battlements built around it as protection from marauding enemies still stands. Some of the city's distinguished wine shippers now use the fortresses as wine cellars.

Just six miles south of the city is the Côte de Meursault, an area scarred by old quarries. It is one of the few hills where the soil is perfectly suited to the Chardonnay vine from which fine white wines are produced in the communes of Meursault, Puligny-Montrachet, and Chassagne-Montrachet.

The Côte de Beaune is known for its outstanding white wines, although there are also some very fine red wines produced. One vineyard in particular, Corton (from the village of Aloxe-Corton), is the only *grand cru* red wine vineyard in the Côte de Beaune.

All of the *grand cru* and the most important *premier cru* wines produced in this area are listed below, under the names of the communes that produce them.

Aloxe-Corton	
Grand cru	**Premier cru**
Le Corton	Corton Renardes
Corton-Charlemagne	Corton Clos du Roi
	Corton Bressandes
	Les Pougets

Pernand-Vergelesses	
None	Ile des Vergelesses
	Les Vergelesses
	Les Fichots
	Creux de la Net

Savigny-Les-Beaune	
None	La Dominode
	Les Jarrons

Beaune	
None	Les Grèves
	Les Fèves
	Les Marconnets
	Les Teurons
	Les Clos des Mouches
	Les Bressandes

Pommard	
None	Les Épenots
	Les Rugiens
	Les Arvelets
	Clos de la Commaraine

Santenay

None

Les Gravières
La Comme
Clos-de-Tavannes
Beauregard

Monthélie

None

Le Chateau-Gaillard
Les Riottes
La Taupine

Auxey-Duresses

None

Les Duresses
Clos du Val
Les Grands-Champs

Meursault

None

La Goutte d'Or
Les Charmes
Les Genevrières
Les Perrières

Puligny-Montrachet

Montrachet
Chevalier-Montrachet
Bâtard-Montrachet
Bienvenues-Bâtard-Montrachet

Le Cailleret
Les Combettes
Les Pucelles

Chassagne-Montrachet

Montrachet
Bâtard-Montrachet
Criots-Bâtard-Montrachet

Clos Saint-Jean
Morgeot
Les Boudriottes
La Maltroie
Les Ruchottes

Volnay	
None	Les Caillerets
	Les Champans
	Le Clos des Chenes
	Santenots

Côte Chalonnaise is a long, low line of hills that extends southward from the Côte de Beaune for about twenty miles. The grape varieties from which its classified red and white wines are made are the same as those grown in the Côte d'Or, but the wines of the Côte Chalonnaise are somewhat lighter and mature faster. The four most important villages in this area are Mercurey, Givry, Rully, and Montagny.

The Mâconnais region takes its name from Mâcon, a rather pretty town on the river Sâone. The local red wine is fruity and very pleasant when young; but the predominant wine here (approximately 70 percent of total production) is white. The region's slopes are covered with vineyards that produce light, dry white wines, such as the world-renowned Pouilly-Fuissé. Other white wines, in ascending order of quality, are Mâcon Blanc, Mâcon Superieur, Mâcon-Villages, St. Véran, and Pouilly-Vinzelles.

The small village of Chardonnay is nestled among the vineyards, just three miles from the celebrated Romanesque church of Tournus; this, supposedly, is where the grape got its name.

Merchants and shippers. There are more than 150 merchant-shippers (*monopoles*) operating in Burgundy. They are responsible for blending wines from several villages or districts and giving the finished wine a brand name. Below is a list of some of the finer *monopoles* of Burgundy:

Albert Bichot	Calvet
Boisseaux Estivant	Domaine Camus
J. C. Boisset	Champy
Bonneau de Martray	Chanson Père et Fils
Bouchard Aîné et Fils	Chateau de Pommard
Bouchard Père et Fils	Clair-Daü
Domaine Dujac	Leroy
Domaine de La Romanee-Conti	Marcilly

Joseph Drouhin	Moillard
Drouhin-Laroze	Mommessin
Dufouleur Freres	Patriarche Père et Fils
Faiveley	Pierre Ponnelle
Pierre Gelin	Jacques Prieur
Domaine J. Germain	Prince de Merode
Henri Gouges	Prosper Mafoux
Heritier-Guyot	Les Fils de Marcel Quancard
Hospices de Beaune	Ropiteau Freres
Louis Jadot	Armand Rousseau Père et Fils
Henri Lamarche	Roland Thevenin
La Reine Pedauque	Tollot-Beault
Louis Latour	Domaine de Varoilles
Domaine Leflaive	Comité Georges de Voguë

Beaujolais

The Beaujolais region is the southernmost district in Burgundy, just south of the vineyards of Mâcon. To the west is the mountain chain of the Monts du Beaujolais; to the east, the river Sâone; and to the south, the region ends just slightly north of Lyon. This is a large and very productive region just over thirty-four miles long, with a total of 49,500 acres which produce 18.5 million gallons each year of the light, fruity red wine that takes its name from the region. (And *Beaujolais* comes from *Beaujeu*, the name of a little town that was the seat of the province in the twelfth century, until the village of Villefranche was built nearer to the Sâone and became the province's capital.)

Beaujolais, produced and consumed in considerable quantities for centuries in the Sâone River Valley just above Lyon, is more popular in the United States than the wines of any other French region. A good percentage of Beaujolais is never even bottled, but goes to market in the barrels from which it is drawn in the restaurants of Paris and Lyon. It is the most popular *vin ordinaire* of France (figure 4-5). In this region in years past, the wine was served free at outdoor restaurants in small bottles known as *pots* (they were about half the size of a normal bottle, and held approximately 17 oz.), to demonstrate the quality of the new wine.

Good Beaujolais should have the fresh, full, fruity nose reminiscent of berries, which is part of its Gamay heritage. On the palate one should taste cherries, strawberries, raspberries, and an overwhelming fresh-

Figure 4-5 Annual Beaujolais Nouveau celebration. (Courtesy Food & Wines from France)

ness. Beaujolais should be young, lively, and joyous. It is the grapiest of all European wines, flowery yet quaffable.

In a prolific year, the region may produce six or seven million cases of wine. Less than one percent of this yield will be white wine, usually without the bouquet or the breed of a good white Burgundy. (The red wines produced in Beaujolais could legally be called Burgundies if the producers adhered to the requirements of the appropriate *Appellation Contrôlée* laws, among them that only the Pinot Noir grape be used.)

Beaujolais is divided into two areas: the Haut-Beaujolais in the north, and the Bas-Beaujolais in the south. One of the special features of Beaujolais is that just south of the town of Pouilly-Fuissé, the soil suddenly becomes granitelike and is composed of manganese, porphyry, and schist or diorite (also granitelike). These elements are not suitable for the Pinot Noir grape. Consequently, growers have slowly switched to using Gamay Noir as the primary grape in the production of the jubilantly light and cherry-colored Beaujolais. (The calcareous soil of the Bas-Beau-jolais is composed mainly of clay and chalk, or limestone.)

The table below indicates the alcohol content requirements for red Beaujolais wines under the *Appellation Contrôlée* laws (*grand cru* wines are listed separately).

Wine	Minimum required strength
Beaujolais	unfermented 9 percent
Beaujolais-Supérieur	unfermented 10 percent
Beaujolais-Villages	unfermented 10 percent
Grand cru	
Saint-Amour	unfermented 10 percent
Moulin-à-Vent	unfermented 10 percent
Morgon	unfermented 10 percent
Juliénas	unfermented 10 percent
Fleurie	unfermented 10 percent
Chiroubles	unfermented 10 percent
Chénas	unfermented 10 percent
Brouilly	unfermented 10 percent
Côte de Brouilly	unfermented 10.5 percent

If the wine does not meet these standards, it will be declassified to a lower level or simply sold as *vin rouge*. A Beaujolais wine at 10 percent alcohol or above, produced from a vineyard that meets yield per acre and other requirements may be sold as Beaujolais Supérieur.

Wines labeled Beaujolais or Beaujolais Supérieur are lighter wines, probably from one of the fifty-nine communes in the Bas-Beaujolais area. Beaujolais with less than 10 percent alcohol is unstable for travel and rarely reaches this country. *Grand cru* vineyards are limited in yield per acre, and their wines must contain a minimum of 10 to 10.5 percent alcohol. Under law, with the exception of "simple" Beaujolais, produced from vineyards whose allowance is 50 hectos per hectare (approximately 445 gallons per acre), all classifications of Beaujolais are produced from vineyards that are permitted a maximum yield of 40 hectos per hectare (approximately 356 gallons per acre). This law became effective on October 19, 1974. The next-highest grade of Beaujolais, Beaujolais-Villages, is produced in thirty-five communes located in the northernmost section of the Haut-Beaujolais area. Like *grand cru* wines, if it comes from vineyards whose yield per acre is too high, it will be dropped in class. Beaujolais-Villages is a little fuller-bodied than the wines from the south, but still rich and charming.

Nine communes that are all located in the northern part of the region, each of which is entitled to its own *appellation*, produce the *grand cru*. (These *grand cru* wines do not use the word *Beaujolais* on their labels, but are sold under the name of the commune that produces them.)

The northernmost of these communes is Saint-Amour, whose grapes have ripened in the full sunlight of hill slopes. The rich red wine is tinged with violet and is less fruity than its eight neighbors. Saint-Amour has a spicy aroma, with hints of kirsch. In parts of Saint-Amour the soil contains some limestone which produces the delightful Beaujolais Blanc—a drier and more delicate wine than Mâcon Blanc, and with slightly less body. Beaujolais Blanc is made from the Aligote rather than Chardonnay grapes.

South of this is the commune of Juliénas, supposedly named after Julius Caesar. The wine produced here is sometimes harsh in its youth, but softens with one to two years of bottle aging. In a normal year, the fresh fruity wine of Juliénas is more assertive and longer-lasting than those of Saint-Amour.

Below Juliénas is Chénas, named after the oak trees *(chenas)* that at one time covered all of the Beaujolais area. The Chénas wines, along with those of Moulin-à-Vent, Juliénas, and Morgon, are the sturdiest of the *grand crus.*

The commune of Moulin-à-Vent (south of Chénas) produces the best-known and probably the finest of all Beaujolais wines. A nearby windmill *(moulin-à-vent)*—still standing, minus its sails—is the source of its name. The character and taste of the wine are due to the granite like quality of the local soil. Moulin-à-Vent is a dark-colored, full-bodied wine that takes a long time to mature; it lasts up to four or five years, but peaks in about three years.

Close by is the commune of Fleurie, probably so named because the wine it produces is known for its delicacy and flowery bouquet. Fleurie is light both in color and body, with a silky flavor, lasting up to three years.

Below Fleurie are the communes of Chiroubles and Morgon. Chiroubles makes robust wines with a distinctive berry flavor. (It also has a special significance as the home of Victor Pulliat, the first person to suggest that American root stocks be grafted to French vines to defeat the *Phylloxera* plague.) Morgon produces a full-bodied but not coarse wine that usually requires nearly a year in the cask and another year in the bottle before it is ready to drink. It takes three years to actually reach its prime. Chiroubles, on the other hand, matures quickly and is often drunk within a few months after harvest.

The two southernmost communes are Brouilly and Côte de Brouilly. Brouilly is the largest producer of the nine *cru* communes, but the wines from the sloping vineyards of Côte de Brouilly are considered to be better than those of Brouilly.

The wines of these nine communes, from lightest to fullest in body, are: Fleurie, Chiroubles, Juliénas, Saint-Amour, Chénas, Brouilly, Côte de Brouilly, Moulin-à-Vent, and Morgon.

Beaujolais Nouveau, also known as Beaujolais Primeur, is the "new" Beaujolais that is rushed through fermentation, then sold only a matter of weeks after harvest. Nouveau is at its best when it first appears on the market. After one year it is tired, and with few exceptions should be forgotten.

Beginning in 1967 the official date of first release or sale of the *nouveaus* was November 15. However, since 1985, the official date is the third Thursday in the month of November, regardless of the specific date.

Some important Beaujolais shippers and producers are:

Paul Beaudet	Louis Jadot
B.&G.	Le Marquisat
Bouchard Père et Fils	Mommessin
Chateau de La Chaize	Père Patriarche
David & Foillard	Piat
Joseph Drouhin	Louis Tete
Georges Duboeuf	

The Compagnons du Beaujolais, formed in 1947, is the wine brotherhood of Beaujolais.

The Loire Valley

The river Loire has a double distinction: it is the longest river in France (625 miles), and the longest of all the world's great rivers that nurture wine grapes along their banks.

The Loire Valley produces mostly dry white wines (75 percent of the total production), the rest being rosé and red wines. Like Alsace, the region lies very far north and doesn't receive sufficient sunshine to fully ripen red grapes.

Most of the wines of the Loire Valley are sold under district or village appellations, such as Anjou, Pouilly Fumé, Saumur, and Vouvray. There is one notable exception: Muscadet, which is sold under its grape varietal name. Technically speaking, the Muscadet grape is actually the Melon de Bourgogne, which was transplanted from Burgundy, by order of King Louis XIV in 1639, and again in 1709.

The best-known wines of the Loire Valley are described below:

Pouilly Fumé is a dry, full-bodied white wine made exclusively from the Sauvignon Blanc grape. Its name comes from the bloom of yeast on the grape's surface, which looks grey (*fumé*: smoked).

Sancerre, also made exclusively from the Sauvignon Blanc grape, lacks the richness and full-bodied quality of Pouilly Fumé.

Vouvray, made exclusively from Chenin Blanc grapes, is known locally in the district of Anjou as Pineau de la Loire or Blanc d'Anjou. The taste of Vouvray can range from bone dry to semisweet and even sweet. There is also a delightful sparkling version produced in limited quantities.

Saumur, a delightfully dry white wine made from Chenin Blanc grapes, is sometimes made into a sparkling wine via the *méthode champenoise*.

Rosé d'Anjou (made from mostly Cabernet Franc grapes), is produced in the northern part of the valley. It is light and delightful, with a fresh and almost floral aroma and flavor. A hint of sweetness in its taste allows it to be enjoyed by most everyone, including those who prefer dry wines.

Muscadet, produced in the far western part of the valley, is a bone-dry, steely, clean, light white wine, usually high in acidity; it is perfect for serving with raw shellfish. The best Muscadet is Sèvre-et-Maine.

The Rhône Valley

Located below Burgundy in the southeast section of France, the Rhône Valley's wine production is almost 100 percent red wines (95 percent to be exact). It is the second-largest AOC wine-producing region (Bordeaux is the largest). The Côtes du Rhône region received its AOC status in 1937. This is the southernmost of France's six major wine regions.

The vineyards—totaling 129,675 acres—stretch along both sides of the Rhône river for about 125 miles, beginning in the south around the famous papal stronghold of Avignon, and extending north to the outskirts of the city of Lyon. In the south the vines work hard to survive in chalky, stone-covered soil; in the northern area they scale palisades towering over the river.

Côtes du Rhône wines are robust and full-bodied, with plenty of bouquet and taste. They are too heavy to be drunk in the summer, but are perfect for cold winter nights. They are higher in alcohol (a minimum of 11 percent) than red Burgundies or Bordeauxs because of their location. They are the farthest southern fine wine-producing region in France.

The red wines of the northern Côtes du Rhône improve with age, sometimes lasting as long as ten to fifteen years, while the whites reach their peak between two and five years of age. In the northern region lies the famous village of Côte Rôtie, encompassing some 150 acres of vineyards. By law, its wine must be made with a minimum of 80 percent Syrah grapes, with the other 20 percent being Viognier; it is only allowed to produce red wines. Côte Rôtie wines are full-bodied and are usually at their best when between six to eight years old.

South of Côte Rôtie is the village of Condrieu, which produces white wines, from the Viognier grape, on some seventeen acres of land; it yields approximately 7,000 gallons of wine per year. These wines are best when they are two to three years old.

South of Condrieu is Château Grillet, the smallest vineyard (six acres) in France, which was granted its *appellation contrôlée* designation in 1936. Château Grillet produces only white wines from the Viognier grape; and because of its small output, its wines are extremely rare and quite expensive.

Yet further south is the 300-acre vineyard of the village of Saint-Joseph. Its wines are relatively recent arrivals on the United States market; it was awarded its AOC designation in 1956. Saint-Joseph produces red, white, and rosé wines. The red wine is made solely from the Syrah grape, which yields a somewhat full-bodied wine. The white wines, also full-bodied, are produced from the Roussanne and Marsanne grapes. Red Saint-Joseph is best when it is four to six years old; and the white and rosé wines two to four years old.

The next southern village is that of Hermitage, which is also the name of the fullest and biggest of all the Rhône Valley red wines; it is able to age for twenty to twenty-five years, and sometimes (depending on the vintage) as long as fifty years. It is produced from 100 percent Syrah grapes which are grown on some 210 acres. The white Hermitage, which has a smell of hazelnuts and is produced from a blend of Roussanne and Marsanne grapes, is difficult to obtain (because of small production), and ages quite elegantly. Red Hermitage wines are best when ten to twelve years old, and white Hermitage wines when three to four years old. The wines of Crozes-Hermitage (about 1,200 acres) are lighter than those of Hermitage and should be drunk when they are younger.

The next village is Cornas, famous for a red wine produced from the Syrah grape on a parcel of about 100 acres. The wine is difficult to find because of small production. It can age for more than twenty years, although most are drinkable in eight to ten years.

The southernmost wine-producing area in the northern half of the Côtes du Rhône is the village of Saint-Peray. Its white wine is one of the lightest of all Rhône whites. Since 1929, some of its production also goes into the making of *brut* and *demisec méthode champenoise* sparkling wines. Saint-Peray is best when it is two to three years old.

The northernmost village in the southern half of the Côtes du Rhône is Gigondas; it covers some 2,000 acres. The red wines, produced from the Grenache Noir, Syrah, Cinsault, and Mourvedre grapes, are some of the most powerful wines of the Rhône Valley. The minimum alcohol content is 12.5 percent for the red wines, which will occasionally last more than twenty years, but are best when seven to nine years old. A small quantity of rosé wine is made here, but it is rarely exported to the United States.

The village of Chateauneuf-du-Pape was the summer residence of Pope Clement V (1309–1377). Chateauneuf-du-Pape wines, the most popular of all Rhône Valley wines, are produced out of some 7,500 acres of vineyards. By law their minimum alcoholic content is 12.5 percent, and although legally they can be made from a blend of thirteen grape varieties, they are usually blends of 65 percent Grenache and 35 percent Syrah grapes. The thirteen grapes that are allowed to be used, under law, are: Bourboulenc, Cinsault, Clairette, Counoise, Grenache, Mourvedre, Muscardin, Picardin, Picpoul, Roussanne, Syrah, Terret Noir, and Vaccarese. Chateauneuf-du-Pape produces predominantly red wines which are light to full-bodied, depending on the year and producer. The lighter ones should be consumed at about five years of age, and the heavier ones at about ten. There are also some fine examples of white Chateauneuf-du-Pape wines; these are rich and full-bodied, with a fine bouquet, loaded with fruit.

Lirac covers some 7,200 acres and produces red, white, and rosé wines. The grape varieties grown here are Grenache, Mourvedre, Cinsault, and Syrah, for the red and rosé wines, and Clairette, Ugni Blanc, and Bourboulenc for the white wines. Most of the wines of Lirac should be consumed fairly young.

The village of Tavel, certainly best-known for its rosé wines, is located on the right bank of the Rhône River. These rosés are soft and plump, with just the right amount of taste and fullness. They are quite dry, and have a light, bright crimson color. They are produced from a blend of Grenache, Cinsault, Clairette, Picpoul, and Bourboulenc grapes. The best known Tavel in the United States is Château d'Aqueria.

The Côtes du Rhône-Villages *appellation contrôlée* was established in 1967 for seventeen villages in the southern half of the Rhône area. The red, white (dry or naturally sweet), and rosé wines of this area can be marketed either under the name of the village where they were produced or under the name of Côtes du Rhône-Villages, if the wine is a blend of wines from several villages. Most wines labeled Côtes du Rhône-Villages are usually quite light and fruity, similar to Beaujolais, and should be consumed very young.

The southernmost vineyard of the entire Rhône Valley is Beaumes-de-Venise, which produces a sweet white wine. A fortified wine, it is made exclusively from Muscat grapes which are allowed to hang on the vines until overripe, then pressed and made into wine using traditional methods. One of the finest examples is produced by Paul Jaboulet.

There are many reputable producers and shippers in the Rhône Valley; the most reputable are listed below.

Chateau de Beaucastel	Chateau Fortia
Chateau La Nerte	Domaine de Cabrieres
Domaine de la Serriere	Domaine de Mont-Redon
La Bernardine	Les Cedres
Max Chapoutier	Marcel Guigal
Paul Jaboulet Aîné	

Suggested Readings

Baxevanis, John J. *The Wines of Bordeaux and Western France*. Totowa, N. J.: Rowman & Littlefield, 1987.

Benson, Jeffrey and Alistair MacKensie. *Sauternes: A Study of the Great Wines of Bordeaux*. London: Sotheby-Park-Bernet, 1979.

Chidgey, Graham. *Guide to the Wines of Burgundy*. London: Monarch, 1977.

Faith, Nicholas. *The Winemasters*. New York: Harper & Row, 1978.

Faith, Nicholas. *Château Marqaux*. London: Christie's Wine Publications, 1980.

Gaertner, Pierre and Robert Frederick. *The Cuisine of Alsace*. New York: Barron's, 1981.

Hanson, Anthony. *Burgundy*. London: Faber and Faber, 1982.

Livingstone-Learmonth, John and Melvyn C. H. Master. *The Wines of the Rhône*. London: Faber and Faber, 1978.

Lichine, Alexis. *Alexis Lichine's Guide to the Wines and Vineyards of France*. New York: Knopf, 1982.

Mouton-Rothschild: Paintings for the Labels. Boston, Mass.: Little Brown, 1983.

Penning-Rowsell, Edmund. *The Wines of Bordeaux, 2d ed*. New York: Scribners, 1981.

Poupon, Pierre and Pierre Forgeot. *The Wines of Burgundy, 5th ed*. Paris: Presses universitaires de France, 1974.

Price, Pamela. *Guide to the Wines of Bordeaux*. London: Monarch, 1978.

Ray, Cyril. *Lafite, 2d ed*. London: Christie's Wine Publications, 1978.

Ray, Cyril. *Mouton-Rothschild*. London: Christie's Wine Publications, 1980.

Wasserman, Sheldon. *The Wines of the Côtes du Rhône*. Briarcliff Manor, N. Y.: Stein and Day, 1977.

Yoxall, Harry W. *The Wines of Burgundy, 2d ed*. (International Wine and Food Society Guide.) Briarcliff Manor, N. Y.: Stein and Day, 1978.

Discussion Topics and Questions

1. Traditionally, French wines have been the benchmark against which all other countries' wines have been judged. Is this still the case today? Cite several reasons for your answer.

2. It has often been stated that wines from Alsace are more Germanic than French in style. Why?

3. Why have the French *Appellation Contrôlée* laws permitted the wines of Alsace to be identified by grape variety rather than, as is traditional, the commune name?

4. How valid is the 1855 classification of Bordeaux wines in today's market? Explain.

5. The wines of Médoc and Sauternes, as well as those made by Château Haut-Brion (in Graves), were classified in 1855. Why weren't the wines from Pomerol and St. Émilion also classified?

6. The five *premier cru* Bordeaux wines once set the pricing standards for all of France, as well as for outside markets. This is no longer the case; cite reasons why.

7. Recently, Bruno Prats of Cos d'Estournel, Bordeaux, France, and Bill Jekel of Jekel Vineyards, California, publicly disputed the importance of soil in France's wine production. To what extent does soil play a part in the making of a great wine?

8. Sauternes was at one time produced in the United States as a dry wine and labeled Sauterne (minus the last *s*). Why?

9. What factors contributed to the fragmentation of Burgundian vineyards into small parcels of land, some only a few acres in size?

10. What differences and similarities exist between French- and U.S.-produced Chablis?

11. Beaujolais is technically considered a Burgundy wine, although the Pinot Noir grape is not used in its production. What reasons prompted the Beaujolais producers to use the Gamay grape instead of the traditional Pinot Noir?

12. The Loire Valley, like Alsace, produces mostly white wines. What climatic factors are responsible?

13. What wine-producing regions of the world are on the same latitude as the Rhône Valley?

5

Wines of Other Countries

This chapter discusses:

- Lesser-known wine-producing countries.
- The grapes grown and types and styles of wines produced in these countries.
- The role played by modern technology in the production of some of these countries' wines.
- Germany's eleven wine-producing regions.
- Spain's Rioja and Catalonia wine-producing regions.
- The table wines of Portugal.
- How governmental wine laws influence quality standards.

At one time if a customer wanted a fine bottle of wine all he would have to do is select from the wines of France, Germany, Italy, or California. Today, although these areas are still considered the leading wine-producing areas, many countries are producing wines close or equal to the quality level of these world leaders.

Modern technology has spread globally; with it, the production of world class wines has surfaced in countries thought not to have the capacity to produce anything better than an inexpensive "jug wine." As these countries' wines enter the American wine market, shelf space will become more and more critical in the attempt to satisfy Americans' ever-growing awareness of quality wines.

Australia

Australia, which is slightly smaller than the United States, has more than three hundred wineries (mostly small) and 180,000 acres of vineyards under cultivation, and produces approximately 100 million gallons of wine per year. Australia is divided into four major grape growing districts.

South Australia

South Australia's main grape growing district is the Barossa Valley, which is approximately thirty-five miles northeast of Adelaide, the state capital. In Australia, the Barossa Valley enjoys a reputation similar to that of the Napa Valley of California. Its most famous winery is the Barossa Valley Cooperative. (Kaiser Stuhl label, translated means "kings seat," named after a German wine region). Other well-known grape growing areas are Clare Valley, Southern Vales, and Coonawarra, home of Australia's famous Riesling wines.

New South Wales

The better-known wineries of this district are Hardy Vineyards, Lindemans, Penfolds Magill Winery, and Rosemount Estates.

Victoria

Victoria has several boutique wineries lying near Mildura, along the Murray and Yarra river valleys. Its better-known wineries are Seppelt and Mildara Wines Limited.

Western Australia

Western Australia's most prominent winery is Leeuwin Estates. Some of the major grape varieties used in this area are:

Red grapes	*White grapes*
Cabernet Sauvignon	Chardonnay
Grenache	Chenin Blanc
Malbec	Muscat of Alexandria
Shiraz	Palomino
	Pedro Ximenez
	Pinot Blanc
	Riesling

Sauvignon Blanc
Sémillon
Thompson Seedless

Austria

Austria's wineries are located mainly in four provinces: Lower Austria, Burgenland, Styria, and Vienna.

Lower Austria produces approximately two-thirds of the country's wines, including Grüner Veltliner, a white grape variety which produces Austria's leading white wine. Other white grapes such as Müller-Thurgau, Rheinriesling, Weisser Burgunder, and Gewürztraminer are grown in this province. Blaufränkisch, a grape that yields a particularly fruity wine with a glowing ruby red color is also cultivated. Eight important regions are located in Lower Austria: Krems, Langenlois, Klosterneuburg, Wachau, Falkenstein, Retz, Gumpoldskirchen, and Vöslau. Wachau, considered the wine paradise of Lower Austria, is noted for its Schluck, a dry white wine made from the Sylvaner grape.

Burgenland, Austria's second-largest wine-producing area, is famed for its Beerenauslese, a sweet white wine made from Riesling, Furmint, and Muskat-Ottonel grapes.

Grape growing in the province of Vienna extends into Austria's capital city, which is flanked by vine-clad hillsides that produce fine white wines. Grinzing, Nussberg, Nussdorf, and Neustift are the best-known villages near the city of Vienna. Further south of Vienna, around Baden, lies the district of the Südbahn, where wines are made from the late-harvested Veltliner, Riesling, and Gewürztraminer grapes.

Styria, in the southernmost area of Austria, produces mostly white wines, which are consumed locally.

Like other great wine-producing countries, Austria regulates and rigidly controls cultivation processes and ensures high quality standards. Its wine laws, which were enacted in 1961, include legally prescribed designations for different wines. The key provisions are:

Wines that have no faults in appearance, aroma, and taste, and are characteristic of their type, can qualify as "quality wines." This is the highest rating. The grower must provide a written statement verifying the geographical origin of the wine. Wines that fulfill these conditions must also pass a two-part official test. First, the wine must undergo a basic laboratory test and meet certain legal standards (listed below). Second, it must pass a taste test, which is conducted by a committee of at least six members of impartial institutions. Each committee member examines the wine in a blind sample and gives his judgment in writing; to pass, the wine must receive at least five favorable judgments. Only wines that successfully meet all of these requirements qualify for the Austrian Wine Quality Seal, which features a government control number. Special attention is paid to residual sugar content, which is strictly specified by law. An ordinary table wine (*Normalwein*), for example, uses grapes whose minimum sugar content is below 15° on the Klosterneuburg Mostwaage Scale (KMW) (equivalent to less than 18.75 Brix).

A quality wine (*Qualitätswein*) must meet the following criteria:

- The juice of the grape must have a minimum original sugar content of 15° KMW (18.75 Brix).
- The wine cannot be fortified.
- The grapes must have been grown in one region and produced from vines designated for that region. The grapes used must be listed in the quality grape register.
- The wine must be typical of wines from the particular vine from which it is produced, especially if the label carries such designation.
- The wine must be harmonious in color, bouquet, and taste, and free from flaws.

A quality wine must be sold under a geographic designation: the wine province, region, district, or village where it was produced.

A *Kabinett* (superior-quality) wine must meet the above conditions for quality wines. In addition, its must has to attain a minimum of 17° KMW (21.25 Brix), and cannot be enriched by the addition of sugar, grape juice or concentrated grape juice, or must.

Spätlese wines are produced from grapes that are fully ripened and gathered later (*spät* means late) than the ordinary harvest time for that particular grape variety. The juice must have a minimum sugar content of 19° KMW (23.75 Brix).

For *Auslese* wines, grapes must be carefully hand picked to select only those that are fully ripened. Their sugar content must be at least 21° KMW (26.25 Brix).

Beerenauslese is an *Auslese* wine made from overripe grapes affected by the "noble rot" (*Botrytis*). Sugar content for this wine must be at least 25° KMW (31.25 Brix).

Trockenbeerenauslese are *Auslese* wines with an even higher sugar content—a minimum of 30° KMW (37.5 Brix)—and are made from raisinlike dehydrated grapes. Although 30° KMW is the specified minimum sugar content, the choicest and rarest of these wines can have an even higher sugar content of their musts—35°, 40°, or even 50° KMW. These rarities can legally be called *Essenz* or *Trockenbeerenauslese-Essenz* and are served in cognac glasses so that their glorious bouquet can be fully enjoyed.

Eiswein is produced exclusively from frozen grapes, which can be harvested as late as mid-January in a great year, and must have a minimum sugar content of 25° KMW (31.25 Brix).

Many different grape varieties are used to produce Austria's fine white wines, which account for approximately 85 percent of total production. The most important varieties and the wines produced from them, are:

Grüner Veltliner: this most commonly used grape is grown extensively in areas of Lower Austria and Vienna. An Austrian specialty, the wine is effervescent and light, with a spicy, fruity taste, and very refreshing.

Müller-Thurgau: an early ripening grape, it produces a mild, aromatic and pleasant wine with a slight Muscat flavor. The wine should be consumed young.

Rheinriesling (White Riesling): this top-quality grape yields an outstanding wine characterized by a unique, delicate bouquet. Maturing slowly, the wine reaches its peak after being aged two to four years.

Neuburger: the wine made from this grape is another Austrian specialty—a full-bodied, mild wine with a particularly fine bouquet.

Weisser Burgunder (Pinot Blanc): from this premium grape are produced wines characterized by their robustness and aromatic bouquet.

Gewürztraminer: the wines have a rich, spicy flavor, pronounced aroma, and a deep golden color.

Muskat-Ottonel: wines made from this grape are distinguished by an exceptionally strong but pleasant Muscat aroma; they are produced primarily in Rust and Neusiedler.

Welschriesling or Wälschriesling: best grown in light soil and in a warm climate, this grape produces a spicy wine which varies in color from pale yellow to gold.

Zierfandler and Rotgipfler: these are two specialties of the Baden vineyards in Lower Austria. They are usually blended, to produce wines that are outstanding in quality. Aging brings out their full body and superior bouquet.

The majority of Austria's red wines are produced from four grape varieties:

Blaufränkisch (red Franconian): this is a popular grape yielding a dry, fruity wine which ranges in color from a light to deep ruby red.

Blauer Portugieser: this grape produces mild wines with a delicate spicy flavor, characterized by a deep red color.

St. Laurent: these grapes are used for high-quality table wines that are deep red in color and have a fine bouquet.

Blauer Burgunder: this grape yields a wine that is dry and rich in body. Mild and spicy, it is noted for its velvety elegance.

Some brand names of Austrian Wines available in the United States are:

Fritz Solomon	Osberger
Klosterkeller Siegendorf	Lenz Moser
Hubert Haimeri	Weingut Dr. Ernst Franz
Weingut Elfenhof	Stiftsweingut Freigut Thallern

Bulgaria

Bulgaria, though not commonly thought of as being a very important wine-producing country, is actually among the top ten countries in total production. The Bulgarian government restricts the consumption, in Bulgaria, of its wines: the bulk of production (about 80 percent) goes to the Soviet Union and other satellite countries. The rest of the wines are exported to Canada, Great Britain, Japan, the Scandinavian countries, West Germany, and the United States.

Bulgaria, located in southeastern Europe, is divided into nine wine-producing areas, each varying in size and overall production. The best white wines come from Shumen in the northeast; the best reds come from Suhindol in the northcentral area.

Some Bulgarian wines have recently been exported to the United States and are marketed collectively under the brand name Trakia (also the name of a local Bulgarian red wine).

Traditional European grape varieties—Cabernet Sauvignon, Merlot, and Chardonnay—grow side by side with native red grapes such as Gamza and Mavrud and white grapes such as Dimiat, Muscat Ottonel,

Rkatsiteli, and Misket (Bulgarian ampelographers state that there is no botanical relation of this grape to the Muscat grape).

Chile

Wine has been made for more than three hundred years in Chile (mostly for sacramental purposes), but it wasn't until about 1851 that the first plantings of *Vitis vinifera* (Cabernet Sauvignon, Sémillon, Grenache, and Sauvignon Blanc) were undertaken.

Chile's Central Valley has a perfect microclimate for grape growing. It is at the same latitude south of the equator as the Northern Hemisphere's best wine-producing regions—Bordeaux and California's Napa Valley, for instance. The soil, which has an ideal balance of limestone and clay, is watered by rivers that flow from nearby mountains. The vineyards bask in the sun, are cooled by the breezes of the Pacific Ocean, and are protected from storms by the Andes Mountains.

Chilean wines have long been appreciated in Europe, but only thirty years ago did they start making their way to the United States. The first Chilean wines introduced were probably from the venerable house of Concha y Toro, founded in 1883 by Marqués Don Melchor de Concha y Toro. Intent upon producing wines of the highest quality, the marqués commissioned M. de Labouchere, a renowned French enologist, to bring over from France the best and most select *Vitis vinifera* vines. These vines were planted in the fertile Maipo Valley in the central region of the country's grape growing area, near the Aconcagua Valley.

Other Chilean wines also available in the United States are Andean and Torres, a Spanish winery which also owns vineyards in Chile.

Germany

Wine is so highly regarded in Germany that the state not only controls labeling but also establishes quality standards. It also maintains institutions which constantly devise new methods of viticulture and vinification to constantly improve Germany's wines.

German wines are confusing to Americans because their names are difficult to pronounce and the labels difficult to decipher. Most of the wine in Germany is produced by 100,000 small landholders whose average vineyard size is only two acres. Therefore, many of the small growers belong to cooperative organizations through which they make and market their wines.

In July 1971 the German government put into effect a wine law that has made Germany's wines among the most carefully regulated in the world. Although the German wine law is too complicated to examine here in all its aspects, its regulations governing the labeling and categorizing of wine are important, and they are described below.

Chaptalization

A limited amount of sugar, set by law, can be added before fermentation when there is not enough natural grape sugar to produce sufficient alcohol during fermentation. Chaptalization (*Anreichern*, in Germany) is only permitted for *Tafelwein*, *Landwein*, and Q.b.A. wines. The *Prädikat* grades of wine are never permitted to be chaptalized.

No sugar can ever be added after fermentation. The sugar that has been added for chaptalization must always be completely converted into alcohol during fermentation.

Süssreserve

In the production of some wines, prior to fermentation some of the grape juice, which is high in natural sugar, is filtered and held under refrigeration. This unfermented juice is called *Süssreserve*. When the fermentation of the rest of the juice is complete, a small amount of this sugar-rich *Süssreserve* is added to the wine, creating a sweet flavor. Under law, this technique is permitted in the production of *Qualitätswein*, *Kabinett*, *Spätlese*, *Auslese*, and even *Beerenauslese* categories of wine.

Öechsle

Öechsle is the term used in Germany to measure the level of sugar present in the must, it was named after Ferdinand Öechsle.

Labeling

The very precise German labeling laws require that wine labels carry a great deal of vital information. All wine labels indicate the grape variety or varieties used, the district (and village name) in which they were grown, the vineyard name, the name of the vineyard's owner, and the vintage (figure 5-1).

A wine must contain at least 85 percent of the grape variety listed on its label. No more than two grape varieties can be used.

Labels must carry any of the following: the name of the *Gebiet*, or region (a region is a division of one of Germany's eleven vineyard areas); the name of the district, *Bereich*, into which regions are further divided; the name of the subdistrict, *Grosslage*, into which districts are still further divided; and, finally, the name of an individual vineyard, or *Lage*. These designated areas are always preceded or followed by the name of the local village; e.g., Bereich Johannisberg. Labels may show a subregion, village, or vineyard name providing that a minimum of 85 percent of the wine originates from such smaller geographical areas inside the specified region.

Almost all German wines use combination names, of which the first word is the town or district name and the second the specific vineyard name. Thus, there are wines called Niersteiner Auflangen, Niersteiner Rehbach, Niersteiner Heiligenbaum, and so on.

There are 2,600 individual vineyard sites registered in Germany. As the supply from each vineyard is limited and the multitude of names can be confusing, most wines shipped are labeled by *Bereich:* Bereich Nierstein, Bereich Bernkastel, etc. They are also labeled with proprietary names such as:

Affenthaler	(monkey or ape wine)
Drachenblut	(dragon's blood)
Liebfraumilch	(milk of the blessed mother)
Moselblümchen	(little flower of the Mosel)
Zeller Schwarze Katz	(black cat)

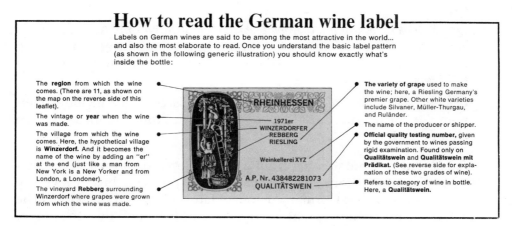

How to read the German wine label

Labels on German wines are said to be among the most attractive in the world... and also the most elaborate to read. Once you understand the basic label pattern (as shown in the following generic illustration) you should know exactly what's inside the bottle:

The **region** from which the wine comes. (There are 11, as shown on the map on the reverse side of this leaflet).

The vintage or **year** when the wine was made.

The village from which the wine comes. Here, the hypothetical village is **Winzerdorf**. And it becomes the name of the wine by adding an "er" at the end (just like a man from New York is a New Yorker and from London, a Londoner).

The vineyard **Rebberg** surrounding Winzerdorf where grapes were grown from which the wine was made.

RHEINHESSEN
1971er
WINZERDORFER
REBBERG
RIESLING
Weinkellerei XYZ
A.P. Nr. 438482281073
QUALITÄTSWEIN

The variety of grape used to make the wine; here, a Riesling Germany's premier grape. Other white varieties include Silvaner, Müller-Thurgau, and Ruländer.

The name of the producer or shipper.

Official quality testing number, given by the government to wines passing rigid examination. Found only on **Qualitätswein** and **Qualitätswein mit Prädikat.** (See reverse side for explanation of these two grades of wine).

Refers to category of wine in bottle. Here, a **Qualitätswein.**

Figure 5-1 A German wine label. (Courtesy German Wine Institute)

As a further safeguard, the wine law requires that each harvest all producers of Q.b.A. and *Prädikat* wines submit two bottles of their wine to an official government panel. The wines are then analyzed and tasted by this panel, which assigns the passing wines an "A.P." *(Amtliche Prüfungsnummer)* number that must appear on its label (see below). If the wine fails this examination, the producer can appeal the decision, make necessary corrections to the wine, and resubmit it. If the wine fails a second time, it cannot be sold to the public. The tasting panel can also declassify the wine, assigning it to a lower category. For example, a *Spätlese* can be downgraded to a *Kabinett* wine.

The A.P. number system is best explained by use of an example. A.P. number 3677030285, for instance, can be broken down as follows:

3 = The approving authority's number.

677 = The number identifying the place of business of the bottler.

030 = The bottler's code or identification number.

2 = The running approval number of the applicant *(not,* as it might seem, the month in which the wine was bottled).

85 = The year in which the wine was submitted for approval (not necessarily the year of harvest.)

Three basic categories of German wines were created under the 1971 law; later, the law was amended to include the following four:

Tafelwein: a very ordinary table wine not normally exported.

Landwein: a step above *Tafelwein* in quality, but again not usually exported.

Qualitätswein bestimmter Anbaugebiete (or simply Q.b.A.): this must come from a particular region *(Gebiet)* and be produced from designated grape varieties. It must also attain a minimum must weight of 60° Öechsle.

Qualitätswein mit Prädikat: traditionally, this category includes Germany's finest and most expensive wines. None of these can be chaptalized.

Prädikat wines must come from a specific area or *Bereich.* This category has six subdivisions that correlate the successively higher levels of sugar produced by the German custom of late and selective picking. (The drawback to this custom is that the riper the grapes—and thus the higher the sugar level—the smaller the quantity of wine produced, as selectivity increases with lateness of harvest.) The *Qualitätswein mit Prädikat* sub-divisions are:

> *Kabinett:* from the first harvest; these wines are the driest. They must attain a minimum must weight of 73° Öechsle.
>
> *Spätlese:* the term literally means "late-harvest"; the harvest, which is predetermined for each village, usually takes place three weeks after the general harvest. These wines must attain a minimum must weight of 85° Öechsle.
>
> *Auslese:* this is a late selective gathering, which means that each individual bunch of grapes is inspected to determine its ripeness. *Auslese* wines are richer and sweeter than *Spätlese* wines. They must attain a minimum must weight of 95° Öechsle.
>
> *Beerenauslese* (sometimes abbreviated as BA): extremely overripe grapes are used for these wines; they are hand selected and picked individually after ripeness has been determined. Out of each bunch of grapes, the pickers might only select one or two berries to use. Obviously the result is an extremely high production cost. In addition, the grapes must have been attacked by the mold *Botrytis cinerea* (known in Germany as *Edelfäule*). These wines must attain a minimum must weight of 125° Öechsle.
>
> *Trockenbeerenauslese* (sometimes abbreviated as TBA): as for the *Beerenauslese* wines, the grapes are selected individually. In this case they are also dried or shriveled up by the action of the *Botrytis*. The wine must attain a minimum must weight of 150° Öechsle.
>
> *Eiswein:* this name is reserved for wines made from grapes of the BA or TBA category, picked and harvested frozen. These frozen grapes produce a wine that is both sweeter and more concentrated than the average *Prädikat* wine.

The practice of making wine from grapes naturally frozen on the vine has long been a part of the wine culture of Germany. With the Rhine and Mosel's best vineyards lying just about as far north as grapes can ripen, working with frozen grapes is not only a tradition but sometimes a necessity as well. German winemakers have built their reputations by exploiting nature, allowing the grapes to hang on the vine past normal harvesting time to further ripen and be affected by *Botrytis*.

The adversary that the vintner faces late in the growing season is cold weather—the chance of an early frost or hard freeze. If the grapes are spared a freezing cold and can sufficiently dry before harvest, wines of incredible lusciousness and complexity can be produced. But if nature wins the battle and a hard freeze hits the vineyards, the winemaker has but one outside chance—to pick and crush the frozen grapes, hopefully producing the rare and unique *Eiswein*. Although this was once a rare product (made only every second or third decade), *Eiswein* is today produced somewhat more frequently because new, colder vineyard sites are allowed to yield frozen grapes.

The production of *Eiswein* is governed by a simple physical law. Water, which freezes at 32°F, constitutes the major portion of the pulp and juice of grapes. As the grapes freeze, it is the water inside them that actually freezes, and not the other elements, of which sugar is the largest component. When these grapes are crushed, the frozen water is not pressed out, only the luscious, sugary nectar of the grapes which is only a fraction of the juice. But while the freeze steals from juice quantity, the must weight gains in concentration. It becomes heavily laden with sugar, sometimes doubling its usual strength; it also has a high level of acidity. The resulting wines are characteristically rich in body with a fine natural sweetness and a mature, complex bouquet and flavor. All the flavors of the grape are intensified and magnified, making this child of considerable risk a prized success for the vintner.

In the production of *Eiswein* the grapevines are wrapped in large plastic covers to protect them from birds, wind, and snow. The grapes are then allowed to hang on the vines in the hope that the already present *Botrytis* will spread throughout the vineyard. When 30 to 40 percent *Botrytis* infection of the vineyard has occurred, vintners hope that cold weather will strike, hard freezing the grapes on the vines. Sustained day/night temperatures in the high teens to low twenties (Fahrenheit) will allow the grapes to become frozen. Sometimes the winemakers will not harvest them until November, December, or even January. However, the longer they wait the greater the chance for the grapes to shrivel up and fall from the vines.

When the grapes are sufficiently frozen, they are harvested (usually early in the morning before the sun can thaw them) and shipped to the winery. There they are pressed in small batches in a basket press, extracting a slight fifty gallons of juice per ton of grapes. The flow of the sweet juice from the press is pencil thin, the grapes yielding less than one-third the normal volume of juice.

Trocken and Halbtrocken Wines

The designations *trocken* and *halbtrocken* went into effect on August 1, 1977 and were created by the wine authority of the Common Market in Brussels. The reason for these new designations was the fact that some people prefer wines drier than most of the German wines on the market. The terms *trocken* (dry) and *halbtrocken* (semidry), which have no connection whatsoever with the *Trockenbeerenauslese* wines, will attempt to lure dry white wine drinkers over to the white wines of Germany.

Contrary to popular belief, the Riesling grape is not the preferred variety for use, because its high acid level (most times over one percent) gives the wine an unbalanced character. (And, German wine-makers never allow contact between the grape skins and the must, because additional acids from the skins will increase the already high acidity level.) Instead, varieties such as Müller-Thurgau, Sylvaner, Weissburgunder (Pinot Blanc), Kerner, and Gutedel, which are lower in acidity, are used. The *trocken* and *halbtrocken* wine categories are described below.

> *Trocken:* these wines contain a maximum of 9 grams per liter of residual sugar (which can also be expressed as 0.9 grams per 100 ml., or 0.9 percent residual sugar). The sugar level cannot exceed the acidity level by more than 2 grams. For example, if a wine has 5 grams of acidity, its maximum sugar level can only be 7 grams per liter.

> *Halbtrocken:* these wines contain a maximum of 18 grams per liter of residual sugar (which can also be expressed as 1.8 grams per 100 ml., or 1.8 percent residual sugar). The variance here can be 10 grams per liter. For example, if the wine contains 5 grams per liter of acidity, the maximum sugar level can only be 15 grams per liter.

Germany's Wine-Producing Regions

In all vine-growing regions, the quality of wine is dependent upon climate, grape variety, soil, and viticulture and vinification techniques. As Germany is the northernmost wine-producing country in the world (most of the vineyards are on the same latitude, 50° north, as Newfoundland), the success of its wine demands a delicate coordination of climate and grape variety. The best-quality grape varieties mature slowly and produce only a moderate quantity of wine; others mature faster and produce large amounts. German grape growers have learned to balance quantity with quality. The state and members of the wine trade work together as an effective control force overseeing this delicate balance.

Although Germany produces predominantly white wine, a relatively small quantity of red wine is made in Germany, mainly in Ahr, the Palatinate, Württemberg, and Baden, usually from the Blauer Spätburgunder (Pinot Noir) grape.

The principal grape varieties grown in Germany are Riesling (which was probably derived from a wild vine, *Vitis vinifera Silvestris*), Sylvaner, and Müller-Thurgau.

The tiny Riesling grape, considered the noblest of all, matures slowly and produces a relatively small amount of wine. Both the Sylvaner and the Müller-Thurgau have larger berries which mature more rapidly and produce a greater, but by no means large, quantity of wine. Most of the high-quality wine in Germany is produced from these three grape varieties, with the Riesling predominating in the Mosel and Rheingau regions, and parts of Rheinhessen.

Professor Hermann Müller, a Swiss ampelographer from Thurgau, developed the Müller-Thurgau in 1882. This was the first hybrid developed by scientists at Geisenheim, Germany. For many years it was thought to be a cross between the Johannisberg Riesling and Sylvaner grapes, but there is no evidence to support this theory. Müller-Thurgau is the most planted grape variety (in acreage) in Germany.

Due to Germany's cold climate, harvest is delayed as long as possible and usually does not take place until late October. By then, the vine has gathered enough summer sun to produce a good balance of sugar and acidity, the hallmark of German wine. German vintners maintain that 100 days of sun between May and October make for a good wine, and 120 days a great wine.

Germany's eleven grape growing regions include: Ahr, Mittelrhein, Nahe, Rheingau, Rheinhessen, Rheinpfalz, Mosel-Saar-Ruwer, Franken, Baden, Württemberg, and Hessische Bergstrasse. Most of the high-quality wines of Germany are grown in the Mosel-Saar-Ruwer, Rheingau, Rheinhessen, Palatinate, Nahe, and Franconia regions.

Mosel-Saar-Ruwer. The grapes of this region, which has been producing wine for more than two thousand years, are grown mainly on slate ground covering the exceedingly steep hillsides of the valleys watered by the Mosel River and its tributaries, the Saar and Ruwer.

Wines here are made primarily from the Riesling grape. They are the lightest of the German wines, being fragrant and flowery, refreshing and clean, with an almost peachy taste. These wines have a low alcoholic content and are best drunk in their youth while they still have all of their charm. Mosel-Saar-Ruwer wines often have a *spritzig* quality: they are characterized by a little natural sparkle. Some of the towns on the Mosel from which these wines come are Piesport, Bernkastel, Wehlen, Graach, Trittenheim, Zeltingen, Brauneberg, and Zell; on the Saar, Ockfen, Serrig, Ayl, and Wiltingen; and on the Ruwer, Waldrach, Kasel, Avelsbach, and Eitelsbach. The wines made on the Saar and Ruwer in outstanding years can be as good, if not better, than the Mosel wines, combining crispness with bouquet and flavor, and being somewhat lighter in body.

Rheingau. This is Germany's smallest grape growing region, and it usually produces the greatest of all German wines. It is almost all one large hillside, facing south and protected against the northern climate by the Taunus mountain chain. The wines made in this area are noble indeed, combining elegance with style and delicacy, and yet substance and fruit as well. Almost every village and vineyard produces a wine whose quality is distinctive, and which an expert can identify. Some of Germany's better-known winemaking estates, such as Schloss Johannisberg, Steinberg, and Schloss Vollrads, are in this area. The main Rheingau villages in which wines are made are Rüdesheim, Johannisberg, Rauenthal, Kiedrich, Erbach, Hattenheim, Oestrich, Hallgarten, Eltville, Geisenheim, and Hochheim. For many years the wines from Hochheim, which contains five vineyards between Mainz and Wiesbaden, were referred to, mainly by the British, as *Hock;* earlier, the British called them "Rhenish" wines.

Rheinhessen. Most of Germany's wine that is exported is made in this region; it produces even larger quantities than Mosel-Saar-Ruwer and Rheingau. Its wines, profiting from a warmer climate, are softer, rounder, and a little fuller than the aristocratic wines of the Rheingau. The main grape varieties of Rheinhessen are the Sylvaner and Müller-Thurgau, which produce very soft, sometimes fairly sweet wines with a delicate bouquet. Because this is a large area, Rheinhessen's wines vary a great deal in their characteristics. In good years, some of the finest, if not *the* finest, *Prädikat* wines of Germany are made here. Some towns with well-known vineyards are Nierstein, Oppenheim, Bodenheim,

Nackenheim, Bingen, Worms, and Guntersblum. It is in Rheinhessen that most of the better Liebfraumilch wine is produced.

Liebfraumilch was at one time produced from a blend of grapes grown in Rheingau, Rheinhessen, Rheinpfalz, and Nahe. However, with changes in the German wine law, vintners no longer can blend grapes from the four regions for Liebfraumilch. Only one of three regions can now be shown as a source for Liebfraumilch—Rheinhessen, Rheinpfalz, or Nahe—and the region must be stated on the label. The word *Liebfraumilch* cannot be shown in type larger than that used to identify the region. The law further specifies that all Liebfraumilch must be made at least 51 percent from one of the following grape varieties: Riesling, Sylvaner, Müller-Thurgau, or Kerner. It is estimated that 60 percent of all wines from Germany are exported under the Liebfraumilch appellation.

The most popular Liebfraumilch in the world is Blue Nun, which was first produced in 1921. In 1925, a small printer in Mainz was asked to design a more "modern" and picturesque label than the ordinary house label which had been used for more than sixty years. He submitted a label picturing nuns dressed in brown habits, working in vineyards under blue skies. In 1930, the words *Blue Nun* appeared on the label; in 1933 Blue Nun made its debut in America. It was not until the 1950s that the nuns (six to be exact) began wearing blue habits.

Rheinpfalz (**also referred to as** *Palatinate*). This is also a large wine-producing area; it is the warmest and driest part of the country. The majority of the high-quality wines here are made from the Sylvaner and Müller-Thurgau grapes, with only 15 percent of the region planted with Riesling. Climate and soil combine here to aid in the production not only of the common wine of the German *Weinstube* or local pub, but also some outstanding wines. Wines from the villages of Forst and Deidesheim are among the finest of the Palatinate, being fuller and sweeter than Mosels, Rheingaus, and even Rheinhessens. They are also meatier and higher in alcohol (there is a saying in Germany that "when you have drunk a bottle of good Palatinate wine, you will find it hard to go home, since it has all gone to your feet"). Other major Rheinpfalz winemaking towns are Wachenheim, Ruppertsberg, Duerkheim, and Ungstein.

Nahe. This region is planted with Riesling, Sylvaner, and Müller-Thurgau grapes, and produces wines of varying taste and quality, some of which are not unlike Rheingau wines. Other wines, however, are heavier and earthier in taste. Though not much wine from this region is shipped to the United States, it does deserve mention. Some of the better-known villages in this region are Schloss Böckelheim, Bad Kreuznach, Niederhausen, Langenlonsheim, and Rüdesheim (not to be confused with the town of the same name in Rheingau).

Franconia. This is the only region from which wine is exported in a *bocksbeutel* or *boxbeutel,* the distinctive, round flagon-style bottle first introduced in 1728. Its wine, although less distinguished than those described above, is made under the close scrutiny of the Frankischer Weinbauverband (Franconian Wine Association), which was founded in 1836.

The wines of Franconia are pleasant, combining dryness with a certain mellowness but lacking somewhat in the varied aromas and bouquets of other German wines. Most Franconian wine is made from Müller-Thurgau, Sylvaner, and Mainriesling grapes, although new varieties such as Albalonga, Bacchus, Kerner, Ortega, Perle, and Rieslaner are being planted on increasingly more acreage.

Other regions. The regions described above are those in which Germany's highest-quality wines are produced. These regions produce less outstanding wines:

Ahr: This northernmost region is noted for its excellent red wines.

Baden: Germany's southernmost winemaking region, Baden is marked by the Kaiserstuhl, an extinct volcano whose soil helps produce wines that are powerful and aromatic.

Württemberg: This region is separated from Baden by the famed Black Forest. Thousands of Württemberg's small growers produce pleasant red and white wines.

Hessische Bergstrasse: This is a very small region, and its wines are produced primarily for local use.

Mittelrhein: Mittelrhein has spectacular vineyards on the steep Rhine slopes; its wines are hearty and stylish.

Although not mandated by law, Rhine wines are always found in brown bottles, while wines from the Mosel region are found in green ones.

Hungary

When one thinks of the wines of Hungary, the rich, naturally sweet, world-renowned Tokay wines immediately come to mind. However,

159

most Hungarian wines entering this country today are table wines whose variety and volume are constantly increasing.

The most popular and easiest to find table wine is Egri Bikavér, a deep, rich, robust, dry red wine often referred to as "bull's blood." This wine is best when drunk before it is three years old. Another popular wine is Green Sylvaner, a pleasantly dry white wine with a delicate aroma, that is enhanced by a slight chilling.

Tokay, by far the most popular dessert wine, comes from the village of Tokaj in northeastern Hungary. Tokay is predominantly made from the Furmint (white grape variety), which can be harvested at various degrees of ripeness. Tokay wines are bone dry to exquisitely sweet white wines.

When a sweet Tokay wine is to be produced, the grapes are left to hang on the vines until they start to shrivel and resemble raisins. It is at this point that a beneficial *Botrytis* mold attacks the grapes, adding a rich scent of honey and increasing the viscosity of their juice. After harvest these grapes (called *Aszús*, meaning dried-out grapes) are placed into wooden tubs called *puttonyos*, which hold about seven gallons of wine. The grapes are crushed and the juice is added to the one-year-old wine that has been stored in *gönci*, small thirty-five-gallon barrels. The number of *puttonyos* (generally up to five), which is indicated on the label, is proportionate to the degree of sweetness of the harvested grapes.

Tokaji Száraz is a dry Tokay wine; Tokaji Édes is a sweet Tokay. The lowest-quality Tokay is Tokaji Pecsenyebor. Among the rarest of all wines is the legendary Tokaji Exzencia, made from the unpressed juice of the *Aszús*. This wine is rarely produced today, perhaps only fifty barrels having been made within the last ten years.

The following names and terms often appear on Tokay wine labels:

Essenz: This term refers to the measurement of sugar levels in the must.

Magyar Állami Pincegazdaság: These are the Hungarian State Cellars.

Monimpex: This is the State Export Monopoly.

Portugal

The best-known Portuguese wines are the delicious, fruity, and refreshing rosé wines and wonderful port wines. But Portugal has quite a bit more to offer than just rosés and port. In fact, some of the greatest wine buys in today's market are the red *reservas* and *garrafeiras* from the fine wine houses of Portugal. These wines are full-bodied and robust, with all the bouquet, flavor, taste, grace, and charm of some of the finest French Bordeauxs, Burgundies, Rhône Valley reds, or of the Italian Barolo and Barbaresco.

Portugal is roughly half the size of California, with a total population slightly less than that of New York City. It appears to be one of the last untapped great wine regions of the world. Portuguese winemakers still produce red wines in the "old style," with plenty of wood aging. Their white wines, on the other hand, have the freshness, lightness, and fruitiness of some of the best in the world.

In the northern part of Portugal, in a hilly region known as Minho, is Vinho Verde (literally, *green wine*), the world's largest demarcated grape growing region. There are ten such demarcated regions in Portugal. Although three-fourths of Minho's production is red wine, this is consumed locally; only the whites find their way to our shores. These wines are often quite young, most of them bottled only four months after harvest, and are not meant to be stored away for prolonged aging. Their charm lies in their youthfulness, "spritzy" character, and absolutely clean, crisp, and refreshing taste. They should be served cold with fish, fruits, cheeses, or cold soups, or just by themselves.

Alianca, Arealva, Aveleda, Garcia, Gatão, Gazela, Mesa do Presidente, and Ouro do Minho are some of the fine brand names available in the United States.

The Dão (pronounced *dow*) is where most of the more popular red wines that are available in the United States originate. Its lovely reds and whites are always found in the traditional Burgundy-shaped bottles. The Dão reds are the softest of all Portuguese reds, meant to be drunk within a few years. These rich-tasting ruby-colored wines are made from the Tourigo do Dão or Tinta Pinheira grape varieties, which tend to produce full-bodied and extremely fruity wines. The Dão's white wines are well made, always dry, with a considerable amount of body and earthiness. Like most other dry whites of the world, they should be consumed young.

Bucelas produces wines that are well balanced because of the cool sea breeze and climate, which actually prevent the grapes from becoming overripe. They retain a high level of natural acidity, yielding wines that are clean, crisp, and very refreshing. These wines, because of their high acidity (not to be confused with sourness), are a natural match for shellfish and other seafood, and of course cheeses. The principal grape variety used is the Arinto.

Bairrada is, without a doubt, one of the finest red wine regions of Portugal. Its deep, dark, very rich-tasting (almost portlike) wines, have a fine fruit-acid structure. The wines are usually high in alcohol (13 percent or more) and are meant to be enjoyed with red meats or other hearty, rich roods. While the reds are big and hearty, the whites are very light and often sparkling. The grape varieties for reds include the Baga, João de Santarém, Castelão, and Tinta Pinheira (Pinot Noir). For white wines they include Bical and Arinto.

The Colares area is probably one of the most difficult places in the world in which to grow grapes. The principal grapevines, Ramisco, must be planted in clay, fifteen feet below the surface of the sandy soil of the wind-blasted shores of the Atlantic Ocean. Cone-shaped holes, several yards across, are dug down through the sand by workers who wear baskets over their heads to allow them to breathe in the event of a cave-in. After planting, the vines are covered with sand. When the vine breaks the sand's surface, bamboo palisades and stone walls have to be built around to protect it against constant ocean gales. This is why so precious little wine is produced in this region, and why it is so expensive. It is, however, well worth searching out.

Algarve and Carcavelos also produce wines of medium body that are quite fruity and are particularly suitable for serving with flavorful or spicy foods.

Two additional wine-producing regions that will not be discussed here are Oporto and Madeira, which are covered in depth in Chapter 6 on aperitifs and fortified wines.

Moscatel de Setúbal is certainly one of the greatest dessert wines in the world. So great in fact, that it has been known to last for well over fifty years.

The Portuguese government has strict laws that govern the labels and seals on its wine exports. A *selo de garantia* (seal of guarantee) bearing the name of the region of origin and a registration number is the formal government stamp of approval. Found around the cork or on the bottle, it assures the buyer that the wine has met standards set by the regional governing bodies. The bottle's label also indicates, when applicable, the wine's region of origin. It also shows the name of the shipper or bottler and may include the wine's alcoholic content, vintage, and brand name. Special terms such as *reserva* (denoting a premium wine from a good-quality harvest) or *garrafeira* (denoting a wine that is from an exceptional harvest, and is a cut above a *reserva*) may also be included on the label.

South Africa

The wine lands of the Cape of Good Hope lie between 32° and 35° south latitude on the southwest corner of the continent, and therefore enjoy a typical Mediterranean climate. The Cape wine area is divided into three main regions: the coastal region, the Boburg region, and the Brede River Valley region. These three regions are divided into sixteen areas of production. As in Bordeaux, a number of smaller districts have also been defined in recognition of important local variations in soil and climate. These districts, sometimes only a few square miles in size, produce wines of great distinction and character.

The coastal region includes the following five grape growing areas: Stellenbosch, Constantia, Durbanville, Paarl, and Swartland. Here the cool Atlantic spring rains, followed by a sunny summer and cooling Indian Ocean winds, create an ideal grape growing climate. This area produces some of South Africa's finest red and white wines, including Cabernet Sauvignon, Shiraz, Cinsault, Pinotage, Chenin Blanc, Clairette Blanche, and Riesling.

A little inland is the Boburg region, a valley sheltered by high mountains. The Tulbagh area in this region is famous for its Rieslings and Gewürztraminers.

The Brede River Valley region has a varied topography; in its sandy valleys, between mountain ranges, grapes grow well and produce superb dry wines.

South Africa's "Wines of Origin" legislation is based essentially on that of the traditional European wine countries and is thus close to the French *appellation contrôlée* laws. Some of its provisions are described below.

> The addition of sugar (chaptalization) is strictly prohibited. The use of sulfur dioxide is limited to a maximum of 200 parts per million (ppm) (mg/l).
>
> An official certificate issued by the South African Wine and Spirits Board certifies the grape variety from which a wine is made, its vintage, and the area of origin. This certificate is attached to the neck of the bottle.
>
> Wine that is classified as a "Wine of Origin" must originate 100 percent from a particular area. Estate wines must be made on a registered estate, from grapes grown on that estate. The highest classification is Wine of Origin Superior (WOS), awarded only to wines of exceptional quality.

The major South African wines available in the United States from the Cape are:

Oude Meester Winery	Oude Libertas
Die Bergkelder	Zonnebloem
Fleur du Cap	Lanzerac
Grunberger	Tasheimer
KWV (Kooperative Wijnbouwers Vereniging)	Meerendal

Most of the grape varieties planted in South Africa are of European ancestry. However, there are some local varieties such as Pinotage (a cross between Pinot Noir and Hermitage), Cinsault, Steen, and Tinta Barocca.

Spain

Spain is most famous for its sherry wines; most of the wines produced in Spain, however, are red, white and rosé table wines.

Spain has 4.2 million acres of vineyards, more than any other country. The average yearly production is about 800 million gallons, placing Spain among the top five wine-producing countries in the world.

The quality and integrity of the wines produced in Spain are assured by a central national system of control regulated by the Instituto Nacional de Denominaciónes de Origen (INDO), which was established in 1972.

Twenty-eight grape growing regions have been defined by the INDO (figure 5-2); wines produced in these regions carry the *denominación de origen* (DO) designation. This system is, like South Africa's, similar to France's *appellation contrôlée* system. More than half of Spain's vineyards are covered by this comprehensive quality control system, which monitors the entire industry from the embryonic stage of grape growing to the finished bottle of wine. The two wine regions of Spain which export the most table wine to the United States are Rioja and Catalonia.

Rioja

Rioja encompasses some eleven million acres of vineyards in northern-central Spain, not far from the western Pyrenees and only two hundred

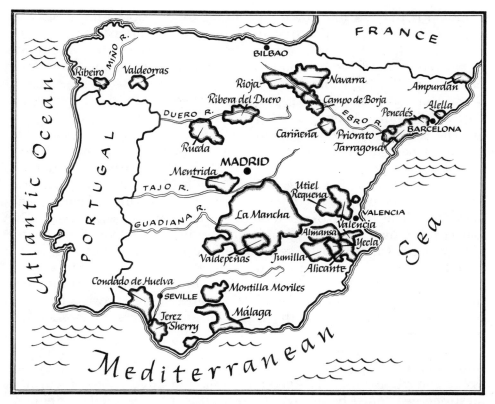

Figure 5-2 Map of the wine regions of Spain. (Courtesy of Bozell, Jacobs, Kenyon and Eckhardt Public Relations, New York)

miles south of Bordeaux, France. There are two major population centers in Rioja. The town of Haro is the traditional center of the wine district and still retains its sixteenth-century appearance, dominated by a magnificent Gothic church. The colorful and modern city of Logroño is the provincial capital and is the business and financial hub. The majority of Rioja wineries, or *bodegas*, are to be found along the roads that run between Logroño and Haro.

The average elevation of Rioja's vineyards is well over 1,500 feet above sea level. These heights produce lighter wines than those that are made from grapes grown in lower and warmer sections of the country. Most of the vineyards are situated on either side of the Ebro River, which flows east from the Pyrenees toward the Mediterranean.

Rioja is divided into three viticultural zones: Rioja Alta, Rioja Alavesa, and Rioja Baja. The first two are in the western portion of the district; the third lies to the east of them. Rioja Alavesa has an altitude in between that of the two other zones which, as is obvious from their names, are the high and low zones of Rioja. The two higher zones, Rioja Alta and Rioja Alavesa, produce the best wines; those from Rioja Baja are considered somewhat harsher and are higher in alcohol.

The premier red wine grape of Rioja is the Tempranillo (planted in up to 30 percent of the vineyards); it is comparable to the Cabernet Sauvignon grape, although it is not related to that particular variety. It is the Tempranillo that gives Rioja's reds a deep color and fine acid balance. Other grapes used for reds are the Graciano, Mazuelo, and Garnacha. The first two are thought to be indigenous to Spain. The Garnacha, which gives the wine body, acidity, and alcoholic strength, and is planted in approximately 40 percent of Rioja's vineyards, is believed to be the Grenache grape from the Rhône Valley of France.

The white wines of Rioja are made from the Viura (called Macabeo in Catalonia), Garnacha, and Malvasia grapes. (The Malvasia bears no resemblance to the grape of the same name used to make dessert wines in California.)

Following fermentation (often in wood), the red wines are racked into 225-liter (59-gallon) oak barrels called *bordelesas*, where they are aged. The *reservas* must be aged a minimum of three years, of which at least one year must be in cask. *Gran reservas* must be aged a minimum of two years in cask and three in bottle.

Although not mandated by law, it is customary for the red wines of Rioja to be aged in white American oak barrels. The whites are fermented and, today, are usually aged in stainless steel (in years past it was customary to age them in oak barrels for two or more years). A general emphasis on wood aging, along with the qualities inherent in the grapes themselves, gives Rioja wines their unique character and taste.

Red Rioja wines that are labeled Tinto are generally full-bodied, with a dark color and lots of tannin; they are shipped in Burgundy-style bottles. Riojas labeled Clarent or Claret are usually lighter in color and body, and are shipped in Bordeaux-type bottles.

In 1560, Rioja vinters formed an association to regulate and guarantee the quality and origin of their exported wines. Today the governing body for wine production in Rioja is the Consejo Regulador de la Denominación de Rioja, which was established in 1925.

Some of the better-known wineries of Rioja are:

Marqués de Riscal	Bodegas Olarra
Marqués de Cáceres	Pedro Domecq
Bodegas Bilbainas	Rioja Santiago
C.U.N.E. (Compania Vinicola	La Rioja Alta
del Norte de España)	Muga
Federico Paternina	Marqués de Murrieta
Muerza	Franco-Españolas
Unidas	Ramon Bilbao
Carlos Serres	Lan
R. Lopez de Heredia	Montecillo
Campo Viejo de Savin	Alavesas
Bodegas Berberana	Palacio

Catalonia

Catalonia is located in the northeast region of Spain where the best-known appellation of origin is Penedes.

Not only the best known, but also the finest producer of Catalonian wines is the Torres Winery. The Torres vineyards are situated in the Mediterranean region of Catalonia, 20 miles west of Barcelona around the city of Vilafranca del Penedes, the capital of the grape growing district of Penedes.

The Torres family has owned vineyards here since the seventeenth century, although it was not until 1870 that Don Jaime Torres Vendrell first began to export his wines to Europe and America. Since then, the business has always been handed down from father to son: the present owner, Miguel Torres, with his son Miguel and his daughter Marimar, are the fourth and fifth generations of the family devoted to the growing, estate bottling, and shipping of wines and brandies. A high regard for tradition, however, does not prevent the Torres family from constantly investigating and adopting the newest enological techniques.

Today, the Torres family produces many different wines by blending traditional Spanish with traditional European grape varieties. The Spanish varieties used are:

Red grapes	*White grapes*
Cariñena	Macabeo
Garnacha	Parellada
Monastrell	
Ull de Llebre (known as Tempranillo in other parts of Spain)	

The traditional European varieties used are:

Red grapes	*White grapes*
Cabernet Sauvignon	Chardonnay
Cabernet Franc	Chenin Blanc
Merlot	Gewürztraminer
Petite Sirah	Muscat d'Alsace
Pinot Noir	Sauvignon Blanc

The Torres family's wines include:

Red wines	*White wines*
Gran Coronas	Viña Sol
Coronas	Gran Viña Sol
Sangre de Toro	San Valentin
Gran Sangre de Toro	Viña Esmeralda
Viña Santa Digna	

Switzerland

Switzerland produces great quantities of table wine, but imports more wine than it produces. Most Swiss wines come from four famous grape-growing areas: Valais (the valley of the Rhône); Lake Geneva; Ticino; and Seeland (the lake area): the Neuchâtel, Bienne, and Morat lakes. In addition, there are many small vineyards all over Switzerland, along the Rhine from Chur to Basel, and on Lake Zurich.

By far the greatest quantity of Swiss wine available in the United States is white wine, predominantly Neuchâtel and Dezaley, although occasionally rosés and reds find their way here.

Valais

One of the most famous wine districts in Switzerland is Valais, a deep, sheltered valley at the headwaters of the Rhône, where carefully cultivated, terraced vineyards step up the mountainsides, reaching very high altitudes (the Visperterminen vineyard, the highest in Europe, is at 4,000 feet). The high Alps shield Valais from winds and storms, giving it one of Switzerland's most temperate climates in summer, although the winters are bitterly cold. Since Valais is the most arid section of Switzerland, the grapevines are irrigated with water taken from mountainside canals fed by the melting glaciers. The rich lowlands of Valais are famous for their lush fruits, especially the pears that are used to make Switzerland's celebrated pear brandy. Winemakers of the Valais district produce delicate white wines and Dôle, a full-bodied red wine.

Lake Geneva

The Lake Geneva area is divided into two grape growing districts—Geneva and Vaud (which is itself divided into three areas).

In the Geneva district, at the easternmost tip of Lake Geneva and north of the city, is the area of Mandement, where Perlana, a fruity, sparkling white wine is made from Chasselas grapes. The Chasselas grape, known locally as the Fendant grape, produces some of the most popular wines in Switzerland. The Geneva district also produces specialty wines made from the Riesling, Sylvaner, Aligoté, and Chardonnay grapes. Light rosés are also made from the Gamay grape.

Vaud's three grape growing areas are Chablais, which is upstream from where the Rhône enters Lake Geneva; Lavaux, bordering the lakefront east of Lausanne; and La Côte, located between Lausanne and Geneva. Nearly all of Vaud's wines are white wines called Dorins (many of which also use the name of the commune or village from which they come on their labels). Charming, fragrant reds, labeled Salvagnins, are also produced throughout Vaud from a blend of Pinot Noir and Gamay grapes.

Seeland

The limestone-rich terrain of the slopes surrounding Lakes Neuchâtel, Bienne, and Morat produces mostly white wines with a light sparkle. The vineyards of Neuchâtel are the source of a light-colored, intriguingly fragrant red wine, and of one of Switzerland's celebrated rosés, Oeil de Perdrix; both are made from the Pinot Noir grape.

Ticino

In the shadow of the St. Gotthard mountains on the southern slopes of the Alps is the Italian-speaking region of Ticino, which produces mostly red wines, all of which are labeled Vino Nostrano.

Tunisia

Tunisia is located in North Africa, between Libya, to the east, and Algeria, to the south and west.

Under Islamic rule in the seventh century A.D., grape growing in Tunisia was limited to table grapes, and wine consumption was forbidden. The wine industry was revived during the French Protectorate (1881–1956), at which time mainly blended wines were produced.

Today the Tunisian vineyards, which cover an area of more than 85,000 acres and are located in the northeastern regions of the country, are being renewed and improved for the production of high-quality wines.

Tunisia produces an average of 25 to 30 million gallons of wine per year, a fifth of which is classified under selected and controlled categories: *vins d'appellation contrôlée* (AOC), *vins supérieurs* (VS), and *vins délimités de qualité superieur* (VDQS). Classified wines must conform with various legal and technical criteria including chemical analyses, bacteriological and organic tests, and tastings by qualified enologists.

To maintain high standards, the cultivation of hybrids is forbidden, as is irrigation of the vineyards. This explains both the low grape yields and their high quality. Chaptalization and watering of the wines are also severely prohibited.

The Tunisian vineyards are planted with traditional vine stocks that have adapted to the Mediterranean climate, including: Carignane, Cinsault, Alicante-Bouschet, Alicante Grenache, Clairette, Beldi, Pedro Ximenez, Muscat of Alexandria, Mourvèdre, Cabernet Sauvignon, and Pinot Noir.

Yugoslavia

Only recently have the Yugoslavs been in a position to develop a world market for their wines. During the 1950s and 1960s, Yugoslavia established markets in most of Europe: in about 1950 the first bottles of the Yugoslavian wine Ljutomer Riesling reached the shores of Great Britain.

Today all Yugoslavian wines entering the United States are labeled as they are on the home market—by grape variety and region. The unfamiliarity of some of the Yugoslav grape and place names will undoubtedly cause confusion. Fortunately, many of the classic grapes have been given the same or similar names in Yugoslavia as they have in the United States and Europe; one can speak, for instance, of a "Cabernet from Istria" or a "Rizling from Fruska Gora."

A wine name such as Opolo from Dalmatia will be a bit more mysterious, but this fresh, fruity, deeply colored rosé should have no trouble establishing a fine reputation for itself. (Dalmatia is, of course, the lovely Adriatic coastal region of Yugoslavia, the two most famous Dalmatian cities being Dubrovnik and Split.) One variety of white grape that prospers in Yugoslavia is the Sipon. The wine of the same name, from Maribor, in Slovenia, is a very pleasing and unique white wine, but its name will certainly not, because of its unfamiliarity, command immediate recognition on a wine list.

The 45° east/west parallel that goes through the north of Yugoslavia also cuts across such celebrated wine regions as the Piedmont region of Italy and the Rhône Valley and Bordeaux region of France. The climate in Yugoslavia ranges from Alpine to Continental to Mediterranean. The topography and soil content are equally varied, of natural combinations contributing to a rich diversity of high-quality wines.

Suggested Readings

Ambrosi, Hans. *Where the Great German Wines Grow.* New York: Hastings House, 1976.

Berberoglu, H. *The World of Wines, Spirits and Beers,* 2d ed., Dubuque, Iowa: Kendall/Hunt, 1984.

Casas, Penelope. *The Foods & Wines of Spain.* New York: Knopf, 1982.

De Blij, Harm Jan. *Wine Regions of the Southern Hemisphere.* Totowa, N.J.: Rowman & Allanheld, 1985.

De Blij, Harm Jan. *Wine: A Geographic Appreciation.* Totowa, N.J.: Rowman & Allanheld, 1983.

German Wine Atlas and Vineyard Register. New York: Hastings House, 1977.

Hallgarten, S. F. *German Wines.* London, 1981.

Johnson, Hugh. *Modern Encyclopedia of Wine.* New York: Simon & Schuster, 1983.

Johnson, Hugh. *The Atlas of German Wines.* New York: Simon & Schuster, 1986.

Johnson, Frank. *The Professional Wine Reference,* 3d ed. New York: Harper & Row, 1983.

Meinhard, Heinrich. *The Wines of Germany,* 2d ed. Briarcliff Manor, N.Y.: Stein and Day, 1980.

Read, Jan. *The Wines of Spain.* London: Faber and Faber, 1982.

Read, Jan. *The Wines of Portugal.* London: Faber and Faber, 1982.

Robards, Terry. *Terry Robard's New Book of Wine,* 2d ed. New York: Putnam, 1984.

Schreiner, John. *The World of Canadian Wine.* British Columbia, Canada: Douglas & McIntyre, 1984.

Sichel, Peter. *The Wines of Germany,* 4th ed. New York: Hastings House, 1980.

Sutcliffe, Serena. *André Simon's Wines of the World,* 2d ed. New York: McGraw-Hill, 1981.

Torres, Marimar. *The Spanish Table: The Cuisines and Wines of Spain.* New York: Doubleday, 1986.

Torres, Miguel A. *Wines and Vineyards of Spain.* 1982.

Discussion Topics and Questions

1. Australia and Chile are considered countries "down under." What are the growing season differences between these two countries and the United States?

2. Australia's wines are becoming more and more popular with each passing year. What grape varieties are used to produce these wines?

3. Why are the wines of Austria and Switzerland not very well known in the United States?

4. The Hungarian government completely controls the exportation and pricing of Hungarian wines in the United States. To what extent does this stunt the growth of sales of these wines?

5. For decades, the wines of Germany have been considered by many to be the finest white wines in the world. Why, then, have

they had such a difficult time selling these wines in the United States?

6. German wine labels are, for some, difficult to decipher. Obtain sample labels and determine why this is so.

7. Spain produces some excellent wines from Rioja and Catalonia. Why, then, when most people think of Spain, does sherry immediately come to mind?

8. Bulgaria, Tunisia, and Yugoslavia have recently begun exporting wines to the United States. What kind of marketing plan could be developed to aid in sales of these wines?

6

Sparkling Wines and Champagne

This chapter discusses:

- The history and geography of the French winemaking region of Champagne, and the grape varieties grown there.
- Five different production methods employed in the making of sparkling wines.
- French rosé champagnes.
- French champagne houses and super-premium bottlings.
- Sparkling wines produced throughout the world.
- Serving and storing sparkling wines.

Sparkling wines, the most elegant of all alcoholic beverages, have been for centuries served to royalty and heads of state, at New Year celebrations and at weddings, births, and other important occasions. "Bubbly," as sparkling wine has come to be known, is the most labor-intensive of all wines, yet its prices scarcely reach those of Bordeaux, Burgundy, and other high-priced wines; its popularity and price seem to grow each year.

French Champagne

History

The Roman chalk quarries of the French Champagne region date from the Roman-Gallo period of the third century A.D. when Reims was the capital of northern Gaul. Excavations made by slaves consisted of large pits that were shaped like pyramids (growing wider as one descended). They were often more than one hundred feet deep; large pulley-type hoists were employed to lift out the huge and heavy blocks of chalk, which were dried and used for building houses and ramparts. In this way, a maximum yield of raw material was obtained with little damage to the ground's surface. Excavations were begun near the ground water level; once completed, they were filled with debris and rubbish and covered by earth.

It was not until centuries later that the people of Champagne rediscovered these pits, and for years they worked to enlarge and connect them, forming the basis of the unique chalk caves which consist of hundreds of miles of tunnels, housing well into hundreds of millions of bottles of champagne (figure 6–1). One of the chief characteristics of the Champagne region is the chalky subsoil in areas where vineyards are planted. The vines thrive in this subsoil, which ensures natural and regular drainage but does not take all of the moisture from the topsoil. This soil has the advantage of storing the heat of the sun and reflecting it back onto the underside of the vines at night; this speeds the growth of the vines and the ripening of the grapes, so that the vintage may be earlier there than in other areas.

The word *champagne* is of Latin derivation, from the time when Julius Caesar's Roman legions arrived unexpectedly in the rolling wooded hills northeast of what is now Paris. Caesar and his men drilled and battled in an open field they called a *campus*; corrupted by the less than elegant soldiers, the word became *campania* in Latin, later to become *champagne*. This name was given to the ancient French province, and is also used for the sparkling wine produced in the region's 62,500 acres (as of 1986) of vineyards in some 250 different villages clustered around the cities of Reims and Epernay.

It was not until the mid-sixteenth century that Dom Pierre Pérignon (1638–1715), a blind Benedictine monk, during his tenure as chief cellar master at Hautvillers (1668–1715), discovered the wine that is now called champagne; he perfected the technique for its production by blending wines to achieve a consistent and harmonious balance, using an oil-soaked hemp rag or the bark of a tree as a temporary bottle stopper. In 1668, Dom Pérignon bottled the first bottle of champagne.

Geography

The Champagne region is ninety miles northeast of Paris. A law passed on July 22, 1927 demarcated a zone of that region that by virtue of its natural characteristics is capable of supporting the vineyards whose product has the exclusive right to be called champagne. The French insist

176

Figure 6–1 A view of the ancient Henriot cellars in Reims where millions of bottles of champagne age to maturity and perfection under ideal conditions. In the background, with Roman arches over their entrances, are the great rooms quarried out of the chalk. They remain today as they were left by the Romans. (Courtesy Henriot Champagne Cellars, France)

that no other wine can legally be called champagne, regardless of how it is made, how it tastes, or how beautifully it bubbles; and there are treaties and trade agreements to support them. The Treaty of Madrid (1891) states that "all goods imported or exported under false appellation are subject to seizure." The Treaty of Versailles (May 6, 1919) forced nations defeated in World War I to accept all the victors' appellation laws and trade names. In 1926 and 1930 there were international conferences

177

of all of the wine-producing countries of the world whose purpose was to limit place names on wine labels; finally, a document known as the "Agreement of Lisbon" was ratified by twelve countries on October 31, 1958: France, Cuba, Czechoslovakia, Greece, Hungary, Israel, Italy, Morocco, Portugal, Spain, Romania, and Turkey. Ratification constituted an agreement to protect product appellations that derive from geographical origin. Today the only notable nonsigners of the agreement are Russia and the United States. Why not the United States? Some claim that the United States simply chose not to attend the relevant conferences; others contend that during Prohibition (1920–1933) the United States had no interest in the matter.

In 1960 the High Court of England issued a judgment ending the use by the Costa Brava Winery of the name "Spanish champagne" for a sparkling wine it produced. In 1973, under a Franco-Spanish agreement, Spanish sparkling wine producers could not use the word *champagne* on their labels after 1978, and could not use it in advertising or promotion after 1983. These sparkling wines are now marketed under the name "Cava." Also, according to a 1973 agreement, Japanese producers cannot use the word *champagne* for their sparkling wines. In addition, legitimate French champagne producers can seek redress for infringements on their rights by foreign wineries that produce or sell sparkling wines labeled "champagne" on Japanese territory.

In the United States, Federal Administration Act wine regulations are enforced by the Bureau of Alcohol, Tobacco, and Firearms (BATF) of the Department of the Treasury. These regulations require that on sparkling wine labels an appellation of origin such as "American," "California," "New York State," and so on must appear "in direct conjunction with, and in lettering substantially as conspicuous as" the word *champagne*. Violations of this regulation are brought to the attention of the BATF and agencies of the French government.

Countries that have either signed the international trade agreement or simply abide by its definition call their sparkling wines by names other than *champagne*. In Italy sparkling wine is known as *spumante*; in France, *mousseux*; in Bulgaria, *champanski*; in Germany and Austria, *schaumwein* or *sekt*; in Spain, *espumosa*; in Catalonia, *xampan*; in Yugoslavia, *sampanjac*; in Hungary, *pezsgo*; and in Portugal and Brazil, *espumante*. In England, in a famous 1960 test case, the courts ruled that the British can no longer market any product called "champagne" unless it is true champagne (made in Champagne, France). Therefore, in England sparkling wine is now called *moussec*.

Grape Varieties

In the production of champagne only three varieties of grapes may be used: Chardonnay (white), Pinot Noir (red), and Pinot Meunier (red). The grapes are usually picked before they reach full maturity and sugar content, generally at 17 to 19 Brix (figure 6–2). At this point they are extremely high in natural grape acidity, which gives champagne its refreshingly clean and crisp taste. The classic champagne blend consists of approximately 70 percent red grapes and 30 percent white grapes. The juice of the red grapes is fermented without the skins, which would otherwise color the wine, making it unsuitable for champagne, more than 98 percent of which is white.

When the grapes have been harvested and pressed, and have fermented, the winemaker then starts to assemble his *cuvée* or blend. He might, for instance, have Chardonnay wine from many different vine-

Figure 6–2 A *vendangeuse* harvesting grapes for champagne in a Moët & Chandon vineyard. (Courtesy of Moët & Chandon, Epernay, France)

yards, sometimes as many as thirty to fifty. From these he chooses wines that display certain desirable characteristics for the final blend; the same is true for the red wines. The next step is to develop a blend of all three wines that captures the particular style of that champagne house. The winemaker has to take into consideration the bottlings of the last fifteen to twenty years and attempt to achieve a sameness of taste, so that this year's bottle will taste like last year's bottle and also next year's bottle. He must consider what the blended wine will taste like after it has gone through the secondary fermentation, when it contains bubbles (figures 6–3 and 6–4). This can drastically change the wine's appearance and taste. Approximately 1.5 kilos (3.3 lbs) of grapes are needed to produce each bottle of champagne.

Figure 6–3 Laboratory analysis of wine destined to be made into champagne. (Courtesy Champagne News & Information Bureau, New York)

Figure 6–4 Cellarmasters blend wine from different vineyards with reserve wines from previous harvests to produce non-vintage champagnes that typify a house style. (Courtesy Moët & Chandon, Epernay, France)

Making Sparkling Wines and Champagnes

Sparkling wines are made in a multitude of ways, from the cheapest—an overnight "charge" of carbon dioxide (CO_2)—to the most costly, the *méthode champenoise*. The various methods of production are described below.

Artificial Carbonation

Probably the quickest and cheapest method of making wines sparkle is similar to the way sodas are made to "fizz"—that is, by pumping them full of carbon dioxide. With this method the bubbles are not an integral part of the wine, and do not last long after it is poured. Sparkling wines made via this method are easy to spot. Their bubbles are very large, and the wine froths up very quickly for a few moments and then appears to go flat.

The Bulk or Charmat Method

The next method is known as "bulk fermentation" or the "Charmat" method, after its inventor Eugéne Charmat, a French wine scientist who developed the process in 1910 to save both the time and money involved in the classic method of producing sparkling wines. The original Charmat process (which is still, with some modifications, used today) requires three tanks. "Still" wine is run into the first tank, artificially aged by being heated for twelve to sixteen hours, and then immediately cooled. This wine is then pumped into a second tank, where yeast and sugar are added; it then ferments for fifteen to twenty days. The wine is then pumped into the third tank, where it is clarified by cooling the tank to about 30°F; this also aids in tartrate stabilization. Finally, the wine is filtered, and bottled under pressure. This method usually produces sparkling wines within one month, and is the least expensive of the higher-quality methods. Because all of the fermentation takes place in temperature-controlled glass-lined, stainless-steel pressurized tanks, bottle breakage is virtually nonexistent. Cooler fermentation allows for greater retention of fresh grapy flavors, and the fermentation can be halted at any point by simply chilling the wine. This method is also known as *cuve close.*

In Italy most of the Asti Spumante is made today in a modified Charmat method, which is favored over the *méthode champenoise.* One of the earlier problems associated with using the classic method to produce Asti Spumante was that the Moscato grape's fresh aroma was lost. Another problem was that it was difficult to maintain the presence of residual sugars, which are necessary for consistent sweetness. When the classic method is used, all of the sugars are metabolized during the secondary fermentation, and the desired sweetness is accomplished later, with the final "dosage." For Asti Spumante the minimum residual sugar after the secondary fermentation must be 75 to 90 grams per liter (or 7.5 to 9.0 grams per 100 ml.), under the Italian DOC regulations. This presented a major problem to Italian winemaker Carlo Gancia (he produced the first bottle of *spumante* in 1865), who experimented with the *méthode champenoise*. At that time countless bottles would explode—often 20 to 30 percent of the entire production. When, in 1910, the Charmat process was discovered, it was immediately put to use in the making of Asti Spumante. The process, which has been greatly modified and advanced, now utilizes such techniques as refrigeration, pasteurization, and sterile filtration and bottling.

Méthode Champenoise
(Champagne Method)

The most costly of all procedures, which produces the finest-quality sparkling wines and champagnes, is the *méthode champenoise*. It was pioneered in France during the nineteenth century. It is the only method that can legally be used to produce French champagnes. The base wine or *cuvée* (blend) must be delicate in flavor, low in alcohol (because there is a one to two percent increase after the secondary fermentation), and relatively high in acidity. This base wine is placed in a champagne bottle, to which is added a measured amount of sugar and yeast dissolved in wine. Too much sugar can result in bursting bottles or a hot (high-alcohol) sparkling wine. Errors are costly, and at this stage of development it is important to choose a yeast that agglomerates readily—that is, clumps up and forms particles large enough to settle out of the wine, rather than remaining in suspension. The yeast used in the secondary fermentation is not the same type as that used in alcohol fermentation; special strains are used that are suitably matched to the base wine and can reproduce in a stoppered bottle. The bottles are then secured with either a metal crown cap or a cork held in place by an *agrafe* (metal clip). They are stacked horizontally to distribute the yeast lengthwise, exposing a greater surface area. Each stack contains about 1,000 bottles; a wooden batten, similar to plaster lath, is placed between each row of bottles, making the stacks quite firm.

While this aging takes place, the bottles are periodically inspected for breaks and leaks and the center bottles (which are the warmest because of the heat given off during fermentation) are interchanged with the outer ones to insure uniformity of fermentation. The bottles remain in cool (50° to 55°F), dark cellars for the secondary fermentation, which normally takes about forty-five days to complete. Five to six atmospheres of pressure, or about 110 pounds per square inch of CO_2 is formed.

During this time, the cell walls of the yeast crack open, allowing the protoplasm present to metabolize the sugar, converting it to more or less equal parts of alcohol and inert CO_2 gas. The finished sparkling wine usually contains 11.5 to 12.5 percent alcohol. Since the CO_2 cannot escape, it is absorbed into the wine over a period of time. After the fermentation in the bottle is complete, the wine is left to age in a cellar. Under AOC regulations, the minimum duration of aging for a nonvintage champagne is one year; for vintage champagne it is three years. Most champagnes are aged from three to nine years on the yeast.

As the yeast cells in the aging champagne break down in a process known as *autolysis*, they release vitamins (such as A, C, D, and E), proteins, peptides, and amino acids, which contribute to the formation of tiny bubbles and add to the complexity and elegance of the wine. When the sparkling wine has aged sufficiently, the bottles are placed on their sides in racks called *pupîtres*—specially constructed A-frame racks invented in 1816 by the champagne house of Veuve Clicquot—for ten to twelve days, during which the sediment in the bottle settles. Riddling begins at this point: experienced riddlers usually place a white paint mark on the bottom of the bottle (punt) at the 6 o'clock position, and rotate the bottles in one-eighth or one-quarter turns. While rotating the bottles the riddlers gently shake them and increase the angle at which they lie to a more vertical position, which moves the sediment that was formed during the secondary fermentation down to the bottle's neck. An experienced riddler can turn 10,000 bottles an hour and as many as 50,000 bottles per day (figure 6–5). Riddling is done on a daily basis for approximately six weeks (see the later section on encapsulated yeasts). When all of the sediment is collected at the neck of the bottles, a process known as *dégorgement*, or disgorgement, takes place.

The bottles are chilled to about 35°F, after which the neck of the bottle is immersed one inch into an extremely cold (−20°F) circulating brine solution or "bath" of propylene glycol, which freezes the neck of the bottle—and the sediment in it—within fifteen minutes. The bottle is immediately turned upright, the cap is removed with pliers, and the pressure of the bottle literally blows out this frozen plug, which contains all of the wine's sediment (figures 6–6 and 6–7). Because the bottle was cooled off before disgorging, there is only a loss of about one atmosphere of pressure during this process, and still plenty of bubble left in the bottle. The bottle is then topped with older wine in which cane sugar has been dissolved, to set its dryness or sweetness. Finally, the bottle is corked, secured with a wire hood, and returned to the aging cellar to rest for a few months while the dosage merges with the wine. This

Figure 6–5 The time-honored method of *remuage* (hand-riddling). (Courtesy Champagne News & Information Bureau, New York)

addition of sugar is known as the "final dosage"; the amount of sugar used in the dosage determines the degree of dryness or sweetness in the wine.

French champagne makers follow the Common Market (EEC) guidelines for the dosage:

Designation	*Common Market standard*
Extra *brut*	less than 6 grams of sugar per liter
Brut	less than 15 grams of sugar per liter (most *brut* champagnes have 8–10 grams per liter)
Extra dry	12–20 grams per liter
Sec	17–35 grams per liter
Demi sec	33–50 grams per liter
Doux	more than 50 grams per liter

Figure 6–6 The traditional, somewhat daring hand method of "disgorgement." (Courtesy Moët & Chandon, Epernay, France)

After the final aging, the sparkling wine is ready for labeling and eventual shipping. Most sparkling wines are sold in the traditional 750-milliliter bottle, and it is not uncommon to find magnums and occasionally double magnums of the same type. However, champagnes found in 750-milliliter bottles, magnums, and double magnums are bottle fermented. When other sizes, either 375-milliliter bottles or bottles larger than double magnums are called for, they are hand filled from a 750-milliliter bottle. (Many of these large bottles, incidentally, have Old Testament names—Jeroboam, Rehoboam, and Nebuchadnezzar, for instance—which were given to them during the 1850s and 1860s by the British negociants, many of whom were Protestants.)

Sparkling wines made in this manner are entitled to indicate so on their labels, displaying either the words *méthode champenoise* or "fermented in this bottle." A three-layer cork, usually two parts solid cork

Figure 6–7 Bollinger R.D. is disgorged by hand to remove the natural sediment on which it has been aging for at least seven years. (Courtesy Niki Singer, Inc., New York)

and one part particle cork, must be used, and the word *champagne* must be stamped on every cork used for this wine.

The Transfer Method

The transfer method was developed in Germany in the 1930s, and is a modification of the *méthode champenoise*. In fact, the two methods are identical, except that the transfer method does not employ the riddling technique. Instead, when the wine has been sufficiently aged, the bottles are moved to a large tank in which pressure is used to remove the corks, suck the wine out of the bottles, and then chill it to below 32°F. After being filtered, the wine is transferred to clean bottles, and the final dosage is added. This does appear to be an easier and certainly cheaper way of making high-quality sparkling wines. However, during the filtering

187

process it has been found that the filtration can strip away the subtlety that the winemaker has worked so hard to create. The reverse is also true—if the winemaker starts off with a mediocre wine, the filtering can improve the wine by clearing it of "off" flavors. Sparkling wines made in this manner are labeled "fermented in the bottle."

Rosé Champagnes

History: Fact or Fancy?

The supposed origin of rosé champagne is part of its romantic charm. One story claims that it was created to match the satin slippers and long dresses of the bridesmaids at a fashionable French wedding; another suggests that it was blended to honor the coronation of a queen. It is more likely that pink or rosé champagne was an accident of nature. During an exceptional growing year in the Champagne province, the vines received more than the usual limited amount of sunshine. This caused some of the pigment in the red grape skins to migrate to the pulp of the fruit, giving the resultant wine a pink or rosé tinge.

Rosé champagne, which has a much longer history than do *blanc de blancs,* is often seen as the quintessential wine of the gay and frivolous late Victorian and Edwardian ages. In the nineteenth century, for instance, it was synonymous with wild and dissolute living. But it is a serious wine, and one of the most difficult and complex to produce.

It was not until the end of the seventeenth century, a period in which great efforts were made to improve French wines, that champagne's tendency to sparkle was analyzed and exploited. Before then the wines of Champagne, although much appreciated, were still, delicate red wines that did not keep well or stand up to travel.

The Production of Pink or Rosé Champagne

Rosé champagne is perhaps the most difficult wine in the world to produce. Of the four basic ways in which rosé champagne can be made, one is illegal in France. This one will be described first. The pink color of rosé champagne was once obtained by artificial coloring. *Cochineal* (the juice of scarlet-colored berries) was often added to "white" champagne, for instance. Other methods included the addition of elderberry juice boiled in cream of tartar (tartaric acid)—known as *teinture de fismes*—or red vegetable dyes or anything else that could produce a red color.

The first legal method used in the production of rosé champagne is seldom used today. Again, champagne is traditionally produced 70 percent from red grapes (Pinot Noir and Pinot Meunier) and 30 percent from white grapes (Chardonnay). If the winemaker decides to make a rosé wine, he or she will simply leave the skins of the red grapes in contact with the fermenting grape juice or must for anywhere from four to twelve hours. During this time both the high acid content of the grapes and the initial stage of alcohol production will draw out some pigmentation from the grape skins giving the must a slight rosé color. (Grape tannins will also be given off during this time.) This method is avoided in the production of the more traditional golden-colored champagnes. One of the most basic problems with the method is that it is difficult to control the stability of the color it produces and its eventual development in the sparkling wine. The rosé color has been known to fade in the bottle or turn to a pale tawny or onionskin color. This method is seldom utilized today.

Another legal method of rosé champagne production, one that is more universally accepted and practiced, is the addition of still red wine (also made in the Champagne region, mostly from Bouzy, but occasionally from Ambonnay, Verzenay, or Trepail, in the Montagne de Reims). The red wine, added in a proportion of 10 to 15 percent in relation to the white champagne gives the sparkling wine the right degree of color. The addition of red wine takes place prior to the secondary fermentation in the bottle.

In either of the above legal methods, the desired color may not "develop" after three to five years in the bottle, since, as stated earlier, the effect of pigmentation is not wholly predictable and could precipitate out at a later date as sediment. It has occasionally been known for the final champagne to emerge yellow, blue, orange, or brown. During this aging period the wine could also take on a pale tawny color, which is why the second method is preferable to deriving the rosé color solely from skin contact.

A final method that is seldom employed is exactly the same (employing the addition of red Bouzy wine) as the method described above, except that the red wine is added *after* the secondary fermentation, when the *liqueur d'expédition* (shipping dosage) is added. The problem with this method is that the red wine never has a chance to "marry" with the existing champagne; therefore, an "off" flavor usually develops.

The Risk of Producing Rosé Champagne

As it is so risky to make this special champagne, most firms producing a rosé do so in limited quantity and only in the finest vintage years when exceptionally mature grapes are available. When one understands the commercial courage needed to produce a rosé champagne (a firm can lose its entire rosé *cuvée* if the color or taste is incorrect), one can also appreciate why production is so small and why it is more expensive than the more common golden champagnes.

Rosé champagne could very easily be made in a *demisec* style. Instead, it is almost always a *brut* champagne, which is much drier than the more traditional golden champagnes. Rosé champagne usually has more tannin and tartness than golden champagne and has a greater aging potential. Rosé champagnes have a characteristic aroma of raspberries and black currants—the light scents that give rosés their charm.

Rosé Champagne Producers

Rosé champagne accounts for approximately one percent of the total production of champagne. Some of the better-known rosé champagnes on the market are:

Nonvintage and Vintage

Ayala	Lanson
Besserat de Bellefon	Laurent-Perrier
Billecart-Salmon	Moët & Chandon
Bollinger	Mumm
Charbaut	Perrier-Jouët
De Castellane	Philipponnat
Deutz	Piper Heidsieck
Nicolas Feuilliatte	Pommery & Greno
Gosset	Louis Roederer
Charles Heidsieck	Pol Roger
Heidsieck Monopole	Ruinart
Henriot	Taittinger
Jacquesson	Veuve Clicquot
Krug	

Prestige Cuvées

Charbaut Certificate	Perrier-Jouët
Dom Perignon	Pol Roger Cuvée de Réserve
Dom Ruinart	Roederer Cristal
Krug	Taittinger Comtes de Champagne

Riddling Machines

The vibrating or automatic riddling racks used to shake bottles in preparation for *dégorgement* were pioneered by the late Adolph Heck of Korbel Champagne Cellars of Sonoma, California more than thirty years ago. There have been many variations on this automated system; one very successful one is used in the sparkling wine house of Domaine Chandon in Yountville, California. Their machine, the VLM (very large machine) is an improved version of the smaller French automatic riddling machine (*gyropalette*), which stood four feet high and was capable of riddling 504 bottles at once. The machine at Domaine Chandon, which stands seventeen feet high, can riddle 4,032 bottles at once! It can also be programmed to turn and/or tilt three times in twenty-four hours. A bottle of sparkling wine can be machine riddled in twelve days (with three movements a day), as opposed to the approximately thirty days of a traditional hand-riddled cycle (figure 6–8).

Encapsulated Yeasts

Over the last ten years the research laboratory at Moët & Chandon has been studying different techniques to facilitate the process of *remuage*. Since 1980, Moët has been studying, in conjunction with the INRA (Institut National de la Recherche Agronomique), a new technology which consists of enclosing the yeasts responsible for the second fermentation in "beads" of alginate, a natural polymer extracted from marine algae. Thus, while activating the second fermentation in exactly the same way as yeasts in their free state, the encapsulated yeasts remain enclosed in these beads even after autolysis (the self-destruction of the cells). During autolysis the molecules that contribute to the flavor and aroma of the wine pass in solution into the champagne, leaving the yeast cells imprisoned in the beads. As these beads have a density that is higher than that of the wine, they settle easily by gravity (rather than floating freely),

Figure 6–8 Domaine Chandon's giant riddling machine mechanically turns 4,032 bottles of sparkling wine at once. (Courtesy Domaine Chandon, Yountville, California)

collecting in the neck of the bottle without the use of the traditional *pupîtres,* or racks. They are then disgorged by the conventional method.

Classically, *remuage,* or riddling, serves to eliminate the yeasts (lees) contained in a bottle of champagne before shipment in a straightforward mechanical operation.

With yeast encapsulation, there are millions of cells in the bottle which create a distinct cloudiness and then leave a very fine deposit which also has to be eliminated by means of *remuage.* Because the yeasts are trapped in beads, the wine remains perfectly limpid throughout the bottle fermentation. With encapsulated yeasts, the usual large number of yeasts is contained in a few hundred beads, each having an average diameter of a few millimeters (approximately one-tenth of an inch) (figure 6–9).

How To Read A Champagne Label

SIZE

Many wine lovers argue that champagne fermented in magnums tastes better. Whatever the evidence, magnums are more festive and practical for crowds — they're BIG!

Here are the main choices:

- *Bottle* — 750ml (Serves 6 flutes)
- *Magnum* — 1.5 liter (Serves 12 flutes)

DRY, DRIER, DRIEST

The amount of sugar used in the dosage determines how dry a finished champagne will taste. Here are the main choices:

- *Brut* — no sweetness
- *Extra Dry* — slightly sweet
- *Sec* — noticeably sweet

(Yes! Brut is *drier* than Extra Dry.)

BRAND

Here's where the champagne producers have done us a favor. They generally stay true to their chosen style through the use of artful blending (whereas still wines are subject to that harvest's characteristics). So once you've found a style you like in a particular brand (e.g., delicate, robust, etc.), you can rely on finding what pleased you again . . . and again.

VINTAGE DATE

A vintage wine is one which contains 95% or more of wines of the year stated. As a rule, there is no quality connotation to a vintage American sparkling wine. Like many wineries, Domaine Chandon does not vintage date its bubblies, blending as much as 30% of reserve wines from previous years to maintain a consistent style.

ALCOHOL CONTENT

Like most table wines, most champagnes contain 12% alcohol by volume. Because people tend to sip wine with foods, it is often referred to as the "beverage of moderation."

VITICULTURAL REGION

This simply tells you that 85% or more of the wine was produced from grapes grown in that designated region.

TYPE

There are three grape varieties which make up the majority of fine champagnes: Pinot Noir, Chardonnay and Pinot Blanc. Champagne vintners are notorious for giving us confusing nomenclature, but here are some simple guidelines:

- *Blanc de Noirs* are generally made from the Pinot Noir grape (dark skin, light juice) and often have an attractive tinge of color.
- *Blanc de Blancs* are made from Chardonnay (light skin, light juice) or other white grapes.
- *Reserve* usually connotes lengthy aging. Chandon Reserve is aged a minimum of four years, for example.

CHAMPAGNE OR SPARKLING WINE?

Where French appellation (wine labeling) law applies, sparkling wine can only be called champagne if it is produced in the Champagne region of France. Here in the U.S., these laws do not apply, so it's up to each producer to decide how to describe his wine. Domaine Chandon sparkling wines are so named out of respect for its parent, Champagne Moët and Chandon. (Note: For simplicity and consistency, the term champagne is used here to mean *any* bubbly wine.)

METHOD OF FERMENTATION

Careful: you get what you paid for.

- *Méthode Champenoise* — A trustworthy signpost. It's the traditional and most expensive process, whereby the bubbly goes through its second fermentation in the same bottle you buy. If you want the best quality, look for it.
- *Charmat* — Also called the "bulk" process, charmat bubblies are fermented in large tanks and often produce champagnes with large, lazy bubbles that disappear too quickly.
- *Fermented in the Bottle* — This phrase indicates that the "transfer" process was used. The bubbly undergoes its second fermentation in a bottle, but unlike the méthode champenoise, the wine is emptied from that bottle, filtered and re-bottled. Many agree it loses some flavor in transit.

Label text: R E S E R V E — NET CONTENTS 1.5 LITERS (50.7 FL OZ) — ALCOHOL 12% BY VOLUME — BRUT — CHANDON Réserve — PRODUCED AND BOTTLED BY DOMAINE CHANDON YOUNTVILLE, CA — NAPA VALLEY SPARKLING WINE METHODE CHAMPENOISE

Figure 6–9 How to read a sparkling wine label. (Courtesy Domaine Chandon, Yountville, California)

Moët & Chandon has studied the selection of yeasts, the qualities of seaweeds used to produce the encapsulating "beads," and methods for preparing the "beads" in laboratory conditions, with a view to producing wine of a quality similar to that obtained by the classical method. Research undertaken in collaboration with the CIVC (Comité Interprofessionel du Vin de Champagne) enables them to say at this stage that, in the method employing encapsulated yeasts, the second fermentation takes place normally; and the panel of specialists has found that the organoleptic properties of champagne that has been produced by this method and that has been aged for up to two years on the lees are indistinguishable from those of champagne containing yeasts in the free state.

It should be noted, however, that the use of this new technique will have virtually no effect on the length of time during which the wines develop and age in the cellars, which will remain approximately three years for nonvintage champagne and between five and seven years for vintage *cuvées*.

According to Edmond Maudière, Moët & Chandon's chief enologist, the first champagnes made by this revolutionary process will probably be sold in the early to mid-1990s.

Bureau of Alcohol, Tobacco, and Firearms (BATF) Regulations

Sparkling wines are wines that contain more than 0.256 grams of CO_2 per millimeter (25.6 grams per 100 ml. or 256 grams per l.) and are not flavored.

Champagne Houses

There are more than one-hundred champagne houses; some of the most popular are:

Bollinger. On February 6, 1829, Jacques Bollinger established the Bollinger champagne house. Bollinger is known for making a super-prestige champagne called R.D. (*récemment dégorgé*, or recently disgorged), first produced with the 1955 vintage and disgorged on January 18, 1968.

Henriot. This champagne house was founded in 1808 by Nicholas Simon Henriot. Almost twenty years ago, Henriot and Baron Philippe de Rothschild of Château Mouton-Rothschild merged their technical expertise, and in 1969 produced a high-quality champagne reserved for the baron and his friends. It was called Réserve Baron Philippe de Rothschild, and since that time has been released to the general public in limited quantity.

Moët & Chandon. 1743 marked the birth of Moët & Chandon and also of Thomas Jefferson, third president of the United States (1743–1826), who would later become extremely fond of this champagne. Moët & Chandon was originally founded by Claude Moët, whose daughter, Adelaide, married Pierre-Gabriel Chandon.

The cellars of Moët & Chandon, which consist of more than eighteen miles of connecting underground caves (approximately 120 feet deep), dug in the beginning of the eighteenth century, are the largest in the world (figure 6–10).

The most popular super-prestige champagne is Dom Pérignon, which is produced by Moët & Chandon. The name originally belonged to another champagne house—Mercier—but was never used by it. When Paul Chandon-Moët married Mercier's daughter, Moët received the rights to the Dom Pérignon name. In 1921, the first vintage of Dom Pérignon champagne was sold in the United States. However, it was not until 1949 that the first vintage (1943) of Dom Pérignon was introduced on the French market.

Moët & Chandon also produces sparkling wines in other countries. Other company production facilities using the Chandon name are Domaine Chandon in California, Proviar in Argentina, Provifin in Brazil, and Chandon Munich in West Germany.

Mumm. Mumm was founded in 1827 by three German brothers, Theophile, Jules, and Edvard Von Mumm, who emigrated to Reims from the Rhine region of Germany. Shortly after World War I, their property was sold to a group of investors and renamed G. H. Mumm & Co.

In 1939, René Lalou, a member of the purchasing group, was appointed president, a post he retained until his death in 1973 at the age of ninety-six. In 1969, in recognition of Lalou's contribution, Mumm introduced a prestigious *tête-de-cuvée* (called René Lalou) bearing his signature.

Cordon Rouge Brut, inspired by the red ribbon (*cordon rouge*) of the French Legion of Honor, was introduced in 1876. The bottle was originally wrapped in red silk ribbons and was first exported to the United States in 1882.

In 1930, Mumm introduced Crémant de Cramant, a 100 percent Chardonnay champagne from the village of Cramant, whose light effervescence is the result of lower than normal pressure in the bottle.

Figure 6–10   Moët & Chandon's cellars, in which millions of bottles of Moët champagne, in various stages of development, are stored. (Courtesy Moët & Chandon, Epernay, France)

In 1956, Seagram Company Ltd. of Montreal, Canada acquired a significant share of the company, providing capital for further expansion.

Pol Roger. Founded in 1849 by Pol Roger, this house's champagne was the favorite of Winston Churchill, who during his tenure as prime minister, consumed some five-hundred cases.

In tribute to the great friendship between the Pol Roger family and Winston Churchill, the labels of the champagne sent to England after his death in 1965 were bordered in black. In 1984, that practice ended with the introduction of a new top-of-the-line champagne. On June 14,

1984, at Blenheim Palace, Churchill's birthplace, Christian de Billy of Pol Roger announced, "Today we are launching a great champagne in memory of a great man. . . . The champagne he loved certainly contributed towards giving Churchill that witty disposition of his and that perhaps enables us to say that there is an indestructible link between the wit of Churchill and the Champagne of France." The creation of a new *cuvée de prestige*, Cuvée Sir Winston, is Roger's permanent tribute to the great statesman.

Pommery. During the late 1800s there was only one champagne—a sweet, heavy wine served as a complement to desserts. It was made by adding to the natural champagne a dosage of thick cane sugar syrup dissolved in wines from the best years. Madame Pommery saw, early on, that this limited champagne sales, and that people were missing the lively, delicate taste of natural champagne. She therefore cut the dosage and introduced a dry and then extra-dry champagne. Madame Pommery's greatest achievement, however, was the premier of Nature 1874, inaugurating the *brut* champagne. Madame Pommery died in 1890.

Ruinart. In 1729 Nicolas Ruinart founded the oldest existing champagne house. Dom Thierry Ruinart (1657–1709), Nicolas' uncle, was a good friend of Dom Pérignon during the late 1600s and early 1700s. In 1963, Ruinart was purchased by the Moët-Hennessy group, which has also owned Mercier champagne since 1970.

Other champagne houses are Charles Heidsieck, Krug, Lanson, Laurent-Perrier, Piper Heidsieck, Perrier-Jouët, Roederer, Taittinger, and Veuve Clicquot.

Super-Prestige Champagnes

In the Champagne region of France, vineyards are rated according to the quality level of the grapes they produce. This official designation, called a "growth," or *cru*, can range from 77 percent (the least distinguished) to 100 percent. Vineyards that produce the best grapes because of the right consistency and drainage of the soil, the most ideal exposure to the sun, and other viticultural and climatic conditions are rated 100 percent. The prices of grapes at harvest time are fixed in relation to the classification of each *cru* in this scale.

Just about every champagne house produces its version of a super-prestige (highest quality) champagne, or *tête-de-cuvée*. Below is a list of champagne producers and the names of their super-prestige champagnes.

Name of producer	Super-prestige champagne
Bollinger	R.D. (recently disgorged) Tradition
Canard-Duchêne	Charles VII
Charbaut	Certificate Blanc de Blancs
De Castellane	Cuvée Commodore
De Venoge	Champagne des Princes
Deutz & Geldermann	Cuvée William Deutz
Charles Heidsieck	Champagne Charlie
Heidsieck Monopole	Diamant Bleu, or Special Reserve
Henriot	Réserve Baron Philippe de Rothschild
Krug	Grand Cuvée
Lanson	Noble Cuvée
Laurent-Perrier	Cuvée Grand Siècle
Moët & Chandon	Dom Pérignon
Mumm	René Lalou, or Mumm de Mumm
Perrier-Jouët	Fleur de Champagne
Philipponnat	Close des Goisses
Piper Heidsieck	Piper Champagne Rare (formerly Florens Louis)
Pommery & Greno	Prestige Pommery
Louis Roederer	Cristal
Pol Roger	Cuvée Sir Winston
Ruinart	Dom Ruinart
Taittinger	Comtes de Champagne
Veuve Clicquot	La Grande Dame

Sparkling Wine Producers of the World

The French, it should be noted, do not have the exclusive market on fine sparkling wines; many excellent bubblys are produced throughout the world. These usually command lower prices, however, than those of the prestigious French champagnes. Some well-known French sparkling wine producers are Bouvet, Gratien & Meyer, Kriter, Monmousseau, and Saint Hilaire.

Germany

Germany's wine law relative to sparkling wines was amended on September 1, 1986 and affected all wines labeled German Sekt or Deutscher

Sekt. The new requirements served to bring the labeling for German sparkling wines more in line with German table wine labeling practices. Under the new provisions, three categories of German sparkling wines were recognized. All must derive exclusively from grapes harvested in Germany. The three categories are:

Deutscher Sekt b.A.: Sparkling wine made from grapes grown exclusively in one of the eleven specified high-quality wine-producing regions in Germany. The letters *b.A.* stand for *bestimmter Anbaugebiete*, or *specified growing region*, indicating wines of delimited origin.

Deutscher Sekt: Sparkling wine that derives 100 percent from German-grown grapes whose origin is not, however, limited to one specific region.

Sekt: This term, where it appears alone, on the label (not preceded by *Deutscher*) indicates that the sparkling wine was processed and bottled in Germany but contains base wine originating from other Common Market countries. Formerly, these wines could be labeled Deutscher Sekt, but this is no longer allowed under the new provision.

Some well-known German sparkling wine producers are Blue Nun, Deinhard, and Henkell.

Italy

On July 9, 1967, four years after the DOC regulations went into effect, Asti Spumante was officially granted its DOC designation. Some *spumante* (sparkling wine) producers who produce Asti and/or Brut spumante are:

Banfi Vintners	Fontanafredda	Équippe 5
Ferrari	Villa Antinori	Bersano
Martini & Rossi	Monte Rossa	Riccadonna
Gancia	Berlucchi	Bosca
Bertani	Bolla	Cavit
Burati	Collavini	Granduca
Contratto		

Spain

Some Spanish sparkling wine producers are:

Borbones	Castellblanch	Codorníu
Dubosc	Freixenet	Juvé y Camps
Lembey	Paul Cheneau	Segura Viudas

United States

Great Western Winery, which began operating on March 15, 1860 in New York, quickly established an international reputation for sparkling wines by winning awards in Paris in 1872 and again in 1873 in Vienna. In March 1871, Mr. Champlin (then owner) sent a case of champagne to his close friend Marshall P. Wilder, a well-known Boston connoisseur. After introducing it at a dinner party at the Parker House, Wilder declared it to be "the great champagne of the Western world." The champagne was thus named Great Western.

Schramsberg Champagne Cellars of Napa Valley, California, was established in 1862 by Jacob Schram. In 1972 Schramsberg became an overnight success when former president Richard M. Nixon took thirteen cases of its sparkling wines to Peking's emperor, to be served during a televised banquet.

Korbel Champagne Cellars of Sonoma County, California, the country's oldest producer of *méthode champenoise* sparkling wines, was established in 1882. Since 1954, it has been owned by the Heck family.

Korbel produces an excellent line of California champagnes which include: Blanc de Blancs, Blanc de Noirs, Natural, Brut, Extra Dry, Sec, and Rosé.

Almaden, California's oldest producer of sparkling wines, made its first sparkling wine from the *cuvée* of 1888. In 1963, Almaden first bottled its Blanc de Blancs (*cuvée* 1959).

Hanns Kornell Champagne Cellars of Napa Valley, California, originally known as the Larkmead Vineyards (this was changed in 1952 to its present name), was established by Hanns Kornell. Among the many fine sparkling wines it produces are Sehr Trocken (first produced in 1964 and released in 1972) and Muscat of Alexandria.

Gallo Winery of Modesto, California bottled a bulk-fermented sparkling wine in 1966 under the label The Vintners of Eden Roc, later changed to Gallo Champagne. This wine is now sold under the name Andre; it is the largest-selling sparkling wine in the United States.

Domaine Chandon, the world-famous sparkling wine producer, was founded in 1973 in Yountville, California. It is owned by the huge Moët-Hennessy conglomerate of France. The winery also houses a renowned restaurant and a tasting salon, which is open to the public. Figure 6-11 shows the Domaine wine cellars. Domaine Chandon is perhaps the finest United States producer of nonvintaged *méthode champenoise* sparkling wines. They are Chandon Brut, Blanc de Noirs, and Reserve Brut, sold in both traditional 750-milliliter bottles and 1.5-liter magnums.

Sterling Winery (wholly owned by Seagram's) and *Domaine Mumm* (partially owned by Seagram's) in a joint venture (1983) with Mumm's Champagne, produced an excellent sparkling wine labeled Domaine Mumm in Napa Valley, California.

Figure 6-11 Stainless steel tanks in the Domaine cellars for primary and reserve wine fermentation. (Courtesy Domaine Chandon, Yountville, California)

Serving and Storing Sparkling Wines

Contrary to popular belief, sparkling wine and champagne do not improve in the bottle. They are at their best when sold for consumption. A good rule of thumb is if the bottle contains a vintage date, purchase the latest year available, and don't purchase bottles more than ten years past the vintage date. If the bottle does not contain a date, it is called a nonvintage (a blend of several years) wine and should be consumed within a six-month to one-year period.

Champagne bottles should be stored horizontally, in a cool (50° to 55°F), relatively low-humidity (55 to 65 percent), dark area that is free from vibration.

To serve champagne, place the bottle in the refrigerator for three to four hours, or use an ice bucket with plenty of ice and cold water to form an "ice bath." Ten to fifteen minutes in this bath is sufficient. Never put champagne in the freezer to quickly chill it, for this can cause the wine to go prematurely flat.

The proper procedure for opening champagne is shown in figure 6–12. To uncork the bottle, carefully remove the foil capsule and then the wire hood, by turning it counterclockwise. Next, hold the bottle at a 45° angle pointed away from you and anyone around you; while holding the cork firmly in one hand, twist the bottle in a downward motion with the other hand. Allow the cork to slowly ease out until a gentle "pop" is heard. Continue to hold the bottle at this angle for a few more moments to equalize the pressure inside the bottle. Stand the bottle up; it is now ready to pour. Pour the champagne gently into each glass until

a   b   c

Figure 6-12 Step-by-step illustration of the proper method of opening bottles of sparkling wine. (Courtesy Sebastiani Vineyards, Somona, California)

it is about three-quarters full. Never add ice cubes to champagne: they dilute the taste and cause the bubbles to quickly dissipate.

Correct glassware is important in serving sparkling wines. During the time of Helen of Troy, milk was served from glasses in the shape of a woman's breast, and today's popular flat saucer-shaped champagne glass derives its shape from a mold of Marie Antoinette's left breast. Because of this glass's large surface area, sparkling wine served in it will prematurely go flat. The proper glassware to use is either a fluted or tulip-shaped glass holding approximately eight to ten ounces.

Suggested Readings

Chandon, Domaine. *A User's Guide to Sparkling Wine*. Yountville: Calif. 1987.

Forbes, Patrick. *Champagne: The Wine, the Land and the People*. New York: William Morrow, 1967.

Kaufman, William I. *Champagne*. New York: Viking, 1973.

Ray, Cyril. *Bollinger: The Story of a World-Famous Champagne*. New York: Pyramid, 1971.

Simon, André. *The History of Champagne*. London: Octopus, 1971.

Wasserman, Sheldon and Pauline Wasserman. *Sparkling Wine*. Piscataway N.J.: New Century, 1984.

Zraly, Kevin. *Windows on the World Complete Wine Course*. New York: Sterling, 1985.

Discussion Topics and Questions

1. What effect does the chalky soil of Champagne have on the flavor of champagne?

2. Although the United States has not signed any trade agreements with the EEC, should we abide by the EEC's international rulings and eliminate the use of the term *champagne* on bottles of American-produced sparkling wines? Cite reasons for your answer.

3. France uses only Chardonnay, Pinot Noir, and Pinot Meunier grape varieties for the production of champagne. Why don't other countries do the same?

4. There are four different production methods that can be used to produce sparkling wines. Why is the *méthode champenoise* considered the best? Describe the methods' differences.

5. The blending of red wine with white wine to produce a rosé is prohibited in most wine-producing countries. However, it is practiced in the making of a rosé champagne. Why?

6. For centuries, hand riddling was the only method utilized for the shaking down of sediment in bottles of sparkling wines. Within the last twenty years, machines have been designed that mechanically accomplish this process. If this mechanical method is superior, why has it not been accepted universally?

7. Are the sparkling wines of other countries equal in quality and taste to authentic French champagnes, or are they inferior simply because they do not come from Champagne? Explain.

8. Although the tulip or fluted champagne glass has been proved to be superior to the flat saucer-shaped one, why have glass manufacturers continued to produce this flat type?

9. What effect does a residue of soap or oil have on a glass that is used for serving sparkling wines?

7

Aperitif and Fortified Wines

This chapter discusses:

- The history and origin of various aperitif and fortified wines.
- Methods of production.
- Different types and styles of aperitif and fortified wines.
- Available brand names.
- Storing and serving aperitif and fortified wines.

For centuries aromatic and fortified wines have been savored like champagne; they have virtually no equal among table wines. Fortified wines have always been considered perfect for both beginning and ending elegant dinners. Aromatized and fortified wines have richer bouquets and tastes than table wines, and a higher alcoholic content.

Although the names *vermouth, sherry, port, Madeira,* and *Marsala* are centuries old, modern production methods have changed and refined not only the wines, but also their patterns of consumption. Today's consumption levels are lower than those of the eighteenth and ninteenth centuries, but interest in these wines is constantly being generated, making the modern-day consumer considerably more knowledgeable about them than his or her ancestors.

Aperitifs and Bitters (Digestives)

Federal regulations define an aperitif wine as one with an alcoholic content of not less than 15 percent, made from grape wine containing added brandy or other spirits. These wines are flavored with various herbs and other natural aromatic flavoring materials and possess the aroma, taste, and characteristics generally attributed to an aperitif wine.

Bitters (known as *amaros* in Italy) were originally produced to soothe and relax the stomach after meals, and are therefore often referred to as "digestives." Alcoholic products from France that have the letter *D* stamped on their labels are also digestives.

Aperire, Latin for *to open* is the origin of our word *aperitif;* a wine that usually "opens" lunch or dinner as a stimulant to the appetite. Most aperitifs have an initial sweet taste with a somewhat bitter aftertaste because of the use of quinine as one of the ingredients. This slight bitterness tends to whet the appetite and cleanse the palate. The French government mandates that aperitifs be produced at least 80 percent from wine with an alcoholic strength of at least 10 percent before more alcohol is added to raise the strength to between 16 and 19 percent.

Aperitifs are usually grouped into categories depending on the nature of their base ingredient:

Spirit-based

Amer Picon	Campari	Suze
Aperol	Cynar	Unicum
Averna	Fernet Branca	
Biancosarti	Ramazzotti	

Wine-based (often fortified with brandy or spirits)

Byrrh	Mistelle	Sercial Madeira
Cap Corse	Panache	Sherry (fino)
Dry Marsala	Port (white)	Sparkling wine*
Dubonnet (red and white)	Punt é Mes	Spritzer*
Kir (white wine and Cassis)*	Ratafia	St. Raphaël
	Rosso Antico	Vermouth (red and white)
Lillet (red and white)		
Manzanilla		

* Not fortified.

Some of the more popular aperitifs are:

Amer Picon (French): First produced in 1837 by Gaetan Picon, a sergeant in the French army serving in Algeria. He blended together local African oranges, gentian root, quinine bark, and alcohol. This wine is best when served with seltzer water and a twist of lemon.

Aperol (Italian; 22 proof): Developed in Italy by Silvio Barbieri in 1919. It has a luminous, distinctive deep orange color and is made from grain neutral spirits with natural flavors.

Averna (Italian; 68 proof): One of Italy's many bittersweet aperitifs/digestives. The aroma is colalike and the taste is bittersweet, with hints of vanilla. It is one of the finest digestives made and is best when served at room temperature after dinner.

Biancosarti (Italian; 56 proof): Produced by Luigi Sarti and Sons of Bologna, since 1885. It is a spirit-based aperitif with a yellow color and a bouquet and initial taste of cloves and cinnamon. Bittersweet, it is reminiscent of vermouth. It is best served chilled from the refrigerator.

Byrrh (French): A proprietary mistelle-based aperitif, it has a ruby red color, hints of cocoa in its taste, and a bittersweet aftertaste. Byrrh is best when served with soda, over ice.

Campari (Italian; 48 proof): First developed by fourteen-year-old Gaspare Campari shortly after 1862, in Milan. This ruby-red, bitter beverage is a mixture of aromatic extractions from herbs, roots, plants, and fruits. In 1932 a premixed Campari and soda was first introduced based upon the overwhelming popularity of that beverage. It is currently sold in more than 170 countries. Campari is best when served with seltzer water and a twist of lemon.

Cynar (Italian; 34 proof): A zesty, bittersweet aperitif, it is made from artichokes. It was conceived in 1950 by Angelo Dalle Molle; the company's current United States president, A. Charles Castelli, says that Cynar "makes what follows taste softer, taste better." This assertion is based in part on a scientific research paper presented in 1934. Dr. Linda Bartoshuk (a Yale taste physiologist) found that after eating globe artichokes 60 percent of 250 participants in her study reported that water tasted different—some claimed that it even tasted sweet. Cynar is best when served over ice with a twist of lemon or orange.

Dubonnet (American; 18 percent alcohol): First formulated by Joseph Dubonnet in 1846 in Chambery, France. The red and white Dubonnet wines have a semidry taste and a full-bodied flavor. Dubonnet was first introduced into the United States in 1934, and because of its popularity is now produced in California, under French license. It is best when served chilled from the refrigerator, or over ice with a twist of lemon.

Fernet Branca (Italian; 80 proof): A very dark, brown-black, extremely bitter beverage first introduced in 1845. It was the only alcoholic beverage that was allowed to be imported into the United States during Prohibition. It is best when served at room temperature as an aperitif.

Kir (French): This drink was named after the late mayor of the City of Dijon, France, Canon Félix Kir. Kir was the favorite drink of the mayor from the 1940s until his death in 1968 at age ninety-two. Originally, Kir was made by mixing Aligoté wine (a highly acidic white wine from Burgundy) with a tablespoon or so of crème de cassis, served chilled. Today just about any white wine is used and mixed with anywhere from several teaspoons to one-third of a glass of crème de cassis. Cassis is a black currant liqueur; to ensure one is using the best cassis, only those labeled Crème de Cassis should be used. Bottles labeled Liqueur de Cassis refer to a liqueur made from black currants macerated in brandy with added sugar.

Lillet (French): The firm was founded by Paul and Raymond Lillet, in 1872, in the small town of Podensac, near Bordeaux. Lillet (both red and white) is dry and full-bodied, with a fruity bouquet and a trace of citrus essence; it has a slightly astringent flavor. It is best when served well chilled, on the rocks with a twist of lemon or slice of orange, or with a splash of tonic or seltzer water.

Mistelles (also known as *mutes*): These are sweet wines produced by arresting or preventing fermentation by the addition of spirits. The process is called *mutage*. Some mistelles are used in the production of aperitifs and vermouths; others stand alone as aperitifs. Some examples are Panache, Pineau de Charentes, and Ratafia de Champagne.

Panache: Produced in California by Domaine Chandon, it is 18 percent alcohol. Panache is a Pinot Noir wine–based aperitif, made by selecting Pinor Noir juice that is either too highly colored or too fruity for sparkling wine production, and blending it with pure spirits (about 192 proof) before the juice ferments. Unlike a Ratafia, Panache is not wood aged, so it retains a brighter color and fresher, fruitier flavor. This is an aperitif with about 10 percent residual sugar, a sprightly acidity, and a fresh, fruity flavor. It is best when served chilled from the refrigerator or over ice with a twist of lemon. One of the best recipes (called a Chandon Judy) using Panache calls for pouring it over ice with a twist of lemon and adding one to two drops of bitters and a splash of Domaine Chandon Brut sparkling wine.

Pineau de Charentes (French; 80 proof): Similar to Panache, it is produced by adding cognac to must, thus stopping the fermentation of the fresh wine. All of the wine used must be at least 10 percent alcohol by volume, and the cognac must be of three-star quality. The combined wine and cognac is placed in casks and aged for two years in Limousin oak. The wine is filtered several times before bottling to clear it of any sediment that has developed. The last filtering is at −10°C; the finished product is 17 percent alcohol. Pineau de Charentes has been produced in the Cognac region since the sixteenth century. French law requires that only growers are permitted to produce Pineau, and only in years when the sugar content in the grape is sufficient to produce wines of 10 percent alcohol by volume. Reynac is the brand name of Pineau supported by the 4,500 growers of Unicoop cooperative.

Ratafia (French): Similar to Panache. The first written reference to ratafia appears in the eighteenth-century records of the French champagne house of Veuve Clicquot, although there is speculation that it was produced much earlier. Ratafias are generally aged for one year in wooden barrels, which gives the final product an oxidized color and taste. United States federal regulations prohibit use of the name for an American-produced product, hence, Domaine Chandon calls its ratafia Panache.

Rosso Antico (Italian): A concoction of wines from Lake Garda, Italy, blended with aromatic herbs; first produced in 1820. A brownish red color, light chocolate overtones in the taste, and a slightly bitter finish and aftertaste is characteristic of this beverage. Rosso Antico is best when served chilled from the refrigerator with a lemon or orange peel and a splash of seltzer water.

Spritzers: Delightful and refreshing drinks made with white, rosé, or red wines topped with seltzer, tonic water, or ginger ale, and garnished with lemon, lime, orange, a sprig of mint, or even a cherry. Spritzers are served on ice.

Unicum (Hungarian): A dark brown, spirit-based beverage produced by the Zwack family of Hungary for over 135 years. It is sold in a round bottle with a white cross on the label.

Serving and Storing Aperitifs

Aperitifs can be served at room temperature or well chilled, either directly from the refrigerator (this is the best way) or with plenty of *fresh* ice. When ice sits for more than three weeks it starts to draw in odors from frozen foods, and actually becomes stale. Wine-based aperitifs are approximately 18 percent alcohol and do not keep forever once opened. Their shelf life (unrefrigerated and opened) is not more than three to four weeks. Therefore, opened bottles should be refrigerated and consumed within six weeks.

Vermouth

According to the Bureau of Alcohol, Tobacco, and Firearms (BATF regulation 1976–C), vermouth is a type of aperitif wine that is made from grape juice and has the taste, aroma, and characteristics generally attributed to vermouth. The BATF regulations also state that aperitif wines fulfilling the characteristics of vermouth shall be so designated.

Vermouth is classified as an "aromatic" or "aromatized" wine, containing between 15 to 21 percent alcohol.

Hippocrates (460–377 B.C.), the Greek physician and "father of medicine" can perhaps be credited with "discovering" vermouth. His flavoring of wine with cinnamon and honey may not have closely resembled present-day vermouth but is certainly the earliest recording of the production of infused wine. More recently, in sixteenth-century Germany, Rhine wines were occasionally flavored with wormwood shrub flowers to give them a rather spicy but pleasant taste. The German word for wormwood is *Wermut*; when the Latin countries emerged as the chief producers of this type of wine in the eighteenth century, the word *Wermut* was written as *vermouth*.

The wine, as we know it today, originated in Turin, Italy in approximately 1757. Antonio Benedetto Carpano didn't introduce vermouth commercially until 1776, under the name Carpano. The French dry version had its birth in 1800, fathered by Joseph Noilly, later to join forces with Claudius Prat.

Since that time, both Italy and France have mastered the art of infusing and fortifying the wine and are the largest producers of high-quality vermouth.

Vermouth's Ingredients

Vermouth, although fortified, is often referred to as an "aromatic" wine, meaning a wine that has been altered by the infusion of *Artemisia absinthium* (any number of related aromatic plants) or bitter herbs. Some of the ingredients used (there are more than one hundred) are: allspice, angelica, angostura, anise, benzoin, bitter almond, bitter orange, celery, chamomile, cinchona, cinnamon, clove, coca, coriander, elder, fennel, gentian, ginger, hop, marjoram, mace, myrtle, nutmeg, peach, quinine, rhubarb, rosemary, saffron, sage, sandalwood, savory (summer), thyme, vanilla, and woodruff (May wine).

Types of Vermouth

The red vermouths, most notably those from Italy and France, are always sweet and contain approximately 130 to 160 grams of sugar per liter (13 to 16 percent residual sugar per 100 ml.). The white vermouths, also mainly from Italy and France, can be dry or semisweet and contain less than 40 grams of sugar per liter (four percent or less residual sugar per 100 ml.).

Vermouth Brand Names

Some of the better-known brands of vermouth are listed below.

Cinzano: The house of Cinzano of Turin, Italy, was established in 1757 by two brothers, Carlo Stefano and Giovanni Giacomo Cinzano. Cinzano produces a sweet red, extra dry white, and sweet white vermouth as well as a special formula labeled Antica.

Noilly Prat: Noilly Prat was established in 1843, when Claudius Prat joined forces with Louis Noilly, whose father had been making Noilly vermouth since 1800 in Marseilles. Noilly Prat makes a dry white and a sweet red vermouth.

Punt é Mes: Perhaps the most famous of all vermouths is this one from the Carpano family of Italy. Punt é Mes' history begins in 1786, in the Piazza Castello in Turin, where Antonio Benedetto Carpano, a well-respected bar and restaurant owner, tailored his vermouths to fit the individual preferences of his customers—adding a bit more of one herb or another, or a higher proportion of bitters (quinine). This was known as ordering vermouth by "points." As the story goes, one evening a group of businessmen involved in the stock exchange, met at Antonio's bar. One of them, still in conversation about the daily fluctuations of the market, absentmindedly told the barman, "Ca'm dag'n punt é mes" ("give me a point and a half," in Piemontese dialect), which caused great laughter in the bar. This story is purported to be fact and was confirmed by its last living witness, Maurizio Boeris, a barman, who died in 1944.

St. Raphaël: This is a French vermouth with a 16 percent alcohol content. Both red and gold varieties are sold; the vermouth was first produced in 1830 by a young Frenchman, Dr. Pierre Juppet of Lyons. St. Raphaël is bittersweet in flavor, and when mixed with equal parts of orange juice and poured over ice, makes a wonderful refreshing drink for any time of the day.

Some other brands of vermouth are Martini & Rossi, Stock, Cora, Boissiere, Duval, Ricadonna, and Berberini.

Serving and Storing Vermouth

Vermouth is basically a wine and should be treated as such. Once opened, it should be refrigerated and consumed within six weeks. After six weeks the sweet, and especially the dry, vermouth takes on a darker color and has a somewhat musty, "off" odor (at this point, it is advisable to use it only in cooking.) When serving vermouth, use plenty of ice and fresh citrus fruits. Dry vermouth is the indisputable and essential ingredient for a gin or vodka martini. If a dry vermouth is to be used only for martinis it is advisable to purchase it in half-bottles (375 ml.) to maintain freshness.

Vermouth can be served chilled "straight up," or over ice with a twist of lemon. A drink called a "blonde and a redhead" is made with equal parts of dry white and sweet red vermouth.

Sherry

Sherry is a fortified and blended nonvintage wine, made via the *solera* system; it contains 17 to 22 percent alcohol. It is traditionally produced in Spain, although certain other countries produce a similar product that they also call sherry.

Sherry originated in southwest Andalusía in the region of Jerez. The town of Jerez was founded by the Phoenicians in 1100 B.C., who brought their sailing ships to an inland city near the Bay of Cádiz off the Atlantic coast, and named it *Xera*. After the Roman conquest, Xera was latinized to *Ceret*, which the Moors pronounced as *Scheris*. This was subsequently hispanicized to *Jerez*, and anglicized, in reference to the beverage, into *sherry*.

The Jerez area is triangular in shape and lies between the Guadalquivir and Guadalete rivers in southwest Spain, with the Atlantic Ocean on the west. The official sherry-producing zone, known as the *zona de Jerez superiore,* or "zone of superior sherry," is bounded by three major towns: Puerto de Santa María, Sanlúcar de Barrameda, and Jerez de la Frontera. The entire Jerez area consists of some 55,000 acres of vineyards.

Law

The Spanish regulatory agency established in 1933 to guarantee the authenticity of sherry is the Consejo Regulador de la Denominación de Origin Jerez-Xérès-Sherry.

The tribunal High Court of England ruled in 1967 that only wine from Jerez may be identified simply as sherry, and that imitations must be labeled by their country of origin.

Grape Varieties Used

Palomino Blanco grapes are pale in color, fairly large, and grow predominantly in *albariza* soil. This grape is used in the production of 85 percent of all sherry wine. The grape is known locally by many different names: *listan*, in Sanlúcar; *horgazuela*, in Puerto de Santa María; in other areas it is known as *alban, temprana,* and *tempranilla.*

Pedro Ximénez and Moscatel grapes are used to sweeten sherry wine. The Pedro Ximénez grapes grow on the lower slopes of the *albariza* and *barro* soil, while Moscatel grapes grow chiefly on *barro* soil.

In the past, the vines were dug out after thirty to thirty-five years, and the land was either left fallow or was planted in other crops for some twenty years to prompt the root louse *Phylloxera* to leave the soil. Today, disease-resistant vines are grafted and utilized.

The Sherry Production Process

Grapes destined to be made into sherry are harvested, crushed and destemmed, and immediately sent to a press, where the first 85 to 90 percent of the liquid obtained is used to produce sherry. The remaining 10 to 15 percent, which is usually of a lower quality, is distilled into brandy, to be used later to fortify the sherry wine.

The must is allowed to ferment in large 130-gallon barrels made of American white oak. After all of the sugar has been metabolized by the yeast, resulting in a wine with 11 to 13 percent alcohol, the wine is racked off the lees (which separates the wine from its sediment, such as dead yeast, pits, and grape solids). It is then put into other barrels which are only partially (about 80 percent) filled and loosely "bunged" (referring to the tightness of the coopering on the barrels), which will help develop a sherry style.

The wine is then fortified with brandy made from the sherry wine, raising its alcoholic content to 15.5 percent. The high alcohol content favors the flor action and is sufficiently high to prevent acetification (vinegar production). Flor is a yeastlike substance *(Saccharomyces cerevisiae)* that forms a whitish film on the surface of certain sherries when the temperature in the cellar is between 60° and 70°F. After a year or so the wine under the flor develops a distinctive yeasty taste, which is technically due to a large increase in the aldehyde content of the wine. The longer the sherry "sits on" the flor, the more flavor it extracts, and the finer it becomes.

All types of sherry start out the same, for some relatively unknown reason flor forms on the surface of some barrels of sherry and not on others. When the flor forms a very thick white blanket, the sherry becomes a *fino*. If a thinner film forms, the sherry becomes an *amontillado*. If no film forms, the sherry becomes an *oloroso*.

After a period of eighteen to twenty-four months of aging undisturbed under the blanket of flor (if it forms) the wine is transferred to the winery's solera system. A *fino* will be sent to the *fino* solera, an *amontillado* to the *amontillado* solera, and so on.

According to some sherry producers, *solera* comes from the word *suelo*, meaning ground or land; and it refers to the butts (casks) nearest to the ground. Others say that it comes from the Spanish word *solar*, which refers to the tradition that holds a family together.

The solera system involves a series of white American oak barrels arranged in rows or tiers, often eight to ten barrels high (figure 7-1). The

Figure 7-1 Rows of barrels containing *oloroso* sherry in various stages of aging in the solera system. (Courtesy Sherry Wine Institute, New York)

arranging of barrels in tiers is not a requirement of the system or of law. The original or bottom row of barrels is called the *solera*, while the upper, or younger, rows, which are on the top, are called the *criaderas* (cradles). Each row is known as a *scale*, and moving the wine from tier to tier is often referred to as "playing the scales."

The wine that is sold first is that on the bottom row, which is then replaced with wine from the second tier, and so on up through as many as ten tiers. The wine from the most recent vintage is poured into the barrels on the top tier, which were not completely filled, thus the youngest wine is blended with a slightly older wine of the same type, which has in turn been blended with a still older wine, and so on down through the tiers. Wines of a superior quality are created in this way.

Wine is not syphoned from tier to tier, but is rather transferred into containers so that wine from various casks on the same level can be blended for even further standardization. By law, the maximum amount that can be drawn out of a barrel of fully mature sherry is 33 percent.

One of the reasons for the blending is to "tame" the young, rough wine. The key to the solera system is that aged sherries in the bottom "educate" the younger ones by giving them character and taste. The wine is also aerated as it passes from tier to tier, and in addition picks up subtle nuances from the oak barrels.

During this entire process, approximately 10 percent of the wine is lost through evaporation, whereas in an aging cellar where the barrels are tightly bunged the amount would be only 1.5 to 2 percent.

Blending. There are basically four types of sherry (in ascending order of sweetness): *fino, amontillado, oloroso,* and cream. These are broken down into subgroups which will be discussed later.

All sherries coming out of the solera are bone dry in taste, since during fermentation all sugar was metabolized by the yeast. During this stage of development a determination of the desired degree of sweetness of the final product is made. The sweet sherries, cream (also brown) and *oloroso,* are made by blending sweet wines made from the juice of Pedro Ximénez and Moscatel grapes. The Pedro Ximénez grapes are left outside in the sun, for twelve to fourteen hours to dry after harvesting, which concentrates their sugar levels. They are then placed on *esporto* mats (made of grass), to further dry. So intense is their sweetness, that fermentation usually stops at about 14 percent alcohol, resulting in a high degree of residual sugar.

Before final bottling, the sherry is, additionally, fortified with brandy, raising its alcoholic content to 17 to 22 percent. The sherry is then re-frigerated for several days to help "stabilize" it, eliminating cloudiness in the final product.

The Major Styles of Sherry

Fino sherries are made entirely from Palomino grapes, and are very dry, light, and pale in color, with a distinctive mild nutty-tangy taste.

Amontillado sherries have more color and body than *finos*, with a medium dry taste and nutty flavor. True *amontillado* sherries are the best to use for cooking, for they impart a nutty-tangy flavor to food. *Fino* sherry is too dry for cooking and seems to lack the *amontillado* sherries' charm and depth, while *oloroso* and cream sherries are simply too sweet.

Oloroso sherries are even fuller-bodied than either *fino* or *amontillado* sherries, and have an even deeper color. *Olorosos* are semisweet and display a more well-rounded flavor than the others.

Cream sherries are a rich, deep amber to a golden brown in color, and usually display an exquisite bouquet. They are very sweet and "creamy" to the taste. (An even sweeter cream sherry, made entirely from Pedro Ximénez grapes is called a "brown" sherry).

Other Sherries

What about the "other" sherries, which are not as popular or easy to find? They are:

Manzanilla. This is the palest, lightest, and driest *fino*-type sherry made. *Manzanilla* sherries are produced in the town of Sanlúcar de Bar-rameda, near the coast, at the mouth of the Guadalquivir River and approximately ten to fifteen miles outside of Jerez.

The grape harvest is usually about one week earlier in Sanlúcar than in other parts of the Jerez district. Therefore, the grapes usually come into the winery with slightly lower sugar levels and a higher level of tartaric acid. In many parts of Jerez it is the usual practice to dry the grapes in the sun to concentrate the grape sugar, but this is frequently eliminated in order to make *manzanilla*. These underripe grapes evolve, with the help of the ocean breezes, into fruit from which can be produced a fresh, clean, delicate, and extremely light and dry sherry. *Manzanillas* are also more astringent or "tonic" in taste than *fino* sherries, which is probably due to both the ocean breezes and the unique soil content of the vineyards where the grapes are grown.

The characteristic saltiness or tanginess of this wine has caused writers and winemakers for decades to speculate on its uniqueness. It was originally believed that because of the salty sea breezes, the grapes and resulting wine retained the salty taste. However, it has been demonstrated that when must or wine from Jerez is transported to Sanlúcar and allowed to obtain its natural flor, the resulting wine acquires the *manzanilla*-type salty taste. Also demonstrated was that when must or wine from Sanlúcar was transported to Jerez, it took on the characteristics of a *fino* sherry, but with more saltiness. A reasonable explanation is that Sanlúcar, because of its close proximity to the sea, has an unusually high water table with numerous shallow wells; it is considered the wettest spot in the entire Jerez area. The sherry flor yeast *Saccharomyces beticus* thrives on this wetness, thereby imparting the unique salty flavor to the wines which can be described as "olive cassee."

Manzanilla sherry is pale green to gold in color, with a bouquet reminiscent of the taste of a ripe apple. It is slightly bitter in taste, and should always be served chilled (not over ice); if refrigerated after opening, it will keep for several weeks. *Manzanillas* are usually at their best if consumed within six months of bottling. *Manzanilla* is equally fine with spicy sausages, heavily smoked ham, tangy shellfish dishes, salted nuts, sharp and strong cheeses, olives, pungent and tangy foods, and piquant snacks. Unfortunately, *manzanilla* is made in small quantities and therefore has a limited distribution in the United States. Two *manzanillas* available are La Guita and La Gitana.

Palo cortado. This is a true rarity among sherries. Although there is no literal translation for *palo cortado*, these sherries have been described as belonging to an intermediate classification—they are the lightest of the *olorosos*. *Palo cortado* has a very fresh and clean bouquet, somewhat resembling a well-made *amontillado*, yet its taste is reminiscent of a full-bodied *oloroso*.

Like all fine sherries, the *palo cortados* are produced from Palomino grapes which are grown in the chalky *albariza* soil unique to the Jerez region. They do not develop any type of flor, and are quite rare. Of a thousand barrels of wine, perhaps only one will develop the distinctive color of brushed gold, the bouquet of almonds, the *amontillado* nose, and the *oloroso* body which are characteristic of *palo cortados*. Therefore, a sherry producer cannot make this style of sherry every year, and its production amounts to less than one percent of the total. The production of *palo cortado* was greatly cut by the devastation of *Phylloxera* during the 1880s.

Palo cortado is an elegant wine and should be enjoyed as one would a brandy or cordial. It will keep for many weeks without refrigeration. This wine is good with moderately sharp cheeses, mild hors d'oeuvres, and soups. Several *palo cortados* are in limited distribution in the United States. As with all sherry styles, each *bodega* (winery) strives for individuality in its brand, so that color, bouquet, and flavor will vary from producer to producer. Williams & Humbert produce a very dry *oloroso* called Dos Cortados which, although not a *palo cortado*, is somewhat similar. One *palo cortado* available is Sandeman's Royal Ambrosante Palo Cortado.

Pedro Ximénez. This is the sweetest and most viscous of the sherries. It is a rich, dark brown and liqueurlike in its concentration. It is traditionally served after meals in place of a brandy or cordial. Pedro Ximénez will keep for many weeks without refrigeration and complements cream pastries, English trifle, flans, sweet desserts, coffee, and hot chocolate. Several brands available are Pedro Domecq Vina No. 25, Zuleta Pedro Domecq, and Argueso Pedro Ximénez.

Serving and Storing Sherry

Sherry is a wine, and storage conditions applicable to wine apply to sherry. Most sherries come in either screw-top bottles or bottles with recorkable tops, and can thus be stored standing up. There is really no reason to store sherry for prolonged periods of time because it does not improve to any great degree with age and is usually ready to drink when bottled.

A *fino* or *amontillado* sherry should be refrigerated when opened and is best when consumed at up to three weeks. *Oloroso* and cream sherries are generally kept unrefrigerated and are best when consumed up to six weeks.

When serving a *fino* or *amontillado* (before dinner, as aperitifs), they should be prechilled, and at no time should be served over ice, which would dilute their flavor. *Oloroso* and cream sherries are best when served at room temperature (65° to 68°F); traditionally they are after-dinner drinks.

The Spaniards have special glasses for sherry—the six-ounce stemmed glass called *copa*, and the four-ounce *copita*. Both glasses allow for a generous serving of sherry with enough space to release the wine's complex bouquet. A four-ounce whiskey sour glass, which is similar in shape, is highly preferable to the two-ounce style filled to the brim, as is often seen in bars and restaurants.

The small, stumpy, and cylindrical glass in which *manzanilla* sherry is traditionally drunk is known as a *canas*.

Port

Port has been the official drink used for toasts by the English royal family for two centuries. In Portugal, its history goes back to before the birth of Christ. In fact, the Douro is the world's second legally demarcated wine region (Italy's Chianti Classico region was demarcated in 1716 by the grand duke of Tuscany). In 1756, during the era of the marquis of Pombal (almost two-hundred years before France's *appellation contrôlée* regulations became law), the Douro region was defined to protect the quality and good name of port (known as *Porto*, in Portugal). In that same year, Pombal reestablished the Oporto Wine Company.

The production of port is limited to a strictly defined area of approximately 1,500 square miles along the River Douro in northern Portugal. The slopes of the Douro, which have a very slatelike soil known as schist, are cut out and terraced for planting with vineyards. These walled terraces prevent erosion of the precious soil.

Grape Varieties Used

More than forty grape varieties are planted in the region and used to produce port; the varieties listed below are those most commonly used:

White	*Red*
Donzelinho	Bastardo
Francisca	Mourisco
Malvasia Fina	Mourisco de Semente
Moscatel Galego	Tinta
Rabigato	Tinta Roriz
	Tinto Cão
	Touriga Francesca
	Touriga Nacional

Production

When a wine master determines that the sugar level in the fermenting must is 12 to 15 percent (measured by an instrument called a *gluco-*

oenometer), he draws off the wine and pours it into casks which already contain a predetermined amount of Portuguese brandy. The two are mixed; the properties are usually 80 percent new wine and 20 percent brandy. At this point, fermentation is arrested by the addition of the brandy, leaving a wine with a high degree of sugar and an alcoholic content of approximately 18 to 22 percent. The wine is then barrel aged for a minimum of three years, except for vintage port, which is aged only two years.

It wasn't until 1678 that brandy or spirits were first added to the musts of port wines made in the Douro region that were destined for export. Brandy was, however, added earlier for wines that were consumed domestically.

Quality Controls and Regulations

The production and marketing of port are strictly controlled by the Instituto do Vinho do Porto (Port Wine Institute). Stringent laws govern the production of all port from the vine to the final product. An official certificate of origin is issued by the Port Wine Institute after careful tasting and examination of each lot. The official seal of guarantee over the neck of the bottle indicates approval by the Port Wine Institute.

The name *Porto* is also specifically protected by law in the United States. Since 1968, the only wine in the United States that can be called *Porto* is the fortified wine produced in Portugal's Douro region. Therefore, if a California wine producer decides to produce a portlike wine, he may not call it *Porto*; it must simply be labeled a port.

Types of Port

White ports. These tend to run from dry and slightly tangy to medium sweet. Generally, the must is allowed to ferment longer (imparting dryness) than for wines destined to become red port. Although some appear to be slightly oxidized, the drier ones are perfect aperitifs for a Portuguese dinner; they may also be enjoyed by themselves, slightly chilled, with some crackers or cheese during warm weather.

Ruby ports. Traditionally, these are the very youngest ports which take their name from their ruby color. Usually rich and fruity, they are best consumed when young. No cellaring is necessary.

Tawny ports. The name is derived from the tawny color of the wine;

this comes from long maturing in barrels, which causes the wine to lose some of its redness. Much smoother than ruby port, tawny port usually spends a minimum of six to eight years in cask (which helps round out the fieriness of the alcohol), resulting in a wine with a smooth texture and a touch of sweetness. Some tawny ports are described as having a nutty smell and taste. Tawny ports do not improve significantly in the bottle, for they have already matured in the cask and are ready to consume.

Late-bottled ports. (These are often referred to as LBVs, the *V* standing for vintage.) These are ports of a single vintage from March 1 to September 30, declared by the shipper during the fourth year after the vintage. The port is bottled between July 1 of that year and December 31 of the sixth year after harvest. Generally, late-bottled vintage ports are vintages not declared as vintage ports (see below), and are usually ready to drink when released.

Vintage ports. These are by far the greatest ports. Vintage ports are produced only in years that are declared by the shippers to be the very best (usually only three or four vintages in a decade). They are aged for two years in wooden casks, then bottled somewhere between July 1 of the second year and June 30 of the third year after the harvest. Vintage port is very difficult to drink in its youth because of its tannin, high alcohol, and concentration of fruit and sugar. However, those who are patient enough to wait fifteen to twenty years will be rewarded with one of the world's greatest fortified wines. Surprisingly, it was not until 1775 that the first vintage port was produced.

Serving Port

Port, because of its high alcohol and sugar levels, is usually best consumed during cool or cold weather.

When it is time to open a bottle of vintage port, the bottle should be stood upright for three to five days, which allows the crusted sediment to settle to the bottom. The bottle should be opened at least one to two hours prior to drinking; this will dissipate any "off" odors or gasses that might have developed under the cork. Port need not be chilled, and is best when drunk at cellar temperature.

Contrary to popular belief, port has a limited shelf life once opened, and should be consumed within several weeks—and vintage port deteriorates eight to twenty-four hours after opening and should be consumed at one sitting.

The English believe that the best accompaniment to port is Stilton cheese (from the blue cheese family) or a well-aged cheddar served with freshly shelled walnuts.

Madeira

The island of Madeira, in the Atlantic Ocean some 360 miles from the coast of Morocco, was discovered in 1418 by a Portuguese explorer nicknamed "O. Zarco the Squinter," during the rule of Prince Henry the Navigator. The island showed no sign of earlier occupation, and because of its dense covering of forest was given the Portuguese name *Madeira*, (island of wood). Before the island could be occupied, huge coast-to-coast forests had to be burned. It was reported that "operation fire" actually lasted some seven years! When the ashes finally blended with the fertile volcanic earth, a unique soil was formed which is composed of deep deposits of wood ash and humus; it is ideal for the making of Madeira wines.

The Production of Madeira

Madeira is a fortified wine (beginning in 1753), with an alcoholic content of 17 to 20 percent due to the addition of a high-proof, 99.6 percent pure alcohol. The sweeter Madeiras (Bual and Malmsey) are fortified with spirits before being put through the *estufagem* process, while the dry styles (Sercial, Verdelho, and Rainwater) are allowed to ferment completely dry, and are then put through the *estufagem* process before being fortified. Madeira owes its characteristic flavor to the fact that it is kept at high temperatures for from ninety days to six months in a special room called an *estufa*. *Estufas* are huge heating chambers or ovens that usually heat the wine at temperatures of 104° to 120°F for the first five months. During the sixth month, the temperature is allowed to drop to normal. The *estufa* gives the wine its characteristic cooked and burnt odor and taste. Madeira is uniquely rich in flavor with a sort of nutty, smoky, silky, burnt raisin taste. Its undertones are unmistakably of burnt wood with a tangy taste.

An accidental discovery was the origin of the use of *estufas*. The original exporters discovered that when Madeira was transported through the tropics in large sailing ships, it was of far better quality when it arrived at its destination than when it left the island. Madeira underwent a transformation from an ordinary table wine to a rich, complex wine with a nutty-tangy flavor. For this reason, and because it made wonderful ballast, Madeira was loaded onto ships bound for the East or West Indies and brought back months later for reexport to Europe. This wine would be called East India Madeira, which in fact greatly contributed to its increasing popularity. At that time, Madeira was shipped in large barrels called *pipes*, which contained 110.5 gallons (418 l.) of wine. In the 1790s, during the Napoleonic wars, it was difficult to find enough ships to make these round-the-world trips; there was also a blockade on all imports to the Americas. The Portuguese producers were therefore forced to find a new way to create the complex Madeiras without the hot voyages. Hence, the *estufagem* system was born.

Types of Madeira

There are five types of Madeira, four of which are named after the grape variety used.

Sercial. The sercial grape variety is viticulturally similar to the German Riesling, and was in fact brought to Madeira from Germany. In reality, however, it bears absolutely no resemblance to the Riesling in taste. Sercial is the driest Madeira; it is similar to a *fino* sherry, although slightly sweeter.

Verdelho. The Verdelho grape is a cross between the Spanish Pedro Ximénez and the Italian Verdea grape varieties. The wine is semidry and has a clean taste and a gentle, smooth flavor.

Rainwater. This wine was believed to have been created by Mr. Habisham, a local Madeira shipper from Savannah, Georgia. Mr. Habisham made very special blends of Sercial and Verdelho that were lighter and quite a bit paler (almost like rainwater) than most of the Madeiras that were consumed during that era (the early nineteenth century).

Bual or Boal. The grape variety is descended from the Pinot Noir of Burgundy, France. The wine is darker in color than either Sercial or Verdelho, with a sort of buttery aroma and a definite sweet taste.

Malmsey. Prince Henry the Navigator transplanted the Malvasia (Malvoisie) vines from Crete to Madeira. Malmsey is a luscious, sweet, rich wine, quite dark in color, similar to a cream sherry but with more character.

Vintage Dating

Since 1900 only thirteen vintages have been declared for Madeira wines. It is a striking fact that for Madeiras, the vintage is not declared until the wines have aged about twenty years; some vintages of the 1960s are now being considered to see if they qualify for vintage dating.

Most Madeiras produced today are either a nonvintage blend or are solera dated (produced basically in the same way as sherry wines).

Serving and Storing Madeiras

Madeiras are fortified wines and therefore will last a great deal longer than tables wines. It is best to keep bottles of Madeira lying on their sides until several days before serving. The bottles should then be carefully stood up to allow any sediment to settle to the bottom, and then decanted. Madeiras, once opened, have an unusually long shelf life provided that they are not exposed to high temperatures or excessive sunlight and air. In serving Madeira, never use ice, but rather chill the wine in the refrigerator. Sercial, Verdelho, and Rainwater Madeiras should be chilled and served as aperitifs. Bual and Malmsey should be served at room temperature after dinner in long tulip-shaped glasses that hold five to seven ounces.

Verdelho is the perfect Madeira to use when cooking, because it lends just enough flavor to the food. It is excellent in sauces, gravies, and in soups, especially turtle soup.

Madeiras are among the longest-lived wines in the world, some lasting as long as two-hundred or more years. Madeiras can legally be made in the United States, but these are a poor imitation at best, and fortunately very little is now produced.

Marsala

Marsala was first produced in the 1760s, when John and William Woodhouse, English merchants from Liverpool, came to Sicily to purchase soda ash to ship back to English soap makers. While in Sicily they tasted the local wine; after noting how similar it was to the already popular wines from Jerez and Madeira, they sent back several casks—60 pipes, or approximately 6,700 gallons—to England. But first they added alcohol, approximately two gallons of it to each barrel of wine, to ensure that it would survive the long voyage. England was so impressed with the quality of the newfound wine that John decided to stay behind with his sons to help cultivate Marsala wine. In 1773 Woodhouse founded a winery to produce Marsala for export to Great Britain.

The name *Marsala* is believed to have been derived from the Arabic *Marsh-El-Alla* (harbor of God).

The Marsala area and rules of production are limited by Law Number 1069, passed on November 4, 1950, which also designates three provinces of Sicily—Trapani, Palermo, and Agrigento—where Marsala can be produced. Marsala was granted its DOC designation on April 2, 1969 by a presidential decree.

The Production of Marsala

Marsala is both the name of a city in northwest Sicily and the name of a blend of grapes, most notably the Catarratto and/or Grillo grapes, with a maximum of 15 percent Inzolia allowed.

Like sherry and port, Marsala is a fortified wine; it bears some resemblance to Madeira, in that one or more of its constituents are cooked or heated during the processing. The white wines, rich in extracts and low in acid, are blended and allowed to ferment until dry. The blend is slowly heated for about twenty-four hours until it has been reduced to about one-third of its original raw volume. During this time the must becomes thick, sweet, and caramel-like. This cooked wine, called *cotto*, is then allowed to age.

The *cotto* is added to a base wine in a proportion of six parts *cotto* and six parts alcohol to one-hundred parts base wine. This process is used to make the sweet Marsala. The dry Marsala is made in the same way, except that less of the *cotto* is used—sometimes as little as one percent.

Marsala is aged in casks from a minimum of four months to as long as five years, and occasionally longer. During this time it takes on a deep brown color, with the original white wine imparting a dry undertaste to the general sweetness, which slowly reduces with age.

Types of Marsala

The Italian DOC law has set production rules for four versions of Marsala. They are:

Marsala vergine. This is considered to be the finest Marsala and is made by the solera system. By law it cannot contain less than 18 percent alcohol. What makes Marsala *vergine* so special is that it is made from the best wines of the vintage and must be aged for at least five years in cask before it can be sold by the producer; it is therefore extremely dry. When properly stored, Marsala *vergine* can be aged for ten to fifteen years.

Marsala fine. This version must be aged for a minimum of four months and have an alcoholic content of no less than 17 percent. It is the most heavily advertised and consumed of all Marsalas in the United States. It is often labeled I.P., for *Italia Particolare* or *Italia.*

Marsala superiore. This version must be aged for two years and have an alcoholic content of no less than 17 percent. It is made in basically two styles, dry and sweet. It is produced with the addition of a heated or cooked must (*cotto*), which gives the wine a delicate bitterness or caramel-like taste. This type of Marsala is occasionally labeled as follows:

L.P.	London Particular
S.O.M.	Superior Old Marsala
G.D.	Garibaldi Dolce
O.P.	Old Particular
P.G.	Particularly Genuine
C.O.M.	Choice Old Marsala

Marsala speciale. This version cannot be sold before the July following the vintage. It must contain a minimum of 18 percent alcohol, but its taste can be changed with other ingredients and flavorings. This version is designed to render the product useful in the preparation of desserts; flavors include strawberry, tangerine, coffee, banana, mocha, almond, cream, and egg.

Some of the best Marsala producers are Rallo, Florio, and Pellegrino.

Serving and Storing Marsala

Normal procedures for proper wine storage apply to Marsalas, except that most Marsalas come in screw-top bottles so that they can be stored upright. There is really no reason to age Marsala for extended periods of time, for it is sufficiently aged prior to bottling. Once opened, Marsala should be refrigerated, which will extend its shelf life to about one month.

Dry Marsala is an excellent aperitif served chilled from the refrigerator (not over ice, which dilutes the taste), while sweet Marsala is excellent after dinner, served at room temperature.

Other Fortified Wines

Commandaria, a fortified dessert wine from Cyprus, was originally known as Nama.

Commandaria is reputed to be one of the longest-lived of all wines, and will often display a solera date on its label.

In Spain, there is a sweet fortified dessert wine known as Malaga; a still sweeter version of this wine is called Lagrima.

Suggested Readings

Allen, H. Warner. *Sherry and Port*. London: Constable and Company, 1952.

Bradford, Sarah. *The Story of Port*. London: Christie's Wine Publications, 1978.

Cossart, Neil. *Madeira: The Island Vineyard*. London: Christie's Wine Publications, 1984.

Delaforce, John. *The Factory House at Oporto*. London: Christie's Wine Publications, 1979.

Jeffs, Julian. *Sherry*, 3d ed. London: Faber and Faber, 1982.

Sandeman, George G. *Port and Sherry: The Story of Two Fine Wines*. No publisher, 1955.

Wasserman, Sheldon and Pauline Wasserman. *Guide to Fortified Wines*. Piscataway, N.J.: Scarborough, 1983.

Discussion Topics and Questions

1. Why have port, sherry, Madeira, and Marsala always been associated with the British?
2. Are most wines that are used as aperitifs also equally as good served after dinner? If so, give several examples.

3. Construct a chart that shows the relative shelf life of fortified wines.

4. Compare the American production of port, sherry, Marsala, and Madeira to that of these wines' respective countries of origin.

5. How would one explain to a customer that although television commercials and print ads suggest that cream sherry be served over ice, it should really be served at room temperature?

6. There was a tradition in England that when a boy was born, a "pipe" of port was laid down for his twenty-first birthday. Is this practical or possible today?

7. To what degree have you noticed an increase or decrease in the consumption of aromatized and fortified wines in the past five years? Be able to back up your answer with statistics.

8. Should aromatized and fortified wines be merchandised to stand on their own, or should they accompany food? Cite examples using *fino, amontillado, oloroso,* and cream sherry.

9. Be able to discuss and describe the differences in taste between cream sherry, Malmsey Madeira, and sweet Marsala.

10. Sherry houses, unlike port houses, have always produced non-vintage sherries for commercial use. Wouldn't vintage dating be advantageous?

8

Brewed Beverages

This chapter discusses:

- Beer's ingredients, and the four-step brewing process.
- Retailer profitability; ways in which retailers can lose profits.
- The perfect glass of beer; and how Beer Clean Glasses can help to achieve it.
- Tips on draft beer.
- Various types of beer brewed throughout the world.
- Sake. How it is made, and various types available; how to serve it.

Beer

Beer is known to have existed 7,000 or more years ago. Pottery from Mesopotamia dating back to 4200 B.C. depicts fermentation scenes and shows kings sipping their version of beer through gold tubes. References to brewing have been found in hieroglyphics on the walls of ancient caves in Egypt. Archaeological discoveries show that beer was familiar not only to the Egyptians but also to the ancient Romans, Greeks, Assyrians, Babylonians, Incas, and Chinese. New York's Metropolitan Museum of Art has on display a wooden model of a c. 2000 B.C. brewery.

In the twenty-third century B.C. in China, beer was known as *Kiu.* Even the Vikings made beer at sea in their war ships and drank it out of the horn of a cow. In the Middle Ages, brewing was done in the home by women who were known as "brewsters."

In more modern times, Peter Minuit, after purchasing "New Amsterdam," established the first public brewery in 1622. William Penn, the famous American statesman, was probably the first to operate (in 1638) a brewery on a large commercial scale; it was located in Pennsbury,

229

Bucks County, Pennsylvania. Other famous patriots who owned breweries were Samuel Adams, Generals Israel Putnam and Charles Sumner, Ethan Allen, and George Washington. President John Adams (1783–1789) even owned and managed his own tavern.

Fraunces Tavern, the oldest tavern in America still in existence, was founded in 1762 by Samuel Fraunces, a black man. It is located at the corner of Pearl and Broad streets in Manhattan, where George Washington said farewell to his officers after a victory in 1783.

Beer's Ingredients

Water. Beer is approximately 90 percent water. Not all water is ideal for beer production, though it can usually be made so. Since water from any two areas is never exactly the same, breweries continually test samples from each plant location. The water is conditioned or treated when necessary to insure uniformity of product.

Malt. Barley that has been steeped (soaked in water) and allowed to germinate (sprout or begin to grow) is called *malt*. Malt is the basic ingredient in brewing and is often referred to as the "soul of beer." It contributes to its color and characteristic flavor. In some parts of the world, malt is the only cereal grain permitted to be used in making beer. (This is according to the German brewing purification law called the *Reinheitsgebot*, or Bavarian Purity Order. It was enacted in 1516 by Bavaria's Duke Wilhelm IV, who decreed that beer could be brewed only from malt, hops, and water, with no other additives except for yeast.)

Corn. The primary reason for adding corn grits to the brew is flavor. Corn grits tend to produce the milder, lighter beer preferred by the American consumer. Like malt, corn is a source of starch that is converted to sugar in the brewing process.

Hops. Hops are the dried, ripe blossoms of a perennial vine (*Humulus lupulus*) that are added to beer brews for flavoring. The characteristic bitter flavor of beer is attributable to the addition of hops or liquid hop extract. Hops also possess antiseptic properties that inhibit the growth of bacteria. This is particularly important in the brewing of the nonpasteurized draft beers.

Brewer's yeast. This is the agent that transforms wort sugars into alcohol and carbon dioxide. It is actually a microscopic cell that multiplies rapidly. At the end of fermentation the yeast population has increased approximately fourfold. It is the enormous number of yeast cells that makes possible the rapid conversion of wort to beer. While all brewer's yeasts have the ability to ferment sugars to alcohol and carbon dioxide, they can differ considerably in their abilities and hence affect beer flavor in various ways.

The Four-Step Brewing Process

Brewhouse. An exact weight of ground malt is mixed with a predetermined amount of corn grits and brewing water in the cooker. The enzymatic action of the malt solubilizes the starches during a precise time/temperature cycle. The solubilized starch is then transferred to the mash tun, which contains the main mash. Another precisely controlled time/temperature cycle converts the starches to fermentable sugars. The clear liquid, called *wort*, is separated from the grain by straining in the lauter tun. The wort is transferred to kettles and boiled. Hops are added in exact amounts to provide the distinctive flavor of beer. At the end of the timed boil period, the hot wort is pumped to a tank to allow settling of unwanted protein.

Fermentation. The wort is converted into beer during this stage. A small amount of brewer's yeast and a quantity of air are injected into the cooled wort as it enters the fermentation tanks. The yeast grows, producing enzymes that convert the sugar in the wort to alcohol and carbon dioxide gas (CO_2). Some of the CO_2 is collected and saved for later use. Fermentation takes about one week. When complete, the beer is filtered to remove yeast and other solids, then pumped to the aging tanks.

Aging. "Green beer" is allowed to rest for an extended period in the aging tanks. When properly aged, the beer is filtered a final time; if the carbonation level is low, additional CO_2 is added. Finished beer is then pumped to the packaging tanks.

Packaging. When the aging process has been completed, the finished beer is then packaged in bottles, cans, and kegs. After packaging, the bottle and can products are pasteurized over a period of approximately half an hour at a temperature that is allowed to rise to 140°F, then cooled down. Because it is pasteurized, packaged beer may be stored at room temperature without damage to the product (figure 8–1).

Product and Handling

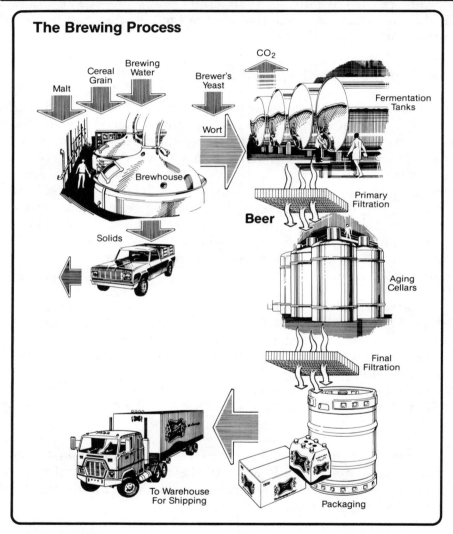

Figure 8–1 The brewing process. (Courtesy Miller Brewing Company, Wisconsin, Copyright 1982)

Draft beer, on the other hand, is not pasteurized. It is of a delicate and perishable nature, just like milk, eggs, and other perishables. Its flavor can be changed if it is not kept under constant refrigeration. The ideal storage temperature for draft beer is 38°F. If the temperature is allowed to rise above 45°F to 50°F for an extended length of time, secondary fermentation may occur, making the beer unpalatable.

Retailer Profitability

Draft: on-premise profitability. The impressive gains in draft beer sales during the last several years are positive indicators for 1980s sales. These gains have been in both the on-premise and off-premise markets. Both markets are of equal importance—the off-premise market because of its potential volume for draft beer, and the on-premise market because that is where consumer brand preference is determined.

Draft beer is the on-premise retailer's most profitable package. At a cost to the retailer of $35.00 per half-barrel, it returns an 81.2 percent profit, or a markup of 431.4 percent (using a 10-oz. hourglass with a ¾" foam head, at a selling price of 75 cents; see figures 8–2 and 8–3.)

Let us take a look at the profitability to the on-premise retailer and what it depends on. In addition to brand demand, the profitability of draft beer depends upon:

Proper temperature

A balanced system

Clean lines

Clean glasses

Proper glass shape and size

Drawing the perfect glass of beer

Four Steps for Pouring the Perfect Glass of Beer

1. Start with a sparkling clean glass that has been wetted in cold water. Place the glass at an angle, about one inch below the faucet. Open the faucet quickly, all the way.

2. Fill the glass until it is half full, gradually bringing it to an upright position.

The Draft Beer Profit Story

Profit per ½ barrel

A. Glass size _____ oz.

   Glass style _____

   Foam head _____

B. Number of glasses per ½ barrel (from Glass Chart) _____

C. Selling price per glass _____

D. Total dollar revenue per ½ barrel _____
   (C x B)

E. Cost per ½ barrel _____

F. Gross profit per ½ barrel _____
   (D - E)

G. % Margin...Profit on Selling Price _____
   (F - D)

H. % Mark-up...Profit on Cost _____
   (F - E)

I. Estimated ½ barrel usage (per week, month or year) _____

J. Gross profit (per time period selected) _____
   (I x F)

Profit per Glass

K. Cost per glass _____
   (E - B)

L. Gross profit per glass _____
   (C - K)

a

Example:

Profit per ½ barrel

A. Glass size ___10___ oz.

   Glass style ___Hour Glass___

   Foam head ___³/₄"___

B. Number of glasses per ½ barrel (from Glass Chart) ___248___

C. Selling price per glass ___75¢___

D. Total dollar revenue per ½ barrel ___$186.00___
   (C x B)

E. Cost per ½ barrel ___$35.00___

F. Gross profit per ½ barrel ___$151.00___
   (D - E)

G. % Margin...Profit on Selling Price ___81.2%___
   (F - D)

H. % Mark-up...Profit on Cost ___431.4%___
   (F - E)

I. Estimated ½ barrel usage (per week, month or year) ___315___

J. Gross profit (per time period selected) ___$47,565.00___
   (I x F)

Profit per Glass

K. Cost per glass ___14.1¢___
   (E - B)

L. Gross profit per glass ___60.9¢___
   (C - K)

b

Figure 8–2a–b The draft beer profit story. (Courtesy Miller Brewing Company, Milwaukee, Wisconsin, Copyright 1982)

Here's how many glasses you can expect from a ½ barrel

TYPE OF GLASS	SIZE	1" HEAD	¾" HEAD	½" HEAD
		APPROXIMATE GLASSES PER ½ BBL.	APPROXIMATE GLASSES PER ½ BBL.	APPROXIMATE GLASSES PER ½ BBL.
SHAM PILSNER	8 oz.	343	325	283
	9 oz.	292	279	260
	10 oz.	265	245	223
	12 oz.	221	204	186
TULIP GOBLET	8 oz.	305	292	275
	10 oz.	248	230	207
	11 oz.	227	209	185
	12 oz.	210	191	167
FOOTED PILSNER	8 oz.	325	292	280
	9 oz.	282	259	245
	10 oz.	250	233	215
SHELL	7 oz.	360	336	315
	8 oz.	315	292	275
	9 oz.	270	255	243
	10 oz.	245	236	220

TYPE OF GLASS	SIZE	1" HEAD	¾" HEAD	½" HEAD
		APPROXIMATE GLASSES PER ½ BBL.	APPROXIMATE GLASSES PER ½ BBL.	APPROXIMATE GLASSES PER ½ BBL.
HOURGLASS	10 oz.	264	248	233
	11 oz.	235	220	205
	12 oz.	220	204	189
	13 oz.	198	184	173
MUG STEIN	10 oz.	248	233	223
	12 oz.	203	189	176
	14 oz.	169	158	153
	16 oz.	149	140	134
HEAVY GOBLET	9 oz.	378	331	294
	10 oz.	330	296	264
	12 oz.	248	220	204
	14 oz.	209	194	172

PITCHER	SIZE	1" HEAD	1½" HEAD
		APPROXIMATE PITCHER PER ½ BBL.	APPROXIMATE PITCHER PER ½ BBL.
	54 oz.	47	50
	60 oz.	39	42
	64 oz.	35	38

275053   LA

Figure 8–3   How many glasses from a half-barrel. (Courtesy Miller Brewing Company, Milwaukee, Wisconsin, Copyright 1982)

3. Let the remaining beer run straight down the middle. This insures a ¾" to 1" head—your source of profit. Do not let the glass touch the faucet.

4. Close the faucet completely and quickly.

It is important to remember that for maximum profit and a glass of beer with eye and taste appeal, it should be served with a good foam head, and that a perfect glass of beer shows a ring of foam after every delicious sip.

A Clean Beer Glass

The glass is the last link between a finely brewed beer and your customer. A clean glass is necessary in order to serve beer at its best—it assures your clientele of the best in taste and eye appeal and tells them that you value their business. How can you maintain your glassware to keep customers coming back again and again? The most effective system is a three-compartment sink.

Sink number one has an overflow pipe with a funnel strainer in which residue from beer glasses is poured (all sinks have overflow pipes to maintain a constant water level). This sink is filled with warm water and glass cleaner.

Sink number two is the rinsing compartment, filled with cool water. A slow but steady stream of cool water should be allowed to run into this compartment throughout the washing operation.

Sink number three is the sanitizer, filled with clean cool water. Where required or preferred it contains a carefully measured amount of sterilizing compound.

The five steps to clean beer glasses are:

1. Thoroughly clean your sinks prior to washing glasses.
2. Empty all contents of the glasses into the funnel located in sink number one. Scrub the glasses vigorously using a low-suds glass-cleaning detergent and, wherever possible, motorized brushes. Use odor-free, nonfat cleaning compounds made especially for beer glass cleaning; oil-based detergents can leave a film on glasses.
3. Thoroughly rinse the glasses in the fresh, cool water that should be constantly flowing into sink number two. Always place the glass bottom down in the rinse to eliminate the chance of air pockets forming and/or improper rinsing.

4. Repeat the same rinse operation in the third sink. Remember that many states require the use of sanitizers. If sanitizers are used, measure the amount very carefully to insure that no odor or taste is left on the glass.

5. Air dry the glass by placing it upside down on a deeply corrugated drainboard, which allows air to enter the inverted glass and complete the drying operation by evaporation. Never dry glasses with a towel or place them on a towel or on a flat surface such as a bar or countertop. Residue from bleaches or detergents in cloth can impart an odor to the glass and spoil the delicate flavor of the beer.

Tips on Draft Beer

The following are important to remember for ideal storage and serving conditions for draft beer:

The walk-in cooler in which draft beer is stored should be kept at 36° to 38°F. Trips into the walk-in cooler should be minimized to maintain a constant temperature. The CO_2 pressure valve should not be tampered with; CO_2 pressure should be left constant to match the specifications of the draft system. *Clean* beer glasses (see above) should always be used. Finally, for ease of tapping, follow these steps: (1) With the tavern head tapping handle in the up position, align lug locks on the tavern head with the lug housing on the top of the keg. Insert the tavern head. (2) Give the tavern head a one-quarter clockwise turn, so that it is secured to the keg. (3) Pull the tapping handle downward to locking position. This will open the beer and CO_2 valves. The keg is now tapped (see figures 8–4 and 8–5).

Problems with Draft Beer

The following, according to the Miller Brewing Company (Milwaukee, Wisconsin) are some common problems that can occur with draft beer equipment, storage, and service. The list indicates both problems and their possible causes:

Flat beer

Greasy glasses
Not enough pressure

Keg Identification

All Miller Brewing Company kegs are dated and carry plant, shift, strength, and product identification. Information is stamped on the aluminum tap cover and printed with ink on two sides of the keg.

Example:

Brand
"Don't sell" date
Plant
Shift
Beer strength

Brand

Each Miller Brewing Company brand is identified with a two letter brand code. In addition, a color coded brand logo is printed on each foil tap cover.

Brand	Code	Foil Tap Cover
Miller High Life	MR	Gold on White
Lite	XX	Blue on White
Lowenbrau Special	NL	Blue on White
Lowenbrau Dark	ND	Brown on White

XX 07162 1 1 Z

"Don't sell" date

A five-digit month/date/year is included in the keg identification. This date is referred to as the "don't sell" date and specifies the last day that the product may be offered for sale in the retail trade.

Example:

07162 would represent the 7th month, 16th day, and 82nd year...or July 16, 1982.

To insure product freshness, the "don't sell" date on all Miller Brewing Company kegs falls 60 days after the keg was racked. All kegs, however, should be sold to the retailer within 45 days. To determine the date, subtract 15 days from the 60-day "don't sell" date. In our example 07162, the keg should be sold to the retailer by July 1, 1982.

July 16, 1982 would be the last day this keg could be sold to the consumer and should be picked up (where legal) and returned to the distributorship any date after July 16, 1982.

XX 07162 1 1 Z

Plant

The following one-digit numbers have been assigned to our plants for the purpose of identification:

Milwaukee	1	Irwindale	6
Fulton	3	Albany	7
Fort Worth	4	Trenton	8
Eden	5		

a

XX 07162 1 1

Shift

This information is provided for quality control purposes.

XX 07162 1 1 Z

Beer strength

Regular strength beer is designated by the letter "Z".

3.2 beer (maximum 3.2% alcohol by weight) is designated by the letter "A" and two vertical red stripes are printed on aluminum tap cover

Keg Information

Receiving and Storing Draft Beer at the Warehouse

When draft beer arrives, it should be immediately transferred to the draft beer cooler and stored at a temperature of 38° Fahrenheit.

Stock Rotation

Each shipment received should be dated to insure proper stock rotation.

Cooling Time

The kegs should be held in storage for a minimum of two days before delivering to the retail trade.

■ The two days holding period allows the beer time to settle and attain the proper temperature for delivery.

Temperature Check Twice Daily

An accurate thermometer placed in a bottle of water (this ensures that when the cooler door is opened the warm air does not affect the thermometer) should be strategically located in the cooler to insure all locations are at the proper temperature.

■ Check the temperature twice daily (morning and evening) and record on the Miller draft beer cooler temperature record chart.

Delivery and Return of Kegs

All kegs full or empty must be handled with care to avoid damage to the container or product.

■ Rope or rubber bumpers should be used to break the fall when unloading kegs from the draft beer truck.

b

Cooperage and Tapping Equipment

Ideally the last keg delivered should be as cold as the first.

■ A refrigerated truck assures this kind of delivery. If volume does not warrant a refrigerated truck, a closed insulated truck can be used. The kegs should be kept cold by covering them with an insulated blanket.

■ During hot months, non-refrigerated trucks should return to the warehouse and exchange warm kegs for cold ones. The warm ones should be put back in the cooler and cooled down to the proper temperature prior to delivery.

Empty kegs must be promptly collected from the retail trade and stored in a protected area until they are returned to the brewery.

■ Prompt return of empty kegs to the brewery will insure a smooth flow of product to the trade. It requires four kegs to maintain one keg in a retail account.

Care and Handling by the Retailer

Every retail account can serve a fine glass of draft beer if careful attention is given to draft

beer equipment, storage facilities, dispensing methods and cleanliness. Storage facilities for draft beer should:

■ Be used for draft beer only. Keep doors closed as much as possible to maintain a constant, uniform temperature of 36° to 38°.

■ Be large enough to handle potential as well as present volume.

■ Be properly insulated.

■ Have an accurate thermometer which is located away from pipes, coils and other cooling equipment.

The retailer's stock should be rotated during delivery of draft beer.

■ Always place the most recently delivered kegs in back of any kegs already in the cooler.

■ In replacing kegs in series, always move a partial keg to the CO_2 source (Position 3) and rotate backup stock into the series nearest the faucet (Position 1).

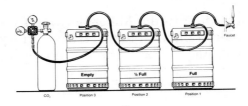

c

Figure 8–4*a–c* Cooperage and tapping equipment. (Courtesy Miller Brewing Company, Milwaukee, Wisconsin, Copyright 1982)

TAP-O-MATIC Tapping Guide

(for Perlick Tavern Head)

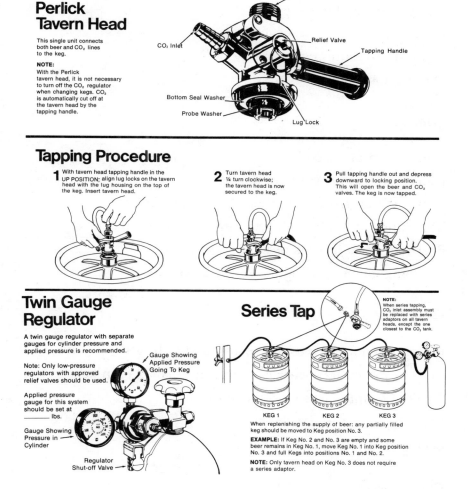

Perlick Tavern Head

This single unit connects both beer and CO₂ lines to the keg.

NOTE:
With the Perlick tavern head, it is not necessary to turn off the CO₂ regulator when changing kegs. CO₂ is automatically cut off at the tavern head by the tapping handle.

Beer Outlet
CO₂ Inlet
Relief Valve
Tapping Handle
Bottom Seal Washer
Probe Washer
Lug Lock

Tapping Procedure

1 With tavern head tapping handle in the UP POSITION; align lug locks on the tavern head with the lug housing on the top of the keg. Insert tavern head.

2 Turn tavern head ¼ turn clockwise; the tavern head is now secured to the keg.

3 Pull tapping handle out and depress downward to locking position. This will open the beer and CO₂ valves. The keg is now tapped.

Twin Gauge Regulator

A twin gauge regulator with separate gauges for cylinder pressure and applied pressure is recommended.

Note: Only low-pressure regulators with approved relief valves should be used.

Applied pressure gauge for this system should be set at _____ lbs.

Gauge Showing Applied Pressure Going To Keg

Gauge Showing Pressure in Cylinder

Regulator Shut-off Valve

Series Tap

NOTE:
When series tapping, CO₂ inlet assembly must be replaced with series adaptors on all tavern heads, except the one closest to the CO₂ tank.

KEG 1   KEG 2   KEG 3

When replenishing the supply of beer: any partially filled keg should be moved to Keg position No. 3.

EXAMPLE: If Keg No. 2 and No. 3 are empty and some beer remains in Keg No. 1, move Keg No. 1 into Keg position No. 3 and full Kegs into positions No. 1 and No. 2.

NOTE: Only tavern head on Keg No. 3 does not require a series adaptor.

Figure 8–5 Tap-O-Matic tapping guide. (Courtesy Miller Brewing Company, Milwaukee, Wisconsin, Copyright 1982)

Flat beer (continued)

Pressure shut off during night

Precooler or coils too cold

Leaky pressure lines

Loose tap or vent connections

Sluggish pressure regulators

Obstruction in lines

Wild beer

Beer drawn improperly

Faucets in bad or worn conditions

Kinks, dents, twists, or other obstructions in lines

Beer runs are too long or lines are not well insulated

Beer too warm in kegs or lines

Creeping gauge causing too much pressure

False head

Pressure required does not correspond to beer temperature

Coils or direct draw beer lines warmer than beer in keg

Small lines into large faucet shanks

Drawing too short a collar

Beer drawn improperly

Cloudy beer

Beer was overchilled or frozen

Beer in keg was too warm at some point

Hot spots in beer lines

Beer lines in poor condition, or dirty

Bad taste

Dirty faucets

Old or dirty beer lines; foul air in lines

Failure to flush beer lines with water after each keg emptied

Unsanitary conditions at the bar

Oily air; greasy kitchen air

Temperature of keg too warm

Dry glasses

Ways to Lose Profits

Beer is very sensitive to temperature and pressure, and foams as a result. If the draft beer is allowed to warm, the liquid and gas will separate and gas bubbles will form in the lines. When beer is drawn, it foams and gasses. This wastes beer, and profits go down the drain: foam is about 25 percent liquid beer.

Beer is best when served in a perfectly clean glass, with a good head of foam—foam that lasts. A thick, rich, creamy foam should cling to the glass as each sip is taken. There is an appearance factor here: the better the beer looks, the more you'll sell. Beer served in a near-clean glass is less than the best. The head goes flat because of an invisible film from inadequate cleaning methods and incompatible petroleum-based sanitizers; the glass must be filled almost to the top, and bubbles stick to its sides. The near-clean glass ruins the beer's appearance and your profits.

Beer served in a ten-ounce hourglass with a one-inch head yields 264 glasses from a half-barrel. The same ten-ounce glass of beer, minus the head, yields only 198 glasses—that's a loss of 66 glasses. At $1.00 per glass, there is $66.00 more gross profit in every half-barrel when beer is properly served (see figure 8–3).

Cans Versus Bottles

There are some major differences in the use of canned versus bottled beers. Although cans chill faster than bottles, they also lose their chill faster; bottles take longer to chill but retain the cold longer. Cans are lighter in weight, easier to stack, and are nonbreakable.

Cans, unlike bottles, have an "image problem" in restaurants and bars; this is the main reason why canned beer is rarely served. Contrary to popular belief, there is absolutely no difference in taste between canned and bottled beer. The cans used today do not give off a metallic taste, as they once did.

Beer Classification

The use of a type of yeast that will generally convert sugars to alcohol and CO_2 at lower temperatures is called *bottom fermentation.* Bottom-fermenting yeast is sometimes referred to as *lager yeast.* Slower fermentations are associated with this yeast. The types of beer described below are bottom fermented.

Lager. Lager was developed in Germany in about the seventh century. It was first introduced into the United States by the Germans in 1840. *Lager* comes from the German word *lagern* (to store), and is applied to bottom-fermented beer in particular because it must be stored at low temperatures for prolonged periods of time. Lagers were traditionally stored in cellars or caves for completion of fermentation. They are bright gold to yellow in color, with a light to medium body, and are usually well carbonated. Unless stated otherwise, virtually every beer made in the United States (more than 90 percent of them) is a lager. Lager is ideally served at 38° to 45°F.

Bock beer. Bock beer is produced from grain that is considerably higher in extracts than the usual grains destined for use in lager beers. *Bock,* in German, means a male goat. Bock beer was originally produced around 1200 A.D. in the town of Einbeck, Germany. Today it is produced in virtually every country, in some form or another, on a seasonal basis, mostly during the winter so that it can be consumed in the early spring. Bock beers are usually quite dark in color with an intense, sharp, sweet aroma. They have a full-bodied flavor, followed by a slightly sweet, malty taste. A stronger version produced in very limited quantities in Germany is called *Doppelbock.* Bock beer is ideally served at 45° to 50°F.

Dark beer. Dark beer is characterized by a very deep, dark color, a full-bodied flavor, and a creamy taste, with overtones of malt, bitterness, sweetness, and caramel. It is usually produced from the addition of roasted barley during the initial brewing stages. It should be served at approximately 45° to 50°F.

Kulmbacher beer. This is beer that comes from Kulmbach, Germany. Some Kulmbacher beers are reported to have as much as 14 percent alcohol by weight, but those exported to the United States have far less. Kulmbacher beer is ideally served at 38° to 45°F.

Light beer. Light beer is usually produced by the dilution of regular beers that have been brewed with the use of high-extract grains or barley and have been allowed to ferment dry. Another method of production involves the addition of enzymes, which reduce the number of calories and the beer's alcoholic content; its flavor is also considerably lighter. The purpose of producing light beer is to make a lower-calorie beer. A regular twelve-ounce beer has 135 to 170 calories; a light beer usually has under 100 calories. There are no current Bureau of Alcohol, Tobacco and Firearms rulings on minimum or maximum calorie levels. Light beers are ideally served at 38° to 45°F.

Malt liquor. This is an American term for a lager beer with a considerably higher level of alcohol (usually above 5 percent) than most lager beers or ales. Tastes vary from brewery to brewery and brand to brand, with some even sweetened with fruit syrup. The name comes from the beer's malty flavor, which has overtones of bitterness. Its color is typically darker than that of regular beers, and its taste is correspondingly heavier and fuller-bodied. Malt liquor is ideally served at 38° to 45°F.

Munich (or Münchener). This type of beer was originally produced in Bavaria; it is now brewed in many parts of the world. It is slightly darker in color than Pilsner-type beers, although milder and less bitter than other German types. It also has a more pronounced malty aroma and taste, with a sweet finish and aftertaste. Munich beer is ideally served at 38° to 45°F.

Pilsner (or pilsener). This is the most popular type or style of beer produced in the world. The word *Pilsner* is taken from the Czech town of Pilsen. Characteristically, these beers are a light golden color, with a highly pronounced hops (referred to as *Bohemian*) flavor and a delightfully clean, crisp taste that refreshes and leaves the palate clean. Pilsner-style beers are usually dry to very dry in taste, although there are some slightly sweet pilsners produced. Pilsners are ideally served at 38° to 45°F.

Top fermentation refers to the use of a type of yeast that generally w⁣ convert sugars to alcohol and CO_2 at temperatures between 60° and 70°F. The beers described below are all top-fermented beers.

Ale. Ale is a top-fermented beer with a slightly darker color than lager beer. It usually has more hops in its aroma and taste and is often lower in carbonation than lager-type beers. Ale is usually bitter to the taste, with a slight tanginess, although some ales can be sweet. Ales are usually fermented at warmer temperatures than lager-type beers (60° to 70°F) for from three to five days, and generally mature faster. Ales should ideally be served at 38° to 45°F.

Cream ale. This is a blend of ale and lager beer. Cream ale is highly carbonated which results in a rich foam and strong effervescence. Cream ale is ideally served at 38° to 45°F.

Porter. This is the predecessor of stout, and is characterized by its intense dark color and persistent bittersweet taste and aroma. It is lower in alcohol than stout and should ideally be served at 55°F. It was invented in 1729 by Ralph Harwood, a London brewer, who named it after the porters who enjoyed drinking it.

Stout. This beer obtains its dark (almost black) color from roasted barley, which has a very high extract level. It contains mostly this roasted barley, which is rendered sterile before germination, and a small amount of malt for added flavor. It is quite thick and malty, with an intense bitterness and underlying sweet taste. Stout is relatively low in carbonation and should be served at 55°F.

Weisse beer (or Weizenbier). This is the German name for a beer made predominantly from wheat. It is usually unfiltered and contains some yeast residue, and therefore is cloudy in appearance. *Weisse* beer is ideally served at 38° to 45°F.

Beer Brands

United States beers

Anchor	Ballantine	Blatz
Andeker	Bergheim	Blue Fox
Augsburger	Black Horse	Break Special

Budweiser	Koch's	Piel's
Bull's Eye	L.A.	Primo
Busch	Lite Beer	Porter
Carling	Lone Star	Prior
Champale	Löwenbräu German	Rainier
Champion	Magnum	Reading
Chesterfield	Matt's	Red, White & Blue
Cold Spring Export	Maximus	Rheingold
Colt 45	McSorley's	Robin Hood
Coors	Meister Bräu	Rolling Rock
Coqui 900	Michelob	Schaefer
Erlanger	Mickeys	Schlitz
Falls City	Miller	Schmidt's
Fort Schuyler	Milwaukee	Schoenling
Fox Head 400	Naragansett	Simon
Gablinger	Natural Light	Stegmaier
Genesee	New Amsterdam	Steinbrau
Gibbons	Olde English	Sterling
Hamm's	Old German	Stroh's
Henry Weinhard	Old Milwaukee	Tuborg
Hudepohl	Olympia	Utica Club
Iroquois	Ortlieb's	Wiedemann
Jax	Pabst	Yuengling
Knickerbocker	Pearl	

Australia

Cooper	Leopard	Tasmanian
Foster's	Swan	Tooths

Austria

Goldfassl	Steffl	Zipfer Urtyp
Gösser		

Belgium

Duvel	Riva 2000	St. Sixtus
Orval Trappist	Rodenbach	

Brazil

Brahma   Rioco

Canada

Canadian 55	Molson	Ontario Special
Grizzly	Moosehead	Trilight
Iron Horse	O'Keefe	Yukon Gold
Labatt's	Old Vienna	

China

Sun Lik   Taiwan   Tsingtao

Czechoslovakia

Pilsner Urquell

Denmark

Carlsberg	Lolland-Falsters	Tuborg
Harboes	Scandia	

Ecuador

Club

England

Bass Ale	London Pride	Tolly
Beaver	Mackeson Stout	Vaux Double Maxim
Charles Wells	Old Peculier	Watney
Cheshire	Samuel Smith	Whitbread
John Courage	Stingo	

Finland

Finlandia   Koff

France

33 Export   Fischer   Kronenbourg

Germany

Altenmunster	Eku	Kulmbacher Mönschof
Augustinerbrau	Euler	Paulaner
Beck's	Fürstenberg	Pinkus
Berliner Weisse	Hacker-Pschorr	Radenberger
Club Weibe	Herrenhauser	Spaten
D.A.B.	Hofbrau	St. Pauli Girl
Dinkelacker	Holsten	Stern
Doppelspaten	Isenbeck	Ur-Märzen
Dortmunder	Kaiserdom	Würzburger

Greece

Aegean Hellas   Spartan

Holland

Amstel Light	Oranjeboom	Three Horses
Grolsch	Royal Dutch	
Heineken	Skol	

India

Eagle

Ireland

Guinness Stout   Harp

Italy

Crystall	Nastro Azzurro	Poretti
Moretti	Peroni	Raffo

Jamaica

Red Stripe

Japan

Asahi	Kirin	Sapporo
Suntory		

Luxembourg

Diekirch

Martinique

Biere Lorraine

Mexico

Bohemia	Dos Equis	Superior	Corona
Carta Blanca	Modelo	Tecate	

New Zealand

Steinlager

Norway

Aass	Ringnes	Rok

Philippines

Manila	San Miguel

Poland

Krakus

Portugal

Sagres

Scotland

Belhaven	McEwan's	NewCastle
Lorimer		

Sweden

Kalback

Switzerland

Cardinal   Hopfenperle

Thailand

Amarit   Payap   Singha

Sake

Sake is an ancient fermented beverage known to have been made since approximately 3000 B.C. in China. But it was not until about six-hundred years ago that sake as we know it today was produced.

In ancient times the making and serving of sake by experienced brewers called *toji,* was only entrusted to women, who had to be virgins. *Sake* means "the essence of the spirit of rice"; it is made from rice and is legally defined as a rice beer.

The rice used to make sake is "polished," so that the part used for final production is much less than the whole grain—often not much more than the heart of the kernel. The quality of the finished sake is based upon the size (the smaller the better) of the rice kernel after polishing: it is accepted that the finest sake is made from rice that has been polished down to 50 percent of its original size. The polished rice is soaked in cold distilled water for twelve to eighteen hours to absorb moisture, then steamed for about forty-five minutes in a *koshiki*—a rice-steaming tub. The rice is then spread out in an area called the *koji* room, where a mold, *Aspergillus oryzae,* is added. This mold converts the rice starch into sugar in thirty to thirty-five hours. The rice, now referred to as *koji,* is mixed with additional steamed rice and water, and instead of depending on traditional wild yeasts, modern sake producers add a pure strain of yeast called *Saccharomyces cerevisiae.* The mash, or *moto,* is put into large wooden or stainless steel containers for the *moroni,* or fermentation. Sake is generally fermented at 60°F for about three weeks. However, the highest-quality sake is fermented cool, at 50°F, for about four weeks. When fermentation is completed, the liquor, which resembles very thick milk, is drawn off (racked). The rice is gently pressed in a machine that resembles a long accordion. The liquid is allowed to settle, then filtered and run into casks to mature for a short period of time, usually ninety to one-hundred days. Finally, the sake is pasteurized before being bottled. This eliminates cloudiness and bacteria contamination, and makes it able to withstand ocean voyages and an extended shelf life. (Today, molasses alcohol, glucose, or grain alcohol is occasionally added to help offset the rising cost of rice in Japan.)

Sake is produced all over Japan, in parts of China, and in other Asian countries, as well as in Hawaii and California. In Japan there is a high-proof spirit distilled from rice called *Awamori*, or *Shochu*. In China it is called *Sochu*. (The ancient Chinese *Alaai* or *Santchoo*, were spirits distilled from rice in about 800 B.C.)

Types of Sake

The type and origin of the rice used in sake production determines what the final product will taste like. For example, sake from Hiroshima is often quite full-bodied and robust; sake from Akita is very heady in its bouquet, often because of its higher alcoholic content. Sake from Kyoto is probably the lightest and driest of all and is the most popular type in the United States. More than one dozen types of sake fall roughly into four styles: *mirin* (*mi* = taste; *rin* = sweet), which is used for cooking; *toso*, which is aged in Yoshino wooden casks which gives it a dark color, fullness of body, and a spicy-sweet taste, is drunk for New Year's celebrations; *nigori*, which is a semirefined sake; and *seishu*, which is also known as *ama-kara-ping* (*ama* = sweet; *kara* = lightly bitter; *ping* = a "delightful effect").

Gekkeikan (meaning *laurel wreath*, the crown that is a symbol of victory in sporting competitions), is Japan's oldest continuously operated sake house; it was established in 1637. Some sake brands available on the marketplace are: Genji; Ozeki; Chiyoda; Gekkeikan; Fuki; Koshu Masamune; Numano; Hakutsuru; Kiku-Masamune; Shirayuki; Akadama; Sawanotsuru; and Shogun.

Serving and Storing Sake

The Japanese traditionally serve sake warm, between 100° to 110°F. At this temperature sake's heady bouquet (which is 12 to 17 percent alcohol) is released. To warm sake, place the opened bottle into a pot of boiling water. Remove it when the sake is 100° to 110°F and immediately replace it with another for later drinking. To serve sake in the Japanese manner, decant the warm sake into the small, beautifully shaped ceramic serving bottles called *tokkuri*, or *ochoko*. Then slowly pour the sake into the tiny porcelain cups or bowls called *sakazuki*, which hold a little more than one ounce. Sake cups are always filled to the brim. (In ancient Japan, these bowls were made of lacquered wood and were quite large—so large, in fact, that the face of the drinker was almost lost in the cup. Sake is traditionally sipped from these bowls.)

Sake is a versatile beverage and can be served chilled, or on the rocks with a twist of lemon. Sake can be an alternative to dry vermouth in a martini, called a "sakini." Sake is almost colorless, with its color ranging from amber to the palest gold. It is technically considered a "still" beverage because of its lack of effervescence. Its bouquet is somewhat earthy, with subtle undertones; it has a slightly sweet initial taste, followed by a dry aftertaste. Sake should be stored in a cool, dark place prior to opening. Sake, unlike wine, does not improve with bottle age, and after opening should be refrigerated to prolong its life.

Suggested Readings

Abel, Bob. *The Book of Beer*. Chicago: Henry Regnery, 1976.

Birmingham, Frederic. *Falstaff's Complete Beer Book*. New York: Award Books, 1970.

Jackson, Michael. *The Pocket Guide to Beer: A Discriminating Guide to the World's Finest Brews*. New York: Pedigree, 1982.

Kondo, Hiroshi. *Sake: A Drinker's Guide*. Tokyo, Japan: Kondansha, 1984.

Robertson, James D. *The Great American Beer Book*. New York: Thornwood, Caroline House Publishers, 1978.

Discussion Topics and Questions

1. In advertisements, both in print and over electronic media, certain breweries state that the unique taste of their beer comes from mountain spring water. Does this really make a big difference, or can water be chemically adjusted to just about any taste? Give arguments for each side.

2. In older publications, photographs often show beer being aged and served from wooden barrels. Why are these not used today?

3. In addition to corn grits, what other ingredients do American brewers use to obtain the light body that makes U.S. beers unique?

4. Sparkling wines are taxed at a higher rate simply because they contain natural carbonation. Beer also contains carbonation. Should it too be taxed at luxury tax rates? In your answer cite other carbonated beverages, both alcoholic and nonalcoholic, and whether or not they should be taxed.

5. Project and explore retailer profitability based on the use of various glass sizes and one-half versus one-quarter kegs.

6. The temperature of beer and the glass in which it is served play an important role in the formation, size, and longevity of a beer head. What temperature should the glass and the beer be when serving a lighter versus a heavier-bodied beer?

7. Most Americans believe that the Europeans, especially the British, drink their beer at room temperature. If this is in fact true, why?

8. When designing the layout of a cocktail lounge, the type of beer you plan to serve will sometimes dictate where the bar will be located. Why?

9. What percentage of bars in your area really serve customers beer from a *truly* clean beer glass?

10. Compare the problems one might have with draft beer with those of premix and postmix soda systems.

11. List areas of the "hospitality industry" in which serving canned beer would be preferable to serving bottled beer.

12. Although sake, like beer, is a brewed product, it is served in a radically different manner. Give several reasons why.

9

Distilled Spirits

This chapter discusses:

- The distillation process.
- Base ingredients of distillation and how they affect the taste of a finished product.
- The charred barrel and its effect on the aging process.
- The minimum and maximum length of time that whiskies age and their varying alcoholic contents.
- The various "brown whiskies" and "white spirits" produced in the United States and other countries.
- The background and history of each type of distilled spirit.
- The major and minor differences between distillates.
- The versatility of "white spirits."
- How distilled spirits should be stored and served.
- Brand names currently available in the United States.

It is believed that the word *whiskey* is derived from the Celtic *uisge baugh* or *uisge beatha*, (roughly, *water of life*). No one knows for sure which country first used the word, but the Scots and Irish claim rightful ownership of the term. We do know that the English found the word much too difficult to pronounce, so it was shortened and anglicized to the present *whisky* (English) or *whiskey* (American).

Brown Whiskies

American-made whiskey was formally defined when the Federal Alcohol Administration Regulations were formulated in 1936. They define whiskey as an alcoholic distillate made from a fermented mash of grain, distilled at less than 190 proof, in such a manner that the distillate possesses the taste, aroma, and characteristics generally associated with whiskey. The minimum proof that a whiskey can be bottled at is 80; there are no maximum proof standards. American whiskey can only be made from grains specified for each category; potatoes and beets, used in vodka production, cannot be used to make whiskey. Whiskey obtains its characteristic brown color from four sources: coloring from the barrel, oxidation, charred barrels, and the addition of caramel for color adjustment.

Blended Whiskey

Blended whiskey is a product containing at least 20 percent by volume 100-proof "straight" whiskey, which is combined with grain whiskey or neutral spirits, and bottled at not less than 80 proof. The blending usually takes place after the whiskies reach full maturity; they are then allowed to rest for further aging. Caramel coloring is usually added prior to bottling.

Blended whiskies made with neutral spirits will carry a label on the back of the bottle showing the percentages it contains of neutral spirits and straight whiskies. Some available brands of blended whiskies are:

Barton Reserve	Four Roses	Seagram's 7 Crown
Calvert Extra	Imperial	Schenley Reserve
Carstairs	Philadelphia	Three Feathers
Fleischmann		

Bourbon: Our National Spirit

Most of Kentucky is "dry," but some of it is "wet": these terms do not refer to the weather, but the status of Kentucky's counties with regard to liquor. Even though seventy-seven of Kentucky's counties are "dry," there are cities in the "dry" areas that are "wet." Some of the "wet" counties require that bourbon be purchased by the bottle and not by the drink. Alcoholic beverages may be sold only to persons twenty-one years of age or older, and usually only until midnight.

In 1789 (the year of George Washington's inauguration as first president of the United States), a Baptist minister, Elijah Craig, made a spirit by combining spring water, corn, rye, and barley malt. Craig lived in Bourbon County, Kentucky, where so much of that state's whiskey was produced that within two generations the name *bourbon* was attached to all Kentucky whiskey—earning the preacher the title of "Father of Bourbon."

At Old Evan Williams Distillery it is argued that in 1783 Evan Williams, an early Kentucky settler and pioneer, earned his permanent role in American history when he built the area's first commercial distillery. Williams also solved pioneer transportation problems by pulverizing about 250 pounds of corn and distilling it into bourbon whiskey. He determined that a single pack horse could easily carry two twenty-gallon kegs of the whiskey (the equivalent of approximately twelve bushels, or a quarter-ton of corn) on a riverboat. Williams' transportation method made the shipment of whiskey much easier; soon after, whiskey was making the long journey to many eastern markets along the Ohio and Mississippi rivers, where it was an immediate success.

The emergence of the bourbon industry. Distillation remained a rather primitive process, subject to much variation from one batch to another until 1835, when scientific procedures were introduced, and emphasis was placed on the careful analysis of the ingredients, the use of such precise measuring instruments as the thermometer and the saccharimeter (which gauge the sugar content of the mash), and above all, sanitation. This led to uniformity in appearance and quality between batches among the distillers. Whiskey was shipped in barrels, along with an empty bottle which was refilled and displayed in retail stores. Even though the bottle was marked with the producing distillers' brand name, this was still no guarantee of quality, for many unscrupulous retailers filled popular brand bottles with cheaper or adulterated products. But even with uncertain quality guarantees, consumers continued to drink bourbon in ever-increasing quantities.

It was not until 1870, however, that George Garvin Brown, a young wholesale drug salesman in Louisville, introduced whiskey in a clear, sealed bottle, to prevent tampering with the final product. The use of a sealed bottle assured the consumer of the genuineness of the bourbon. The individual bottling of bourbon brands became widely accepted during the late 1800s. It was more expensive for the distillers, but it assured that valued customers were getting the whiskey they paid for. Many distillers quickly capitalized on the idea and soon were bottling, sealing, stamping, and labeling their whiskies at the distillery.

In 1890, there were 1,576 registered distilleries throughout the state. These distilleries were not the corporations we now recognize, but rather family-owned or partnership operations, each on a relatively small scale, with each one professing to have a premium product. These small distilleries continued production until 1906, when President Taft signed the Food and Drug Act, which required certain standards of identification for whiskey and imposed greater federal control on the production of distilled spirits. This act marked the turning point in bourbon quality.

In 1933 citizens voted for the repeal of Prohibition by the adoption of the Twenty-First Amendment, thus making the alcoholic beverage industry the only business existing in this country today as a result of a vote of the people. After the repeal of Prohibition, Kentucky was in the enviable position of having many medium-sized workable distilleries intact, which could begin operating in a short time. But times had changed. The small distiller did not have the capital to start operating on a large scale, and many of the smaller companies soon failed or were sold. Most of those who had survived had to seek corporate capital by raising money through the sale of stocks and bonds. Thus the high number of family-operated distilleries existing prior to 1920 promptly shrank to less than one-hundred producing distilleries; that number is substantially smaller today. On May 4, 1964, the United States Senate passed a resolution recognizing bourbon whiskey as a "distinctive product of the United States," with no other country having authority to call their whiskey products bourbon. And, because consumers associate Kentucky with bourbon whiskey, the United States government permits only Kentucky to use its name on the label to identify the product.

The use of charred barrels. Early distillers chose white oak barrels for shipping their whiskies. The sturdy cooperage proved strong enough to withstand rough handling aboard the river boats.

A charred white oak barrel is essential in the production of bourbon whiskey. The nature of the barrel's role came about accidentally. Supposedly, a nineteenth-century barrel maker was steaming and bending oak staves over an open fire. Through his negligence, the staves began to char. Being a frugal sort, he used them anyway, without bothering to tell the distiller. The distiller who used the barrel found that his whiskey improved in flavor and had picked up a rich color. He then insisted on charred staves for all his barrels. The charred inner surface of the barrel is key in maturing bourbon; it produces its color, bouquet, and most of its flavor and taste characteristics.

Vital to the flavor and color of good bourbon are the uniformity and depth of the two thin charred layers of the barrel's inner surface. The first layer of pure carbon and the second "red layer" of caramelized wood sugars give bourbon its rich, dark color; the deeper layers contribute tannin and vanillin. The barrels are first toasted, then charred; the whiskey thus benefits from consistent char layers and the wood resins that are brought to the barrel surface by the toasting process. The charring of the barrels takes only about thirty seconds. The proper selection, cutting, and air drying of white oak for barrel heads and staves is essential to the proper "breathing" of the barrel, which helps to mature the whiskey. White oak comes from the central United States, including Kentucky. Federal law specifies that bourbon must be stored at not more than 125 proof in new charred white oak barrels. The Blue Grass Cooperage Company is the leading producer of new white oak whiskey barrels in the United States.

Producing bourbon whiskey. The making of bourbon whiskey today is a combination of art and a highly developed science. No two distillers are exactly alike in their operations. And, while the manufacture of bourbon is closely regulated and somewhat standardized by the federal government, the actual process differs from one distiller to the next. Federal regulations require that bourbon be made from a minimum of 51 percent corn; generally, 65 to 75 percent is used. When the corn in the mash reaches 80 percent the product, by government definition, becomes corn whiskey—not bourbon. The higher the corn content and the lower the percentage of other grains, the lighter the whiskey. The blend of the other grains is dictated by the distiller's own private formula; rye, wheat, or barley malt can be used in the grain mix. All distillers, however, go through five essential steps: grain handling and milling, mashing, fermenting, distilling, and maturing.

Natural, mineral-free limestone water plays an important role in the production of bourbon. Underground alkaline springs act as a perfect filtering agent for fresh water and provide it in almost unlimited quantities, free of minerals and iron deposits.

Grain handling and milling. Grain handling involves the selection of corn, rye, and barley malt according to standards on moisture content, ripeness, and purity. Only the finest grains that are free of odor, available in sufficient quantity, have at least 60 percent starch, and have less than 13 percent moisture (more moisture will cause mold and bacterial contamination) can be used. Once selected, the grains are individually shipped to distillery mills in special rail cars called *hopper cars.* At the mills, the grain is cleaned and sorted, then ground to a meal for cooking, and finally moved to separate containers for weighing and proportioning.

Mashing. Before a fermentation can take place, the starch contained in the grains must be converted into usable sugar. This is accomplished by an enzymatic process which causes the grains, which have been mixed with limestone water, to malt or sprout, and changes the starch into maltose sugars. The various grains are mixed, warmed, and pumped into a sterile fermentation tank and inoculated with a special yeast strain. Fermentation takes three to five days, converting the sugar in the mash to alcohol, which eventually reaches 8 to 9 percent of the mash. The distillers call the fermented mash *beer*. Once fermented, the mash is heated in a still until the alcohol, which was produced by the yeast strain digesting the mashed grain sugars, vaporizes. Traces of flavoring components called *congeners* are also produced during the fermenting process. Congeners are fusel oils, esters, tannins, acids, aldehydes, and so on. In proper proportion with other elements, these congeners will eventually help develop and determine the aroma, body, and taste of the final product.

Distilling. Distillation involves the separation of alcohol from the fermented mash. Since alcohol boils at 173.1°F and water boils at 212°F, it is relatively easy to separate the alcohol and flavoring components from the mash. The higher the heat, the greater the volume of neutral spirits. The lower the heat, the greater the amount of true bourbon flavor that is carried through distillation. The mash enters near the top of a continuous still or column still, while steam enters near the still's bottom chambers, thus vaporizing the alcohol and flavoring components. When the vapor is drawn off, it condenses into a liquid, known as *low wine*, with an alcoholic content of anywhere from 45 to 65 percent. The low wine is redistilled, or futher refined, allowing the alcohol to reach an even higher concentration and further removing unwanted impurities and flavors. The resulting liquid is called *high wine*, or new whiskey; it is crystal clear and ready for maturing.

The double distallation is expensive, but well worth it if a distiller wants a premium bourbon. Some distillers double distill, some don't. Although the maximum proof at which whiskey can leave the still is 160, most bourbon whiskey is actually distilled at about 130 proof. If distilled at 160 proof, the higher-proof bourbon tends to pick up too much of a woody taste during aging.

The spent grains and fluids (called *slop*) which are drawn off from the bottom of the continuous still are dried and used as high-protein feed supplements for both livestock and poultry.

Maturing. The new whiskey is pumped into a cistern room where it is reduced to a lower proof by the addition of demineralized limestone water. The bourbon must be barreled at not less than 80 proof and not more than 125 proof. The raw bourbon is then put into new, large charred white oak barrels ranging in capacity from 50 to 66 gallons, which are filled and then stored in large warehouses. Due to heating and cooling in the warehouse, the whiskey both expands and contracts. Higher temperatures cause the whiskey to expand and penetrate the carmelized or "red layer" of wood behind the char. As the temperature drops, the whiskey contracts out of the wood. With each succeeding cycle, the harsh flavoring components in the new whiskey are further filtered out. The charred oak gives the bourbon its color, while time develops and mellows the flavoring components that give the bourbon its distinctive flavor and bouquet. Bourbon whiskey, by law, must be aged for a minimum of two years; most distillers age their bourbon anywhere from four to ten years. Throughout this stage, test samples and periodic inspections of each barrel ensure that the distiller's standards are being met. Occasionally a leak is discovered in one of the barrels. Most leaks are repaired with wood slivers which are driven into the leak spot, then cut flush with the barrel surface. A portion of the bourbon volume is lost every year from soakage and evaporation (amounting to as much as 15 percent after four years), but in the end a unique distilled product is achieved. After aging, the barrels are removed from the warehouse, opened, and filtered, removing the heavier sediment and solids that have formed on the bottom of the barrel. During bottling the proof or alcohol content is adjusted (usually by the addition of demineralized water).

Bourbon, technically, can be produced anywhere in the United States, although in practice Indiana, Illinois and Virginia are the only states besides Kentucky that produce this unique whiskey. Today sixteen companies produce 80 percent of the world's supply of bourbon, which amounts to approximately 65 million gallons. Some well-known brands of bourbon are:

Ancient Age	I. W. Harper	Old Forester
Benchmark	Jim Beam	Old Grand-Dad
Ezra Brooks	Kentucky Tavern	Ten High
Evan Williams	Maker's Mark	Wild Turkey
Heaven Hill	Old Crow	

Sour mash production method. Federal regulations require that a minimum of 25 percent of the volume of the fermenting mash must be stillage (cooled, screened liquid recovered from the base discharge of the whiskey-separating column) and the fermenting time be at least seventy two hours. Sour mash is actually made from a yeast mash "soured" with a lactic acid culture for a minimum of six hours to promote the growth of the yeast and at the same time inhibit the growth of any other organisms. In the sour mash process, spent beer from the previous fermentation is added, together with fresh yeast, to the grain mash. This does not change the flavor or taste, but it does provide continuity of flavor, body, and bouquet in the whiskey, and reinforces the individual characteristics that mark the bourbon brand. Sour mash is a distiller's term, and there is nothing actually sour about sour mash bourbon.

Bottled in bond bourbon. Bourbon that is bottled in bond is bourbon that by federal regulations must be produced by one distillery in one distilling season, aged a minimum of four years in new charred oak barrels, and bottled at 100 proof. Bourbon that is bottled in bond has also been stored and bottled in a Treasury Department bonded warehouse; no excise tax is paid on the bourbon until the beverage is withdrawn or shipped from the warehouse. The term *bonded* on a label therefore does not refer to quality; it means nothing more than that the treasury agent was present to collect the taxes.

Blended bourbon whiskey. If a minimum of 51 percent straight bourbon whiskey is used in a blend, the whiskey label must state that it is "blended bourbon whiskey" or "bourbon whiskey—a blend."

Canadian Whisky

Although Canadian whisky (in Canada, it is spelled *whisky*) is a distinctive product of Canada, the Canadian government doesn't set regulations relative to the mixture of the grain blend, the proof level at which it is distilled, or the type of barrel used. Distillers are allowed to make their own whisky as they see fit. Canadian whisky is matured in white oak barrels (mostly used), and for the American market is bottled at a minimum of 80 proof. Canadian whisky is made only from grains (corn, rye, and barley malt) and may be bottled after three years of age. Canadian whisky sold in the United States is generally four to six years old. Canadian whisky cannot be designated as a "straight" whisky. Some better-known brands are:

Black Velvet	Canadian Mist
Canadian Club	Lord Calvert

Schenley O.F.C. (Old Fine Canadian)	Seagram's V.O. (Very Old)
Seagram's Crown Royal	Windsor Supreme

Corn Whiskey

Legally, corn whiskey is distilled at a proof not exceeding 160 from a fermented mash of at least 80 percent corn. Corn whiskey must be stored in uncharred oak barrels or used charred oak barrels at not more than 125 proof. It must be aged for a minimum of two years—yet there are some corn whiskies on the marketplace that for some unknown reason do not meet this requirement. Because of its dominant corn content, corn whiskey is extremely light in flavor.

Irish Whiskey

Irish whiskey is a distinctive product of Ireland, manufactured in compliance with the guidelines of Irish Distillers, Ltd. It is commonly thought that Irish whiskey is produced from potatoes, mainly because of the general association between the Irish and potatoes; this is not true. Irish whiskey is not a single malt or pure malt whiskey—it is a blend. It is made from a mash of cereal grains, mostly barley (malted and unmalted), wheat, oats, corn, and rye. Most Irish whiskey is produced in pot stills, which help give it a unique taste.

There are basically two types of stills used for distilling: the pot still and the continuous still. The pot still is in the shape of a kettle and produces only single batches of distilled spirits. After each batch has been distilled, the pot still must be refilled again. Pot stills produce the finest quality as well as the highest priced distilled spirits. The continuous still was developed in 1832 by Aeneas Coffey, an Irishman. The continuous still is often referred to as a column still, Coffey still, and even patent still. The continuous still is continuously fed and saves time, but doesn't produce the same high quality as the pot still.

Irish whiskey must be aged a minimum of three years, but is usually aged five to eight years prior to shipping. It is light and mild to the taste, with a complex, rich and distinctive flavor. Some better-known brands are:

Dunphy's	Murphy's	Paddy
Jameson	Bushmills	Tullamore Dew
John Powers		

Light Whiskey

Light whiskey is a product of various cereal grains distilled at 160 to 189 proof before being reduced and stored in used or uncharred new oak barrels. It is lighter than other whiskies in flavor, aroma, and taste because the flavor congeners are removed during the distillation at a high proof. This whiskey was first authorized for production in 1972.

Rye Whiskey

Rye whiskey is the most misunderstood of all whiskies offered for sale in the United States. In many states, when people order "rye," they almost always really want a blended whiskey. Rye whiskey—real rye—is not to everyone's taste, for it has a strong and distinctive flavor of caraway seeds. Rye is produced from a mixture of various grains, with a predominance (51 percent minimum, by law) of rye. It cannot be distilled at higher than 160 proof, and thus retains most of the congeners that contribute to its flavor. It must be aged in new charred barrels for a minimum of two years, although four years is the standard.

The top name brands available are:

Jim Beam Rye Whiskey Wild Turkey Rye Whiskey

Old Overholt Straight Rye Whiskey

Scotch Whisky

Scotch whisky is a specific product of Scotland (see figure 9-1), made in compliance with the laws of Great Britain. Scotch's unique flavor and character come from the water used in its production, and the type and amount of malt whisky used. Its distinctive smoky taste comes from the peat fires over which the barley malt is dried.

The malting of barley is the first stage in making Scotch whisky; this may be done by one of several processes. In the older floor malting method, the barley, after being soaked in water for two to three days, was spread on a kiln floor for germination or sprouting, which generally took eight to twelve days (figure 9-2). This process has been largely replaced by mechanical maltings of one type or another, but the principle of the process remains the same.

During this malting period, an enzyme called *diastase* is secreted by the barley, converting the starch in it into a readily fermentable sugar. The germination is stopped by drying and smoking the malted barley

Figure 9-1 This typical Scotch distillery has a pastoral setting, with swans gliding on the adjacent lake. (Courtesy Scotch Whisky Information Bureau)

over peat fires in open malt kilns; this helps to give Scotch its unique smoky taste. Peat is a soft, not fully formed coal in a primary state; it is made up of decomposed vegetal material often found in swamps (figure 9-3). During the smoking process, the barley lies above the smoking peat on screens, which allows the burning vapors to permeate the barley, swirling around and under it. This not only dries out the barley but infuses it with a unique smoky aroma and taste.

The barley is then mixed with water and poured into deep vessels, and yeast is added. In two or three days, the sugar in the liquid will have been converted by fermentation into alcohol. After this, the liquid is piped into stills, where it is double distilled, until the correct proof is reached (figure 9-4). Generally speaking, malt Scotches are distilled in the proof range of 120 to 140, whereas the lighter grain whiskies are generally distilled in the 180 to 188 proof range.

Blended Scotch Whisky

Scotch is made from a blend of as many as fifty different malt and grain whiskies. The lighter Scotches are made with greater amounts of grain

Figure 9-2 Kiln floor: malted barley being dried in kiln. (Courtesy Scotch Whisky Information Bureau)

Scotch whiskies, distilled in column stills at higher proofs from malted and unmalted barley, corn, and other cereals.

The blended Scotches, as we know them today, did not really come into existence until about 1860. Prior to that, Scotches were distilled in old-fashioned pot stills at lower proof levels which produced Scotches with a full body and heavy taste. In 1832, the column still was perfected by Aeneas Coffey for use in the distillation of Scotch whisky. This enabled distillers to produce lighter bodied and flavored Scotch whiskies, which were then blended with the heavier malted Scotches. In 1853, in Edinburgh, Andrew Usher produced the first blended Scotch whisky.

After distillation is completed, Scotch is put into used American oak bourbon whiskey or wine barrels, where it ages for a minimum (by law) of three years (figure 9-5). However, in practice most whiskies mature for much longer, often five to ten years or even longer, depending on the distiller. Scotch sold in the United States is generally aged a minimum of four years; if it's less than four years old, the bottle must carry

Figure 9-3 Peat being dug out from dried-out marsh lands. (Courtesy Scotch Whisky Information Bureau)

an age label. When there is an age stated on the label of a blended Scotch whisky, it identifies the youngest whisky in the blend.

After maturing in wooden barrels, the Scotch is blended and its proof reduced by the addition of distilled water. At this point it is allowed to blend for several months, before being filtered and finally bottled.

It is commonly thought that the longer a Scotch whisky (or any other whiskey, for that matter) ages, the better or smoother it becomes. Actually, after twelve to fifteen years the whisky does not improve significantly, and with prolonged barrel aging it could start picking up a woody

265

Figure 9-4 Huge copper pot stills used for the distillation of Scotch whisky. (Courtesy Scotch Whisky Information Bureau)

flavor and start to deteriorate. Whisky does not continue to age or improve after being removed from the cask—one's twenty-five-year-old Scotch will still be only twenty-five years old (quality wise) after fifty years.

Scotch can be distilled in Scotland, yet be bottled in the United States, which saves large sums of money, with little or no sacrifice to the product's quality. Some better-known brands of blended Scotch whisky are:

Ambassador	John Begg	Black Bull
Ballantine	Bell's	Black & White

Figure 9-5 Barrels containing Scotch whisky being loaded onto racks for aging. (Courtesy Scotch Whisky Information Bureau)

Chivas Regal	J.&B.	Teacher's
Cutty Sark	Ne Plus Ultra	Tomatin
Dewar's White Label	Old Rarity	Usher's
Grant's	Old Smuggler	Usquaebach
Haig	100 Pipers	Vat 69
Harvey's	Passport	White Horse
Johnnie Walker		

Malt Scotch. Malt Scotch, often referred to as single-malt Scotch, is produced by the pot still method from a mash consisting of only malted barley. A *single-malt* whisky means a malt produced by a single distillery. By way of contrast, *blended* Scotch means a blend of pot-stilled malt whiskies with whiskies produced in Scotland by the column still method from a cereal mix that may contain unmalted as well as malted barley and other grains.

Malt Scotches are generally darker in color than blended Scotches, because of increased aging in cask; they are traditionally served at room temperature. Some brands of single-malt Scotch whisky are:

Auchentoshan	Glendronach	Glenordie
Aultmore	Glenfarclas	Knockando
Balvenie	Glenfiddich	Laphroaig
Cardhu	Glenlivet	The Macallan
The Edradour	Glenmorangie	Talisker

Serving and storing Scotch. Scotch, because of its high alcohol content (minimum 80 proof), will last almost indefinitely either opened or unopened, unless it is subjected to extremely hot or cold temperatures for prolonged periods of time or constantly exposed to movement or vibrations.

Scotch can be served "neat" (without ice, seltzer, water, and so on); over ice; with water or seltzer; or in a multitude of mixed drinks. It is best to use blended Scotches under twelve years of age for mixed drinks that contain sugar, fruit, or lemon flavors. Twelve-year-old single-malt Scotches and well-aged Scotches (often up to thirty years) are best served straight or with a splash of water or seltzer, over ice.

Tennessee Whiskey

Tennessee distillers choose to identify their product as Tennessee whiskey, yet it may be technically identified with bourbon. Tennessee whiskey is leached or filtered through vats of compacted maple charcoal, which eliminates congeners and adds to its flavor prior to aging. To make the special charcoal filtration system the distillers of Tennessee whiskey cut down maple trees during the cold winter months when the sap level is minimal so that a resin or sugar taste is not added to the whiskey.

Then the hard maple wood is cut lengthwise into long six-foot strips, and set on fire. During the burning process, the strips are periodically wet down to slow the burning process and force the wood to become charred rather than disintegrate into ashes. The wood is then pulverized and tightly packed into large tanks at the distillery. When ready, the whiskey is poured in at the top and allowed to run through the charred wood (twelve solid feet of it) very slowly, giving a strong maple flavor to the whiskey, which is then filtered and bottled.

The only two brands of Tennessee whiskey currently available are Jack Daniel's and George Dickel.

White Spirits

The term white spirits or "white goods" refers to those distillates that are clear in color and are usually not aged in wood. These spirits lack the distinctive flavor generally associated with whiskey and are perceived as being light by most consumers.

Gin

Under federal regulations gin must be bottled at a minimum of 80 proof (except in the case of flavored gins). Gin must have a juniper berry flavor and can be made either by direct distillation or by redistillation. Most gins are not aged, and federal regulations do not permit age claims. Distilled gins are allowed to use the word *distilled* on the label, although gins made through the *compound method* (see below) are not.

Gin was invented in about 1650 by Franciscus de la Boe (1614–1672), who was known as Dr. Sylvius. Dr. Sylvius was a physician and professor of medicine at Holland's famed University of Leyden (or Leiden). Dr. Sylvius was attempting to produce a therapeutic medicine that was both palatable and inexpensive and could be made by distilling pure alcohol in the presence of juniper berries, which come from evergreen trees. He was aware of medical theory and archaic pharmacology: the Latin *Juniperus communis* literally means *youth-giving*. At that time it was believed that the oils contained in juniper berries offered diuretic properties that could relieve the bladder and also treat kidney ailments. For some reason Dr. Sylvius proposed the use of the French name *genievre*

269

for his juniper berry elixir. The Dutch, however, preferred to use their word for juniper berry, and called it *genever*.

England's introduction to gin came when British soldiers, returning from the wars in the Netherlands, sampled the juniper-flavored spirit and nicknamed it "Dutch Courage" or "Hollands." The soldiers found it to their liking and brought back the recipe, along with the name *geneva*, mistakenly thought to be a product from Switzerland. The name was changed to *gen*, which was later anglicized to *gin*. In no time at all gin became the national drink of England, which it still is today.

Gin Production. The important differences among gins are the result of the type of mash from which the neutral grain spirits are distilled and the quality of the juniper berries and other botanicals used in the redistillation process. United States federal law standards of identity permit gin to be produced from any of the following base materials: corn, rye, wheat, barley malt, and sugar cane among others. Most gins are produced by private formulas which are the distillers' most closely guarded secrets. Known ingredients or botanicals besides juniper berries that are often used in small proportions are: angelica root, anise, bitter almonds, calamus, caraway seeds, cardamon, cassia bark, cinnamon, cocoa nibs, coriander seeds, fennel, ginger, lemons or dried lemon peels, licorice, limes, orange peel, orris root, and other seeds, and almost a limitless number of barks, herbs, and roots. Technically, gin could be called a liqueur or cordial, if it were sweetened.

The United States federal government acknowledges the existence of a number of different styles of gin; however, it only defines two types. They are *distilled* gin and *compound* gin.

Distilled gin is a distillate obtained from the original distillate of mash or the redistillation of distilled spirits with juniper berries and other aromatics customarily used in the production of gin. Gin derives its characteristic flavor from juniper berries, and is reduced at time of bottling to not less than 80 proof.

Compound gin is produced by mixing high-proof neutral spirits with extracts or oils of juniper berry and other botanicals and flavorings. This gin is of a lower quality than distilled gin, and therefore very little gin is produced today using this method. This is, however, a federally approved definition that recalls the days of Prohibition, when members of households mixed neutral spirits (often using methanol, or wood alcohol, which is lethal, instead of ethanol or ethyl alcohol) with juniper or "gin flavoring" to produce a bootleg spirit called "bathtub gin" or "hooch," which was revolting to the taste.

Gin is usually distilled at a high proof, somewhere between 180 to 190, and is therefore clean and free of "off" flavors and undesirable odors. After the initial distillation the producer uses many different methods to produce the characteristic juniper aroma and flavor. One method, often called *original distillation*, is to suspend the cracked and crushed juniper berries on mesh trays, baskets, or perforated racks called *gin heads*. This allows rising vapors to pass from the still through and around the berries, picking up essences and becoming impregnated with the aromatic flavoring oils of the botanicals, which remain in the condensed distillate. The proof of the gin is corrected with distilled water, and then bottled. Another similar method is to distill the original mash at 190 proof, then redistill it in the presence of the gin head. Although the second method is more common, both methods are acceptable in the United States. The flavoring content of the botanicals used change from year to year, depending on rainfall, amount of sunshine received, and so on, so the distiller must alter his formula every year in order to achieve the same taste and smell, bottle after bottle.

Types of gin

British or London dry gin. In England gin mash usually contains less corn and more barley, because English distillers feel that this produces a spirit of extraordinary smoothness. Their gins are distilled at a high proof, then redistilled in the presence of juniper berries. English gins have a lightly balanced aromatic juniper bouquet and flavor; they are light, dry, crisp, and clean, with the delicate flavoring of the juniper berry, although this is slightly toned down. These gins are ideal for drinking straight, in martinis, or mixed in cocktails. London dry gins, although originally produced only in or near London, are now produced all over the world, and the term presently has little meaning.

American dry gin. American gins are usually produced by one of two methods, distilling or compounding. They are often labeled "dry" or "extra dry," although these terms have little actual meaning, and gins labeled as such are not actually any drier than other gins. American dry gins are ideal for use in mixed drinks.

Dutch gin/Holland gin/Genever gin, or Schiedam gin. The production of Dutch gin is slightly different than that of other gin; the Dutch usually begin with a grain mash of equal parts of barley malt, corn, and rye, distilled in a pot still at around 100 proof. The initial distillate, known as *malt wine*, is then redistilled in the presence of juniper berries in another pot still at a low proof (around 100 to 110), which carries flavoring congeners and produces Dutch gin's full-bodied character. Dutch gins are usually heavy, with very complex, malty aromas and flavors; they have a pungent, full taste of juniper berries. They also have a pronounced grain flavor and, surprisingly, are often slightly sweet. Because of their heaviness of taste they are usually drunk straight and cold, especially in Holland.

Schiedan gin is named after one of the Dutch towns in which it is manufactured.

Old Tom gin. This is a dry gin, usually sweetened by the addition of sugar syrup, that was quite popular during the eighteenth century. It is rarely seen today.

Plymouth gin. This is actually an *appellation*, and is only produced by the Coates firm of Plymouth, England, which was founded in 1798. It is an aromatic gin, sometimes pink in color from the addition of angostura bitters. Its taste lies somewhere between that of Dutch and London dry gin. Plymouth gin was originally associated with the British Royal Navy which, as legend has it, invented this gin as a tolerable way of drinking bitters, which helped control intestinal disorders. They often mixed it with lime juice; hence the nickname "limey," which is frequently applied to the British.

Unfortunately, the production of Plymouth gin has dwindled in recent years.

Steinhager (or Steinhaeger) gin. This is a German gin similar to London dry types, but with slightly more of a juniper taste.

Golden gins. These gins are aged in wood for a short period of time and have a light golden-brown color, which is extracted from the barrel. Golden gin is difficult to find today.

Sloe gin. This is not really a gin; it is a cordial made from sloe berries (actually, small plur.is), which give it a rather tart flavor.

Flavored gins. According to United States federal regulations, flavored gins are gins to which natural flavoring materials (apple, lemon, mint, orange, and pineapple, with or without the addition of sugar) have been added. They are bottled at not less than 70 proof, and the name of the predominant flavor must appear as part of the designation. The famous British Damson Gin, for instance, is flavored with damson plums.

Some well-known gin brands are:

Beefeater	Boodles	Burnett's
Bellows	Boord's	Doornkaat
Bombay	Booth's	Fockink

Gilbey's   Seagram's   Tanqueray
Gordon's

Rum

Rum is a spirit resulting from an alcoholic fermentation and the distillation of sugarcane, sugarcane syrup, molasses, sugar beets, maple sap, or other sugarcane by-products, at less than 190 proof. Rum, in order to be designated as such, by United States federal law, should possess the characteristics that are generally attributed to it (aroma, taste, and so on) and cannot be less than 80 proof (40 percent alcohol). The distillation must also occur within the area of production of the sugarcane.

Rum production. Sugarcane, minus the leaves, is cut and shredded by heavy rollers; the juice is collected, strained, decanted, and filtered. Rum, unlike other distilled spirits, has its own natural sugar for fermentation and does not depend on various added enzymes to convert the starch in the cereals to a readily fermentable sugar.

The sugarcane juice is first boiled to evaporate the water, which crystalizes the sugar and separates it from the thick, black molasses. The juice is fermented for one to two days, producing a small amount of alcohol, then double distilled in column stills to about 180 proof. Dark, full-bodied rums are distilled in a pot still at a lower proof, maintaining some of the flavor components in the final distillate.

Both light and dark rums come out of the still almost colorless, although they may taste quite different. The light rums are generally kept in glass or stainless steel vats, so that they do not acquire color from barrels, while dark rums are kept in lightly charred oak barrels.

Types of rum

Basically, there are three types of rum; light or amber; dark, full-bodied; and aromatic rums.

Light or amber rums. Light rum, also labeled "white" or "silver" rum, is clear in color and displays either a very light, molasses flavor or the neutrality of vodka. It must be aged a minimum of one year in either glass or stainless steel containers, but more traditionally is aged in uncharred barrels. If aged in barrels, it is further treated through carbon filtration systems, which eliminates any color that may have been picked up from the barrel.

Amber rum, also labeled "gold" rum, is aged in wooden barrels for a minimum of three years. It contains more flavor than light rum, and is darker in color because of the addition of caramel coloring.

Every rum producer also makes a high-quality, well-aged rum which is often labeled as Añejo or Muy Añejo.

Light-bodied rums are generally produced in Puerto Rico, the Virgin Islands, Cuba, the Dominican Republic, and Haiti.

Full-bodied rum. The method of production for the dark, full-bodied, pungent rums of Jamaica, Barbados, Martinique, Trinidad, and Guyana's Demerara are slightly different from that for the light-bodied rums, making the resulting product very popular for mixed drinks.

The skimmings of sugar from previous distillations are added to the sugarcane molasses and allowed to slowly ferment for twelve to twenty days. The mash is distilled twice in pot stills and is run off at between 140 to 160 proof. The rum is then aged and blended, and at bottling the proof is adjusted with distilled water. It is this special fermentation process that gives the dark rums a pungent bouquet and more pronounced flavor of butter and molasses. Full-bodied rum is aged from five to seven years in oak barrels, and at the time of bottling considerably more caramel is added than is the case for lighter rums to give it a deep mahogany color.

Aromatic rum. The combination of the special quality of the river water on the island of Java in Indonesia and the addition of dried red Javanese rice cakes, which are added to the mash during fementation, results in the highly aromatic nature and dry taste of this rum. Aromatic rum is generally aged for three to four years in Java, then shipped to the Netherlands where additional aging takes place prior to blending and bottling. One brand available in the United States is Batavia Arak. (According to legend, ancient Arabian seafarers voyaging to the Caribbean islands gave this unusual product its name.)

Some of the more popular brands of rum are:

Appleton	Mount Gay	Rhum Saint James
Bacardi	Myers's	Ron Rico
Cockspur		

Serving and storing rum. With the exception of well-aged rum, white, gold and dark rums are best enjoyed in mixed drinks, which usually contain coconut milk, pineapple juice, or the juice of citrus fruits.

Rum is an extremely versatile beverage that can, in most cases, be substituted in drinks calling for gin or vodka and occasionally even tequila. Rum, like gin, vodka, and tequila, is a highly stable alcoholic beverage that is not adversely affected by vibrations or changes in temperature; in most cases it will last indefinitely, either opened or unopened.

Well-aged rums should be given the same treatment as brandies or cognacs; they are served in brandy snifters at room temperature.

Tequila

Tequila is distilled from the fermented juice or sap of a single variety of the maguey or mezcal (actually, there are more than four hundred varieties), a type of agave plant called Tequilana Weber (blue variety) that resembles cactus. It is known in the United States as the American aloe or century plant, because it was mistakenly believed to bloom only every one hundred years. The maguey plant takes between eight and twelve years to mature before it can be used, and only the heart of the plant, often called the *pina*, or "head," is used.

Tequila, by government decree, can only come from a specific geographic area of Mexico known as Tequila, which is within the state of Jalisco, about 40 miles from Guadalajara. If produced outside these geographical limits, it is called mezcal.

Tequila production. The heart or base of the maguey plant, often weighing between 75 and 125 pounds, contains what the distiller calls the sap or *aguamiel* (honey water). The plant is first split in half, then steamed until the starchy pulp turns a mushy brown color. The pulp goes into a shredder which opens up and crushes the fibers, allowing the juice to run off. It is collected in large vats, then mixed with cane sugar (up to 49 percent maximum) and yeast, and fermented for two to three days. The liquid is double distilled in copper pot stills between 104 to 106 proof and filtered through charcoal.

Tequila may be aged or unaged and is usually bottled at 80 to 86 proof for U.S. consumption.

The clear (often described as white or silver) tequila is not aged and is bottled after proofage reduction by distilled water. The brown or gold tequila is aged in oak casks. *Añejo* is tequila that has been aged for a minimum of one year in oak barrels. If the tequila is aged for from two to four years, it may be called *muy añejo*.

Pulque, a milky-white alcoholic beverage fermented from the juice of agave plants, was enjoyed for centuries before the art of distilling came to Mexico from Spain. Because of its rather low alcoholic content and susceptibility to spoilage, it is consumed locally, and rarely reaches the United States.

A final category of tequila, known as *crema de tequila* or *almendrado*, is a liqueur which is rarely exported to the United States.

Direccion General de Normas. In an effort to control the production and quality of tequila, the Mexican government has devised a set of strict regulations known as the *Direccion General de Normas*. These regulations have since become somewhat more restricted and defined and will be known in the future as *Norma Official Mexicana de Calidad* (NOM).

Tequila's worm? One will occasionally hear of a person finding a worm at the bottom of a bottle of tequila. In fact the worm is not found in bottles of tequila, only genuine mezcal, which is made from the agave plant in Oaxaca province. According to the locals, it tastes delicious. One brand of mezcal available in the United States which occasionally is bottled with a worm inside is Monte Alban (80 proof).

Serving and storing tequila. Tequila, like other clear or white spirits, has a minimum of 80 proof, which eliminates the possibility of freezing. With the exception of one or two "super-prestige" brands, there is really no need to chill tequila. It has an extremely long shelf life, either opened or unopened, and reacts quite well to direct sunlight. Although some people enjoy drinking it straight, it is mostly used in mixed drinks.

Tequila has a very unusual and distinctive taste quite different from that of other clear spirits. Its flavor is somewhat herbaceous, grassy, and vegetal in nature, and has a natural affinity to salt and lemon juice.

There are many brands available in the United States. Among the most popular are:

Don Emilio	Jose Cuervo	Sauza
Gavilan	Montezuma	Torado
Herradura	Pedro Domecq	Two Fingers

Vodka

Vodka is an alcoholic distillate made from a fermented mash primarily of grain, which is distilled at a high proof, and processed further to extract all congeners with the use of activated charcoal. According to United States federal standards of identity, the final product must be "without *distinctive* character, aroma, taste or color." However, no federal law requires vodka to be *entirely* without aroma or taste; therefore, some vodkas display distinctive characteristics in aroma *and* taste. Federal law governs the production of vodkas in the United States.

Vodka seems to have first appeared in either Russia or Poland around the twelfth century, when it was first known as *zhizenennia voda* (water of life) in the Russian monastery-fort of Viatka. The word *vodka* is a diminutive of the Russian word for water, *voda* (although it has been proved that the Russians took this word from the Poles). By the fourteenth century, vodka began to be used as a beverage; formerly, it was mainly used in perfumes and cosmetics. However, it was primarily employed as the base ingredient of many "wonder drugs" or "cure-all" elixirs. During the fifteenth century, Poland produced many types of vodka as well as several "grades" which varied according to the number of times the vodka was distilled and refined.

Vodka was originally made from the most plentiful and least expensive ingredient available, which in most cases was the potato. Today, grain rules as the main base ingredient for vodka throughout the world. The early vodkas, even if made from grains, were strongly flavored, and therefore it became a common practice to add certain spices to mask the sometimes harsh, raw taste of the grain. It was not discovered until the early 1800s, that charcoal could be used to absorb most or all of the aromas and flavors of congeners in the vodka—thus the relatively tasteless, colorless vodka that is produced today.

Vodka production. Vodka can be made from any fermentable material, including rye, potatoes, corn, beets, grapes, and even sugarcane. Vodkas produced from grain are accepted as the finest; those produced from other materials often display a "distinctive" aroma or taste. To begin with, neutral spirits, which are highly refined distillates (with a minimum of 190 proof), are taken from the still and reduced in proof by the addition of pure water. They are then slowly and continuously run through tanks containing vegetable charcoal for a period of not less than eight hours. Filtration systems do not have to use charcoal; in fact, some vodka producers actually use fine sand, which is made from pulverized silicon dioxide. The famed Russian vodka producer Stolichnaya, for example, is proud of its special combination quartz-sand and activated charcoal filtering system.

The type of charcoal used in filtration, what kind of wood it comes from, the duration of the char process, and how long the charcoal was air dried also determine the taste, or lack of distinctive taste, of a vodka.

Vodka may be stored in containers of stainless steel, porcelain, concrete, glass, paraffin, or any other neutral material—rarely ever wood. Vodka produced in the United States is never aged, so that no age claim can be made. Vodkas are generally bottled between 80 and 100 proof, although higher-proof vodkas do exist.

Vodka enters the U.S. Peter Smirnoff first began making vodka in Russia in 1818 (actually, the Smirnoff family was not Russian; they came from Lvov, Poland). Immediately after World War I, the Bolsheviks gained control of the nation and Vladimir Smirnoff (decendant of Peter) was forced into exile in Paris.

It wasn't until 1934 that vodka was first introduced commercially into the United States by Rudolph Kunett. He was of Ukrainian extraction, and his father sold grain and alcohol to the Iron Bridge Distillery of Moscow. Kunett bought the American rights to Smirnoff from Vladimir Smirnoff. Kunett originally set up business in Bethel, Connecticut with the American branch of Societé Pierre (Peter) Smirnoff et Fils, but did not prosper. He then met John G. Martin, the English-born president of the small but long-respected Hartford-based firm of Heublein. Against strong opposition Martin arranged to retain Kunett, and in 1939 Heublein purchased the Smirnoff name and formula for a mere $14,000 (plus some royalties), taking over its manufacture and sales. For many years Smirnoff vodka used the slogan, "It will leave you breathless."

Today's market. Today, there are more than two hundred brands of vodka sold in the United States, including imports from the Baltic countries, Canada, China, Czechoslovakia, England, Finland, France, Germany, Israel, Japan, Poland, Russia, Sweden, and Turkey.

Some notable vodka name brands.

Absolut (Swedish). The name *Absolut* comes from the phrase *"Absolut renat Brannvin,"* which means "absolutely pure vodka." Absolut vodka, made from wheat, was first produced in Sweden in 1879, but was not introduced into the United States until 1979. In 1986 a pepper-flavored Absolut, called Peppar, was introduced into the United States. Peppar, which is clear in color, is made from a blend of natural jalapeño pepper and paprika.

Finlandia (Finnish). This vodka was first produced in 1888, but was not introduced into the United States until 1970. Its distinctive bottle is the creation of Finland's most famous designer, Tipio Wirkkala. The cracked ice surface of the glass bottle and its classic label portraying two white reindeer in combat under the red midnight sun of Lapland form a unique package.

Stolichnaya (Russian). This vodka was first introduced into the United States in 1973. In addition to the traditional vodka, Stolichnaya also produces Limonnaya, Okhotnichya, and Pertsovka (see below).

Other vodka brands are:

Anatevka, and Carmel (Israel)	Sermeq (Danish)
Burrough's (English)	Silhouette (Canadian)
Great Wall, and Tsing Tao (Chinese)	Suntory (Japanese)
Izmira (Turkish)	Wodka Wyborowa (Polish)

Flavored vodkas. Flavored vodkas are vodkas that are made with the addition of any natural flavoring materials, with or without sugar. The name of the flavoring *must* appear on the label. Some examples of flavored vodkas are:

Limonnaya. The base vodka is flavored with the aromatics of fresh lemon peels. It is made in the USSR.

Okhotnichya. This is a 90-proof "hunter's vodka," made in the USSR, that has a deep straw color and slightly herbal aroma. It is infused with many ingredients including sugar, giving it a honeylike sweetness, making it ideal for serving with desserts or after dinner. The ingredients are ginger, tormentil (an herb), ash woodroots, cloves, red and black pepper, juniper, coffee, anise, orange and lemon peels, white port, and sugar. The aging process takes several months. (The term "hunter's vodka" originates from the tradition in which the aristocrats of Czarist Russia drank such vodkas to celebrate a successful hunt.)

Pertsovka. This is a 70-proof vodka made in the USSR, with an infusion of red, white, and black pepper (capsicum, cayenne, and cubeb, which is another berry from the pepper family). Pertsovka is aged for several months in wood or metal casks, then strained and bottled for export. It is brown in color and can be fiery hot.

Starka. This 86-proof vodka made in the USSR, is amber in color. Starka is one of the few available aged vodkas (up to ten years) that has hints of brandy, vanilla, honey, and port, and a scent of the leaves of several different types of Crimean apple and pear trees.

Zubrowka. This is a flavored vodka produced in Slavic countries; it has a yellow-green tinge and a distinctive smell and taste, which is derived from various botanicals that have been added. Bottles of it at one time contained a single blade of grass, but these are no longer available in the United States, because U.S. scientists believed that the grass contained *coumarin*, a toxic compound found in some plants, which was said to cause liver cancer. The vodka, minus the grass, is available in the United States and is free from anything harmful.

Serving and storing vodka. Vodka's taste is that of ethyl alcohol or ethanol, which is indeed a definite flavor.

Bottles of premium vodka should be stored in the freezer. They won't freeze because of their high alcohol content. They will, however, become somewhat thick and almost syrupy, adding to one's enjoyment of it. Vodka can be drunk neat (straight, without ice), chilled, or even Arctic cold, served in Y-shaped glasses and downed in one gulp. Vodka is the perfect accompaniment to caviar, anchovies, sardines, potatoes and sour cream, pickled herring, various breads, and smoked fishes, especially salmon, as well as to spicy foods such as Thai, Szechwan, Hunan, Mexican and Indian foods.

There are many different drinks that can be made from this most versatile spirit, including Bloody Marys, screwdrivers, Moscow Mules, martinis, vodka and tonics, Black Russians, and White Russians.

Suggested Readings

Cooper, Derek and Dione Pattullo. *Enjoying Scotch*. London, England: Johnston and Bacon, 1980.

Ford, Gene. *Wines, Brews and Spirits*. Dubuque, Iowa, William C. Brown, 1983.

Getz, Oscar. *Whiskey: An American Pictorial History*. New York: David McKay, 1978.

Gorman, Marion and Felipe P. de Alba. *The Tequila Book*. Chicago: Contemporary, 1978.

Discussion Topics and Questions

1. Why do most customers on the East Coast ask for "rye" whiskey when what they really want is a blended whiskey?

2. Jack Daniel's is often referred to erroneously on many beverage lists as a bourbon. Why does this error continually occur?

3. What differences exist between bourbon and Tennessee whiskey?

4. Is it appropriate to call Tennessee whiskey "sour mash" when the sour mash procedure also applies to bourbon whiskey?

5. Compare and contrast the minimum aging requirements for all types of "brown whiskies."

6. What, if any, are the major differences between Scotch and Irish whiskies?

7. Seagram's has on several occasions petitioned the United States federal government to lower the minimum proof level of distilled spirits, thus making them better able to compete in today's trend toward "lightness" in alcoholic beverages. Do you agree or disagree with this practice? Be able to back up your opinions.

8. Single-malt Scotches have existed for well over one hundred years. Why the sudden interest in them now?

9. Why has the consumption of "white spirits" dramatically overtaken that of the more traditional "brown whiskies?"

10. To what extent have Mexican-type restaurants influenced the growth of tequila as a separate spirits category?

11. If you were in charge of a public relations program to promote bourbon as our only national spirit, what steps would you take?

12. Is the rise in popularity of flavored gins and vodkas merely part of a cycle that ebbs and flows, or is it permanent?

13. Set up a back bar with brand names of "white spirits" that need refrigeration or that should be stored in the freezer.

14. Are the traditional cocktails of the 1950s and 1960s becoming popular again, and if so what effect will this have on today's growth level of distilled spirits?

10

Brandy, Liqueurs, and Other Distillates

This chapter discusses:

- Brandy, and how it is made.
- American-produced brandies; brandies produced in Europe, Mexico, and Peru.
- Fruit brandies of the world and how they are made.
- Fruit-flavored brandies; how they differ from fruit brandies and liqueurs.
- Calvados: France's apple brandy; how it is made, understanding its label, and brand names.
- The history, geography, and production methods of Armagnac and Cognac; blending and aging; labeling terminology; how to serve them.
- Lesser-known distillates.
- Various types of liqueurs; generic and proprietary names; how they are made and what they are made from; and how to serve them.

Brandy has for many years been known as the ideal after-dinner beverage, or the drink that warms one up on a cold day. The name *brandy* originates with the Dutch, who are believed to have been the first great connoisseurs of this drink; they called it *brandewijn*, meaning *burnt wine*. This referred to the process by which brandy was made: wine was heated, and the resulting vapor distilled. This term was carried over into Germany as *branntwein* (*weinbrand*) and into France as *brandevin*. The English adopted the word as *brandywine*, which was later shortened to *brandy*.

In addition to brandy, there are many other high-proof distillates; some are flavored after distillation, while others are flavored by their base ingredients.

The liqueurs we know today—alcoholic beverages made from natural flavorings such as fruits, berries, and juices—have come a long way from the medicinal "magic potions" concocted by medieval monks.

More than 2,300 years ago, Hippocrates, the Greek physician, wrote about a certain cordial called *Hydromel*, which was made of wine, honey, and aromatic herbs and botanicals. During that era, alchemists strove to develop recipes for use as love potions, cure-alls for man's ailments, guarantees of everlasting life or rejuvenation, and aphrodisiacs.

In 1533 during the High Renaissance of sixteenth-century Italy, Queen Catherine de Medici introduced France to liqueurs, when she brought *rosolio,* an Italian liqueur (as well as many other sweet liqueurs), to France. Thereafter it became fashionable to serve liqueurs at court.

Increased sea trade in the seventeenth-century brought new fruits, herbs, and spices to Europe. Many were used in liqueurs, which became more varied.

In the 1700s, when Louis XIV's doctor used an herbal liqueur to cure the king's stomach ailments, liqueurs became even more popular in France. In Victorian times, they became customary at formal dinners.

Bistros all over France were serving exotic, colorful liqueurs to their regulars when the cocktail craze of the 1920s caught on. Liqueurs were used in such drinks as parfait amour, monkey gland, and forbidden fruit.

Brandy

Brandy is a spirit made by distilling wines or the fermented mash of fruit, which is then suitably aged in oak barrels. The varying characteristics of different brandies are the result of differences in fruit and grape varieties, climate, soil, and production methods, which vary from district to district and country to country.

Generally speaking, the wines used in the production of brandy are not of drinkable quality; they tend to be rather acidic and harsh.

Brandy is distilled either by the pot still (this produces the highest-quality brandy) or by the more common and modern patent still (also called the continuous still). In the pot still method, the distillation process is carried out in single batches, which is laborious, time-consuming, and expensive. Using the patent still saves time because the distillation is a continuous process.

The pot still resembles a large copper pot with a broad rounded base, topped by a long column. Initially, anywhere from 250 to 2,600 gallons of wine (depending on the still's size) are loaded into the base of the pot still. The wine is then heated and kept simmering until the alcohol is vaporized and rises up into the column, taking with it flavors from the wine; this gives brandy its characteristic aroma and taste. When the vapor rises to a certain point in the column, it comes into contact with a cold condenser, which turns the vapor into liquid alcohol (in this case, brandy). In the pot still method, there are two distillations. The initial distillation is collected at a strength of 30 percent alcohol; this is then redistilled to approximately 70 to 80 percent alcohol. (The brandy, before it is redistilled, is called *singlings*.) Only the middle or "heart" of a distillation is collected, and the first and last runs, called "heads" and "tails," are redistilled before they can be used.

The patent or continuous still operates in the manner described above, except that it can be continuously fed with wine.

The brandy, after the second distillation, is colorless and 70 to 80 percent alcohol (140 to 160 proof). It is put into charred oak barrels to soften the fiery, rough liquid. The barrel, because of its composition, will allow a slight oxidation to take place; the brandy also absorbs various flavoring substances from it. When the distiller feels that the brandy has aged sufficiently, its alcoholic content will be cut with the addition of distilled water to a level of not less than 80 proof. At this point, caramel coloring can be added to the brandy to "adjust" its color. The brandy will then be filtered to remove any suspended particles, and finally bottled.

Brandy is expensive simply because ten gallons of wine are needed to produce one gallon of brandy.

American Brandy

Approximately 95 percent of all American-made brandies come from California; therefore, the following information will be based on California production methods and types of brandy.

California brandy was first made by Spanish missionaries, after they had produced several successive vintages of wine. Jean Louis Vignes, a Frenchman, is credited with producing, in about 1837, California's first brandy. Captain John Sutter later produced brandy at Sutter's Fort in 1841, but after encountering serious problems, decided to stop production. The brandy industry didn't really develop until about 1867, when Almaden Vineyards of Madera (the first and also oldest producer of brandy in California) began to produce brandy. In 1955, the firm of Fromm & Sichel marketed a premixed drink, the Dry Brandini, which was displayed for promotion in a martini stem glass with a twist of lemon peel. It consisted of one part dry vermouth and four parts brandy. In 1968, E. & J. Gallo brandy was sold for the first time. In 1972, the Christian Brothers Winery of Napa Valley first introduced X-O Rare Reserve brandy. Other fine producers are Korbel Champagne Cellars, Paul Masson, and The Woodbury Winery.

By law, all California brandy must be made from grapes grown and distilled in California. It must be aged a minimum of two years in oak barrels, and if aged for less time, it must be labeled an "immature brandy." For brandies that are aged for more than two years, the age may be stated on the label.

There is no required grape variety for use in brandy production in California; many different varieties are used. Most distillers use the Thompson Seedless or Flame Tokay grapes to make brandy, as they are inexpensive, nondescript, and produce a fairly good product.

Brandies of Other Countries

Germany. Asbach Uralt was first produced in 1907 by Hugo Asbach. He was also the first to register a brand name of brandy (also in 1907) at the Imperial Patent Office in Berlin.

Greece. Metaxa Distillery was founded in 1888 by Spyros Metaxa.

Italy. Stock 84 is produced by the Stock Distillery of Trieste; Vecchia Romagna VSOP was first produced in 1820 under the name of Buton (after Jean Buton moved to Emilia-Romagna, Italy, he changed its name to Vecchia Romagna).

Mexico. Presidente brandy is produced by the Pedro Domecq Distillery.

Peru. Inca Pisco brandy is distilled from Muscat or Mission grapes.

Spain. Fundador brandy is produced by Pedro Domecq, a wine and brandy producer since 1730. Carlos I is the name of the finest brandy produced by Pedro Domecq. Other Spanish brandy producers are Torres, Duff-Gordon, Sandeman, Gonzalez-Byass, and Terry.

Fruit Brandy

Fruit brandies may be produced from almost any kind of fruit. Wild or cultivated fruits containing stones or seeds, and even most berries, will yield a suitable-tasting brandy. The production method is simple: basically, the fruit is thoroughly washed, then chopped or ground until it resembles a slurry, known as the *mash*. At this point water and a specially cultivated yeast is added; the mixture is then allowed to ferment until all of the sugar has been metabolized. The mash is then pressed, and the liquid collected; the solid mash is discarded or used as animal feed. The liquid is distilled either in a continuous or pot still until the desired proof is reached. The brandy may also be aged in oak barrels. Fruit brandies state on their labels the name of the fruit used, or use accepted European names such as those listed below.

Fruit brandies

Applejack or apple brandy: Made from apples; similar to Calvados. The premier producer of applejack is the Laird's & Co. Distillery. Laird's, the oldest U.S. distillery, was established in 1851 in Scobeyville, New Jersey.

Barack Pálinka: Made from apricots; produced in Austria and Hungary.

Calvados: (See the later section specifically on Calvados.)

Fraise: Made from strawberries; French.

Framboise (called Himbeergeist in Germany and parts of Switzerland): Made from raspberries.

Kirsch (French); Kirschwasser (Swiss): Made from small, semiwild cherries which generally come from the Black Forest (Germany), the Vosges (France), or parts of Switzerland.

Mirabelle: Made from yellow plums; French.

Poire: Made from pears, mostly in Switzerland and occasionally France. The best-known is Poire Williams, each bottle of which contains a fully mature pear—not an easy accomplishment. When the pear is about the size of a grape, it is placed, still on the branch, in the bottle. When the pear is mature, the branch is cut away, the pear washed, and the bottle filled with pear brandy.

Quetsch: Made from blue plums; usually produced in Alsace, France.

Slivovitz: Made from blue plums; usually produced in central Europe and Hungary.

Calvados

Calvados is made from different varieties of apples that grow in the Normandy, Brittany, and Maine regions of northwest France. Calvados is actually an *eau-de-vie* of cider, or a brandy distilled from either cider or the juice of fresh apples. The Swiss call their apple brandy *Batzi*.

The name *Calvados* is not French, but of Spanish origin. It comes from the name of a Spanish ship, El Calvador, of Phillip II's fleet, which sank off the French coast of Normandy in 1588.

Cider brandy was first distilled in about 1553 by Giles de Bouberville, a Norman farmer. As early as 1600, during the reign of Henri IV, Norman cider brandy distillers had formed a corporation.

In 1941, when the French government was instituting regulations to ensure consistent excellence for the region's distilled apple brandy, Calvados was legally baptized.

Calvados production is controlled by French law. Those carrying an *appellation contrôlée* designation on their labels must be made from apples grown in the legally established Calvados regions. They must also be pressed into cider and distilled there. They are generally double distilled in pot stills and suitably aged in oak barrels; these are considered the finest Calvados. Calvados labeled *appellation réglementée* is produced by the continuous still method and may use apples from other designated parts of Normandy; it is considered to be of a lower quality than that made in Calvados.

The production process. Calvados is made by crushing apples into juice, which is fermented in oak barrels until it reaches between 4 to 6 degrees of alcohol. This takes approximately one month. The juice is then transferred to a still, in which it is double distilled.

According to a 1971 rule, Calvados must be aged in Limousin oak barrels of varying size (400 to 45,000 l.) for a period of not less than one year, before being sold commercially. Generally, Calvados is aged for up to three or four years.

The alcoholic content of Calvados ranges between 75 and 84 proof. The color, which is not an indication of age or lightness of body, varies among producers.

Younger Calvados are drier and retain an appley taste. The older blends acquire a more refined and subtle taste in aging.

Label designations. Calvados labeled "three stars" is at least two years old. The terms *old*, *réserve*, or *vieux* denote three years of age; *VO* (*vielle réserve*) indicates an age of four years. *VSOP*, or *grand réserve*, indicates an age of five years. The terms *extra Napoleon, hors d'age*, or *age inconnu* apply solely to Calvados that are more than five years old.

Brand Names. The following are some of the better-known brands of Calvados:

Boulard	Morice
Busnel	Norois
Chevalier de Brevil	Pere Magloire
Montgommery	

Fruit-Flavored Brandies

These brandies are produced in basically the same manner as fruit brandies, except that a minimum of 2.5 percent sugar is added, along with natural coloring and flavoring derived from the base fruit. In addition to fruits, other ingredients can also be used—coffee beans and anise seeds, for example. Under U.S. federal law, fruit-flavored brandies are classified as cordials and cannot be bottled at less than 70 proof.

Armagnac

Although Armagnac is technically a brandy, it is often confused with its close cousin, Cognac. However, Armagnac's taste is fuller and richer than that of Cognac, and is generally described as less "burning," and more mellow.

Armagnac has been distilled in Gascony (in southwest France, 150 miles southeast of Bordeaux) since 1422, making it the world's oldest brandy. However, it was not until the mid-1600s that it was first exported, by the Dutch.

The demarcated region of Armagnac comprises approximately 52,000 acres of quite sandy soil, mixed with some limestone, clay, and chalk. It is bounded roughly by the Garonne Valley to the north, Toulouse to the east, Bayonne and Bordeaux to the west, and the Pyrenees to the south. Its average annual production of wine is under 79 million gallons.

About one-quarter of this wine is distilled into brandy; the remainder is consumed as table wine.

The Armagnac region is divided into three zones: Upper Armagnac (Haut-Armagnac), the smallest area (3 percent of the total brandy production comes from this zone), which is often called "White Armagnac" because of its chalky, limestone-containing calcareous soil; Lower Armagnac (Bas-Armagnac), which is by far the largest zone (57 percent of production), and is often called "Black Armagnac," because of its forests; and Tenareze (40 percent of production). The quality, style, and taste of Armagnac varies from zone to zone, and it is generally agreed that the finest Armagnacs come from the Bas-Armagnac zone (whose name appears on bottle labels).

On May 25, 1909, the French government officially granted the region of Armagnac its own *appellation contrôlée*. Since then the production, viticulture, distillation process, and aging of Armagnac are subject to detailed official inspection and strict controls. These regulations have, since 1909, became more specific: more accurate definitions were introduced in 1936, and perfected in 1972.

The production process. The quality of Armagnac is based on several factors: the grapes, the wine, the distillation process, and the aging and blending processes.

The production of Armagnac involves a multistep process. Major white grape varieties, such as the famed St. Émilion, Colombard, Folle Blanche, and Baco 22A (a cross between the American Noah and Folle Blanche), are used, as well as approximately half a dozen minor varieties. These grapes all have two things in common: they yield wines low in alcohol, and are high in natural acidity.

After the juice ferments into wine, it is not racked, but instead is left in contact with the lees to extract additional flavoring components, which add more complexity. The wine is then transferred to continuous copper stills called *alembic armagnacais* (permitted since 1973), a term that has Moorish origins. The wine is distilled in one continuous, slow process (unlike Cognac production, in which there are two) to produce a colorless brandy with a powerful bouquet and flavor (sometimes described as *eau-de-feu*: fire-water). According to French law, all distillation must be completed by April 30 of the year following the grape harvest.

The brandies made from different varieties of grapes are aged separately for a minimum of three years. During this time there is constant evaporation due to changes in temperature, humidity, and the porosity of the wooden barrels. The amount that evaporates is approximately 3 percent of annual production (15 million bottles); it is known as "the angels' share." In most aging cellars in Armagnac the walls and ceilings are covered with a microscopic grey mold, the *Torula* fungus, which feeds on the alcohol vapors.

Armagnac is aged in black, sappy, tannic-rich, fine-grained, 400-liter oak casks from the Monlezun forest of France. The development of Armagnac's complex flavor and deep amber color is dependent on ridges in the wooden casks used: coopers, using axes, shape each stave along the grain to expose more of the wood's surface area (from which the flavor and color is absorbed) to the brandy.

During this aging process a slow oxidation also takes place which intensifies the brandy's color and smooths out its raw flavor. The Armagnac also acquires a musky aroma, reminiscent of hazelnuts, peaches, plums, prunes, and other fruits.

After proper aging, the last and perhaps most important part of the process takes place: blending, the secret to the production of an excellent Armagnac. Armagnac brandies of different origins and ages are skillfully blended under the strictest quality controls; this is an art that has been handed down generation after generation, for centuries.

After blending, the brandy's alcohol level is adjusted by adding distilled water, and its color corrected by adding caramel. Armagnac is kept in large vats for an additional six months to allow for the proper curing, or "marrying," of the blend.

Label designations. Most Armagnacs that are shipped to the United States are classified VSOP (very superior old pale), VO (very old), or *réserve*. For all of these classifications, the youngest brandy in the blend will be at least four-and-a-half years old.

Extra, Napoleon, XO, *vielle réserve*, and similar label designations indicate that the youngest brandy used in the blend is at least five-and-a-half years old (although larger amounts of older Armagnacs have been used). If, for example, a distiller chooses to blend a thirty-year-old Armagnac with a four-year-old Armagnac, the blend will always be described as being four years old.

Generally, the longer an Armagnac remains in wood, the finer and smoother its taste is. But after about forty years in cask, there has been so much evaporation of alcohol and water that the remaining Armagnac starts to become concentrated and viscous.

Legislation enacted on January 1, 1977 rules that if a vintage date appears on the label of a bottle of Armagnac, it signifies the year in which the product was *distilled*, not the year in which the grapes were harvested. (No indication is given of how many years the Armagnac remained in wood.) All Armagnac must come from the year indicated on the label, and cannot have been blended with Armagnacs from other years.

Brand names. Some brands of Armagnac that are available in the United States are:

Château de Laubade	Loubere
Cles des Ducs	Malliac
Clos de Moutouguet	Maniban
De Montal	Marquis de Caussade
Francis Darroze	Marquis de Monod
Janneau	Marquis de Montesquiou
Laberdolive	Samalens
Lafontan	Sempé
Lapostolle	St. Vivant
Larressingle	

Cognac

Cognac, a small medieval town in southwest France, just north of Bordeaux, originally became known because of its proximity to the town of Angoulême, where the train from Paris once stopped on its way to Bordeaux, and then Spain. Many foreign buyers of wines and spirits thus found their way to Cognac and, once there, could always be assured of accommodation by the Cognac families.

Cognac is located in the departments of Charente and Charente Maritime (which were established in 1791, by combining the provinces of Aunis, Saintonge, and Angoumois). The Cognac region's stony, chalk-rich soil (which is probably due to ancient oyster beds), its climate, and the specific grape varieties grown there, as well as the methods used in distilling, blending, and aging the brandy, give that beverage its unique flavor.

Cognac (the brandy) was first produced more or less by accident; until the fifteenth century Charente was strictly a wine-producing area. Unfortunately, its stony chalky soil was mainly suitable for growing varieties of grapes (Saint Émilion, Folle Blanche, and Colombard) that made for an exceedingly acidic white wine. These wines did not stand up well on long sea voyages, and were far less appealing than the delicious white wines produced by grape growers on the nearby Atlantic coast; and, the fact that these poor, thin, acidic wines were being taxed at the same rate as better-quality wines hardly increased their popularity.

Undaunted, the industrious farmers of the Charente decided to make an experiment. Seamen from Britain and Scandinavia regularly visited the area to obtain salt, which was much sought after by cod and herring preservers. The Cognac vintners realized that they could develop an export market, utilizing these foreign cargo ships, for their rather ordinary wine if they distilled it. This, they reasoned, would save ship cargo space and reduce export taxes, which at that time were based on bulk. The original idea was that the distilled spirit, which had an alcohol content of 75 percent, would later be reconstituted by adding water.

During this time trade routes were blockaded because of the War of Spanish Succession (1701–1714), and export sales to England and the Netherlands were halted; the distilled wine from Cognac thus had to be stored for a time. When trade resumed, the Limousin oak–aged distilled wine was found to have lost its fiery taste and to have taken on a beautiful golden amber color. Its flavor had also improved, and it had acquired a great mellowness.

To accomplish the distillation, the vintners had used an onion-shaped pot still called an *alembic*, which had been brought to the region five centuries earlier by invading Moors, who had used it to distill the nectar of flowers for perfume. (Later, it was used by medieval alchemists in attempts to turn nonprecious metals into gold.) The distillation process, to everyone's astonishment, had resulted in a drink that was delicious in its own right. Since the new drink was as clear as water, the vintners dubbed it *eau-de-vie* (water of life). This "water of life," which was drunk straight, enjoyed tremendous success on the medieval export market.

Word about the discovery spread quickly. Naturally, vintners in other areas tried to copy the production techniques that were fast making the farmers of Cognac the wealthiest in the land, but it seemed that nature had balanced the scales. The vintners of Cognac had struggled unsuccessfully for centuries to produce good wines from grapes grown in their light gray, stony, chalky soil; but when growing grapes for the distilled brandy, they found that the chalkier the soil the better. Other areas simply were not able to produce a comparable product.

Would-be imitators flourished nonetheless, until on May 1, 1909, the French government passed a law proclaiming that only the product made in a sharply defined "delimited area"—139,000 acres surrounding the town of Cognac—could be called Cognac. All other brandies, however good, must be called by some other name.

The Cognac production area. In 1936, the French government officially divided the delimited Cognac area (see figure 10-1) into seven sections (the Bois Ordinaires and Bois à Terroir are usually grouped together; there is thus sometimes confusion over whether there are six or seven districts). The seven sections, which—very roughly—describe

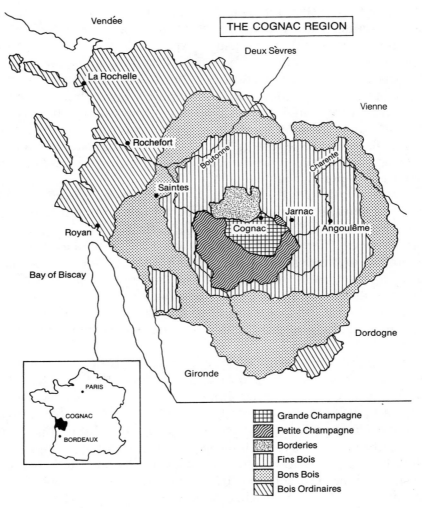

Figure 10-1 Map of the Cognac region.

concentric circles around the town of Cognac, are: Grande Champagne; Petite Champagne; Borderies; Fin Bois; Bon Bois; and Bois Ordinaire and Bois à Terroir (also called Bois à Communs). The highest-quality Cognacs are produced in Grande Champagne and Petite Champagne.

The production process. Under French law, only these major grape varieties may be used in the production of Cognac: St. Émilion (known as Ugni Blanc in California, and Trebbiano in Italy), Folle Blanche, and Colombard. The grapes are generally harvested quite early, when sugars barely reach 17° Brix, ensuring a wine with a low alcohol content (about 8 percent), and a very high acid level (usually above 1 percent).

After the juice ferments into wine, it is slowly warmed and transferred into copper pot stills (figure 10-2), which are heated by gas or coal. The first distillation lasts between eight and twelve hours, producing the *brouillis*, which is a distillate of approximately 50 to 60 proof. This is heated a second time for about twelve hours in an extremely critical process; many years of experience are necessary before one can control temperature, climate, and distillate strength—all in the proper balance. The new colorless liquid (called the *bonne chauffe*) that is produced by the second distillation is a youthful, overstrong Cognac, which must now be matured. French law states that the final distillate must not have an alcohol content exceeding 72 percent; if it does, it may not be called Cognac. Distillation at this proof allows for the retention of substantial amounts of flavoring congeners.

Under French law, the capacity of these stills may not exceed 793 gallons; this restriction prevents the swift conversion of wine to spirit. It allows for pinpoint accuracy, however, in restricting or facilitating the flow of the distillate. French law also dictates that distillation must be completed by March 31, while the wine is in its bloom of youth, fruity and unoxidized.

Aging. After Cognac has been distilled for the second time, it is placed into barrels (which hold about 55 gallons) that are made of oak wood from the Limousin and Troncais forests. The oak used has a considerable influence on the bouquet and taste of the Cognac; it introduces soluble substances such as aromatic aldehydes, lignin derivatives, gum, polyphenols, salts, and sugars. When Cognac is first placed in the barrel it is about 70 percent alcohol, and is crystal clear in color. During the aging process, the oak from the casks imparts its taste, color, and odor to the final product, turning the clear *eau-de-vie* into a mellow, golden drink.

Figure 10-2 A classic Cognac alambic, or copper pot still, which has been used continuously from 1880 through 1973 by the Hennessy Company in France. (Courtesy of Moet-Hennessy, France)

Aging is a critical step in the production process and, in conjunction with soil qualities, is a key factor in determining the quality and price of the final spirit. The older a Cognac becomes, the smoother its flavor, the more subtle its aroma, and the more it costs. No Cognac sold contains spirits of only a single vintage. All Cognacs are ultimately blends that combine spirits from varying sections and vintages into a final product. Today, in the town of Cognac, there are barrels of spirits that have been aging for a hundred years or more.

Aging barrels of Cognac are stored in warehouses that are usually built on stilts above the ground so that air can circulate freely through the casks, allowing the Cognac to "breathe." During this time, there is constant evaporation due to changes in temperature, humidity, and the porosity of the wooden barrels, reducing the alcoholic content of the Cognac to approximately 40 percent. Approximately 3 to 5 percent of annual Cognac production per year is lost through evaporation (this amounts to 22 million bottles, or one-fourth of annual world sales). In order to compensate for this loss, distillers regularly "top off" the barrels with similar Cognacs.

Once bottled, Cognac remains unchanged: unlike wines that age in the bottle, Cognac ages only in cask. Therefore, a Cognac that has aged three years in oak is a three-year old Cognac, even if it has been sitting in a musty cellar for one hundred years.

Aging casks of Cognac virtually fill the town of Cognac. The stone-walled warehouses of the largest firms often hold as many as 200,000 barrels, stacked in three tiers. A single warehouse may contain 30,000 barrels. Casks of young, middle-aged, and old Cognacs are stored in each of the warehouses. This way, if there is a fire, a firm will not be left with a shortage of Cognac of a certain year.

Blending. The last critical phase of Cognac production is the blending of the final spirit. There are currently some 320 Cognac firms, each of which has its own master taster/blender who must reproduce, year after year, the distinctive character and flavor that have become the trademark of the company's product. The possibilities are endless: some firms produce blends that are hefty and full-bodied; others create spirits that are fruity and mellow, or light and smooth. It is the master blender's job to maintain the integrity of the company's signature taste.

In order to keep his nose and taste buds in top form, the master blender lives under the rigid routine of an athlete. His is a difficult job: he must be able to discern, by taste and smell, the year in which the grapes of a certain Cognac were grown and from which sections of the region the grapes came—even from which section within a section. Since the same section may produce quite a different variety of Cognacs in different years, the taster's job is as much an art as a science. He must, in effect, analyze with one sniff the life history of each sample brought to him.

The master blender works for two hours in the morning every day of the year. First, he holds his glass (a small tulip-shaped vessel, rather than a traditional wide-brimmed brandy snifter) up to the daylight to determine the color of the Cognac. He then twirls the glass slowly by the stem, allowing the bouquet to come out at full flower. Next, he warms the glass in his hands, "encouraging" the aroma. Finally, he thrusts his nose directly into the opening and inhales. In fact, the master is tasting almost entirely with his nose. His taste buds would become desensitized were he to take an oral sampling of the forty to fifty specimens brought to him each morning. Any mistake can cost the firm thousands of dollars.

When the tasting is complete, the master selects the Cognacs that he will use to produce this year's blends. He then writes out various formulas and creates samples using the old, middle-aged, and young Cognacs that he has selected. He tastes the samples, and sips, smells, and compares them to the established brands he is trying to duplicate. When there is the slightest difference, he revises his formula and has new samples prepared. The process goes on until the precisely correct bouquet and taste have been obtained.

Labels. The ultimate results of the blender's efforts will be a line of Cognacs that represent a range of average ages and prices. The Cognac drinker can tell a great deal about the particular blend he is purchasing from the label on the bottle.

The following letters are used on Cognac labels in abbreviated designations of various classifications:

E = extra

O = old

P = pale

S = superior

V = very

X = extremely

These designations are commonly found:

VS (or three stars): This means that the average aging period of the Cognac in the blend is five to nine years, and the youngest Cognac in the blend is under four-and-a-half years old.

VO, VSOP, or réserve: These mean that the average age of the Cognac used in the blend is from twelve to twenty years. The youngest Cognac in this blend is at least four-and-a-half years old. In 1946, by French law, these designations became legal for use.

XO, Napoleon, VVSOP, cordon bleu, vielle réserve, grand réserve, royal, and vieux: These terms apply to Cognacs that contain a very high percentage of Cognac that has been aged for twenty, thirty, or forty years or more. The youngest Cognac in this blend is at least five-and-a-half years old.

Grande Fine Champagne, or Grande Champagne: These terms identify Cognacs made exclusively from grapes grown in the Grande Champagne section of Cognac.

Petite Fine Champagne, or Petite Champagne: These terms mean that the Cognac is a blend made from grapes grown in the Grande Champagne and Petite Champagne sections of Cognac; at least 50 percent of it must be from grapes grown in the Grande Champagne section.

The terms *fine Cognac* and *grande fine*, which may also be found on Cognac labels, have no legally defined meaning. The designations *extra old* (EO) and *very old pale* (VOP) are not officially recognized by the Bureau du Cognac.

In 1963, a French law was passed prohibiting the placement of vintage labels on Cognac bottles.

Serving and storing Cognac. Cognac can be enjoyed in a variety of ways. It has traditionally been regarded as an after-dinner drink, but in some countries (the Japanese, for example, mix it with seltzer) it is served before or with a meal almost like wine. Purists prefer to enjoy the older, finer Cognacs unmixed. A Cognac should be clear in color, but depth of tint is no indication of quality. Traditionally, Cognacs are served in tulip-shaped glasses tall enough to allow a reasonable aroma to build, yet small enough to be cradled entirely in one hand (the hand provides an overall gentle warmth that encourages the aroma). This is the type of glass used by the master blenders (figure 10-3).

Since traditional cognac glasses are not widely available in this country, most people prefer to drink the spirit from classic balloon-shaped brandy snifters. The main consideration is to select a glass that will enhance the beverage's bouquet. The glass should be large enough (10 oz.) to enable the liquid to move around with ease, spreading the bouquet over a wide surface area. Ideally, the neck should be slightly indented to help the spirit retain its bouquet. Unfortunately, many people choose much larger snifters, some holding as much as 32 ounces. The major problem with such glasses is that if a couple of ounces of Cognac are poured and the glass swirled, most of the Cognac adheres to the sides of the enlarged glass. At $25.00 or more per bottle of Cognac, that can be quite expensive.

Another popular item, often sold in specialty stores or catalogues, is a "brandy heater." It features a brandy snifter, perched at a 45-degree angle on a metal holder, above a short candle. According to the direc-

Figure 10-3 Proper glassware for serving Cognac. (Courtesy Cognac Information Bureau)

tions; pour some Cognac into the glass, light the candle below the bowl of the glass, and allow the candle to gently warm the liquid. In reality, if one follows these directions one will burn one's hands on the glass. And, subjected to an intensified heat, the Cognac's vapors, which are an intrinsic part of its enjoyment, will "burn off."

Although most people prefer not to mix older Cognacs, younger (VS, or three-star) Cognacs make delightful highballs when mixed with soda water, leaving the palate more receptive to wines. Cognac and freshly squeezed orange juice make an excellent cocktail. After dinner, Cognac is the perfect companion to coffee.

Younger Cognacs are also excellent for use in cooking. As the Cognac heats, it releases vapors that impart a subtle and distinctive aroma to the dish. Creating a flambé, in particular, is a dramatic but simple culinary technique that adds excitement and flavor to a variety of plain and fancy fare. The alcoholic content of the spirit is burned off during the process.

Some available brands of Cognac are:

Armand Roux	Hardy	Odeon
Bisquit	Hennessy	Otard
Camus	Hine	Prince Hubert de Polignac
Château de Fontpinot	Leyrat	Ragnaud
Courvoisier	Martell	Remy Martin
Delamain	M. Tiffon	Renault
Denise-Mounie	Monnet	Salignac
Gaston de LaGrange		

Other Spirits

Akvavit/Aquavit and Schnapps

Akvavit is a high-proof spirit made from a distillate of caraway seeds; because of its potency it was nicknamed "Black Death." It is quite popular in the Scandinavian countries, where it is known as Akvavit, Aquavit, or, in some locales, Brannvin.

Schnapps is a high-proof distillate flavored with numerous aromatic herbs; it is produced in Germany, Holland, and most Scandinavian countries. (It should not be confused with peppermint schnapps, which is a liqueur.)

Anise-Flavored Spirits

Anise-based spirits are produced by either infusion or the addition of flavoring, and have a high alcoholic content.

Absinthe is an aromatic, yellow-green spirit, flavored with oil of wormwood. This anise-based spirit was officially banned throughout most of the world on March 16, 1915. The technical name of the main ingredient was *Artemisia absinthium* (wormwood), an Old World plant or herb which grows about three feet high and is botanically related to our southwestern sagebrush. The oil from the leaves, called *absinthol*, contains a rather strong narcotic, *thujone* ($C_{10}H_{16}O$), which is poisonous in large doses.

Some of the problems associated with absinthe ingestion were: convulsions, mania, gastrointestinal irritation, extreme nervousness, drugged stupor, hallucination, and loss of hearing and sight. In large doses, absinthe induced a coma or even death. In 1905, a drunken and crazed man killed his wife and two daughters but failed to kill himself. His daily alcoholic consumption was six quarts of wine, six brandies, and a couple of absinthes; he was said to be in an absinthe-induced delirium. Stories of the outrage spread throughout the world, fired by temperance groups, causing the courts to ban the production of absinthe first in Switzerland, then in France. The French government on the pretext that alcohol was needed for the manufacture of gunpowder for the war, finally prohibited the manufacture and sale of absinthe in 1915, putting an end to a century of popularity.

Absinthe, with its dry, bitter, licoricelike flavor and herbal aroma, was resurrected in 1922 under the name Pernod, minus the toxic wormwood. In its place, anise was substituted; the alcohol content was lowered to 86 proof, and the drink's popularity was once again on the rise.

The French drink their anise spirits in a tall glass with ice-cold water, one part anise spirit to five parts water. When you drink anise spirits either chilled directly from the refrigerator or over ice, you may notice a cloudiness or opalescence, which adds to the beauty of the drink.

Other anise-based spirits are:

Anesone (Italy)
Chinchon (Spain)
Herbisant (United States)
Masticha (Greece)
Ojen (Spain)
Ouzo (Greece)
Pastis/Ricard (France)
Pernod (France)

Grappa and Marc

Grappa, also known as *vinaccia* (Italy) and *marc* (France) is a distillate made from the stems, pulp, skins, and pits (known as the *pomace*) of grapes—the remains from the pressing grapes for winemaking. It is estimated that 224 pounds of residue or pomace yields approximately five liters of pure alcohol. The residue of pressed fruit such as apples, apricots, and pears can also be used.

In the production process, water is added to the pomace (which may be from either red or white grapes), along with yeast and sugar. After the pomace finishes refermenting, the resulting liquid is double distilled, usually in small pot stills, and is removed from the still at between 100 to 130 proof.

This distillate is usually stored in stainless steel containers; it is bottled when quite young and is usually clear in color. However, if it is determined that the distillate should be aged, then oak barrels are used.

This distillate is quite raw, rough, and coarse in its youth, and it is several years before it becomes palatable. Traditionally, it is served after dinner as a digestive; it is consumed straight, either at room temperature, or well chilled.

The origin of the name *grappa* comes from a town called Bassano del Grappa in the Veneto region of Italy, where grappa was originally produced. In Portugal, the distillate is known as *Bagaceira*; in Spain, *Aguardiente*; in Germany, *Tresterschnapps*; and in South Africa, *Dop Brandy*.

Cordials and Liqueurs

The word *cordial* is derived from the Latin word *cor* or *cordis*, meaning *heart*; because the earliest cordials were administered to the sick to stimulate the heart and lighten the spirit. *Liqueur* is derived from the Latin world *liquefacere*, and means to dissolve or melt. The words *cordial* and *liqueur* are identical in meaning and are so indistinguishable from the point of view of nomenclature that they are always mentioned together in federal and state laws and regulations. *Liqueur* is generally accepted as the European name, and *cordial* as the American.

Cordials and liqueurs sold in the United States must contain a minimum of 2.5 percent sugar by weight. In practice, most cordials/liqueurs contain large percentages (up to 35 percent) of some sweetening agent. While there is no minimum alcohol level mandated by the federal government, most cordials/liqueurs are between 34 and 60 proof, while others are as high as 100 proof.

Production Process

The aromas, flavors, and tastes of cordials and liqueurs are produced by the addition of herbs, seeds, barks, roots, plants, flowers, fruit, fruit stones, and peels. The alcohol base can be brandy or neutral grain spirits.

Cordials and liqueurs are made by any of three different methods: maceration (also known as infusion); percolation; and distillation. Maceration and percolation are also known as the *cold methods*, because the flavoring materials are sensitive to heat and would be damaged by it. The cold method is a lengthy process that can take as long as one year.

Maceration is not unlike the brewing of tea. Fruit or other ingredients are placed directly into the spirit or brandy and allowed to steep until sufficient amounts of the aroma and flavor have been extracted into the spirit. Each ingredient has its own unique aroma and taste. After the steeping is complete, the spirit is drawn off and filtered; water is added and the color adjusted, and it is finally blended with sugar syrup or occasionally honey for consistency of taste. It is allowed to age or "marry" from several months to one year, in order to blend the flavors before bottling.

The percolation method is similar to the percolation of coffee. Spirits are put into the bottom of a tank and the botanicals (fruits, flowers, etc.) are placed in a basketlike container at the top of the tank. The spirits from the bottom of the tank are then pumped to the top where they are sprayed over the botanicals, dripping back to the bottom to be repercolated over and over until the desired flavor has been extracted.

Distillation, also known as the *hot extraction method*, is the process that is usually employed with most seeds, peels, flowers, roots, barks, plants, or some combination. These materials can withstand heat and benefit from a quicker extraction of flavor. The ingredients are first "softened" by soaking in brandy for several days before being transferred to a pot still.

Since all distillates are colorless, harmless artificial (and natural) colorants are added, along with sugar syrup.

Proprietary and Generic Liqueurs

France, Italy, and Holland produce more than 50 percent of all liqueurs available today; the following table gives information on many of these (asterisks denote proprietary brands).

PROPRIETARY AND GENERIC LIQUEURS

Liqueur	Flavor	Color	Proof	Country
Abisante	anise-herb	yellow-green	120	Many
Advokatt/Advocaat	eggnog	creamy yellow	30	Holland, Germany
Aki*	plum	red	49	Japan
Alize*	passion fruit, Cognac	yellow	32	France
Amaretto	almond, apricot	russet	54–56	Many
Amaretto di Saronno*	almond, apricot	russet	56	Italy
Ambrosia*	caramel	amber	56	Canada
Anisette	licorice	clear	50–60	Many
Abricotine*	apricot	orange-amber	60–70	France
Apricot liqueur	apricot	orange-amber	60–70	Many
Apry*	apricot	orange-amber	60	France
Ashanti Gold*	Armagnac, cacao	chocolate	56	Denmark
Aurum*	orange	orange	80	Italy
Bailey's Irish Cream*	Irish whiskey, cream	beige	34	Ireland
Blackberry liqueur	blackberry	red-purple	60	Many
Boggs Cranberry	cranberry	red	40	U.S.A.
Cafe Brizard*	coffee	dark brown	50	France
Caffe Lolita*	coffee	brown	53	U.S.A.
Carolan's Irish Cream*	Irish whiskey, cream	beige	34	Ireland
Chambord*	raspberry	red	33	France
Cheri-Suisse*	chocolate, cherry	dark brown	52	Switz.
CherriStock*	cherry	red	50	Italy
Cherry liqueur	cherry	red	50–60	Many
Cherry Marnier*	cherry	dark red	48	France
Chocolate liqueur	chocolate	dark brown	50–56	Many
CocoRibe*	rum, coconut	clear	42	U.S.A.
Coffee liqueur	coffee	dark brown	48–56	Many
Cointreau*	orange	clear	80	France
Cordial Medoc*	brandy, fruit	red	80	France

PROPRIETARY AND GENERIC LIQUEURS (continued)

Liqueur	Flavor	Color	Proof	Country
Crème de Almond	almond	red or clear	54–56	Many
Crème de Ananas	pineapple	clear	48–56	Many
Crème de Banana	banana	yellow	50–60	Many
Crème de Cacao	cocoa, vanilla	dark brown or clear	50–60	Many
Crème de Cafe	coffee	dark brown	50–60	Many
Crème de Cassis	black currant	red-brown	30–50	Many
Crème de Celery	celery	yellow or clear	50–60	Many
Crème de Fraise	strawberry	red	50–60	Many
Crème de Framboise	raspberry	red-purple	50–60	Many
Crème de Mandarine	tangerine, orange	orange	50–60	Many
Crème de Menthe	mint	green or clear	50–60	Many
Crème de Moka	coffee	dark brown	50–60	Many
Crème de Noyaux or Crème de Noya	almond	red or clear	50–60	Many
Crème de Prunelle	plum	brown-purple	50–80	Many
Crème de Rose	rose petal	light red	50–60	Many
Crème d'Yvette	violet, bubblegum	lavender	50–60	Many
Curacao	orange	clear, blue, or orange	54–80	Many
Devonshire Cream liqueur*	Scotch whisky, cream	beige	34	Scotland
Drambuie*	Scotch whisky, honey, herbs	amber	70	Scotland
Dunphy's Original Cream*	Irish whiskey, cream	beige	34	Ireland
Emmet Irish Cream*	Irish whiskey, cream	beige	34	Ireland
Fior d'Alpi*	anise, fruit	yellow	92	Italy
Forbidden Fruit*	grapefruit and other fruits	amber	64	U.S.A.

Frangelico*	hazelnuts	amber	56	Italy
Galacafe*	coffee, cream	dark red	53	Italy
Galliano*	vanilla, licorice	yellow	70	Italy
Get Peppermint*	mint	green or clear	60	France
Ginger schnapps	ginger	clear	60	Many
Glayva*	herbs	amber	80	Scotland
Grasshopper	cacao, mint	green	55	Many
Greensleeves Cream*	Irish whiskey, cream	beige	34	Ireland
Grenadine	pomegranate	red	34–50	Many
Haagen-Dazs*	Cognac, cocoa	beige	34	Holland
Honey Dew Melon*	honeydew, lime	lime	30	U.S.A.
Iced Tea	blended tea	dark gold	60	U.S.A.
Irish Mist*	Irish whiskey, honey	amber	70	Ireland
Irish Velvet*	Irish whiskey, coffee	amber	46	Ireland
Izarra*	brandy, honey	yellow-green	86, 100	France
Jägermeister*	herbs, fruits	dark red	70	Germany
Jeremiah Weed*	Bourbon whiskey, fruit	amber	100	U.S.A.
Kahlua*	coffee	dark brown	53	Mexico
Kirsch liqueur	cherry	clear	90–100	Many
Krupnik	honey	amber	80	Poland
Kümmel	caraway	clear	54–70	Many
Licor 43 (Cuarenta y Tres)*	vanilla, citrus	yellow	68	Spain
Lochan Ora*	Scotch whisky, honey, herbs	gold	70	Scotland
Malibu*	coconut	clear	56	Canada
Mandarine Napoleon*	tangerine	orange	80	France
Maraschino	cherry	clear	50–60	Many
Midori*	melon	green	46	Japan
Nassau Royale*	herbs, fruit	red	67	Bahamas
Nocello*	walnut	amber	48	Italy
Orange liqueur	orange	orange or clear	50–60	Many
Peach liqueur	peach	clear	50–60	Many
Pear liqueur	pear	clear	50–60	Many

PROPRIETARY AND GENERIC LIQUEURS (continued)

Liqueur	Flavor	Color	Proof	Country
Peppermint Schnapps	mint	clear	50–60	Many
Peter Heering*	cherry	dark red	49	Denmark
Pistachio	pistachio	green	50–60	U.S.A.
Praline*	vanilla, pecan	amber	40	U.S.A.
Raspberry liqueur	raspberry	red-purple	50–60	Many
Rock & Rye	whiskey, fruit	gold	48–80	U.S.A.
Roiano*	herbs, spices	yellow	80	Italy
Rosolio*	rose petal, spices	red	60	Italy
Rumona*	honey, spices	amber	63	Jamaica
Sabra*	chocolate, orange	brown	60	Israel
Sambuca	anise	clear	84	Italy
Sloe Gin	wild plum	red	42–60	Many
Southern Comfort*	Bourbon whiskey, peach	amber	80, 100	U.S.A.
Strawberry liqueur	strawberry	red	50–60	Many
Strega*	herbs, spices	yellow	80	Italy
Tia Maria*	coffee	dark brown	53	Jamaica
Tilus*	truffle	amber	70	Italy
Triple Sec	orange	orange or clear	50–70	Many
Tuaca*	caramel, vanilla	gold	84	Italy
Vandermint*	chocolate, mint	dark brown	52	Turkey
Venetian Cream*	brandy, cream	beige	40	Italy
Vieille Cure*	herbs, vanilla	green-yellow	86, 100	France
VOV*	eggnog	cream	18	Italy
Waterford Cream*	Irish whiskey, cream	beige	34	Ireland
Wild Turkey liqueur*	Bourbon whiskey, fruit	amber	80	U.S.A.
Wisniak	cherry	dark red	50–60	Many
Wisniowka*	cherry	dark red	80	Poland
Yukon Jack*	whiskey, fruit	amber	100	Canada

Other Liqueurs

Benedictine. In 1510, Monk Dom Bernardo Vincelli formulated the recipe for this world-famous French liqueur while at the abbey in Fecamp, Normandy.

During the French Revolution of 1789, the abbey was totally destroyed and the production of the liqueur was halted. In 1863, Alexandre Le Grand, a noted wine merchant in Fecamp, obtained part of the recipe, and with some help was able to resurrect the original recipe. Since that time, Benedictine has been made by the firm of Le Grand. The formula has never been duplicated by anyone: in fact, there is a room in the reconstructed abbey that is called the *Salon de Contrefacon* (the Hall of Counterfeits). The room's walls are adorned with more than eight hundred recipes and bottles that were created in an attempt to duplicate Benedictine, obviously without success.

Benedictine, unlike most other liqueurs, is aged about four years after the blending takes place, prior to final bottling. In 1937, after discovering that some Americans were adding brandy to Benedictine to make a "drier" drink, the distillery introduced Benedictine & Brandy: five- to six-year-old Cognac (the amount is about 40 percent of the final mixture) was added to the Benedictine, and they are allowed to "marry" for a specified time before bottling. Incidentally, the Cognac used is Comandon, made by a Benedictine-owned distillery. The letters DOM which appear on the label stand for *Deo Optimo Maximo* (to God, the most good, the most great).

Benedictine is dark amber in color and 80 proof.

Chartreuse. This world-famous liqueur was originally formulated in 1605, in Grenoble, France.

Chartreuse is made from more than 130 herbs and spices which are allowed to steep in a brandy base. The yellow, which was first introduced in 1838, is 80 proof and slightly sweet (from the addition of honey, rather than sugar). The green, considerably drier, with a spicy, peppermint taste, is 110 proof. The original elixir of Chartreuse liqueur was white (colorless) and is still produced, but not sent to the United States (it would probably be classified as a "medicine" because of its high proof and "secret" recipe, and would therefore be open to government scrutiny). The initials VEP on twelve-year-old bottles of Chartreuse stand for *viellissement exceptionnellement prolongé.*

Creme liqueurs. These are not dairy creams; the term means that they are sweet liqueurs, generally sugared. This term could in fact be used to describe most cordials/liqueurs.

Grand Marnier. In 1827 Grand Marnier was formulated by J. B. Lapostolle, in France. In 1859, Eugene Lapostolle started using Cognac as the base spirit in its production. However, it was not until Marnier Lapostolle (of a later generation) first came up with a special blend that Grand Marnier as we know it today was produced. This amber-colored liqueur is made from the peels of bitter oranges, which are macerated in Cognac.

Falernum. This is a colorless, slightly alcoholic spiced syrup originating in the Caribbean, used as a flavoring in rum drinks.

Goldwasser. This is an orange-based liqueur. Alchemists believed for many centuries that by mixing pure gold with alcohol, they could create "liquid gold" or the elixir of passion, stamina, and good health, for use as an aphrodisiac or even a guarantee of immortality. By the end of the sixteenth century, a beverage was made in Europe in which flakes of gold were combined with alcohol; it was called *goldwasser*. The current production uses 23-karat gold leaf, which is quite pure and harmless to ingest. In fact, it is so thin and light (technically, it is classified as of double-X thinness) that when the bottle is shaken, the flakes appear to be suspended and float indefinitely. The gold is purchased in thin sheets resembling tissue paper; in fact, they cost more than gold in solid form. The reason is simple: the labor needed to prepare this paper-thin gold leaf is considerable. The gold is added to the liqueur and immediately blended with rapid movements. As the liquid is agitated, the gold breaks up into tiny flecks.

Petite Liqueur. This first-produced and only existing sparkling liqueur in the world, is produced by Moët & Chandon of France. Petite Liqueur (36 proof) is produced from a sparkling wine base and reserve wines and spirits, including old Cognacs. It has a deep gold hue and "lazy" bubbles reminiscent of very old champagne. It smells of honey and has a ripe plum taste with hints of coffee, and a fruity quality. It is housed in a 200-milliliter bottle, and is closed with a champagne cork with a wire hood and foil capsule.

Cordial/liqueur producers. Some of the major producers of these beverages are:

Arrow	Garnier	Patrician
Bols	Hiram Walker	Peter Hagen
Cointreau	Jacquin	Stock
Cusenier	Leroux	WF
DeKuyper	Marie Brizard	
DuBouchett	Old Mr. Boston	

Serving and Storing Cordials and Liqueurs

There is really no need to refrigerate cordials either before or after opening. Because of their alcohol and sugar levels, they have a very long shelf life and will take changes in temperature and humidity quite well. However, it is advisable to keep them out of direct sunlight because the rays could cause a slight color change.

Traditionally, most cordials are served after dinner because of their high sugar levels. Cordials are also natural digestives, because they contain many different bitter botanicals.

Cordials can be served at room temperature, chilled from the refrigerator, or over ice. A cordial served with crushed or shaved ice is called a *frappé*. Cordials are also suitable as "long drinks" (with soda water) and in mixed drinks, and can be used in cooking.

Suggested Readings

Goolden, Jill. *Armagnac*. London: Christie's Wine Publication, 1980.

Greenberg, Emanuel and Madeline Greenberg. *The Pocket Guide to Spirits and Liqueurs*. New York: Putnam, 1983.

Hallgarten, Peter. *Spirits and Liqueurs,* 2d ed. London: Faber and Faber, 1983.

Henriques, E. Frank. *The Signet Encyclopedia of Whiskey Brandy and All Other Spirits*. New York: Signet, 1979.

Ray, Cyril. *Cognac*. Briarcliff Manor, New York: Stein and Day, 1973.

Discussion Topics and Questions

1. Brandy is an instant "body heat rejuvenator." What happens to the temperature of the body when an excessive amount of brandy is consumed?

2. Why have the U.S.-produced brandies not received the same recognition as the brandies coming from Armagnac and Cognac in France?

3. Do you feel that there is too much "hype" placed on imported brandy products, while U.S. brandies are perceived to be of a lower quality? If the answer is yes, what steps would you take to elevate U.S.-produced brandies to the same status as imports?

4. How much of the base price of a bottle of twenty-five-year-old Cognac derives from its superior quality, and how much is based on brand identification, producer prestige, etc.? Be able to back up your statements with figures.

5. Name the types of brandies that have a distinctive fruit aroma and taste.

6. Most classes on beverages taught in colleges are described as "beverage management" courses. Why is it important to spend considerable time learning about each type of alcoholic beverage?

7. Consumer loyalty aside, are there significant differences between brands of brandy? In what respect?

8. European fruit brandies tend to be drier than similar brandies produced in the United States. Why?

9. If a customer orders Cognac and orange juice, would it be acceptable to substitute Armagnac if one ran out of Cognac? Is it acceptable to substitute it without first asking permission, even if the customer couldn't tell the difference?

10. What differences, if any, exist between schnapps and peppermint schnapps?

11. Some customers find the taste of grappa and marc objectionable. If your storeroom had several cases of this product, how could it be merchandised and effectively sold in light of the objections?

12. What difference does it make if you use green crème de menthe instead of white in a mixed drink?

13. A generic amaretto is generally lower in price than the proprietary brand Amaretto di Saronno. Under what circumstances would the proprietary brand be required?

11

Preparing a Beverage List

This chapter discusses:

- The most important points a wine list must cover: breadth, depth, balance, and inventory.
- The preliminaries of preparing beverage lists: competition; product availability; the length of the lists; how many lists to prepare.
- The preparation of an aperitif list.
- Purchasing wines.
- Dual and multiuse wines.
- Selling wine by the glass: preserving and dispensing systems; pricing methods.
- Beer lists, and major brands and types of beer available.
- Distilled spirits lists: standard mixed drinks and brand names.

Wine is one of the great pleasures of the civilized world. Customer awareness of and demand for wine has grown dramatically in the last ten years. The increase is not just in the quantity of wine drunk, but in the interest in wine, especially fine wines. The savvy restaurateur naturally wants to profit by this wine boom, but to do so she must understand the needs and concerns of her new, more knowledgeable, more demanding customers.

A beverage list (covering wine, beer, and distilled spirits) must be given the same careful thought and attention to detail and market trends that is involved in the planning of a food menu. The beverage list must complement the selections on the menu to satisfy discerning customers.

Many restaurateurs view the creation of a beverage list as a Herculean task better left to consultants; or, more than often, it is ignored. Often when there is a discussion concerning beverage lists, restaurateurs can rattle off dozens of reasons for why their list is mediocre: "No room for storage. . . . It won't sell in my restaurant. . . . I don't know a thing about the stuff. . . . My staff doesn't know one end of a corkscrew or shot glass from another, etc." With so many responsibilities and problems to contend with, it may be understandable why restaurateurs often put beverages in last place; but it is important to note the profit potential in a good beverage list.

Beverages make up approximately 35 percent of restaurant check sales and often account for more than 40 percent of its profits. Beverage sales can significantly boost check averages and impact positively on the bottom line. It does not make sense to lose out on those extra dollars by presenting a beverage list that presents incomplete information and a poor selection, or one that is overpriced, misleading, and not matched to menu selections. Careful attention to planning and purchasing of beverages can prevent such a profit loss.

The Wine List

Customers used to judge a restaurant primarily on ambiance, service, and food quality. Now a fourth criteria has been added: wine. Wine selection, service, and pricing are on an equal footing with ambiance, service, and food. Restaurant reviews routinely make mention of the breadth, depth, and price structure of the wine list when rating the restaurant. But what criteria do the reviewers use and what do these terms mean?

Breadth

Breadth refers to the actual number of different selections on the list. (It is important to remember, however, that mere quantity is not enough; reviewers and customers weigh quality just as heavily.) France, Italy, and California produce so many wines that it is easy to offer the customer great breadth; and, when reviewers tout a restaurant because of the size of its wine list, it increases the volume of business to some degree.

Depth

Depth refers to the extent to which particular regions and/or vintages of certain wines are represented. A list with good depth in Bordeaux would feature five or six classified wines, along with several shippers' or regional wines. A depth of vintages requires offering at least three or more vintages of the same wine, for example Banfi Vintners Brunello di Montalcino 1978, 1979, and 1981. Restaurants may find it difficult to offer a depth of vintages, as older wines are almost impossible to find and are often quite expensive. Those restaurants with a large range of vintages generally have extensive cellars that have enabled them to lay away wine for future consumption.

Balance

Balance refers to the overall range of styles offered and the balance between the different countries and regions represented on the list. France, Italy, California, and Germany are the primary producers of fine wines, so it is natural to include a broad selection of these wines on your list. You may choose to balance your list with wines from these major wine-producing regions, or you may specialize in just one region or country. Specialization is not a negative trait on a wine list. By highlighting one region within your list, you might place yourself in a unique marketing position, as you are offering something that your competitors do not.

Some restaurants are now including wines from local wineries, setting their restaurant apart from competitors. Some customers have a sense of pride in their community; by the use of locally produced wines, patronage might be increased. In addition, customers from outside areas might be tempted to try the local "brew" as an alternative to other wines.

Inventory

Inventory refers to the approximate number of wines kept on hand. Smaller restaurants often cannot make a capital investment in very large inventories or sacrifice the space necessary for storage. The benefits of a large inventory are in ensuring a continuity of supply and in buying wines for aging and buying large stocks when prices are most favorable.

The customer who has made a reservation at a fine restaurant and is thus prepared to part with hard-earned dollars will order a better wine to complement his meal than he might drink at home. He will experiment, and will explore wine selections if the breadth, depth, and pricing of your list encourages him to do so.

The Preliminaries

Check the competition. Find out what is and what isn't being done with wine in your area. Visit the restaurants in your area that have the

315

same customer base as yours, as well as restaurants above and below your price range. Study how they merchandise wine and how competent their wine service is, and obtain a copy of their wine list if possible. Notice how well it is written, what wines it highlights, and what prices are charged.

Check the availability. You may decide that you want to feature a rare, old, or hard-to-find wine—but have you checked its availability? Contact the suppliers in your area and explain your objectives to them. Ask them to supply a list of the wines they carry including vintages, prices, and projected availability. Ask them to assist you with your wine list. Many distributors have people who have been trained to be knowledgeable about wines and whose main job is to work with restaurateurs on their wine lists, merchandising, training, and promotion. It is important to remember, however, that their suggestions are not carved in stone, and you are under no obligation to use them or their products.

How Large a List?

The size of your wine list is in part determined by the size of your storeroom. Wine requires specific storage conditions, and storing it improperly jeopardizes your investment. Your capital investment also figures prominently in determining the size of your wine list. However, in order to attain any degree of balance and variety in your list, you should have a minimum of forty to fifty wines. If your restaurant is small, this figure may seem high, but when you consider that these forty to fifty wines are divided among aperitifs; sparkling wines and champagnes; and white, red, rosé, and dessert wines from different regions or countries, then forty to fifty begins to sound like a very conservative number. In fact, it could be considered the minimum number that will allow you the flexibility to offer a range of wines appealing to different tastes and ability to pay, suitable for casual drinking or special celebrations.

Some establishments feel that when customers are presented with a list containing two hundred or more wines, they tend to order wine with more frequency. It is felt that this communicates the idea that the restaurant specializes in wine, the management is knowledgeable, and the wines will be of excellent quality. Perhaps when customers view this type of list, they will even purchase a better-quality (usually higher-priced) wine.

How Many Wine Lists?

If your wine list contains well over one hundred entries, you should have two separate and distinct lists. Very few if any of your customers are going to spend an entire evening reading through your wine list. Most customers would certainly be intimidated and overwhelmed by the array of names, types, and prices of wine on such a list. The first list should contain the most popular wines, which have immediate brand name recognition. Brand name recognition has bred loyalty among consumers; and many customers have only a superficial knowledge about wine and do not want to spend large sums of money on a product they generally don't drink at home anyway. They often order wines to be sociable among friends or family, and so this list should be merchandised accordingly. Also, this abbreviated list should incorporate low-, medium-, and fairly high-priced items, which will cover most occasions.

If the customer, after looking at this list, decides that he would prefer a better-quality wine, a more comprehensive list should then be made available.

Another reason for having two beverage lists is for increased beverage sales. A good portion of the American public enjoys two things about their beverages; the fact that they are cold and sweet. Most consumers talk dry, but drink sweet, or at least semisweet wines. This can easily be demonstrated by the tremendous sales of Lambrusco, wine coolers, etc. As a matter of fact, of the ten best-selling imports, seven of them are semisweet or sweet wines. If there is room on your menu, list simple wines that are both profitable and popular and that most customers will immediately recognize. Customers feel comfortable with wine names they can pronounce and recognize; and if your customer is more familiar with wines, the second, more extensive list can be asked for and presented.

The Aperitif List

Perhaps the most overlooked part of the wine list is the aperitif list. Very few restaurants effectively merchandise aperitifs, and because of this loss of revenue runs quite high. In fact, better than 90 percent of all restaurants across the country don't have an aperitif list as part of their wine lists.

It is not enough for your server to ask customers if they would like a "drink from the bar," or "perhaps a glass of white wine." In today's marketplace, if everything is equal, then why would a customer want to eat, drink, or socialize in your establishment? You must offer the customer something unique or different: an unusual theme or specialized service, for instance.

If you had a listing of various aperitifs that a customer could consult, this would increase beverage sales. If you can sell an aperitif, you have one sale; then, at dinner, if a bottle of wine is sold, that's two sales.

By developing an aperitif list, you can pick up additional sales. Many people are getting tired of a glass of nondescript white wine that costs them as much as a mixed drink containing liquor. They may have heard that wine is lighter and contains fewer calories than liquor and want to try some, but are simply afraid to or uneducated in the art of ordering wine. An aperitif list can be placed on the table, awaiting the customers' arrival, showing eight to twelve alternative aperitif drinks besides martinis or white wine.

What is an aperitif? There are many factors that must be considered: the beverage should be dry, light, chillable, and refreshing; it should be relatively acidic, to cleanse the palate; it should perhaps also be slightly bitter.

The popularity of aperitifs lies partly in the fact that they are lighter and lower in alcohol than traditional mixed drinks or cocktails such as martinis or Manhattans. They can be more interesting than liquor-based drinks; most of them are quite flavorful. They also contain fewer calories, and stand up to ice better than white wines (which tend to become diluted). They are today's "in" drinks when one is ordering at a bar or restaurant. (See the chapter on aperitifs and fortified wines for examples of aperitifs.)

The Wine List and the Menu

Your wine list must relate to your menu offerings. If your menu is primarily seafood, your list should include a larger proportion of white wines, which are well matched with seafood. Conversely, if beef and lamb predominate, then a concentration of red wines would be a logical focus.

Tasting Wines Before Purchasing

One of the biggest mistakes restaurant/bar owners can make is not first tasting the wine they are purchasing, but rather taking the word of a customer, employee, or salesman. There is no way, unless you taste a wine, to determine where it should be placed on the wine list, or what food or foods it will go with. It is foolish to have wines on the list that do not complement your foods. Unfortunately, in some restaurants the quality of food far outshines the quality of wine, which makes a poor balance for the customer.

Before purchasing wines for your list, first determine, with the aid of your chef, the food item you would like to match. Let's say that by prior tasting, an Alsatian Riesling would go well with a certain fish dish featured on the menu. But which Alsatian Riesling would you purchase?

Before you place your order, contact all of the distributors from whom you purchase, and ask them to drop off a bottle of every Alsatian Riesling they carry. Then, properly chill the wines and taste them blind; either by putting the bottle into a brown paper bag or decanting it into a carafe, making sure that no one, including yourself, is able to see the label. This avoids the possibility of your being influenced by price or label. Have tasting sheets made up so that you will have a written record of the results of the tastings. Evaluate each wine using the criteria of taste; compatibility with menu items; suitability as an aperitif; availability; and, most of all, price. Expect to taste at least three times as many wines as you will actually have on your list.

Taste no more than eight to ten wines at once to avoid palate fatigue, and try to plan the tasting for midmorning (10:30–11:00 A.M.); this is when your palate is the keenest.

Have your staff participate in the tastings. They will begin to learn about wines and develop an enthusiasm for your offerings that will translate into increased sales. Taste the wines alone and then with your menu items to make sure you are choosing wines that marry well with the food you serve. This will alert your staff to wine and food combinations they can recommend to customers.

Tally up the results and determine the order in which you have ranked each of the wines. Before you automatically purchase the wine that tasted best, there are a number of factors that must be considered, including price. If your highest-priced entree is $10.00 and the number-one Alsatian Riesling wholesales for $8.00, that translates to approximately $18.00 per bottle, and will be a tough sale. In this case, the second- or even third-choice wine might have to be considered. Thus you do not, perhaps, purchase the finest Alsatian Riesling produced, but you *do* purchase the finest Alsatian Riesling for your restaurant.

You should, however, take one more thing into consideration before the final purchase order is written: could this wine be designated a "dual" or "multiuse" type of beverage? A dual or multiuse wine is one that can be merchandised as an aperitif, to be sold by the glass, as well as fitting nicely into your wine list.

Dual and Multiuse Wine Brands

Many restaurants have limited storage space, and simply lack the shelf area necessary to hold many competing brands. But most of the suggested aperitifs you will already have on hand: dry vermouth, for example. This is the indispensable ingredient for a martini, and since the way most people drink martinis today is in a ratio of sixteen parts gin or vodka to one part dry vermouth, you will probably get ninety-nine drinks out of a liter. Dry vermouth is an aromatized wine with about 17 percent alcohol, and it has an optimum shelf life of six weeks, refrigerated. So if after six weeks a check of the underbar refrigerator shows that there is still two-thirds to three-fourths of the liter remaining, you should consider two things. First, remove the vermouth to the kitchen for cooking, for marinating or sauteeing mushrooms, for example. Second, the next time you purchase vermouth, only purchase 375-milliliter (12.7 oz.) bottles. How should you merchandise this multiuse drink? Further possibilities are: dry vermouth on the rocks, with a twist of lemon; chilled straight up; mixed with equal parts of sweet vermouth; served as a long drink; a dry Manhattan; a dry Rob Roy; a substitution for white wine in spritzers, Kirs, etc. That makes nine different ways to merchandise a brand you *already* have in the bar. By effectively selling the vermouth in larger quantities, you could also lower the A.P. (as purchased price) by volume buying, and post-offs, usually ranging from 2 to 3 percent on three to five cases, cutting down the beverage cost, thereby increasing the profit margin.

Pricing Wines

Today's customers are well aware of the price of a bottle of wine available in local wine shops, and understand that a restaurant must charge additional money for labor and to make a profit. What they do not understand is why some restaurants charge inordinately high prices. Price gouging on wine results in diminished sales and disgruntled customers. Offering good wines at fair prices will lead to more sales. Customers are already intimidated in relation to wine, and astronomically high prices alienate them further; and, many may feel, as well, that the restaurateur knows little about marketing and cares little for repeat patronage.

For a customer to desire a bottle of wine, it must be within his reach and be fairly priced. The pricing strategy suggested below guarantees a fair return per bottle for the restaurant, while at the same time encouraging customers to make initial and repeat purchases.

WINE PRICING FORMULA BY THE BOTTLE

Cost per bottle (750 ml.)	Percentage mark-up	Selling price	Gross profit
Up to $ 4.00	200%	$12.00	$ 8.00
Up to $ 7.00	150%	$17.50	$10.50
Up to $10.00	125%	$22.50	$12.50
Up to $15.00	100%	$30.00	$15.00
Up to $25.00	75%	$43.75	$18.75
Over $25.00	50%		

To determine the selling price, take the cost per bottle, multiply by percentage mark-up, then add the two numbers. After the selling price has been established, round it off to the nearest quarter and add $1.00 to cover breakage, spillage, and insurance.

Selling Wines by the Glass

More and more restaurants are offering fine wines by the glass. Machines that preserve the quality of open bottles are now available, allowing you to pour a variety of wines by the glass. With today's sophisticated beverage-dispensing systems, some restaurants can offer just about every wine on their list by the glass. Your restaurant does not have to have an expensive beverage system, or any beverage system, to offer such a program. Just remember that red wines, after opening, generally have a shelf life of two to three days if refrigerated, while whites will last up to five days before serious deterioration takes place. Several types of recorkers are available which are suitable for still or sparkling wines. If you do a very high volume of business and have a fast turnover rate, then perhaps an expensive system is unnecessary.

Champagnes and sparkling wines, sold by the glass, are continually growing in popularity. Selling wine this way allows a customer to try several different wines while keeping down total alcohol consumption.

Wine-preserving and dispensing systems. Wherever fine wines are served by the glass, by the bottle, or even by the sip, wine-dispensing systems can be found.

Restaurants have begun to allow customers to taste several wines to determine which they would prefer to drink while dining. This also offers customers the opportunity to select a variety of wines to be served throughout the meal: champagne before dinner; Chardonnay with the fish; Chianti with the main course; and a Sauternes with dessert, for example.

Wine-preserving and dispensing systems offer numerous avenues of promotion: "awareness advertising"; suggestive selling with dinner orders; and wine-tasting events. In addition, these systems are a visual marketing tool: people see them and ask about them—and generally order a glass of wine. Sales and profits are thus increased.

Consumers may find, where such systems are used, that a glass of fine wine is more easily within their reach. For the first time novice wine drinkers can afford to taste the many varietals and discover the differences between them. Wine connoisseurs find themselves able to broaden their expertise of the finest wines, and producers find new markets for their premium lines. In addition, with such systems customers are able to taste truly great wines that they would not otherwise be able to afford.

These systems, in short, allow more people to be served a variety of wines, while at the same time increasing the profit margin in single-glass sales, with virtually no risk of spoilage. Some features of these systems are:

> Most systems are designed to keep the contents of opened wine bottles for up to about six weeks, as fresh as when they were uncorked, without spoilage due to oxidation. Inert nitrogen gas, injected under gentle pressure through a sealed stopper, replaces the wine as it is removed from the bottle, and preserves the wine by keeping it oxygen free. The wine may be quickly dispensed and easily stored after use.

> A fast, reliable bottle-changing system is available that generally entails a simple changing of siphon tubes from one bottle to another.

> The nitrogen system fits both 750-milliliter and 1.5-liter bottles.

> Wines are chilled quickly, and proper temperatures of fast-moving wines are electronically controlled and maintained.

> Most dispenser systems display temperature, wine pressure, and gas flow, and have open-door signals.

Systems are available to accommodate single bottles or up to thirty-two bottles; see-through cases are available.

Wine-by-the-glass systems increase your profits dramatically, and the profits realized by serving premium wines by the glass will pay for the system, generally within a few months.

The systems increase the sale of premium wines and your per-unit profit rate. Unique or special wines such as dessert wines, Port, or rare red wines that are ordinarily too expensive to stock may be opened, and only as much as is desired drawn off and served. Because a bottle of wine is sold by the portion, more can be charged for it than when selling it by the bottle. Discriminating customers tasting a glass of wine they like may purchase the entire bottle.

The wine-dispensing system does not replace your present wine list, but adds to your selection and increases the profitability of your entire wine program. Some manufacturers of these systems are:

Le Cruvinet	Winekeeper
Vintage Keeper	Wine Systems Int.
Winebar	

BATF rulings: Effective on August 2, 1985, the Bureau of Alcohol, Tobacco and Firearms permits the use of carbon dioxide for dispensing wine from original wine containers, if the carbon dioxide is not injected into the wine and the carbon dioxide level of the wine is not increased. Advances in modern technology permit many containers to be equipped with dispensing devices that allow carbon dioxide to be added *only* to the headspace of the container. This use of carbon dioxide results neither in potential jeopardy to tax revenues nor in unauthorized cellar treatment of the wine. (Under federal law still wine is taxed at $.17 per gallon, and artificially carbonated wine at $2.40 per gallon. Any addition of carbon dioxide into wine itself is considered a cellar treatment and can be conducted only on the premises of a bonded wine cellar.)

Pricing methods. When developing a wine-by-the-glass program, there are two separate and distinct pricing methods, depending on the quality of the wine and the size of the bottles you use. Each portion served should be six ounces, which gives the customer a high level of perceived value.

The pricing formula is similar to that for per-bottle service, but in this case you only round off to the nearest quarter and do not add the $1.00 to cover breakage, spillage, and insurance.

WINE PRICING FORMULA BY THE GLASS

Cost per bottle (750 ml.)	Percentage mark-up
Up to $ 4.00	250 percent
Up to $ 7.00	200 percent
Up to $15.00	175 percent
Up to $25.00	100 percent
Over $25.00	75 percent
From bulk (3 or 4 l. or larger)	250 percent

Wine-on-tap systems. Most of these systems utilize the latest state-of-the-art aluminum canisters, which vary in dimension and capacity from producer to producer. Most are also equipped with inert nitrogen gas systems that replace the wine as it is removed from the keg, which preserves the wine by keeping it oxygen free. Delicato Winery and Banfi Vintners both use a system that does not utilize nitrogen, but rather uses any gas or compressed air (oxygen included). The principle of its operation is that compressed gas sucks out the wine rather than replacing it with costly nitrogen gas. In both types of systems, the wine may be quickly dispensed and easily stored after use. The systems can be made portable for catering purposes. Paul Masson, for example, uses 30-liter (7.9 gal. or 1,014 oz.) and 58.6-liter (15.5 gal. or 1,981 oz.) canisters which weigh 83.6 pounds and 160.4 pounds full, respectively, and 18.4 pounds and 31.4 pounds, respectively, empty.

The advantages of such systems are listed below.

Eliminates:	*Reduces:*
Breakage	Inventory carrying costs
Spillage	Refrigeration
Pilferage	Storage space
Trash accumulation	Bar restocking

324

Leakage   Employee handling

Space needed for empties

Deposit and return (of bottles)

Other benefits of the system are: more consistent quality of wines; lower operating costs; greater ease of operation; greater labor efficiency (improved through quicker service); reduced labor costs (through minimum handling); and elimination of waste (virtually all of the wine is deliverable through the system, and there are no disposal costs, and no trash).

Wine sold in kegs is generally generic in nature (Chablis, Rhine, Burgundy, etc.), but some wineries do offer varietal wines such as Chardonnay, Chenin Blanc, French Colombard, Ruby Cabernet, White Zinfandel, and so on.

Some tap wine system producers are:

Almaden Vineyards

Anheuser-Busch: Master Cellars

Banfi Vintners: Entree Wines

Delicato

Heublein: Inglenook

Gallo: Wm. Wycliff

Louis Glunz: Coastal Valley Cellars

Vintners International: Paul Masson and Taylor California Cellars

How to Write a Wine List

Wine lists can come in impressive leather-bound books or on computer printouts, yet they all should follow a basic structure. Wine lists should be divided into sections on aperitifs, champagnes and sparkling wines, dry white, dry red, rosé, and dessert and fortified wines, in that order.

Under each main category, the wine list can be subdivided. For example, under red wines, you can list Italian red wines, or even list those by region: red wines of Tuscany, etc. There must be at least three or more wines of a similar type to justify the use of subheadings.

Some restaurateurs attempt to list white wines from the driest to the sweetest, which presents all sorts of problems. First, with the exception of some California wines, you have no idea at all of what the residual sugar content of the wine is. Second, most people confuse the taste of fruit in the wine with sugar. Third, and most important, the perceived sweetness is directly related to the amount of acidity contained in the wine. Two wines with identical residual sugar contents but different levels of acidity will taste different. A wine with a higher level of acidity will taste far drier than the wine with less acidity. Even professional tasters are occasionally fooled by various acid levels.

After you have established your basic outline, it is time to compile the listing for each individual wine. The following information should appear on your wine list.

Bin number. While not absolutely mandatory, this information simplifies wine storage, inventory, and reordering. It also assists both customers and staff with difficult pronunciations. If the customer can just say, "I'll have number 45," rather than trying to stumble over an unfamiliar name, he will feel more comfortable about ordering. It is a proven fact that people will not order food or drink items they are not familiar with or can't pronounce. If the customer pronounces the wine's name incorrectly, the waiter does not need to correct him, but can say, for instance, "Yes, sir/madam, bin number 45 is an excellent choice with the steak."

Vintage. Never leave out the vintage on your list; it is an insult to your customer's intelligence. Grapes are an agricultural crop, and some years are naturally better than others. Also, after a period of time, some reds and most white wines are beyond drinkability and should not be offered to the customer. The customer has a right to choose. If a wine is nonvintage, then the letters *NV* should be used.

Many restaurateurs leave the vintage date off the wine list because they say they cannot be assured of a steady supply of a particular wine or vintage. However, many restaurants have chosen to print wine lists on word processors or by an inexpensive offset process to ensure that the information is accurate and up to date. This also avoids the all-too-common problem of out-of-stock wines, and is preferable for the customer who cares more about wine than elegant calligraphy. Leaving out the vintage date creates a lack of wine-buying enthusiasm on the part of your customer, either because he does not want to bother the waiter for specific vintages or does not want to have to ask the vintage dates of several or more wines; and this additional step adds to the amount of time your guest stays in your restaurant without purchasing food or beverage.

If, for one reason or another, you still do not wish to place the vintage date on the list, then on a plain three-by-five index card list each and every wine and its vintage. This card should be carried by the waiter or sommelier and referred to when he is asked what vintage a particular wine is.

The name of the wine. The complete name of the wine must appear and be correctly spelled. The wine's name could be varietal (the name of the predominant grape variety used)—for example, Chardonnay; generic (the place name)—for example, Bordeaux, or even proprietary (a made-up name)—for example, Blue Nun. An incomplete listing only confuses the customer.

The name of the shipper or winery. This is extremely important for wines that come from the French regions of Bourgogne and Côtes du Rhône, where many small vineyards operate whose production is bought and bottled by shippers. For wines from regions such as Bordeaux, where the best wine bears the name of an individual château, or California, where the name of the winery is listed on the label, the shipper's name is not needed.

The country or state of origin. Every wine list should state the country of origin, or if it is an American wine, the state where it was produced. The term *domestic* should be avoided, because it has the connotation of a cheap replica or imitation. Instead, use the term *American*.

Many customers have an allegiance to a certain country or even state. This can translate into increased sales—for instance, when a customer finds a wine that comes from the country or state of his birth.

Bottle size. The traditional size of bottle in which almost all wines come is the 750-milliliter (25.4-oz.) bottle, and unless you are serving a wine that comes in a bottle of a different size, it is unnecessary to list this information. Other bottle sizes that could be brought to the table are 375-milliliter (12.7-oz.) or 1.5-liter (50.8-oz.) bottles (the latter is also known as a magnum).

Most customers will order the 750-milliliter size, which will be sufficient for dinner. However, by offering half-bottles (375 ml., or 12.7 oz.), the customer is given an opportunity of trying one, two, or more different wines, while still consuming only as much wine as if he had ordered one 750-milliliter bottle.

On the other hand, magnum (50.8-oz.) bottles of wine offer larger parties the opportunity to order one large bottle of a particular wine.

Types of Wine Lists

The information contained in the wine list can be given in many formats. The wine list should always be automatically presented with the menu, and because of this many restaurateurs choose a cover similar in design to their menu cover.

Paper quality and type size affect the readability of the list. Colored, textured paper and fancy typefaces are not only expensive, but in the low light of some restaurants may make the list difficult to read. Avoid using only upper- or lower-case type on the wine list; instead use a combination of both, which is easier on the eyes. Italics or script should be avoided because it is difficult to follow and tiring to read.

Choose a format that is easily read, with boldface titles and spaces between categories so that customers can scan the list easily. When the list is ready to be printed, assign a minimum of two people as proof-readers to ensure accuracy.

One of the fastest ways to lose a current or prospective customer is to list incorrect prices or vintages. If a listed wine is out of stock, the sommelier or server should inform the customer of this when the wine list is presented.

Remember that the wine list should be kept neat, clean, and up to date. Soiled wine lists reflect on the overall cleanliness of the restaurant.

Follow-up. Once you've written your list, the work is not over. It is important to track wines' popularity to ascertain if the selections you have made are the wines your customers want.

Keep a count of the number of bottles sold per customer (divide the number of covers by the number of bottles sold). If this number is less than 0.5, you need to seriously consider changing your selection and merchandising strategies. Include your staff in discussions.

Figure the proportion of white wine to red wine sold. If you are selling 57 percent white wine (the national average) and you stock 70 percent red, you may need to adjust your ratio.

Analyze the average price of a bottle of wine sold over a three-month period. If your average sale is $16.00, yet most of your wines are $24.00 and over, you need to stock more moderate-priced wines.

Rank the ten most popular wines on the list, and analyze what they have in common. This will assist you when you revise your list. If the ten most popular wines are all whites under $20.00, then you may want to focus the bulk of your list on wines such as these.

Wine Consumption

Americans generally speak about the per capita consumption of wine in the United States as it compares to that of Europeans. In the late 1960s some industry experts predicted that the U.S. per capita consumption would be 5 gallons by 1990 (the consumption was approximately 1 gallon at the time). In 1986, the consumption level was approximately 2.42 gallons.

The Beer List

Beer is steadily growing in popularity: consumers drink it before, during, and after dinner. This type of consumer might be one who simply refuses to pay for exorbitantly high wine prices, and instead drinks beer during dinner; or he may be a true beer lover or someone seeking a drink low in alcohol. Beer consumption also increases in hot weather. In any case, it is wise to consider having a beer list on hand in those establishments that cater completely or even partially to beer-consuming customers.

Beer drinking today is not only trendy but also sophisticated, and most restaurants are taking note of what brands of beer their clientele drink. The annual consumption of beer in the United States was listed as 23.9 gallons per capita in 1986. This is quite high compared to the 2.42 gallons of wine and 1.6 gallons of distilled spirits that are consumed (per capita, per year). The beer-consumption figure is low, however, compared to what is found in other countries: West Germany, at 39.18 gallons; Czechoslovakia, at 39.05 gallons; and East Germany, at 38.84 gallons (all 1983 figures). Actually, of all countries where beer is consumed, the United States in total beer consumption, ranks twelve.

In spite of the increasing number of beer drinkers, many restaurateurs do not realize the potentially large revenues to be gained from promoting beer in their establishments.

Major brands of beer. The ten most popular brands of American beer are, in order of popularity:

1. Budweiser	**6.** Coors Light
2. Miller Lite	**7.** Bud Light
3. Miller High Life	**8.** Busch
4. Coors	**9.** Michelob
5. Old Milwaukee	**10.** Stroh's

Source: Beverage World, March 1987.

The best-selling imported brands of beer in the United States are:

1. Heineken (Holland)
2. Molson (Canada)
3. Corona Extra (Mexico)
4. Beck's (Germany)
5. Moosehead (Canada)
6. Labatt (Canada)
7. St. Pauli Girl (Germany)
8. Amstel Light (Holland)
9. Tecate (Mexico)
10. Dos Equis (Mexico)

Source: National Association of Beverage Importers, 1986.

The figures listed above represent the most popular brands sold in the United States; figures for restaurant popularity on a national basis are somewhat limited. The most popular restaurant brands, according to *Nation's Restaurant News*, are:

American

1. Budweiser
2. Miller Lite
3. Michelob
4. Coors
5. Michelob Light
6. Miller High Life
7. Stroh's

Imports

1. Heineken (Holland)
2. Beck's (Germany)
3. St. Pauli Girl (Germany)
4. Molson (Canada)
5. Moosehead (Canada)
6. Kronenbourg (France)
7. Dos Equis (Mexico)

A good beer list that most restaurants could start with contains a total of twelve beers: five American beers and seven imports, chosen from the above list, with substitutions for local or regional preferences or for locally produced beers. It is extremely important to let your customers know whether the beers are available in bottles or by the draught pump. Avoid selling beer by the can in restaurants, because of the image problem associated with cans.

Ethnic restaurants, may need a different selection: for example, a German restaurant may need more German beers. Some restaurants across the United States call themselves "American" restaurants; therefore, most or all the beers served would be produced in the United States.

For restaurants with a larger beer-drinking clientele, a list containing twelve imports and six American beers would be proper. Restaurants with an even larger beer-drinking clientele would do well with a minimum of twenty imports and seven American beers.

Types of beer to include. The most popular type of beer is lager, which is produced worldwide. Other popular types that could be included on a restaurant's beer list are:

Ales	Pilsners
"Light" beers (low in calories)	Stout
Dark beers	Malt liquors

The Distilled Spirits List

Although lists containing solely distilled spirits are apparently not in vogue in today's primarily wine-drinking environment, good restaurant profit still lies in the popularity and diversity of distilled spirits. Mixed drinks are still preferred by some customers over both wine and beer when it comes to cocktail parties, weddings, banquets, and especially before, during, and after dinner. Making up a list that includes only the spirits currently available in your restaurant could very well be off the mark when it comes to consumer preferences. For one thing, in the 1970s and 1980s the popularity of "white spirits" (gin, rum, tequila, and vodka) has increased over that of the traditional "brown spirits" (whiskies) that existed before Prohibition. Consumers view white spirits as versatile, mixable with most fruit juices; they taste less of alcohol and not as strong as whiskies (although their alcoholic content is often the same).

The trend toward white spirits shows little sign of weakening. Of the ten best-selling brands of spirits in the United States, Bacardi rum and Smirnoff vodka are clearly at the top of the list. These top ten spirits, in order of popularity are:

Brand name	Category	Cases sold in millions
1. Bacardi	Rum	7.4
2. Smirnoff	Vodka	5.8
3. Jim Beam	Bourbon	4.0

Brand name	Category	Cases sold in millions
4. Seagram's 7 Crown	Blended	3.9
5. Canadian Mist	Canadian	3.3
6. Popov	Vodka	3.2
7. Seagram's V.O.	Canadian	3.1
8. Canadian Club	Canadian	3.1
9. De Kuyper liqueur	Cordial	3.1
10. Jack Daniels Black	Tennessee	2.8

Source: Pat Kennedy's Executive Newsletter: 1987.

The List

Your spirits list is an excellent merchandising tool for selling mixed drinks. It can be enhanced with color photographs and/or descriptions.

According to the American Bartender's Association, the ten drinks that are most often ordered in a bar are, in order of popularity:

1. Vodka and tonic
2. Gin and tonic
3. Rum and Coke
4. Bloody Mary
5. Beer
6. Chablis wine
7. Margarita
8. Martini/Manhattan
9. Shooters
10. Long Island Iced Tea

Standard mixed drinks that are often ordered are listed below, under the name of their main ingredient (the spirit used):

Gin or vodka

Black Russian
Bloody Mary
Gibson
Gimlet
Gin or vodka and tonic
Gin rickey

Mimosa
Orange blossom
Salty Dog
Screwdriver
Singapore Gin sling
Tom Collins

Harvey Wallbanger   White Russian
Martini

Tequila or rum

Bacardi	Piña colada
Daiquiri	Planter's punch
Fruit daiquiri	Rum and Coke
Mai Tai	Tequila sunrise
Margarita	Zombie

Scotch

Godfather	Rusty nail
Godmother	Scotch and soda
Rob Roy	Sours

Whiskey

Highball	Old-fashioned
Jack Rose	Seven and seven
Manhattan	Sours
Mint julep	

Other mixed drinks

Americano	Long Island Iced Tea
Bee's knees	Negroni
Bellini	Orgasm
Brandy Alexander	Screaming orgasm
Cobbler	Sidecar
Copacabana	Slippery nipple
Glögg	Sloe and comfortable screw
Golden Cadillac	Sloe gin fizz
Grasshopper	Stinger
Jelly bean	Swampwater
Kir	Tom and Jerry
Kir royale	

Name brand and super-premium spirits. The spirits list can contain name brand (also referred to as *call brand*) as well as super-premium (also referred to as top-shelf or super-call) spirits from each category; some of these are listed below.

Blended whiskey

Barton Reserve	Imperial
Calvert Extra	Philadelphia (aged 8 years)
Carstairs	Schenley Reserve
Fleischmann	Seagram's 7
Four Roses	Three Feathers

Bourbon and Tennessee whiskey

Benchmark	Jim Beam
Ezra Brooks	Kentucky Tavern
Evan Williams	Maker's Mark
George Dickel (Tennessee whiskey)	Old Crow
Heaven Hill	Old Forester
I.W. Harper	Old Grand Dad
Jack Daniels (Tennessee whiskey)	Wild Turkey

Canadian whisky

Black Velvet	Seagram's Crown Royal
Canadian Club	Seagram's VO
Canadian Mist	Windsor Supreme
O. F. C. Schenley	

Gin

Beefeater	Burnett's
Bellows	Gilbey's
Bombay	Gordon's
Boodles	Seagram's
Boord's	Tanqueray
Booth's	

Irish whiskey

Dunphy's	Paddys
John Jameson	Power's

Murphy's   Tullamore Dew
Old Bushmills

Rum

Appleton   Myers's Dark
Bacardi   Rhum St. James
Cruzan   Ron Castillo
Don Q   Ron Rico
Mount Gay

Scotch whisky

Ambassador   J. & B.
Ballantine   Johnnie Walker Red
Bell's   John Begg
Black Bull   Laphroaig
Black & White   Ne Plus Ultra
Cardhu   Old Rarity
Chivas Regal   Old Smuggler
Cutty Sark   Passport
Dewar's White Label   Pinch
Excalibur Excellence Teacher's
Glenfarclas   The Macallan
Glenfiddich   Tomatin
Glenlivet   Usher's
Glenmorangie   Usquaebach
Grant's   Vat 69
Haig & Haig   White Horse
Harvey's   100 Pipers

Tequila

Don Emilio   Montezuma
Gavilan   Pedro Domecq
Herradura   Sauza
Jose Cuervo   Torado
Monte Alban   Two Fingers

Vodka

Absolut	Silhouette
Burrough's	Smirnoff
Finlandia	Stolichnaya
Gordon's	Wyborowa
Popov	

After-dinner cordials/liqueurs and brandies. Some recommended generic and proprietary brands of after-dinner drinks that can be included on the spirits list (or on a separate list) are listed below.

Amaretto	Grappa
Anisette	Grenadine
Applejack	Irish Mist
Apricot-flavored brandy	Jagermeister
Akvavit (or aquavit)	Kahlua
Alizé	Kirschwasser
Armagnac	Kummel
Asbach Uralt brandy	Lochan Ora
Averna	Malibu
Baileys Irish Cream	Mandarine Napoleon
Benedictine	Maraschino liqueur
Benedictine & Brandy	Marc
Blackberry-flavored brandy	Metaxa (Greek brandy)
Blackberry liqueur	Midori
Brandy	Mirabelle (plum brandy)
Calvados (apple brandy)	Nocello
Campari	Ouzo
Chambord (raspberry liqueur)	Peach-flavored brandy
Chartreuse (green or yellow)	Peppermint schnapps (or other flavors)
Cherry-flavored brandy	
Coffee-flavored brandy	Pernod
Cognac	Peter Heering (cherry liqueur)
Cointreau	Petite Liqueur
Crème de banana	Pisco brandy (Peru)
Crème de cacao (brown and white)	Poire (pear brandy)
	Ramazzotti
Crème de cassis	Rock and rye

Crème de menthe (green and white)
Curacao (orange or blue)
Cynar
Drambuie
Emmets Irish Cream
Fernet Branca
Frangelico
Fraise (strawberry brandy)
Framboise (raspberry brandy)
Galliano
Goldwasser
Grand Marnier

Sabra
Sambuca
Slivovitz
Sloe Gin
Southern Comfort
Strawberry liqueur
Strega
Tia Maria
Triple Sec
Tuaca
Vandermint

Suggested Readings

Kreck, Lothar A. *Menus: Analysis and Planning,* 2d ed. New York: CBI, 1984.
Seaberg, Albin G. *Menu Design: Merchandising and Marketing,* 3d ed. New York: CBI, 1983.

Discussion Topics and Questions

1. If instead of a full-service restaurant you decided to open a local "mom and pop" restaurant whose clientele primarily drinks "jug" wines, what sort of wine list would be needed?

2. Before purchasing wines, how does a restaurateur ascertain who the local distributors are?

3. What advantages or disadvantages are there in making the wine list part of the menu?

4. Suppose that you have just been retained as a consultant for a restaurant whose beverage manager informs you that even though the ten best-selling brands of beer are available in the restaurant, beer sales are poor. What advice would you give?

5. What problems would you encounter if you decided to sell every wine on your list by the glass?

6. Should white wines that are included on the regular wine list also

be offered as aperitifs? If so, how does one decide which ones to offer?

7. How would you list a martini on your beverage list: as a martini, or a gin martini or vodka martini? If you listed both types, wouldn't you have to do the same for almost every other drink? Explain.

8. Most restaurants present customers with a wine list that simply lists "house wines," including reds, whites, and rosés, which are sold "by the glass or carafe." Is this sufficient information for most customers? If not, what additional information would be needed?

9. Suppose that as a newly appointed beverage manager, you notice that your competitor is doing a considerable business with wines. Are you able to obtain both his wine list and prices? Qualify your answer.

12

Purchasing, Storage, and Cost Controls

This chapter discusses:

- Ordering and establishing a "par stock."
- Various sizes of alcoholic beverage bottles (metric measurements are given).
- Procedures for receiving alcoholic beverages.
- Proper storage conditions for wine.
- The use of plastic bottles for alcoholic beverages.
- How to price various types of banquets.
- Beverage cost controls and forecasting.
- Portion-controlled liquor-dispensing machines.
- In-room bars.
- Ice-making machines.

The purchasing function is one of the most overlooked aspects of running an effective beverage business. All alcoholic beverages are not the same, and therefore a practice that might pertain to distilled spirits will have little relevance to wine or beer. Distilled spirits, with few exceptions, have an extremely long shelf life and do not require atmospherically controlled storage areas, as do wine and beer. Beer and wine, to some extent, are perishable items and are adversely affected by temperature fluctuations and exposure to light. Careful ordering, receiving, and storing practices must be strictly adhered to.

Most beverage managers are concerned with the financial running of an operation and rely heavily on beverage controls. Automation has provided the industry with many types of control systems, some costing as little as a few dollars, while other more sophisticated systems may cost well into the tens of thousands of dollars. As the beverage operation moves into hotels, special customer-operated in-room bars have been developed which control each and every purchase. With increasing business from conventions and corporate meetings, banquet managing has also become more sophisticated.

One of the most important pieces of equipment that every beverage operation needs, without exception, is an ice-making machine. The machine should be chosen based on the general needs of the operation, taking into consideration peak and future needs.

Alcoholic Beverage Bottles

The Bureau of Alcohol, Tobacco and Firearms (BATF) has eliminated the future use, in the United States, of 500-milliliter bottles for distilled spirits. Beginning on January 1, 1989, importers and bottlers can no longer import or bottle distilled spirits in 500-milliliter containers; this bottle size is said to confuse consumers because of its similarity to the 375- and 750-milliliter sizes.

In order to provide the consumer with clearer and more useful information on labels for distilled spirits, the BATF also issued new regulations (on November 10, 1986) for labeling: alcohol content must be indicated by percentage—not just in proof. This is a more readily understood way to convey alcohol content to the purchaser.

Since the repeal of Prohibition, the requirement that labels state alcohol content (formerly expressed in degrees of proof) has remained unchanged. Proof is a traditional term for alcohol content (equal to twice the percentage by volume). Thus, 80 proof means 40 percent alcohol by volume; 100 proof means 50 percent alcohol by volume, and so on.

According to the new regulations, labels *must* show percentage by volume of alcohol, but both forms (proof and percentage) may be used. If a proof statement is used, it must be shown in direct conjunction with the percent by volume, emphasizing the fact that both expressions mean the same thing. Distillers have until October 1988 to make the transition solely to percentage listings.

BOTTLE SIZES FOR WINES AND DISTILLED SPIRITS

Wines (all types)

Bottle size	Capacity in ounces
4 l.	135.2
3 l.	101.4
1.5 l.	50.8
1 l.	33.8
750 ml.	25.4
375 ml.	12.7
187 ml.	6.3
100 ml.	3.4

Champagne

Bottle size	Name	Capacity in ounces
15 l.	Nebuchadnezzar	540.93
12 l.	Balthazar	432.74
9 l.	Salmanazar	324.46
6 l.	Methuselah	216.37
3 l.	Jeroboam	108.19
1.5 l.	Magnum	54.09
750 ml.	Bottle	25.4
375 ml.	Half-bottle	12.7
187 ml.	Split	6.76

Distilled spirits (all types)

Bottle size	Capacity in ounces
1.75 l.	59.2
1 l.	33.8
750 ml.	25.4
200 ml.	6.8
50 ml.	1.7

Ordering and Par Stock

Reordering must be done before one has completely run out of a product. Many beverage managers have what they call a "reorder point," at which there is sufficient lead time for deliveries, yet customers can still be satisfied with what is on hand.

It is suggested that, whenever a bottle is ordered from the storeroom, a record of this requisition be made, then sent to the storeroom at the close of the day for the purpose of inventory and eventual replacement. Another possibility is to use metal-edged numbered tags on bottles, which can be removed as bottles are sold and deposited in a box, from which requisitions for replacements are made up at the close of the day. Some establishments use a "bottle-for-bottle" policy; a practice of requiring an empty bottle be turned in before a replacement bottle is issued.

An inventory system should be set up with adequate space for wines, distilled spirits, and beers; if possible, these should be separated. Sometimes a "perpetual inventory" system is utilized: simply put, this is a bookkeeping system that adds to and subtracts from the inventory as bottles enter and leave the storeroom. In this case, the perpetual inventory should correspond with the actual inventory figures. Beverage managers should check inventory on a weekly basis and report any discrepancies immediately.

Ordering effectively can only be accomplished by determining from past inventories what was sold, in what quantities, and how fast. From patterns established over several weeks it is easy to determine how much of a certain product is needed at the bar. The *par stock* is the minimum amount of a product that must be on hand to satisfy customers' needs for a specific period of time. It might be wise to establish different par stocks for weekends, holidays, parties, and so on. If this is not possible, then plan on those occasions to have on hand one-and-a-half times the needs of your busiest day. Keeping a par stock helps in determining an ordering schedule, since it sets up an inventory level of merchandise. For several reasons, it is unwise to go above your predetermined inventory level: excess capital will be tied up that could be put to better use; space will be used that could be put to other or better use; and the interest you are paying on your tied-up money may not be regained.

Another point to consider when purchasing is the possible trade-offs involved in certain decisions: Do you want to purchase a particular case of red wine now, when the price is low, although it will not be drinkable or saleable for five years, or should you wait five years, when the purchase price is considerably higher, before purchasing? A decision should be based on the following considerations:

Five years later the wine might not be available.

How much storage space do you have? Are your storage conditions ideal?

What is your cash flow?

What interest rates would be charged against money borrowed for the purchase?

What dollar amount would you save by purchasing the wine when it first appears, as opposed to buying it at a higher price in five years?

How secure against theft or fire is your facility?

If the purchase is made, in what quantity?

What is the market like: how willing will your clientele be to purchase the wine?

Does the wine complement any of the food items on your menu?

Sales Representatives

When it is time to order or reorder, be sure that you are purchasing from a reputable distributor or wholesaler. This could make the difference between prompt service and service that costs you business and money because of delays.

Establish a good rapport with sales representatives. In addition to selling you a product, they can give advice and assistance. If problems arise with deliveries, immediately call the sales representative, inform him or her of the situation, and seek immediate remedies.

Most distributors/wholesalers will not sell you a "broken" case (a case of twelve bottles made up of several brands or types of wine or distilled spirits, according to your specifications), but a good working relationship with your sales representatives could result in several broken cases being delivered.

Receiving

Assign the manager or bar manager to handle deliveries; insist that they are "rear" delivered (delivered at the service entrance), if possible. When deliveries are received, invoices must be checked against merchandise delivered. Simply counting the number of cases received does not ensure that you are getting what was ordered. It is necessary to either open the cases or check labels stamped on the box sides that indicate their contents. This is essential with wines that carry a vintage date, to ensure that you are getting the vintage that was ordered.

Whenever possible, make sure that the contents delivered are not damaged or broken. A simple eye check should immediately pick up such damage, or even missing bottles. Occasionally, through rough handling, boxes are dropped, and one or more bottles in the case are broken. If the case is left untouched for several months, the cardboard will dry out, and unless the case is shook the break will not be detected. This type of breakage is referred to as a "dry break."

Wine Storage

Wine's enemies are temperature (too high, too low, or widely fluctuating), vibration, light, and excessively high or low humidity. You do not have to spend thousands of dollars building a special cellar, but you do have to use common sense when choosing a storage area.

If your bulk wine storage is far away from the dining room, be sure to requisition a day's supply and keep it behind the bar or in another convenient area. If servers have to travel too far to get bottles of wine or can't find a bucket, they will find ways not to sell wine.

Light

Strong light, particularly sunlight, can be harmful to wine if a bottle is exposed for long periods. It is not necessary to reproduce sealed darkroom conditions, but wine should be protected from light as much as possible. For this reason most wines are packaged in green or brown bottles.

Temperature and Humidity

Wide and frequent fluctuations in temperature should be avoided. The proper cellar temperature is 52° to 55°F, but a few degrees higher or lower is satisfactory, providing that the temperature is constant. Wines can be safely stored for years in a fairly stable temperature ranging from 55° to 70°F. The cooler the bottle's aging conditions, the more a young wine's character is retained, for a longer period of time. Temperatures are cooler at floor level and on interior walls or closets; exterior walls are affected by sunlight and daily temperature changes. Uninsulated rooms should not be used, as their wide temperature changes damage the wine and shorten its life.

The correct level of humidity for a wine cellar is between 55 and 65 percent. If the humidity begins to rise, reaching 80 percent or more, mold may form and corks may leak as the wine in the bottle expands. There is also a long-term effect; bottle labels begin to deteriorate, and with long-term exposure will actually disintegrate. Conversely, if the humidity falls well below 55 percent, the corks begin to dry out, as do the wooden wine racks and supports.

Wine racks should be positioned away from water heaters, stoves, and heat ducts. Store white wines and sparkling wines and champagnes close to the floor, where it is cooler. A room equipped with an air conditioner will help maintain a consistent temperature and humidity, ensuring that the wine your customer orders arrives in the best possible condition.

Vibrations

Wines should rest quietly. Constant vibration can damage their flavor, and storage areas should not be located adjacent to loading docks or dishwashers. Other poor choices are areas near air conditioner or heat exhaust ducts.

Wine bottles should be stored with their labels facing up for easy identification of the type and brand of wine. If the bottle has been stored with the label facing down, chances are that it probably shows abrasions from repeated handling. Since some customers like to save empty bottles, or soak off the labels as souvenirs, this could be a problem. Another, and more important reason why labels should face up is so that they can be easily identified in the periodic checks that are made (called *candling*) to determine the amount of sediment, if any, that has formed in the bottle. To candle the bottle, carefully hold it, horizontally, in front of an exposed light bulb (60 to 100 watts) so that light penetrates the glass, displaying any sediment on the bottom side of the bottle. Knowing which wines have started to "throw" sediment aids in serving wines.

Wine Racks

Wine racks should be designed so that wine bottles are stored horizontally, allowing the cork to remain in contact with the wine, which ensures that it stays moist and pliable. A moist cork provides the best seal for a bottle of wine. If the bottle is allowed to stand upright for prolonged periods of time (two months or longer) the cork will dry out, allowing air to enter the bottle, which eventually causes oxidation, and finally spoilage. (The only exception to the rule of horizontal storage is for bottles that are sealed with plastic corks or metal screw caps; these may be safely stored upright.) Horizontal rack designs should allow air to circulate and permit, when possible, each bottle to be removed without disturbing its neighbor. Several types of shelving are available that absorb vibrations.

There are basically two ways to correctly store cork-finished wine bottles; either horizontally, or with the neck of the bottle tilted slightly upward. (Some wine racks are also designed so that the neck of the bottle is pointed down. This leads to trouble, for it is not uncommon for wine bottles to leak at the neck or through the cork.)

The other problem associated with storing bottles with the necks pointed either slightly up or down is that it wastes cellar space. In an average storage room, whose ceiling is eight feet high, space is at a premium. The diameter of a wine or champagne bottle at its widest point can be up to four inches. If another four inches are allowed for retrieval, and two additional inches for movement, a total of ten inches (vertically) is used in horizontal storage. If the neck is pointed upward or downward, another six inches is used for a total (vertical) space of sixteen inches.

Purchasing Nonvintage Wines

Perhaps the biggest problem associated with wines that do not carry a vintage date is that one has no way to determine how long it was stored in the warehouse prior to purchase. It happens quite often that warehouse workers who have little or no knowledge of wines simply place the new merchandise in front of the old; rotation of stock, under these circumstances, is rarely accomplished. As the stock is depleted, the older wines start appearing—wines that may have been stored there for several years.

Therefore, it is imperative that you purchase nonvintage wines only from very reputable distributors who have temperature-controlled warehouses and insist on rotation of stock. Do not purchase more nonvintage wine than will be consumed within six months.

It is a good idea to mark cases or even the individual bottles of nonvintage wine with a piece of removable tape showing the date it was received. And, always insist that your own stock is rotated.

Plastic Bottles

Distilled Spirits

Airlines have been switching to plastic liquor and wine bottles to trim fuel costs. The main reasons why products are packaged in plastic bottles are well documented: they are light-weight, cost-effective, easy to transport and handle, and, most important, they are break resistant. Safety is also a factor, and is another reason why glass is rarely used on airlines.

In 1983, British Airways switched a 747's entire normal flight complement of one thousand miniature bottles of liquor from glass to plastic, which saved about $25,000 per year for each of the airline's twenty-six jumbo jets used on transatlantic flights. (A nine-gram miniature plastic bottle is 86 percent lighter than glass.) British Airways estimates that every pound of weight reduction on a 747 saves about $82 (under current exchange rates) per year in fuel.

There are many distilled spirits available in plastic miniature bottles as well as 750-milliliters. Among them are: Jim Beam (the first liquor from an American distiller); Smirnoff, Popov, and Relska vodkas; Johnnie Walker Red and Black Scotch; Tanqueray gin; Campari; Pernod; Murphy's Irish whiskey; and many others.

Wine

Distributors and retailers are receptive to large-size plastic bottles because their reduced weight and their compactness means lower freight costs; there is also no breakage. The use of plastic reduces the overall weight of a filled bottle by at least one-third.

Eastern Airlines and Piedmont, in addition to plastic miniature bottles, also carry plastic 187 milliliter bottles of wine. A package kit (of ninety) of these plastic bottles weighs only twenty-four pounds, compared to forty-six pounds for glass.

Some California wineries also bottle their wines in plastic jugs, which they report are not only light-weight, but easier for store personnel to move around. Plastic containers also make pouring easier for bartenders. These light-weight wine bottles provide outbound freight savings in excess of 20 percent by increasing the number of cases per truck or railcar. An empty plastic 3-liter bottle weighs 3.6 ounces, compared to 38 ounces for equivalent glass containers. An empty 4-liter plastic bottle weighs 4.5 ounces, versus 42 ounces for a glass jug.

The success of economically priced table wines sold in large, light-weight plastic bottles may prompt more wine producers to eventually switch over to plastic.

Banquets

To effectively sell alcoholic beverages at banquets, bars must be attractive to guests and be stocked with a good assortment of brand name alcoholic beverages.

For efficient service, a minimum of one bartender is generally needed for every fifty guests, with two being optimum. When one bartender is responsible for fifty guests, speed, efficiency, and organization is extremely important. The bar, which is usually portable, must be entirely set up before the banquet begins; all necessary supplies—alcoholic beverages, ice, glasses, and so on—must be within immediate reach of the bartender. Because of the small size of most catering bars, the number of beverage brands one can supply is limited, and careful selection of the most popular brands is essential.

It is extremely important that the catering staff be instructed on proper pouring of wines at banquets, conventions, meetings, and so on. Stress the importance to your waiters of not filling glasses with wine when the dinner is about to break. As much as 50 percent of what is spent on wine can be saved by insisting on proper pouring. In addition, specify in writing exactly how much wine waiters must pour; six or even eight ounces is more than sufficient. One of the best ways to ensure proper pouring is by using automatic pouring tops that fit all bottle sizes. Proper glassware size is also important, as it guarantees the correct liquor-to-mixer ratio.

A complete and total bar inventory must take place prior to and immediately following any and all events.

Pricing Banquets

Prices should be flexible enough to guarantee a sizable profit, while at the same time making your premise accessible to (affordable by) the general public. The pricing structure that follows is a suggested one that can easily be modified to suit individual needs.

Hosted bars, on a per-person basis. This pricing structure provides for unlimited drinks for a minimum of fifty guests, and serves name brand liquors. The prices are estimated on a per-person basis, and include the cost of employing two bartenders per every fifty guests:

One hour	$ 9.00 × 50 guests = $450.00
Two hours	$11.00 × 50 guests = $550.00
Three hours	$13.00 × 50 guests = $650.00
Four hours or more	$15.00 × 50 guests = $750.00

Hosted bars, on a per-drink basis. This pricing structure is based on the service of name brand liquor drinks, but with no minimum set for the number of guests. Either the organization pays the final tab, calculated by each drink, or each guest pays for his/her own individual drinks. When guests pay for individual drinks, fixed prices for drink categories must be standardized, to avoid the necessity of committing to memory each individual brand's selling price. These per-drink prices do not include the cost of employing bartenders, which would be covered separately:

Name brand liquor	$3.25
Premium brand liquor	$3.50
Name brand liqueurs	$3.00
Premium brand liqueurs	$3.50
House wines (white, red, rosé)	$2.25
American beers	$2.50
Imported beers	$3.00

Hosted bars, on a per-bottle basis. This pricing structure is based on the cost of name brand bottles of liquor; it entails no established minimum number of guests. The sponsoring organization pays the final tab, calculated by each bottle opened, regardless of whether the contents have been totally consumed. Some state liquor laws permit the organization to claim any opened, unempty bottles (often referred to as "stubs"), while other states prohibit such actions. The drink prices would not reflect a charge of $50.00 per bartender, which would be covered separately.

Beverage Cost Forecasting

There is no such thing as a perfect cost percentage to be accepted by all beverage managers as an industry standard. Every beverage cost percentage must and should be considered in relation to a particular establishment.

In determining a reasonable beverage cost percentage, we could consider utilizing a "bottom-up approach." In using this method, we first consider an acceptable return on investment out of every dollar, then anticipate controllable and noncontrollable expenses. Other than the cost of the beverage add these variables, and then subtract from $1.00; this will give us a "target" beverage cost.

For example: $.13 represents desired profit from each
dollar of sale

.20 represents projected noncontrollable expenses
per dollar of sale

.40 represents projected controllable expenses
per dollar of sale

$.73 is the gross profit
per dollar of sale

We now subtract this $.73 gross profit per dollar of sale from $1.00, arriving at a targeted beverage cost of $.27 per dollar of sale.

To change this figure to a percentage, simply convert all monetary figures to percentages; e.g., $1.00 to 100 percent, $.73 to 73 percent, and so on. This $.27 or 27 percent represents the percentage of the dollar that we have targeted to pay for *all* of our beverage costs. It should be noted that we are solely using the aforementioned figures for demonstration purposes; again, they do not represent any type of industry standard.

There are numerous resources available in print that can be used where projected feasibility returns on investments along with payment of expenses can be determined. Armed with this information, the entrepreneur can predict with justifiable accuracy an acceptable beverage cost percentage for his particular establishment.

Every year, the National Restaurant Association publishes a Restaurant Industry Operations Report which is prepared by Laventhol & Horwath, certified public accountants. At the end of each report the reader is presented with a method by which to analyze his or her existing or future operation. Statistics are presented on national averages for certain types of establishments, and which can be compared to our projected sales and expenses, with net income treated as an expense. Once these projections are targeted, we can then target *minimum* selling prices (maximum selling prices are determined solely by what the market will bear).

Determining the Sale Price of a Drink

To determine the price of a single drink, there are several points that must be considered: the size and price of the bottle, and individual drink size. With today's automatic pourers, bars have a choice of exactly what size of drink they pour.

In the following example, a liter bottle of Scotch is used, which costs (wholesale) $10.00. You have determined that a 1.5-ounce drink will be poured to each customer, and wish to determine how much each drink will cost. Thus:

$$\frac{\text{Bottle size}}{\text{Drink size}} = \text{Number of drinks}$$

(Note: The bottle size is not rounded off, because of the fractions used in the size of the drink.) So, for example:

$$\frac{33.8 \text{ oz.}}{1.50 \text{ (1.5 oz.)}} = 22.5, \text{ or 22 drinks}$$

When rounding off the number of drinks, always round off lower, simply because you cannot divide a drink.

To determine the cost of those twenty-two drinks, use this formula:

$$\frac{\text{Cost of bottle}}{\text{Number of drinks}} = \text{cost per drink}$$

For example:

$$\frac{\$10.00}{22} = .454, \text{ or 45 cents}$$

There are two methods of determining the projected beverage cost:

The divisional method. To find out the potential selling price, divide the actual beverage cost by the projected beverage cost percentage:

$$\frac{\text{Actual beverage cost}}{\text{Projected cost percentage}} = \text{Potential selling price}$$

For example: A single drink of Scotch costs 45 cents and you are working with a projected 27 percent beverage cost. The selling price would be determined as follows:

$$\frac{45 \text{ cents}}{27 \text{ cents (or 27 percent)}} = \$1.666, \text{ or } \$1.67$$

The price multiplier method. Continuing our example, to determine a minimum selling price per drink, divide 27 into 100, which will give us a price multiplier of 3.70. Take the cost of any drink, and multiply it by 3.70 to determine a *minimum selling price.* We will use the cost of 45 cents:

$$45 \text{ cents} \times 3.70 = \$1.665, \text{ or } \$1.67$$

From this point we can establish common prices for each drink category: well, call, and super-premium. Adjustments will be necessary based on clientele and demand. However, we must target all pricing to *average* a 27 percent beverage cost should we want to maintain and *control* this targeted beverage cost.

Determining the Projected Cost Percentage

The formula used to project cost percentages is the following:

$$\frac{\text{Actual beverage cost}}{\text{Potential selling price}} = \text{Projected cost percentage}$$

Using the same figures as used in determining the selling price, for example:

$$\frac{45 \text{ cents}}{\$1.67} = .269 \text{ (or 27 percent)}$$

Determining the Actual Beverage Cost

If you determine the potential selling price and projected cost percentage of a certain drink, it is easy to determine the actual beverage cost: multiply the potential selling price by the projected cost percentage. For example:

$$\$1.67 \times .27 = 45 \text{ cents}$$

Determining Gross Profit on a Full Bottle

It has been established that there are twenty-two drinks in a liter bottle of Scotch (1.5-oz. drinks), which costs $10.00; the potential selling price of each drink is $1.67. To determine total sales from the entire bottle, simply multiply the number of drinks by the potential selling price per drink; for example:

$$22 \text{ (drinks)} \times \$1.67 \text{ (selling price)} = \$36.74 \text{ (total sales)}$$

To determine gross profit, subtract the bottle cost from the total sales; for example:

$$\$36.74 - \$10.00 = \$26.74 \text{ (gross profit per bottle)}$$

Pricing Mixed Drinks

There are many ways to price individual drinks. One method is to take the prime ingredient (liquor) and use that as the base, then add the other ingredients to come up with a total cost.

For example, we would like to make a martini, and from our standard recipe determine that 2 ounces of vodka, .25 ounces dry white vermouth, and one green cocktail olive are needed. Olives come in various sizes, with the "small" designation being the correct size for a martini. Depending on the purveyor you choose, the price can vary greatly. Purveyor A sells them in the following way:

$11.00 per large #10 can

Contains 51 oz. (drained weight)

Count of 578 olives

Average number of olives per lb. = 177–193

If we divide the cost of the can ($11.00) by the number of olives in the can (578), we find out that each olive costs $.0190 cents, or 2 cents. This figure is added to the cost of the vodka.

To determine how much 2 ounces of vodka costs, divide the cost per bottle by the number of ounces in that bottle; for example:

$$\frac{\$10.00 \text{ (cost of bottle)}}{33 \text{ oz.}} = .303, \text{ or 30 cents per ounce}$$

To determine what $\frac{1}{4}$ ounce of dry vermouth will cost, we first find out the cost per liter. If a liter costs $4.24, how many quarter-ounce drinks will we get, and how much will each of them cost?

$$\frac{33.8 \text{ oz. (size of bottle)}}{\frac{1}{4} \text{ oz. (or .25 oz.)}} = 135.2, \text{ or } 135 \text{ (quarter-ounce) drinks}$$

$$\frac{\$4.24 \text{ (cost of bottle)}}{135 \text{ drinks}} = .031, \text{ or } 3 \text{ cents per drink}$$

To determine the cost of the whole drink, add:

Cost of vodka (2 oz. at @ .30 per oz.)	60 cents
Cost of vermouth (.25 oz.)	03 cents
Cost of olive	02 cents
Cost of drink	65 cents

Now, by using our formula for determining a selling price, we find that our drink sells for:

$$\frac{65 \text{ cents (actual beverage cost)}}{27 \text{ cents (projected cost percentage)}} = \begin{array}{c} \text{(selling price)} \\ \$2.407, \text{ or } \$2.41 \end{array}$$

Another method for determining this price is to use what is known as a "kicker": automatically adding 5 to 10 cents to the base cost of the drink, instead of figuring out each and every ingredient. If, for example, a Scotch and soda is requested by a customer, the standard recipe might call for 1.25 ounces of Scotch, 6 ounces of seltzer water, and ice cubes. Instead of figuring how much the seltzer water costs, 10 cents is added to base liquor cost of the drink; for example:

Cost of Scotch, per 1.25 oz.	45 cents
Seltzer (10 cents "kicker")	10 cents
Cost of drink	55 cents

Then:

$$\frac{55 \text{ cents (beverage cost)}}{27 \text{ percent (cost percentage)}} = \$2.037, \text{ or } \$2.04$$

Determining Average Beverage Sales

To determine average beverage sales per customer, divide total beverage sales by the number of customers present during that period of time. For example, if the total wine sales (by the bottle) for an evening are $2,350.00, and there were 150 customers present:

$$\frac{\$2,350.00}{150 \text{ customers}} = \$15.666, \text{ or } \$15.67 \text{ (sales per customer)}$$

Making or Buying Beverage Mixes

Occasionally you will be faced with deciding whether to purchase pre-mixed beverage mixes — for Bloody Marys, piña coladas, Margaritas, etc.—or make them yourself. The decision should be based not only on the quality of the premix versus homemade blends, but on the relative cost of each of them. For example: You are able to purchase Sour Mix at a cost of $23.50 per (12 qt.) case; there is a 2 percent "post-off" on three cases. Your bartender makes an equally fine sour mix, but you don't know how much it costs to make. What you do know is that his mix yields two gallons, and that the raw ingredients cost you $11.45. In addition, it takes him 25 minutes to make, and you pay him $4.85 per hour, with 15 percent in fringe benefits. To determine the cost of the purchased mix:

$$
\begin{array}{r}
\$23.50 \text{ (case cost)} \\
\times \quad 2 \text{ percent (post-off)} \\
\hline
47 \text{ cents (post-off)}
\end{array}
$$

$$
\begin{array}{r}
\$23.50 \text{ (cost of case)} \\
- \quad 47 \text{ cents (post off)} \\
\hline
\$23.03 \text{ (case cost after post-off)}
\end{array}
$$

$$\frac{\$23.03 \text{ (case cost)}}{12 \text{ quarts}} = \$1.919, \text{ or } \$1.92 \text{ per quart}$$

To determine the cost of the homemade mix:

$$\frac{\$11.45 \text{ (2 gal.)}}{8 \text{ quarts (2 gal.)}} = \$1.43 \text{ per quart}$$

$4.85 (hourly salary) × 15 percent (fringe benefit) = 73 cents

$4.85 (hourly salary)
+ 73 cents (fringe benefit)
$5.58 per hour

$$\frac{\$5.58 \text{ (per hour)}}{60 \text{ (minutes in one hour)}} = \$.093 \text{ per minute}$$

$.093 (per minute) × 25 (minutes) = $2.325, or $2.33 for 25 minutes of work

$$\frac{\$2.33 \text{ (25 minutes of labor)}}{8 \text{ quarts}} = \$.29 \text{ per quart (labor)}$$

Product cost $1.43 per quart
Labor costs .29 per quart
$1.72 per quart

So, it costs $1.92 per quart to buy the sour mix and $1.72 per quart to make the blend. The difference is 20 cents for 2 gallons. You must determine how many gallons of sour mix you need per week to find out if it really pays to make your own.

Percentage Increases/Decreases (Mark-ups)

Often a beverage manager wants to determine how much (as percentages) the costs/selling prices of drinks either increased or decreased over a specified period of time. For example, five years ago a bottle of Scotch cost $3.85; now it costs $8.50. To determine how much the cost of the Scotch has increased, the following formula is applied:

$$\frac{DT \text{ (distance traveled)}}{SP \text{ (starting point)}} = Percentage$$

$8.50 (current cost)
− $3.85 (old cost)
$4.65 (difference expressed in dollars)

Now, by using the formula, we have:

$$\frac{\$4.65 \text{ (DT)}}{\$3.85 \text{ (SP)}} = 1.208, \text{ or a 121 percent increase}$$

Another way to use this formula is illustrated in this example: A wine shop owner sells a bottle of Beaujolais wine for $5.59; he bought it for $3.83. To determine the mark-up percentage in this case we can utilize the same formula:

$$\begin{array}{r} \$5.59 \text{ (current selling price)} \\ - \ \$3.83 \text{ (original cost per bottle)} \\ \hline \$1.76 \text{ (difference)} \end{array}$$

$$\frac{\$1.76 \text{ (DT)}}{\$3.83 \text{ (SP)}} = .46, \text{ or a 46 percent mark-up}$$

Determining a "Better Buy"

When purchasing wines or distilled spirits, you must determine what bottle size or sizes you will need; the traditional 750-milliliter size; the larger liter bottle; 1.5-liter bottle (wine only); or a 1.75-liter bottle (distilled spirits). Which one is the better buy, or are they priced exactly the same, per ounce?

Let us say that a certain Scotch wholesales per bottle for:

$11.41 for 750 ml.

$14.62 for 1 l.

$23.20 for 1.75 l.

Which one of these (perhaps they are all the same price) is the better buy? Use the following formula:

$$\frac{\text{Cost per bottle}}{\text{Number of ounces in the bottle}} = \text{Price per ounce}$$

1. 750-ml. bottle $\dfrac{\$11.41}{25.4 \text{ oz.}} = .449, \text{ or } \$.45 \text{ per ounce}$

2. 1-l. bottle $\dfrac{\$14.62}{33.8 \text{ oz.}} = .432, \text{ or } \$.43 \text{ per ounce}$

3. 1.75-l. bottle $\dfrac{\$23.20}{59.2 \text{ oz.}} = .391, \text{ or } \$.39 \text{ per ounce}$

The better buy in this case is number 3, the Scotch that wholesales for $23.20 per bottle. Before you purchase this 1.75-liter size, however, determine the size and space of your speed racks, back bar, and underbar, and the frequency with which the brand is chosen by customers. For an extra few cents, it may pay to purchase the 750-milliliter bottle (for size) or the 1-liter bottle (for frequency of drinks).

Pouring Spouts

Constant price increases, rising liquor taxes, and tougher drunk-driving laws make it essential not to overpour drinks. You could be losing a considerable amount of money by allowing your bartenders to freely pour liquor by using the uncontrollable plastic spouts many bars use. Instead, consider using the portion control pourer, which saves money and increases profits.

For example, if you use a liter bottle of Scotch (33.8 oz.) and pour one-ounce shots, or thirty-three drinks, charging $3.00 per drink, that totals $99.00 in sales. But, if because of overpouring, spillage, or guess-work when using the free pourer, only twenty-six drinks are yielded from the bottle ($78.00), that's a loss of $21.00 in sales per liter. If the bartender pours five cases of Scotch per week by the free-pour method, that's a loss of $252.00 per case ($21.00 × 12 bottles), or $1,260.00 per five cases. This is the loss for only one type of liquor served; you could be losing tens of thousands of dollars every year.

The national average loss for all types of bars—from spillage, over-pouring, dead inventory, unauthorized giveaways, dishonesty, and poor recordkeeping—is five drinks per bottle. Losses in many bars are actually higher—sometimes six to seven drinks per bottle. By using the portion control pourer, you can guarantee that a controlled amount of liquor is always dispensed. Because a consistent drink is poured every time, service speed is increased (most pourers have a half-second to one full second recycle time), more drinks are sold, and profits are increased. Use of controlled pourers relieves bartender tension and eliminates the cost and constant washing of shot glasses. Cocktail waitresses can also serve more customers in less time.

By using controlled pourers, you can consistently pour whatever size of shot you want—without offending your customers. They also guarantee uniformity of drink taste and assure perfectly blended cocktails. Automatic pourers are made for drinks of many sizes, including the following: $\frac{1}{2}$, $\frac{5}{8}$, $\frac{3}{4}$, $\frac{7}{8}$, 1, $1\frac{1}{8}$, $1\frac{1}{4}$, $1\frac{1}{2}$, and 2 ounces. Many manufacturers even color code their pourers for quick recognition. Some manufacturers even offer flip-top caps which protect beverages not only from dust but also from insects, especially fruit flies. Dust caps are now required in many areas of the country by government health departments.

In another controlled dispensing system, liquor bottles are placed upside down in a plastic dispenser. To operate it, a glass is placed underneath and a lever on the dispenser is pushed up to pour out, with 100 percent accuracy, a measured amount of liquor. At the same time a meter registers, and shows in a visible readout, each drink and how many drinks per bottle have been dispensed. This simplifies inventory control, and gives a full accounting of *all* sales.

Computerized Beverage Control Systems

To effectively cope with rapidly rising costs, bar managers must have access to accurate, timely, and complete information relating to sales, inventory, guest check control, employee productivity, and beverage and labor costs. This vital information must be available on a minute-to-minute basis. Combining the finest in modern technology and management tools, computerized control systems provide the total control of profit and inventory that is essential in today's market.

In the fiercely competitive beverage business it is imperative that you have the full use of all profits, both to satisfy current commitments and to meet capital needs for future growth. Control systems provide you with the consistency, quality, speed, and total control that you need. It is not enough to partially control products poured at the bar; every liquor, liqueur, wine, cocktail, highball, soft drink, and even draft beer must be poured accurately, rapidly, and with total accountability.

In-Room Bars

In-room computerized bars offer hotel guests the opportunity to enjoy alcoholic beverages in the privacy of their rooms while the management maintains absolute control over purchases. Upon guest check-in, the room unit is activated, and a key is provided to the registrant. Guests can select from a range of different items in privacy, and charges are instantly transferred for addition to the room charge. In such computerized systems printouts are instantaneous, and provide a wealth of information, from restocking reports to usage tracked by room type. Computerized in-room systems eliminate the problems associated with "honor" bars. Some of the benefits of such systems are:

By providing beverages and light snacks, they free room service personnel for larger and more profitable orders.

They are profitable amenities that differentiate your hotel or resort from others.

They are virtually pilfer proof.

They comply with liquor laws through computer controls.

They promote impulse purchases, which otherwise would not be made.

They serve the in-room guest, while at the same time not detracting from lounge sales.

The computerized restocking report saves time and money.

Detailed statistical printouts provide instant accountability of all sales, tracked through a variety of checkpoints.

Some manufacturers of in-room alcoholic beverage control systems are:

ABC Computer Bar (American Beverage Control) (Mogadore, Ohio)

Bar-Vender (Posen, Illinois)

Dometic Mini-Bar (Elkhart, Indiana)

NCR Corporation (Dayton, Ohio)

ServiBar (Tysons Corner, Virginia)

Ice-Making Machines

In the beverage business a ready supply of ice is always a necessity. One of the most important pieces of equipment you will need is a reliable and efficient ice-making machine that suits the individual needs of your establishment. There are basically two types of machines: one produces cubes; the other, flakes.

Some questions to be asked prior to purchasing an ice-making machine are:

What type and size ice cubes are needed?

What is the total storage capacity of the machine?

How many pounds of ice does it produce per hour?

How large a machine is needed?

The Operating Cycle

Although ice-making machines vary considerably in methods of forming and releasing ice, the operating cycles are similar in most cases. The water-contact or water-container surfaces are chilled to below the freezing point in the ice-making cycle. When the ice reaches a certain thickness, the water-contact or water-container surface is heated briefly to release the ice. This is called the *harvest cycle*. The cycling process is automatic.

The Electrical System

The electrical system consists of a compressor, a condenser, fans, and various thermostats. The elements required for harvesting ice are also part of the electrical system; in certain machines the harvest is controlled by a solenoid valve that transmits hot gas to the copper freezing surfaces.

The Water System

The water system includes a pump and one or more water pans. The water level in the pan(s) is usually controlled by a float-operated valve. The other parts of the water system depend on the type of freezing system used: in certain machines water is distributed in an even sheet over freezing surfaces; in others, it is sprayed on freezing surfaces or into freezing containers.

Operation and Maintenance

Ice-making machines operate automatically. Kitchen personnel should not adjust the machine except to set the cube-or-chip control. Wash the exterior of the ice-making machine as necessary with a clean cloth dampened in a warm detergent solution. Wipe with a cloth dampened in clear warm water, and dry with a clean cloth.

Crushed Ice

Crushed ice is required for cold pans. If a dining facility ice-making machine produces cubes only, an ice-crushing machine may be installed as an attachment to the ice-making machine. If two or more ice-making machines are used, one should provide crushed ice, or both cubes and chips.

Ice Cube Dispensers

Many types and styles of dispensers are available. Among the most popular types are countertop, trigger, pushbutton/key, and coin/token models.

The Storage Compartment

The ice storage compartment is a large well with a drain. The compartment temperature is controlled by a thermostat. An automatic element in the compartment senses the level of ice in storage. When the compartment is filled with ice, the element activates a switch to interrupt the power supply to the ice-making machinery; as ice is removed from the storage compartment, the element deactivates the switch so that power is restored to the ice-making machinery and the supply of ice is automatically replenished.

Storage capacity can range from 220 to 2,000 pounds, and occasionally even more.

Production

Modern ice-making machines can produce from 100 to 3,300 pounds of ice per hour, depending on the make and model purchased. It is important to note that most ice-making machines give varying production ratings for different temperature levels of the air-cooled or water-cooled condenser unit, as well as for different temperatures of water used. Examples of such varying production are given below.

24-Hour Production (lbs.)

Air temperature	Water temperature		
	50°F	*70°F*	*90°F*
	Air-cooled unit		
70°F	100	95	90
80°F	90	85	80
90°F	80	75	70

Water-cooled unit			
70°F	100	95	90
80°F	95	90	85
90°F	90	85	80

Ice Cube Size

Most later-model ice-making machines can be adjusted to produce either ice cubes or ice chips. In these machines, the capillary sheath that governs ice formation is adjusted to be close to the freezing surface, for chip ice, or farther from the freezing surfaces, for ice cubes.

There are many different sizes of ice cubes produced by various manufacturers' ice machines; some of them have been dubbed: "crescent" cubes; "cubelets"; "flake ice"; "flat" cubes; "gourmet" cubes; "full" cubes (also called "dice"); "half-cubes" (also called "half-dice"); "ice nuggets"; and "regular" and "square" cubes. Of these, the standard sizes are:

Regular ($1\frac{1}{8}'' \times 1\frac{1}{8}'' \times \frac{7}{8}''$; 30 cubes per pound)

Full (also called "dice") ($\frac{7}{8}'' \times \frac{7}{8}'' \times \frac{7}{8}''$; 48 cubes per pound)

Half-cubes (also called "half-dice") ($\frac{3}{8}'' \times \frac{7}{8}'' \times \frac{7}{8}''$; 96 cubes per pound)

Sizing guidelines. Daily ice needs in any business are rarely stable; there are always minimum and peak ice usage levels. Daily ice needs in summer are usually greater than winter, and on weekends are greater than on weekdays. Therefore, size your ice machine and storage bin based on what your peak ice usage needs will be.

Avoid sizing a new ice machine solely on the basis of the performance of your existing ice-making machine. The age and mechanical condition of your existing ice machine may mislead you in determining the quantity of ice you need. Remember: surrounding air and incoming water temperatures affect the quantity of ice a machine produces. Determine what these temperatures will be during peak ice needs and verify your model selection from its ice-production chart.

Use the ice usage guide shown below to calculate your ice usage based on your peak ice needs. After calculating how much ice you must have, add to that figure a 20 percent safety factor to accommodate future business growth. Taking time to correctly size ice-making equipment ensures an always adequate ice supply.

ICE USAGE GUIDE

Hospitality	Approximate ice cube/flake ice needs per day
Restaurant	1.5 lbs. ice per person
Cocktail	3 lbs. ice per person/seat
Salad bar	30–40 lbs. ice per cubic foot
Fast food	4–5 oz. ice per 7–10-oz. drink
	8 oz. ice per 12–16-oz. drink
	12 oz. ice per 18–24-oz. drink
Guest ice room service	5 lbs. ice per room
Catering	1 lb. ice per person

Health care	
Hospital	10 lbs. ice per bed
Hospital cafeteria	1 lb. ice per person
Nursing home	6 lbs. ice per bed

Convenience stores	
Beverages	6 oz. ice per 12-oz. drink
	10 oz. ice per 20-oz. drink
	16 oz. ice per 32-oz. drink
Cold plates	50% more ice per day
Packaged ice	lbs. per bag × bags sold per day

Some manufacturers of ice-making machines are:

Crystal Tips	Manitowoc	Saxony
Hoshizaki	Reynolds/Alco	Scotsman
Ice-O-Matic	Ross Temp	

Suggested Readings

Coltman, Michael M. *Cost Control for the Hospitality Industry.* New York: CBI, 1980.

Crawford, Hollie W. and Milton C. McDowell. *Math Workbook for Foodservice/ Lodging,* 2d ed. New York: CBI, 1981.

Dittmer, Paul R. and Gerald G. Griffin. *Principles of Food, Beverage and Labor Cost Controls for Hotels and Restaurants,* 3d ed. New York: CBI, 1984.

Miller, Jack. *Menu Pricing and Strategy,* 2d ed. New York: CBI, 1987.

Stefanelli, John. *Purchasing: Selection and Procurement for the Hospitality Industry,* 2d ed. New York: John Wiley, 1985.

Van Kleek, Peter E. *Beverage Management and Bartendering*. New York: CBI, 1981.

Discussion Topics and Questions

1. You have just been appointed assistant beverage manager for a hotel chain. While taking physical inventory, you notice five cases of apparently "over-the-hill" white wines. What do you do with them, and what steps must be taken to avoid this problem in the future?

2. Which (metric) bottle sizes for vodka would be most appropriate to use behind the bar? Explain.

3. While attempting to fill your "par stock," you discover that there are still three cases of bottles to stock, but there is no more room. What should you do?

4. Is it wise to deal with more than one liquor distributor at the same time? Explain.

5. While checking deliveries of beer, you notice that one of the cases contains two broken bottles. Who should you notify?

6. You have just been appointed beverage manager of a resort in Florida and are informed that because of the close proximity to water, no cellar exists for wine storage. How could wines be stored properly?

7. Your local salesman informs you that he has a close-out special on cases of white wine that are already five years old. What should you do?

8. More and more airlines are moving toward plastic bottles for wines and distilled spirits. What about stocking your bar with plastic bottles? What effect do you think it will have on patronage and image?

9. How important is it to pay close attention to beverage forecasting figures if your bar is making excellent profits year after year?

10. How would you handle a complaint from a corporate president who demands he be given paid-for bottles of liquor which were not completely finished from a recent banquet?

11. Analyze this situation: Recently you have installed a pouring system that totally eliminates overpouring, spillage, buy-backs,

and pilferage. However, because of this, customers have gone elsewhere and sales have dropped! What happened, and why?

12. Do hotel cocktail lounges suffer from the implementation of in-room bars? Cite reasons for your answer.

13. When purchasing ice-making machines and deciding between models, how important is it to take into consideration its intended location in your establishment?

13

Merchandising and Marketing

This chapter discusses:

- The marketing of alcoholic and nonalcoholic beverages.
- Planning a promotion.
- Boosting sales through promotions.
- Suggestive selling.
- Ideas for profit.
- Low-alcohol and nonalcoholic beverages.

The marketing phase of a beverage operation is, some experts suggest, the most important one. By researching current consumer likes and dislikes and general trends, long- and short-term goals can be established and plans for reaching these goals developed.

An integral part of any marketing plan is proper merchandising and effective selling. Promotions can make the difference between surviving, or just making ends meet, and financial success. And, in addition to promotions, there are many other ways to increase profits and enlarge the customer base. Some ideas are based solely on intuition, while others incorporate research and experience.

Today's society is moving toward lighter beverages and those that are lower in alcohol. Most people are drinking less, but when they do drink, they demand a high-quality product. Consumer demand for low-alcohol and nonalcoholic beverages has increased recently, due in part to recently passed drunk driving legislation. To make up for loss of revenue due to lower drinking levels, marketing and merchandising plans must be developed to alert customers to alternatives to alcoholic beverages.

Marketing

"Bellyspace"

This concept, introduced more than two decades ago by San Francisco wine industry consultant Lou Gomberg, is important, because while many beverage industry executives don't appreciate the point, no seller of beverages is competing solely against other sellers of the same category of product: each beverage, to a greater or lesser degree, is competing against everything else that's potable—beer against soft drinks, soft drinks against milk, milk against fruit juice, fruit juice against wine, wine against liquor, and all of them against all others, as well as against tap water.

Over the past couple of decades, thanks in large part to the marketing skills of sellers of beverages (and thanks also, of course, to the affluence of the American population), tap water has been the big loser. In 1968, Americans consumed about 19 ounces of tap water daily versus 41.1 ounces of commercially produced beverages. By 1985, tap water's share of America's "bellyspace" had fallen to 14 ounces per day, and commercially produced beverages' share had risen to 50.3 ounces (see the tables below).

It helps, of course, that tap water in many locales is foul tasting and/ or suspected by the citizenry of being contaminated. But that is secondary to the major point, which is that the average American in 1985 paid for 9.2 ounces of beverages per day that he or she was not paying for seventeen years ago; 3,358 ounces of commercially produced beverages are consumed per person per year (or roughly 100 liters per person per year). There are approximately 230 million Americans, so one can estimate that approximately 23 billion liters more of beverages were being purchased in 1985 than were purchased in 1968.

Someone is selling that extra 23 billion liters of beverages, and whoever is selling it is taking business away from whoever is not.

DAILY AVERAGE U.S. CONSUMPTION OF LIQUIDS IN 1985

Beverage	Ounces consumed	Percentage of commercially produced beverages	Percentage of all beverages (including water)
Soft drinks	15.6	31	24.4
Tap water	14	———	21.9
Coffee	9.2	18.2	14.4
Beer	8.3	16.7	13
Milk	7	13.9	10.9
Tea	2.5	5	3.9
Fruit juice	2.2	4.4	3.4
Powdered drinks	2.1	4.2	3.3

Bottled water	1.8	3.6	2.8
Wine	0.8	1.6	1.3
Liquor	0.6	1.2	0.9

Source: *The Wine Investor*, Los Angeles, California.

An average of 50.3 ounces of commercially produced beverages is consumed daily.

DAILY AVERAGE U.S. CONSUMPTION OF LIQUIDS IN 1968

Beverage	Ounces consumed	Percentage of commercially produced beverages	Percentage of all beverages (including water)
Tap water	19	———	29.7
Coffee	13	31.6	20.3
Milk	9	21.9	14.1
Soft drinks	8.2	20	12.8
Beer	6.1	14.8	9.5
Tea	2.3	5.6	3.6
Fruit juice	1.6	3.9	2.5
Liquor	0.6	1.5	0.9
Wine	0.4	1	0.6

Source: *The Wine Investor*, Los Angeles, California.

An average of 41.1 ounces of commercially produced beverages was consumed daily in 1968.

All figures in the tables above take into account the proportion of a given beverage that is actually water. However, the figure for liquor consumption does not take into account the various other beverages with which it might be mixed before being consumed: water, soda water, fruit juices, etc. These items are reported under their respective categories. All percentages are rounded out. Therefore, they may in some instances total less or more than 100 percent.

The figures listed in these tables and discussed in the immediately following text were obtained from Paul Gillette, "California Beverage Hotline," *The Wine Investor* (Los Angeles, Calif., October 1986).

There is only so much bellyspace. The typical human consumes about half a gallon of liquid per day. In 1968, 29.7 percent of it was tap water, 20.3 percent was coffee, 14.1 percent milk, and 12.8 percent soft drinks. By 1985, soft drinks had staked a claim on 24.4 percent of the nation's bellyspace, with tap water falling to 21.9 percent (a drop of 7.8 percentage points), coffee to 14.4 percent (a drop of 5.9 percentage points), and milk to 10.9 percent (a drop of 3.2 percentage points).

In 1968, two beverage categories that appear in the 1985 table were statistically insignificant: bottled water and powdered drinks. In 1985, each was doing more than twice as much business (in liquid volume) as wine and more than three times as much as spirits.

These are national figures. In affluent California, with its much higher percentage of "yuppies" and other free-spending types, commercially produced beverages almost certainly command several additional percentage points of bellyspace.

Once again, there is only so much bellyspace—and there is only so much business you can take away from tap water. So if you are selling soft drinks or beer, congratulations are due for your success over the past seventeen years; sales in these categories have increased, rising in the aggregate from 22.3 percent to 38.8 percent of the nation's bellyspace. If you are selling coffee or milk, sales of which have declined in the aggregate from 34.4 percent to 25.3 percent of the nation's bellyspace, what should you do to try to rebuild your business? Whatever you decide, keep in mind that you are *not* selling exclusively or even mainly against other brands in your own category; you are selling against everything else that is potable.

Distilled Spirits: America's Dinnertime Favorite

When Americans drink alcoholic beverages with their dinner, they are more likely to have a drink made with distilled spirits, rather than beer or wine, according to several recent studies. *Restaurants and Institutions Magazine* conducted a nationwide survey in 1985 of 1,381 people, and found that 36.9 percent had ordered a cocktail or mixed drink at least once with dinner outside the home during the preceding month. This compares with 33.6 percent who ordered wine and 26.4 percent who ordered beer.

In July of 1985, *Impact Newsletter* published a study by National Family Opinion, Inc. based on consumption diaries maintained by 12,000 people. This study reported the percentage of total comsumption for various beverages in various locations. The Distilled Spirits Council of the United States, Inc. (DISCUS) has converted those percentage of volume figures into figures for standard servings for beer, wine, and distilled spirits. This analysis shows that drinks made with distilled spirits are indeed the favorite of Americans when they are at restaurants. DISCUS calculations based on the National Family Opinion research show that Americans ordered 6,196,000,000 servings per year of distilled spirits in restaurants, compared with 1,652,000,000 servings of wine and 2,776,000,000 servings of beer.

Combined, these figures represent the equivalent of America's 100 million adult drinkers eating out once per week and consuming two drinks per occasion. Other studies, including the latest Gallup poll, suggest that these are reasonable assumptions.

The analysis also showed that the greatest volume of spirits are consumed at home, with restaurants being the second most important location. For both beer and wine, the two most popular drinking locations are one's own home and the homes of other people.

Several participants in the National Family Opinion study also indicated their beverage choice for certain occasions. Assuming standard serving sizes of 5 ounces for wine, 12 ounces for beer, and 1.25 ounces for distilled spirits, the data suggests that Americans are most likely to order spirits with dinner (whether at or away from home). Their second choice is beer, and wine is the least frequently chosen form of alcoholic beverage for dinnertime consumption.

In a third study conducted for DISCUS by the Gallup Organization, a representative national sample of 1,202 adults were asked, among other things, what their beverage preferences were and how many drinks they had consumed on their last drinking occasion. According to this study, the average number of drinks consumed per occasion by Americans is 2.2. Only 6 percent of the drinkers claimed to have consumed six or more drinks on their last drinking occasion. For those who prefer distilled spirits, the average number of drinks consumed on their last drinking occasion was 2.0. Those who preferred wine consumed 1.6 drinks, and those who consumed beer, 2.7 drinks. Eleven percent of beer drinkers claim to have consumed six or more drinks on their last drinking occasion, compared to one percent of wine drinkers and three percent of distilled spirits drinkers.

The data obtained in these studies confirm that most Americans drink moderately and responsibly and that distilled spirits are far more popular as an accompaniment to meals than is commonly believed. It has been long recommended that the safest policy is to consume food with or prior to drinking since this slows the absorption of alcohol into the bloodstream. It seems clear that many Americans are following this advice. It is also clear that, despite the myth that beer and wine are the most popular mealtime choices of America's drinkers, distilled spirits are indeed well established as the form of alcohol most frequently ordered with dinner.

What Customers Are Ordering

Where do people order the most beer? Wine? Spirits? Beer is sold most in bars: an average of 53 percent of bar customers order beer, according to operators surveyed; spirits sell best in hotels; and wine sells well in restaurants (see the table below).

PERCENTAGES OF CUSTOMERS ORDERING ALCOHOLIC BEVERAGES IN VARIOUS SEGMENTS OF THE HOSPITALITY INDUSTRY

	Spirits	*Beer*	*Wine*
Restaurants	44%	33%	23%
Bar/tavern/lounge	35%	53%	13%
Hotel/motel/resort/club	49%	34%	17%

Source: Cahners Bureau of Foodservice Research (copyright 1985, *Bar Business Magazine*, a Cahners publication).

In an annual survey of 1,381 households, 37 percent of respondents said they ordered mixed drinks with dinner. Beer, wine, and mixed drinks were neck-and-neck at lunchtime:

Beverage type	*Lunch*	*Dinner*
Beer	16%	26%
Wine	15%	34%
Mixed drinks/cocktails	16%	37%

Source: *Restaurants & Institutions Magazine* Annual Tastes of America Survey, 1984.

Merchandising Wine

A well-written wine list is only the first step in realizing the profit potential of wine sales.

Wine of the month

Perhaps your distributor has already alerted you that he has a limited quantity of special wine. You don't wish to put it on your regular wine list, as the availability is limited. However, you can merchandise it as a "wine of the month." Menu clip-ons make useful beverage recommendations and at the same time remind guests of the wine currently being promoted. Blackboards, placed in front of the restaurant, let customers know what is featured. Table "tents" expose customers to special beverage promotions even before they receive the menu and wine list.

Promoting a "wine of the month" can be used to draw special attention to a wine on your regular list that doesn't seem to be moving. Make sure that your staff knows the wine, and encourage them to actively promote it.

Staff Competitions

Many restaurants have been successful in boosting wine sales by holding staff competitions. A goal is set, such as thirty bottles sold per month; anyone who exceeds this goal is "in the running," and the top salesperson receives a prize at the end of the competition. Track wine sales on a large board in the kitchen to create enthusiasm for the competition. The prize does not have to be large to generate excitement and increased wine sales.

Have staff meetings at which you explain that for every bottle of wine sold the amount of the dinner check is increased, out of which staff receive 15 percent. On a $20.00 bottle of wine a $3.00 tip is received; if five extra bottles are sold, an additional $15.00 per shift is gained—this amounts to an additional $75.00 per week, or $300.00 per month.

Educating Your Staff

One of the most overlooked and underutilized tools for increasing profits is the wine list. Most or all restaurants have at least one, and some have two.

How do we effectively sell what's on the wine list to our customers? By educating our servers, who are after all salespeople who make commissions on sales (tips). Education and training of servers is a top priority, regardless of how little or how much knowledge they already possess about wine.

It is strongly recommended that on an "off" or slow day, you gather all of your servers and present a one-hour lecture (at *your* expense) on how to effectively sell wine. How much will this cost? Let us say that you pay your servers $6.00 per hour (this is relatively high) and there are ten servers; that is $60.00 per hour. During this hour, the servers become a "captive audience." It should be explained that while company profits increase from additional beverage sales, servers' tips also increase. Each and every wine on the list should be identified, and ways to properly chill, open, and pour the wine explained; you should also discuss which foods on the menu the wine will complement. It should be instilled in the servers' minds that they are salespeople working on commission; workable quotas that servers *must* meet could be the sale of a certain number of bottles of wine per week or month.

Let us see if that $60.00 for one hour, or even $120.00 for two hours that you will spend on the lecture can be recaptured. If every server, working a five-day week, sells one additional bottle of wine per day, and you have ten servers, you will sell an additional two hundred bottles of wine per month. A $6.00 bottle of wine (wholesale) sold at a 150 percent mark-up sells for $15.00, or a $9.00 gross profit per bottle. This $9.00 times 200 bottles equals an additional $1,800.00 per month in gross sales, or $21,600.00 per year: all of this for a simple $60.00 or $120.00 investment.

Wine-Selling Tips

Selling wine is fun, and it should be done in a manner that is not intimidating to the customer. Though most customers have little trouble selecting food courses, they may occasionally feel uncomfortable in making a wine selection. Helping your customer choose a wine makes you much more important to that customer. In addition to ensuring larger tips, your knowledge of wine selling and service will yield personal and professional satisfaction. Here are some steps to follow for successful wine sales that have been suggested by Sebastiani Vineyards (Sonoma, California):

1. Always assume that your customers will want wine.
2. Present the wine list along with the dinner menu. Do not wait to be asked for it. A comment on the fine wine selection available would be appropriate and could ensure that your customer orders wine.
3. When you return to take the food order, be sure to ask which wine has been selected; this is a positive suggestion and makes

the sale. Never ask, "Do you want anything to drink?" This is a negative suggestion that leaves open the possibility of getting a "No" for an answer.

4. If you recommend a wine based on the food ordered, give the customer a choice, rather than risking rejection of a single recommendation. Your two recommendations should represent different price categories.

   If your customers seem hesitant to choose a wine, ask what type of wines they enjoy. From the answer, you can make a suitable recommendation.

5. Do your best to sell wine to your first customers, for as others come into the dining room and observe wine being consumed, they are more likely to order it also.

6. Let the inclusion of bin numbers on your wine list be an aid to your customers, who may have difficulty pronouncing the name of a wine. You should not refer to the wine by the bin number, but rather by its name. Never correct a customer's mispronunciation or disagree with his or her wine selection.

7. When you have taken the wine order, return with the wine without delay.

8. Serve the wine immediately. When the wine is promptly poured the guest has more time to enjoy it; the bottle is finished earlier, and this creates an extra selling opportunity.

Wine Fact Sheets

Another promotional strategy is to present customers with a card on which pertinent information about the wine they have ordered is given. A label reproduction may be included. Customers are encouraged to keep the fact sheets; this serves as a reminder of the restaurant in which the wine was enjoyed and helps build the customer's bank of wine knowledge. Regular customers are often inspired to experiment with different wines, as they enjoy collecting these fact sheets.

Table Settings

Another overlooked merchandising strategy is to have wine glasses already placed on the table prior to the arrival of your customers; this is a very suggestive way of selling a glass or bottle of wine.

Korbel Champagne Cellars of California includes, as part of their merchandising program suggestions, champagne buckets, table "tents," and wine list menu clip-ons. These tools aid in the promotion of their sparkling wine, the best-selling *méthode champenoise* sparkling wine in the United States.

Tracking Business

For the future of your business it is very important to "track" sales, and if need be divide them demographically to determine future additions to your wine list. First, determine the number of bottles of each type of wine sold by individual category; e.g., red, white, rosé, sparkling, sweet, dry, and so on. Then, determine the ratio of sales of one type to another. What was the average price of a bottle of wine sold during a certain period of time (usually three-month intervals)? What are the most profitable and popular wines on your list? Lastly, are there any wines that don't "move" for one reason or another? Base your future wine list on the answers to these questions.

Wine Tastings

Consider holding wine tastings for special customers. Highlight one country/region or type of wine and encourage guests to discuss these wines while they taste. Contact your distributor to see if he has a lecturer available. Customers love to be singled out for such special events and you are not only building good will but are creating knowledgeable customers. The following tips are offered for organizing a successful tasting:

Have a large supply of clean glasses on hand. If you would generally plan on using one glass per person (with tasters rinsing glasses between tastes), have two glasses per person on hand for emergencies.

After removing the glasses from a storage box, put them through a water (no detergent) rinse.

Make sure you have adequate chilling facilities.

Make sure that there is adequate drinking water available—ideally, at each wine station. Avoid bottled club soda, for it contains salt. Instead, choose an unflavored "still" or carbonated water. Using bottled water will let people know that the water is for drinking, not for rinsing glasses.

Make sure that you have an adequate supply of spittoons and pour buckets—generally two spittoons or pour buckets at each wine station.

Always have one staff member circulating at all times to empty the pour buckets.

Always supply a basic French-type bread or plain crackers (preferably low-salt, matzoh-type crackers). Make sure you have a back-up supply of bread on hand.

Keep the temperature of the room cooler than usual. People will be moving around or seated in close proximity to each other and consuming alcohol, which is warming.

Set up the tasting room several hours in advance. The red wines should be set out in the order in which they are to be poured. The whites and sparkling wines should be chilling, so that they are completely chilled well before the event begins.

If you have several stations where wines are being poured, vary the number of wines at each station. The first station should have no more than two wines to avoid "traffic jams."

Provide clean name tags for the staff.

Don't overcrowd the room. The number of participants should be limited to one-half to two-thirds of the maximum capacity of the room.

Don't allow smoking.

Don't overpour: 1 to 1.5 ounces is adequate for tasting.

Don't give away open bottles of wine at the end of the tasting. You could lose your liquor license in certain states, and your insurance may not cover any damages that could result.

Don't let the event last more than two hours. People should not linger at tastings—especially stand-up tastings.

These suggestions were provided by Rory P. Callahan of the California Wine Institute's New York office.

Wine Festivals

Build a festival or promotion around a particular wine-producing region or country. Offer a selection of wines by the glass and feature regional dishes as specials. Decorate your restaurant with posters of the country and give departing guests informational material to take with them. Informational material is usually available free of charge from public relations firms that promote the wines of a specific country or region.

Staff training. At least one week before the festival, schedule an intensive staff training session. At this meeting explain the purpose and theme of the festival, making sure that the staff is thoroughly trained in proper wine and food service. Present background information on the featured wines and make sure all servers are able to pronounce each wine's name. Finally, give the staff an opportunity to taste the featured wines and foods; this helps in suggestive selling.

Publicity. A well-planned promotion can result in free publicity for the restaurant in local newspapers and on television and radio. Before you start imagining yourself on the evening news, however, remember that members of the press are looking for a unique story angle. The simple fact that you are holding a French, Italian, or California wine promotion does not make a riveting story. Develop a press kit that includes stories on the chef, background information on the food and wine, and recipes home cooks can recreate. Hold a press party one week prior to the opening of the festival so newspapers and TV stations have time to run your story and the public has time to respond to the publicity before the festival is over. Consumers are more likely to attend a promotion once they've read about it.

Increase cover counts. A promotion can significantly boost business during normally slow periods. A special event creates excitement and increases customer cover counts. It can inspire customers who may have never been in your restaurant to try it—and to come back again after the promotion is over.

Create a positive image. A well-conceived and well-executed ethnic promotion (French, Italian, German, and so on) can enhance your reputation for quality, originality, and value. Customers will regard your restaurant as one that is exciting and innovative.

Increase your profits. A successful promotion should increase average amounts and in turn increase profits. An increase in beverage sales will be shown as customers experiment with aperitifs, wines, and after-dinner drinks. Customers will add on appetizers and desserts because they are anxious to try new experiences and enjoy the ethnic ambiance—without purchasing an airline ticket!

Time is of the essence. Allow sufficient lead time to plan your promotions properly. Many important details must be arranged months in advance. Develop a checklist to help you plan a timetable. Be sure to assign deadlines to each task and appoint a specific person to be responsible for its completion.

Contacts with sponsors. If you are trying to secure a partial sponsorship of your promotion, begin to do so at least ninety days before the start of the festival. Potential sponsors are airlines, food and beverage importers and distributors, and information bureaus, which are public relations arms of major beverage- and food-producing countries. You may receive assistance in paying for the airfare of a guest chef or winemaker, or be promised a trip to be awarded as a prize. Many companies will also provide food and beverage products as prizes. Some information bureaus are listed below.

Information bureaus

Arizona Winegrowers' Association
P.O. Box D18
Vail, Arizona 85641

Arkansas Wine Producers
   Association
Wiederkehr Wine Cellars
R.R. 1, Box 14
Altus, Arkansas 72821
501–468–2611

Armagnac
(Food and Wines from France)
24 E. 21st Street
New York, New York 10010
212–477–9800

Association of Tequila Producers
P.O. Box 58083
147 World Trade Center Hall of
   Nations
Dallas, Texas 75258
214–744–5711

Association of Wisconsin Wineries
321 Mill Street
Algoma, Wisconsin 54201
414–487–3814

Australian Trade Commission
636 Fifth Avenue
New York, New York 10111
212–245–4000

Austrian Trade Commission
845 Third Avenue
New York, New York 10011
212–421–5250

Beer Institute
1225 Eye Street, N.W.
Washington, D.C. 20005
202–737–2337

Bordeaux Wine News Information
Bureau
16 E. 32d Street
New York, New York 10016
212–685–8000

California Association of
Winegrape Growers
926 J Street, Suite 709
Sacramento, California
916–441–1455

California Raisin Advisory Board
3636 North 1st, Suite 148
P.O. Box 5335
Fresno, California 93755
209–224–7010

California Table Grape
Commission
2975 N. Maroa Avenue
Fresno, California
209–224–4997

Canadian Wine Institute
89 The Queensway West
Mississauga, Ontario, Canada
L5B 2V2
416–273–5610

Champagne News and
Information Bureau
355 Lexington Avenue
New York, New York 10017
212–949–8475

Cognac Information Bureau
380 Madison Avenue
New York, New York 10017
212–986–6100

Connecticut Grape Growers and
Winemakers Association
RFD 1

N. Grosvenor Dale, Connecticut
06255

Cyprus Trade Center
13 E. 40th Street
New York, New York 10016
212–686–6016

Distilled Spirits Council of the
United States (DISCUS)
1250 Eye Street, N.W.
Suite 900
Washington, D.C. 20005
202–628–3544

Finger Lakes Wine Growers
Association
Canandaigua Wine Co., Inc.
116 Buffalo Street
Canandaigua, New York 14424
716–394–3630

Florida Grape Growers
Association
Rte. 3, P.O. Box 3966
Havana, Florida 32333

Food and Wines from France
24 E. 21st Street
New York, New York 10010
212–477–9800

Georgia Grape Growers
Association
Spring Water Farm
Rte. 3, P.O. Box 259
Ball Ground, Georgia 30107

German Wine Information Bureau
79 Madison Avenue
New York, New York 10016
212–213–7028

Hudson River Region Wine
    Council
c/o Baldwin Vineyards
Harenburgh Road
Pine Bush, New York 12566
914–744–2226

Irish Whiskey Information Bureau
123 Main Street
White Plains, New York 10601
914–328–1400

Italian Wine Center
499 Park Avenue
New York, New York 10022
212–980–1100

Italian Wine and Food Institute
One World Trade Center
Suite 1513
New York, New York 10048
212–432–2000

Kansas Grape Growers and
    Winemakers Association
801 S. Crawford
Fort Scott, Kansas 66701
316–223–0866

Kentucky Distillers Association
714 McClure Building
Frankfort, Kentucky 40601
502–223–2436

Maryland Grape Growers
    Association
18517 Kingshill Road
Germantown, Maryland 20874
301–972–1325

Mexican Food and Beverage Board
575 Madison Avenue
New York, New York 10022

Michigan Grape Society
226 E. Michigan
Paw Paw, Michigan 49079

Michigan Wine Institute
116 W. Ottawa Street
Lansing, Michigan 48933
517–374–6050

Minnesota Grape Growers
    Association
Plant Science Department, UWRF
River Falls, Minnesota 54022
715–425–3851

Mississippi Grape Growers
    Association
The Winery Rushing
Merigold, Mississippi 38759
601–748–2731

Missouri Grape Growers
    Association
Gray's Creek Vineyard
Rte. 5, Scott Station Rd.
Jefferson City, Missouri 65101

Missouri Grape and Wine
    Advisory Board
Missouri Department of
    Agriculture
P.O. Box 630
Jefferson City, Missouri 65102
314–751–3374

Missouri Vintners Association
501 S. Main
St. Charles, Missouri 63301
314–946–9339

Monterey Wine Country
    Association
P.O. Box 1793
Monterey, California 93940

Napa Valley Vintners
900 Meadowood Lane
Box 141
St. Helena, California 94574
707–963–0148

National Association of Beverage
    Importers, Inc.
1025 Vermont Avenue, N.W.
Suite 1205
Washington, D.C. 20005
202–638–1617

National Beer Wholesalers
    Association, Inc.
5205 Leesburg Pike
Suite 505
Falls Church, Virginia 22041
703–578–4300

National Liquor Stores Association
    (NLSA)
5101 River Road
Suite 108
Bethesda, Maryland 20816
301–656–1494

New Mexico Vine and Wine
    Society
P.O. Box 26751
Albuquerque, New Mexico 87125

New York State Wine Grape
    Growers, Inc.
201 Elm Street
Penn Yan, New York 14527
315–536–2853

New York Wine Foundation
Elm and Liberty Streets
Penn Yan, New York 14527
315–536–7442

Ohio Wine Advisory Board
822 North Tote Road
Austinburg, Ohio 44010
216–466–4417

Oregon Wine Advisory Board
1324 S.W. 21st Avenue
Portland, Oregon 97201
503–224–8167

Oregon Winegrowers Association
P.O. Box 6590
Portland, Oregon 97228

Pennsylvania Wine Association
Rte. 3, P.O. Box 424
Stewartstown, Pennsylvania 17363

Portuguese Trade Commission
548 5th Avenue, 5th Floor
New York, New York 10036
212–354–4610

Rioja Wine Information Bureau
220 E. 42d Street
New York, New York 10017
212–907–9385

Santa Clara Valley Wine Growers
    Association
1645 San Pedro
Morgan Hill, California 95037
408–779–7389

Santa Cruz Mountain Vintners
22020 Mount Eden Road
Saratoga, California 95070

The Scotch Whisky Information
    Center
415 Madison Avenue
New York, New York 10017
212–688–3392

Sonoma County Grape Growers
  Association
850 2d Street, Suite B
Santa Rosa, California 95404
707–576–3110

Sonoma County Wine Growers
  Association
50 Mark West Springs Road
Santa Rosa, California 95401
707–527–7701

Tennessee Viticultural and
  Enological Society
5538 Woodburn Drive
Knoxville, Tennessee 37919
615–584–9555

Texas Grape Growers Association
One Turtle Creek Village
Suite 618
Dallas, Texas 75219
214–559–2023

Vinifera Wine Growers
  Association
P.O. Box P
The Plains, Virginia 22171
703–754–8564

Virginia Wineries Association
P.O. Box 527
Richmond, Virginia 23204

The Vodka Information Bureau
201 E. 42d Street
New York, New York 10017
212–687–1196

Washington State Grape Society
P.O. Box 117
Grandview, Washington 98930
509–882–4029

Washington Wine Institute
1932 1st Avenue
Room 510
Seattle, Washington 98101
206–441–1892

Wine and Spirits Wholesalers of
  America, Inc. (WSWA)
2033 M Street, N.W.
Suite 400
Washington, D.C. 20036
202–293–9220

Wine Institute of California
165 Post Street
San Francisco, California 94108
415–986–0878

Wine Institute of California, New
  York Branch
79 Fifth Avenue
New York, New York 10003
212–206–6750

Wine Institute of New England
P.O. Box 454
Back Bay Annex
Boston, Massachusetts 02117
617–588–3067

Wines of Spain
405 Lexington Avenue
New York, New York 10174
212–661–4814

Spirits Promotions

One way to increase sales of spirits is to adopt the policy of special theme nights on which the customer purchases a drink whose price includes that of the glass. For example, on "Margarita night," when special 25-ounce frozen margaritas are sold for $6.00, the customer can take home a traditional Margarita glass that is not available in most department stores or specialty glass shops. Not only will customers treasure the glass and enjoy serving Margaritas in it at home, but you will benefit from having your business name, address, and telephone number displayed somewhere on the glass, which increases repeat patronage. The concept illustrated here can be extended to other items, such as ceramic Irish coffee mugs, fluted or tulip-shaped champagne glasses, liqueur glasses, and so on. The list is endless.

Tony May, a well-known New York City restaurateur, heads the operation of three restaurants: La Camelia, Palio, and Sandro's. At Sandro's, printed cards bearing the following message to customers are on every table: "Would you like to take home the dishes, the silverware, the salt cellars, the pepper mill? Maybe a teapot. Or a jug of balsamic vinegar. Everything's for sale. Except the chef."

There are many other ways to increase profits from spirits sales, and some of them won't cost you a cent. Many beverage distributors and food purveyors have public relations or promotional budgets which can be tapped. One promotion concept, for example, uses both beverage and food purveyors. It was conceived by Vlasic Foodservice, which took a standard drink recipe and, by changing it slightly, converted it into a big seller. Based on the popular Bloody Mary, this new drink, called the Pregnant Mary, is created from a flavorful recipe and is, of course, topped off with one of Vlasic's Kosher Pickle Spears to give customers a crunchy, fresh-tasting treat to go along with their drink. Here is the recipe:

    4 cups tomato juice
    2 tablespoons Vlasic pickle juice
    1 teaspoon prepared horseradish
    2 teaspoons Worcestershire sauce
    2 teaspoons lemon juice
    Tabasco sauce, to taste
    salt and pepper, to taste
    Vlasic Deli Dill or Kosher Spears

Blend all ingredients except pickle spears in a covered container and chill well. To prepare the drink, add 1.5 ounces of vodka to an 8-ounce glass of ice, and fill with the prepared mix. Blend, and garnish with Vlasic Deli Dill or Kosher Spears and serve. The recipe makes approximately six drinks. (Note: Vlasic also offers excellent merchandising tools to help you tell your customers about the Pregnant Mary, including swizzle sticks that feature the trademark Vlasic stork.)

Holiday and Seasonal Promotions

A good idea for sales promotions is to use a calendar to determine what important holidays, events, or celebrations take place each month. It's then a simple task to choose which special event fits within the theme of your restaurant. A plan for its incorporation should then be formulated. A sample calendar might include:

January

New Year's Day (January 1)

Post-holiday blues

National Pizza Week

Superbowl

February

Ground Hog Day (February 1)

Lincoln's birthday (February 12)

Valentine's Day (February 14)

Chinese New Year (February 17)

Washington's birthday (February 22)

Mardi Gras

National Cherry Month (all month)

March

St. Patrick's Day (March 17)

First day of spring (March 21)

April

April Fool's Day (April 1)
Easter and Passover
Post-income-tax-filing celebration (April 15)
National Secretaries' Week
Arbor Day

May

May Day (May 1)
Armed Forces Day
Memorial Day (May 30)
Mothers' Day
Kentucky Derby Day
National Pickle Week
National Tavern Month
Victoria Day (Canada)

June

Flag Day (June 14)
First day of summer (June 21)
Fathers' Day

July

Canada Day (July 1)
Independence Day (July 4)
Bastille Day (July 14)

August

Washington State Wine Month
Tailgate parties
Picnics

September

Labor Day
Back-to-school party
Grandparents' Day
First day of autumn (September 21)

October

Columbus Day (October 12)
United Nations Day (October 24)
National Wine Month
National Restaurant Month
World Series
Halloween

November

Election Day
New York State Wine Month
Veteran's Day (November 11)
National Split Pea Soup Week (second week of the month)
Thanksgiving Day

December

Repeal of Prohibition Celebration (December 5, 1933)
Pearl Harbor Day (December 7)
First day of winter (December 21)
Christmas Day (December 25)
Boxing Day (December 26; celebrated in England, Canada, and Australia)

In general, it is extremely important for your servers to make appropriate drink suggestions on the basis of season or climate. For customers who come in during cold weather and want something to warm them up, a brandy or Cognac could be suggested. An alternative suggestion is brandy served with coffee or tea, either mixed or separately, to help eliminate winter's nip. Hot weather demands that servers suggest cold, refreshing drinks that are appealing in appearance, smell, and taste. Most warm-weather drinks can easily be made with fruit juices or a customer's favorite mixes.

Increasing Beverage Profits Through Food Sales

Americans today live mobile, active lives. The traditional three meal periods have been transformed into flexible "on demand" eating occasions. The National Restaurant Association cites five separate meal occasions—breakfast, lunch, midafternoon, dinner, and late supper—that have evolved as a result of "on demand" eating patterns. Many of these occasions can be made more profitable by adding creative and exciting alcoholic beverage service.

Brunch as a Way of Merchandising Drinks

Those who eat brunch outside of their homes are predominantly between the ages of twenty-five and fifty-four. This means that they are well past the twenty-one-year-old drinking age, generally have more disposable income, and can enjoy a leisurely dining experience. Brunch is a fashionable but casual meal that offers unlimited opportunity for creativity with food and beverage service. In fact, brunch is an excellent occasion for the promotion of specialty drinks. Eye-openers such as Bloody Marys, screwdrivers, mimosas, and Ramos gin fizzes are popular brunch choices, as are fresh fruit daiquiris, Margaritas, piña coladas, Tom Collinses, and of course champagne and dry sparkling wines. Many operators successfully promote a free drink with brunch (its cost is built into the price of the meal), which often results in a reorder of the drink at the regular price.

Other Ideas for Increasing Profits

According to a report in *Independent Restaurants Magazine* (December 1983) T-shirts that show a restaurant logo and message can stimulate word-of-mouth advertising.

When a customer phones in a reservation, consider placing a small table "tent" on the reserved table with a simple note thanking them for calling in advance, with a small cut-out on the table tent holding a quarter, along with your restaurant's name, address, and telephone number.

Take a promotional tip from the airlines and have a "frequent diners' club." Customers receive points for the amount of money they spend and with the number of persons in their party.

If your restaurant is full and there is a long line of waiting customers, have a server pour them some house wine. This eases their wait and stimulates appetites. Very few if any customers will leave; and these customers will tell others about "what they got" at your restaurant while standing in line. If you pour each person 3 ounces of an inexpensive house wine, and there are twenty-five people waiting in line, you will serve a total of 75 ounces and, at a usual cost of less than five cents per ounce, this strategy will at most cost you $2.25.

Low-Alcohol and Nonalcoholic Beverages

There is a growing need for and trend toward nonalcoholic beverages and "mocktails" (mixed drinks without alcohol). The potential profits they can bring for restaurant and bar owners is limitless.

According to recent statistics released by the U.S. Department of Agriculture's Economic Research Service, 108.3 gallons of nonalcoholic beverages were consumed by every man, woman, and child in the United States in 1984. This is a significant increase over the 101.6 and 97.5 gallons consumed in 1974 and 1964.

Between 1982 and 1985 there was a 43 percent increase in the number of occasions at which diet drinks were ordered in restaurants, according to the CREST Household Report for 1985. Much of this increase has been attributed to the tastes of working women, a group that typically consumes the most diet soft drinks.

According to a 1985 Gallup survey, one out of every four consumers indicated that they would be likely to order caffeine-free sodas if they were available in restaurants.

There are many new low-alcohol and nonalcoholic beverages along with some not so new drinks. Some of the most popular are: sodas (traditional colas and new natural fruit-flavored sodas); juices; seltzers; mineral water (both carbonated and still); cocktail mixers; malt beverages; nonalcoholic wines; wine beverages such as Riunite Sunny Apple, Natural Peach, and Royal Raspberry; low-alcohol and nonalcoholic beers; sparkling ciders; and, of course, wine coolers.

Bottled Waters: Mineral and Spring

With today's health-conscious American consumers, restaurants and bars should consider carrying one or more brands or flavors of mineral water. Mineral water comes in basically two types, sparkling and still. The most popular version by far is sparkling water, which is apparent from the enormous growth in sales of such brands as Perrier and San Pellegrino. Some producers are even flavoring their mineral waters with natural citrus extracts such as mandarin orange, lemon, and lime.

Bottled mineral water can also be marketed toward consumers who seek an alternative to alcoholic beverages. Increased awareness of drunk driving laws, coupled with the public's health and fitness consciousness, could actually be used to the advantage of a canny restaurateur. Consumers also want to be able to choose a beverage that has no artificial coloring or flavors, artificial sweeteners, salt, sugar, other additives, or chemical preservatives. Sparkling mineral water is not only reputed to be a healthy drink; it is a trendy item that is considered chic by many consumers. A 1985 Gallup consumer poll found that 33 percent of those surveyed said they don't consume alcohol, and 14 percent of those who do consume alcohol said that they planned to reduce their alcohol consumption. This trend creates opportunities for growth in other beverage categories.

Mineral and spring water are best served chilled. It is strongly recommended you do not use ice, as the cubes are usually made from tap water which can alter the fine, light taste of bottled water.

Nonsparkling bottled water can be served in place of tap water on the table. Have your servers display the bottle's label, then wrap a napkin around the bottle and fill large (10 to 12 oz.) stemmed wine glasses.

The definition of mineral water. In most countries of Western Europe where bottled mineral waters are a common household beverage, no drinking water can be classified as a "natural mineral water" unless it contains dissolved minerals in its natural state. Italian law requires that mineral water be bottled only at its source.

All mineral water contains some minerals, but to be classified a "natural mineral water" in Europe, the water must have at least 500 milligrams of minerals per liter as it flows from the ground—minerals that are collected in the water as it travels over great distances through geological formations. The minerals are thus dissolved and become an integral part of the water. Minerals are thought to be more readily absorbed by the body when in solution than as a component of solid food.

The U.S. federal government has not established a formal definition for mineral water. In 1979, however, California set a minimum standard of total dissolved solids for mineral water sold in that state at 500 milligrams per liter. This means that a water cannot be called a mineral water unless it has at least 500 milligrams of minerals dissolved in it.

The mineral content of bottled waters varies from state to state, country to country, and producer to producer. In addition to being basically low in sodium, and virtually calorie and carbohydrate free, mineral water contains many trace elements and minerals, which also vary in their interest to consumers.

Among these elements and minerals are aluminum, ammonia, bicarbonate, boron, bromide, calcium, carbonate, chloride, chromium, cobalt, copper, fluoride, iodine, iron, lithium, magnesium, manganese, nickel, nitrate, phosphorus, potassium, selenium, silica, sodium, strontium, sulfates, zinc, and others.

Some brands of bottled mineral and spring water are listed below.

United States

Aqua Essence Mineral Water (Pennsylvania)

Arrowhead Spring Water

Artesia Mineral Water (Texas)

Bartlett Mineral Springs (California)

Calistoga Mineral Water (California)

Crystal Geyser Mineral Water (California)

Deer Park Spring Water (Maryland)

Kentwood Spring Water (New Orleans)

La Croix Mineral Water (Minnesota)

Mendocino Mineral Water (California)

Mountain Valley Spring Water (Arkansas)

Poland Springs Mineral Water (Maine)

A Sante Mineral Water (New York; owned by Anheuser-Busch)

Saratoga Mineral Water (New York)

Vittel Mineral Water (California)

Austria

Voslau Mineral Water

Belgium

Spa Light Mineral Water

Canada

Montclair Mineral Water
Naya Spring Water

France

Evian Spring Water
Perrier Mineral Water (flavored versions include lemon, lime, and mandarin orange)
Vichy Celestins Naturally Alkaline Mineral Water
Volvic Spring Water

Germany

Apollinaris Mineral Water

Ireland

Glenpatrick Spring Water
Tipperary Spring Water

Italy

Acqua de Nepi
Ferrarelle Mineral Water
Fiuggi Mineral Water
Sangemini Mineral Water
San Pellegrino Mineral Water

Spain

Cabreiroa Mineral Water

Sweden

Rämlosa Mineral Water (comes in a distinctive blue glass bottle)

Switzerland

Alp Water Mineral Water

Swiss Altima

Valser Mineral Water

"Mocktails"

"Mocktails" are well-known mixed drinks minus the alcohol (often referred to as "virgin" drinks). To help merchandise these drinks, some restaurant and bar owners have come up with fanciful names such as "softtails," "virgin territory," etc.

When creating "mocktails," let your imagination run wild. Develop "signature mocktails," the favorite drink concoction of the bar, which can be called by just about any name you choose. A separate beverage list can be developed to present these drinks, with appropriate descriptive terminology and drink ingredients. They can be served in the same type of glasses used for liquor-based drinks, and may include garnishes and plenty of fruit.

Holiday Inn has established the following policy to deal with the demand for alternatives to alcohol. A nonalcoholic drink menu is provided to Holiday Inn hotel lounge customers that lists healthy, tasty, and safe alternatives to alcoholic beverages. Drinks featured on the menu include Citrus Collins, a blend of fresh orange, grapefruit, and lemon juices; Summer Sipper, a mixture of fresh honeydew and watermelon accented with lime juice and ginger; Strawberry Limonade, a combination of fresh lime and lemon juices mixed with strawberries; Orange Banana Frosty, a blend of banana, orange, and lime juices mixed with milk and cream; and Fresh Vegetable Cooler, a spicy combination of vegetable and clam juices. The menu also includes nonalcoholic versions of traditional cocktails such as piña coladas, Tom Collinses, frozen daiquiris, Bloody Marys, and sunrises.

In addition to offering nonalcoholic drinks, managers at company-owned and operated Holiday Inn hotels are being encouraged to discontinue two-for-one drink promotions and set up designated driver programs that will offer drivers nonalcoholic beverages either free or at a discount. To further discourage overindulgence, Holiday Inn also has a bar food menu that offers lounge patrons light meals, as well as appetizers. Holiday Inn wants its customers to participate in the social atmosphere of the lounges, enjoying tasty, refreshing beverages, while at the same time staying safe and healthy. Its nonalcoholic beverage offerings make this possible.

Nonalcoholic and "Alcohol-Free" Malt Beverages

According to the Bureau of Alcohol, Tobacco and Firearms, effective April 1, 1986, producers of "nonalcoholic" malt beverages must indicate on labels and in advertising that their product "contains less than 0.5 percent alcohol by volume." Malt beverages labeled "Alcohol free" may contain no alcohol whatsoever. "Nonalcoholic" malt beverages cannot be labeled or advertised as beer, lager, ale, porter, stout, or any other designation commonly associated with malt beverages. Some available brands of nonalcoholic and alcohol-free beverages are listed below.

Brand names

Barbican (England)

Birell (Pennsylvania)

Clausthaler (Germany)

Goetz Pale Near Beer (United States)

Kaliber (brewed by Guinness of Ireland)

Kingsbury Brew Near Beer (brewed by G. Heileman, Wisconsin)

Metbrau Near Beer (New Jersey)

Moussy (Switzerland)

Norsk (Norway)

Santor (France)

Schmidt's Select Malt Beverage (Pennsylvania)

Steinbrau Malt Beverage (New Jersey)

Texas Select (Texas)

Warteck (Switzerland)

Alcohol-Free "Wine"

Alcohol-free "wines" are wines whose alcohol is removed after fermentation; they are virtually 99.5 percent alcohol free. Some brands are:

Ariél (J. Lohr Winery, California)

Carl Jung sparkling and still wine (Germany)

Giovane Sparkling Wine (Italy)

Marcelino Sangria (Spain)

Petillion (France)

Sante sparkling and still wine (California)

St. Regis red, white, and rosé (Seagram's, California)

Toselli Spumante (Italy)

Wine Coolers

Wine coolers are simply a blend of wine, fruit juices, carbonated water, and sugar. There are more than two dozen in the marketplace across the United States. Some producers also bottle flavored wine-, spirit-, and malt-based coolers. The more readily identifiable brands are:

Bartles & Jaymes Premium Wine Cooler (Gallo)

California Cooler (Brown-Forman)

Calvin Coolers (Joseph Victori)

Citronet Cooler (Heublein)

Fletcher & Oakes (spirit based; produced by Jim Beam)

La Croix

Manischewitz Wine Cooler

Matilda Bay (Miller Brewing Company)

Mogen David Wine Cooler

Seagram's Cooler (also a spirits cooler)

Steidl's Cooler (Paddington Imports)

Sun Country Cooler (Canandaigua)

T.J. Swann (Heublein)

White Mountain Cooler (malt based; produced by Stroh's)

20/20 Cooler (The Wine Group)

Widmer Cellars Cooler

Sparkling Cider

French sparkling cider is to cider what champagne is to sparkling wine—its zenith. Soft, fruity, and light, this unfussy yet sophisticated nonalcoholic beverage is a perfect accompaniment to many foods and delicious all by itself. Although French sparkling ciders are nonalcoholic, most other ciders are probably approximately 5 to 6 percent alcohol, with a few listed as 10 to 12 percent alcohol (the same as table wine). A drink for daily consumption or special occasions, sparkling cider from France contains no added sugar or preservatives, making it an appealing alternative for today's health-conscious customer. Extremely healthy and loaded with B and C vitamins and essential mineral salts, this festive drink is said to have purifying qualities as well as being uniquely refreshing. The time is right for a fresh alternative to alcohol—an upscale beverage that's festive, with the clean bright taste of cider apples.

Merchandising cider. Nonalcoholic drinks must be merchandised with flair, pizzazz, and dramatic appeal. French sparkling cider has the cachet of an import and a fresh, fruity flavor; it provides taste without guilt or unpleasant consequences the morning after. It is not sugary sweet, yet it sparkles. Sold in individual serving-size bottles, it is easy to price and to control. It can also be poured from larger-size bottles during peak periods at a bar or for banquets.

Merchandise sparkling cider during the traditional "happy hour" time slot. Serve it in stemmed glasses or champagne flutes for an appropriately upscale image, and garnish it imaginatively with a slice or ring of apple (dipped in lemon juice to prevent discoloration) and a sprig of mint. Or, add a spiral of orange peel studded with a few cloves. Its taste, effervescence, and visual appeal will have customers ordering again and again.

Lunch is the perfect time to feature sparkling cider in your restaurant. Use a blackboard or menu clip-on to alert customers that they can enjoy a beverage that goes well with food yet won't hamper their judgment in their afternoon meetings. Brunch, too, demands something that sparkles, and cider fills the bill. Even children will enjoy its crisp fruit flavor.

Sparkling cider has the qualities that customers are looking for. Print its name on your menu, write it on your blackboard, display bottles near the restaurant entrance, and inspire your staff to do some suggestive selling. To serve it as a special nonalcoholic aperitif, add a splash of nonalcoholic fruit syrup such as cassis or orange. Don't forget the fresh fruit garnish.

Individual serving-size bottles are perfect for room service. Include them in your minibar and use them in VIP set-ups. Another suggestion is to have chilled sparkling cider available on tennis courts or golf courses.

Some available brands are:

Apple Amber	El Gaitero	Le Duc
Bel Normande	Fleuret	Le Petite
Bulmer's London	Grand Cru	Normand
Dry	Grand Real	Purpom
Challand	Hudson Valley	Richards
Chamay	Jacques Detoy	Santa Ana
Double Six		

Suggested Readings

Nykiel, Ronald A. *Marketing in the Hospitality Industry*. New York: Van Nostrand Reinhold, 2d ed., 1989.

Reid, Robert D. *Foodservice and Restaurant Marketing*. New York: CBI, 1983.

Splaver, Bernard R. *Successful Catering*. New York: CBI, 1975.

Discussion Topics and Questions

1. Why is it more important to market your operation to the customer rather than making the customer purchase what you have to offer?

2. Discuss the advantages and disadvantages of holding a wine festival.

3. To what extent should you pay attention to surveys and polls relating to drinking trends of consumers?

4. At what point should you change your current mode of operation after being informed that some of your current mixed drinks are out of vogue?

5. Should monetary and nonmonetary incentives be offered to your beverage servers? Explain.

6. "You can't effectively sell a product you don't know; and the more you know about your product, the easier the sale." Explain this statement.

7. Develop a merchandising plan for bottled mineral and spring water sold in a restaurant.

8. Compare "personal" drink selling to the more conventional table "tents" and beverage lists.

9. Some restaurants invite a different beverage importer or distributor each week to present their line of wines to customers at tastings. Cite reasons why this type of promotion is beneficial to the restaurant.

14

Alcoholic Beverage Service

This chapter discusses:

- Developing schedules for bartenders.
- Set-up procedures for bars, including necessary equipment and supplies.
- Purchasing and proper handling of glassware.
- Beverage service and staff training.
- Customer demand for quality products.
- Liquor liability: methods of protection; staff training; alternatives to "happy hours."

The bar is an important part of the total concept of a restaurant. In order for the entire restaurant to run smoothly, certain criteria must be addressed. Price must be equal to quality to attract new customers and maintain the current customer base. Part of the total concept is staff training in the proper service of alcoholic beverages, both at the bar and at tables. Server and bartender attire must be addressed with the same care given to the food and drink. Decor should also be part of the restaurant's total package. Every aspect of the entire bar and beverage facility is important.

The era of liquor liability is upon us in full force, and unless we take steps to curb alcohol abuse, more stringent laws will be enacted, further restricting the selling and serving of alcoholic beverages. The National Restaurant Association, in cooperation with local, state, and federal officials, has spearheaded a program to train personnel in the awareness of alcohol abuse. Today's beverage manager must compensate for loss of revenue resulting from liquor liability laws and society's trend toward lighter, less alcoholic beverages and develop programs that will provide adequate financial rewards.

Bar Operations

For the development of a well-run bar, rules must be established pertaining to the duties of each bartender. These rules, along with guidelines and procedures, should be followed up by a training program. Develop a work schedule for the bar that enables it to be run efficiently, with a smooth scheduling of bartender shifts.

Scheduling of Bartenders

Examples of shifts for two bartenders are:

Day shift	Night shift
10:00 A.M.–6:30 P.M.	6:30 P.M.–2:30 A.M.
11:00 A.M.–7:30 P.M.	6:30 P.M.–3:00 A.M.

During weekends, "happy hours," and peak season times, three bartenders might be needed. Examples of work schedules with three bartenders are:

Day shift	Relief shift	Night shift
10:00 A.M.–6:30 P.M.	3:00 P.M.–11:30 P.M.	6:30 P.M.–2:30 A.M.
10:00 A.M.–6:30 P.M.	4:00 P.M.–12:00 midnight	7:00 P.M.–3:00 A.M.
10:00 A.M.–6:30 P.M.	6:00 P.M.–2:30 A.M.	8:00 P.M.–3:30 A.M.

The productivity of bartenders should be taken into consideration before work schedules are developed. Bartenders can mix and serve up to 125 drinks per hour depending on their experience, their expertise, the difficulty of drink recipes, the efficiency of bar design (the proximity of beverages in the work area and the location of ice machines and the cash register), and the hour of the day or night.

Bartenders should memorize basic drink recipes along with house specials for every drink the bar serves. This cuts down on wasted time searching recipe books and adds professionalism to the operation. Sometimes, if the bartender is not sure of the ingredients of a requested drink, the customer should be asked for the recipe and the suggested way of preparing and serving it.

Day Shift Bartender Duties

The daytime bartender should check fruit from the previous day and if necessary throw out spoiled or dried-out fruit and thoroughly wash fruit trays and troughs.

When using fruit for garnishes, select only the freshest and choicest available. To extract more juice from citrus fruits, slightly warm the fruit under warm running water. Then roll the fruit from side to side with the palm of the hand, which separates the juice from the pulp.

Fruits should be cut to proper size with a clean, sharp knife and on a clean cutting board—*not* the bar top. Citrus fruits such as lemons, limes, and oranges should be cut into three distinct shapes depending on the kind and type of drink served: wheels, peels, and wedges. When cutting for wheels and wedges, the cut piece should contain the outer skin (zest), the inner bitter white surface (pith), and either a little or a lot of the fleshy pulp. A peel contains only the zest and pith. A slice (wheel) of lemon, lime, or orange, cut to an almost transparent thinness, shimmers on the surface of a clear white wine spritzer. Wedges are used in drinks such as vodka and tonic, in which a healthy squeeze of the fruit is a necessary ingredient. Peels are intended for those drinks (martinis, for example) in which a "twist" of fruit is desirable. The purpose of the "twist" is to physically crack the skin of the fruit, exposing its oils, which contain both fragrance and flavor. The cracked portion should be rubbed along the rim of the glass, then discarded. Avoid dropping peels into the drink, for the alcohol will absorb some bitterness from the exposed pith.

Cut enough fruit for the entire day and night shifts. The amount will be determined by the number of bartenders, the number of waitress stations, and previously determined needs. Refill trays with the freshly cut fruits (lemons, limes, oranges, pineapples, etc.) and cover them immediately to protect them from dust, oxidation, and insects. Cherries, olives, and onions should be covered and stored in their own juices to retain freshness and visual appeal. Be sure to refrigerate the cherries, olives, onions, celery, and possibly bananas.

Punches can be served from large bowls with fresh fruit and sprigs of spearmint or peppermint floating on top. They can even be color coordinated to match table cloths or party themes.

If juices are called for in drinks, avoid using bottled extracts or reconstituted juices. After opening cans of juice, immediately pour the juice into sanitized containers and store in the refrigerator. Juices left over from the previous day should be checked to ensure that they are still fresh and are not fermenting. Rotate them so that the "first in, first out" policy is adhered to. Shake the juices prior to the start of each shift to avoid settling and separation of contents.

Other responsibilities of day shift bartenders are:

Milk and cream should be smelled daily to ensure that they are not in the process of souring.

Postmix soda guns should be inspected.

Beer taps should be inspected and cleaned.

Make sure that back-up kegs of beer are available.

Make sure that an adequate supply of chilled bottled beer is available. Wash tubs can also be filled with plenty of ice and bottled beer for fast chilling and service.

Ice machines should be inspected and ice troughs adequately filled.

Bartenders should be responsible for maintaining "par stock" levels and keep a running list of empty bottles that can be checked later against inventory.

Back bar and speed racks must be cleaned and filled.

Sinks should be filled with appropriate wash and rinse waters.

All glassware must be washed and available.

Beer mugs must be adequately chilled.

The cash register must be opened for the day.

When you are ready to open for business, be sure that garbage and other wastes are disposed of. The bar and surrounding areas should be clean and dry.

Bar stools should be wiped clean and neatly lined up.

Outside and inside lights should be turned on.

Night Shift Bartender Duties

When reporting for duty, the day shift bartender should close out his register, and a new "bank" should be established for the night bartender.

When closing up for the night, the following procedures should be adhered to:

Night bartenders should tally up the register, putting all monies into security bags and then into the safe.

Inventory sheets should be filled out relative to empty bottles.

All fruits, juices, and other perishables should be put into the refrigerator.

Bottled beer should be taken out of wash tubs and stored in the refrigerator.

The beer tap should be cleaned and hot water poured down the drain to help clean it out.

The ice maker should be wiped down with a damp cloth; check that its door is tightly closed.

Speed racks should be cleaned out.

All glassware and bar utensils should be cleaned.

Blenders should be emptied out and washed.

Drainboards must be washed down.

All sinks must be totally drained and scrubbed with steel wool.

The bar top must be wiped clean.

All dirty towels should be gathered and placed into a laundry bag.

The juke box and other machines should be shut down.

All lights should be turned off.

The door should be locked and the alarm set.

Bar Set-Ups

Each bar and service station should have the following beverages and equipment present.

The basics

Distilled spirits	Wine coolers
Bottled beer	Nonalcoholic beer
Red, white, and rosé wines	Hot coffee (optional)

Carbonated mixes

Coke or other cola sodas

Diet soda

Ginger ale

Mineral water (sparkling)

Seltzer

Sprite

Tonic water (quinine water)

7-Up or lemon-flavored carbonated mixes

Flavored sodas such as root beer, Dr. Pepper, orange soda, etc., depending on your geographic location and customer taste preferences.

Juices and juice-based mixes

Apple juice	Orange juice
Cranberry juice	Pineapple juice
Grapefruit juice	Tomato juice or V-8

Other liquids for mixing

Beef bouillon	Piña colada mix
Bloody Mary mix	Rose's Lime Juice (brand name)
Coconut milk or cream of coconut	Sour mix
Falernum or Orgeat syrup for rum-based fruit drinks	Simple syrup (sugar syrup)
Grenadine syrup	Tom Collins mix
Milk or cream	

Miscellaneous bar ingredients

Eggs, fresh and hard boiled	Cube sugar
Horseradish	Brown sugar
Mint (spearmint or peppermint)	Tabasco sauce or other hot pepper sauce
Black and cayenne pepper	Worcestershire sauce

Salt (also celery salt and coarse salt)

Bitters (Angostura and orange)

Superfine sugar

Nutmeg, vanilla, cloves, cinnamon, and cinnamon sticks

Bar equipment and utensils

Shaker glass with stainless steel shaker

Tooth picks

Electric blender

Napkins and straws

Shot glasses

Coasters for beer

Bar spoon and funnel

Wine lists

Fruit squeezer

Food menus

Strainer

Corkscrew that contains a knife

Muddler

Can or bottle opener

Garnish tray

Automatic pourers or free pourers

Cutting board

Serving trays

Knife

Guest register checks

Adequate glassware

Guest check trays

Carafes for wine

Bar towels

Water pitchers

Pens, pencils, and paper

Sufficient amount of ice

Matches and ashtrays

Plastic ice scoop or tongs

Bar snacks such as pretzels, potato chips, peanuts, and popcorn should also be available.

Glass Rimmers

When serving such drinks as Bloody Marys, Margaritas, Salty Dogs, Gimlets, Pink Squirrels, Sours, and so on, it is important to have the correct amount of salt or sugar on the rim of the glass. Too much or too little can ruin an otherwise perfect drink.

There are "rimmers" available on the marketplace that consist of two self-contained circular swing trays. Lemon or lime juice, or a combination of both, is placed in one tray. In the other tray is either coarse salt or superfine sugar. The use of a rimmer guarantees that quick and consistent rims of salt or sugar are effortlessly applied to any of your cocktail glasses. Most glass rimmers manufactured are designed to accommodate all sizes of glasses up to 6.75 inches in diameter. They can easily be fastened under the bar.

To use a rimmer, place the glass upside down in the liquid tray, then immediately into the salt or sugar tray which leaves a thin layer of either on the rim of the glass.

Correct Glassware

Many glass manufacturers used to (and still do today) dictate the kinds, types, and amount of glassware needed at the bar. If one accepted their recommendations the average bar would need as many as thirty different kinds of glasses. Unfortunately writers, consultants, restaurant/bar owners, and even books continued this exploitation by suggesting that a different glass type is needed for Bordeaux, Burgundy, and Rhine wines; champagne; cordials and liqueurs; Port; Sherry; and so on.

Today's restaurants simply don't have the shelf space to accommodate such a multitude of glasses, nor the storage facilities needed for back-ups and replacements. Confusion is also engendered for bartenders and service personnel when they have to remember which glass is needed for which drink. Attempting to memorize this list or taking time out to read the restaurant's manual on which type of glass to use for which drink is a waste of valuable time.

Purchasing Glassware

Selecting the right glass can be the key to more profitable beverage service. Plan on purchasing two to four times the number of glasses as the number of drinks you expect to serve during peak hours of operation. Purchasing or using the wrong glass size can result in a drink being too weak or "burned" (containing too much alcohol).

Glassware can be the most dramatic and least expensive way to create atmosphere or improve the appearance of a table setting. The glassware showcased on the tables and behind the bar should reflect the style and atmosphere of the restaurant's decor. Coordinating the shapes and sizes of the glassware with the decor and ambiance of the dining room will make a positive statement.

Interesting or distinctive glassware can enhance appearance, atmosphere, and/or merchandising appeal while improving your service and increasing your business. Durable glassware ensures safety and savings (from decreased breakage). The result: a more profitable beverage service. You might find it necessary to upgrade your glassware because of increased volume in your beverage service. Extra durability can be achieved by replacing your existing glassware with heat-treated glasses. Their added strength and improved resistance to mechanical and thermal shock lower replacement costs and improve service life.

Upgrading your glassware for merchandising appeal will increase sales and profits by increasing the perceived value of service.

Set a mood by using wine glasses at each place setting to promote wine with dinner. An oversized bowl on a wine glass suggests a larger serving and allows the customer to enjoy the fragrance of the wine.

A number of factors should be considered prior to purchasing glassware. Among them is the washing/sterilizing equipment needed, initial costs versus replacement costs, future availability, storage space needed, the needs of the restaurant/bar, and the fragility of the glass or its resistence to breakage.

Types of glassware. For serving wine, champagne, brandy, and liqueurs, stemmed glasses that are crystal clear and free of color and etchings should be used in place of the ordinary water glass or tumbler. The glasses listed below should always be stemware:

Cordial/liqueur; Sherry and Port glasses (4–6 oz.)

White wine glass (8–10 oz.)

Red wine glass (10–12 oz. or larger)

Flute or tulip-shaped champagne glasses (8–10 oz.)

Brandy/Cognac glasses (8 oz.)

Also needed are the following types and sizes of glasses, which are not necessarily stemware:

Shot glasses (1.5 oz.)

Water goblet (8–10 oz.)

Rocks or "old-fashioned" glasses (6–8 oz.)

Sour or parfait glasses (4–6 oz.)

All-purpose beverage glasses (8–10 oz.)

Pilsner glasses (10 oz.)

Beer steins or mugs (10–12 oz.)

Highball glasses (10–12 oz.)

Margarita glasses (6 oz.)

Handling Glassware

Libbey Glassware in Toledo, Ohio, offers the following tips on handling glassware for safety and profitability (see figure 14-1).

Persons handling glassware should be advised of the fine qualities of glassware and how it should be treated and handled. These tips are designed to improve the handling of glassware in your business. Improved handling means less breakage, and this means higher productivity and less chance of injury through accident. There are two causes of glass breakage: mechanical impact and thermal shock.

Mechanical impact. Mechanical impact is contact with another object. It may be a spoon, a beer tap, or another glass. This contact can cause minute abrasions that are invisible to the eye. These abrasions weaken the glass and make it more susceptible to breakage from further impact or thermal shock. Any severely abraded glass must be removed from service.

Thermal shock. Thermal shock is the result of temperature change. Glass holds temperature, and quick temperature changes can cause enough stress in the glass to cause breakage. For example, glass with ice in it cannot be emptied and put directly into the dishwasher. Similarly, glass coming out of the dishwasher cannot be put directly into service. In both cases the glass must be given time to reach room temperature. Never put cold water or ice into a warm or hot glass. Cracks that result from thermal shock usually form around abrasions caused by mechanical impact. Remember, the thicker the glass the more time it needs to reach room temperature.

Other tips. You should also always adhere to the following when handling glassware:

Handling Glassware
for safety and profitability

Persons handling glassware should be advised of the fine qualities of glassware and how glassware should be treated and handled. These tips are designed to improve the handling of glassware in your operation. Improved handling means less breakage and this translates into higher productivity and less chance of an injury accident. There are two causes of glass breakage...Mechanical Impact and Thermal Shock.

Mechanical Impact

 is the result of contact with another object. It may be a spoon, a beer tap, or another glass. This contact can cause a minute abrasion, invisible to the eye. These abrasions weaken the glass and make it more susceptible to breakage from impact and thermal shock. Any severely abraded glass must be removed from service.

Thermal Shock

 is the result of temperature change. Glass holds temperature, and quick temperature change can cause enough stress in the glass to cause breakage. For example, glass with ice in it cannot be emptied and put directly into the dishwasher. Similarly, glass coming out of the dishwasher cannot be put directly into service. In both cases the glass must be allowed a few minutes to reach room temperature. Never put cold water or ice into a warm or hot glass. Cracks that result from thermal shock usually form around abrasions caused by mechanical impact. Any severely abrased glass must be removed from service. Remember, the thicker the glass the more time it needs to reach room temperature.

General

- Keep adequate supplies of glass to prevent recently washed glasses from going directly into service.
- Place guides on scrap table for busboys to place glass, china, and silverware in separate areas.
- Check dishwasher temperature twice daily.
- Instruct busboys to "BE QUIET. No one wants to eat in a noisy place." This rule will cut down on breakage of glassware and china, as well as help create atmosphere.
- Always use plastic scoops in ice bins. Metal scoops sometimes chip the glassware. Never scoop ice with the glass.
- Never put cold water or ice into a warm or hot glass.
- Ideally, bus glassware directly into racks, or use divided bus trays with silver baskets.
- Color code your racks for different glassware items.
- Any severely abraded glass must be removed from service.

Figure 14-1 Handling glassware for safety and profitability. (Courtesy Libbey Glassware)

Keep adequate supplies of glass on hand to prevent recently washed glasses from going directly into service.

Place guides on scrap tables so that busboys can place glass, china, and silverware in separate areas.

Check the dishwasher temperature twice daily. Replace worn glass washer brushes.

Instruct busboys to *be quiet.* No one wants to eat in a noisy place. This rule will cut down on breakage of glassware and china as well as help create atmosphere.

Always use plastic scoops in ice bins. Metal scoops sometimes chip glassware. Never scoop ice with the glass.

Ideally, bus glassware directly into racks, or use divided bus trays with silver baskets.

Color code your racks for different glassware items.

Food and Beverage Service

Is the service in your restaurant/bar perfect? If not, your sales might be considerably lower than expected, and unless steps are taken to resolve all problems, sales will continue on a downward trend.

Unfortunately the level of service in the United States is usually far from excellent. This statement will certainly ruffle more than a few feathers among those in the industry; nevertheless, it is true. Go out to dinner or even for a drink one evening and carefully make note of the level of service you are receiving. Are all of your questions regarding food and drink answered correctly and with authority, or does the server use these familiar phrases when being asked simple questions: "I don't know; I'll find out; I'll be right back!" Then, do an honest analysis of your own business. You might be surprised by the results. Too many establishments give customers unsatisfactory or even poor service. The majority of customers might accept it once or twice, but not a third time.

Customers look upon servers as if they are looking at you. Servers are an extension of yourself; therefore steps must be taken to ensure that customers are receiving the service they deserve and demand.

Personal appearance: Unless you specify either uniforms or a dress code, you could have a department store syndrome on your hands: customers will not be able to distinguish your servers from the other customers. Many books and pamphlets are available from purveyors showing uniforms for virtually every type of establishment. Uniforms or approved clothing must be clean, fresh, and pressed. Shabby, torn, worn, undersized, or oversized clothing should be avoided.

Clean hair neatly cut, tied, or covered in a hair net is a necessity, as are trimmed beards and mustaches. Personal hygiene includes general cleanliness as well as clean hands and fingernails and fresh-smelling breath. Some restaurants and bars even make a dish of breath mints available to employees. Colognes and perfumes, as pleasant as they may be, often compete with the subtle aromas of the wines and foods and should be used sparingly, if at all.

Common courtesy: All too often a server's poor attitude will spoil a customer's dinner, leaving you with one less customer, who will certainly not recommend your establishment to others. Therefore it is important to "screen" all current employees and prospective new ones on their attitudes and use of common courtesy. A simple greeting or goodbye (never use the customer's first name) followed by a sincere and pleasant smile can win over new customers and "revive" old ones. It is a proven fact that if a customer likes your establishment, he will tell three people; but if he dislikes it, he will tell ten!

Salesmanship: "You can't effectively sell a product you don't know; and the more you know about your product, the easier the sale." This slogan should be the cornerstone of all employee training and be re-emphasized periodically. Servers are really salesmen; after all, they are paid a salary, and like a salesman work on commission, the tip. The better the service and the higher the check, the larger the commission will be. Therefore, servers should be completely familiar with all food items in the kitchen, as well as wines appearing on the wine list and the ingredients of the most popular cocktails. This is commonly known as "product knowledge," and its impact on the restaurant's sales can be dramatic.

It is suggested that all employees, prior to the start of their shifts, familiarize themselves with the daily specials and their ingredients, as well as the cooking techniques and so on used for all items on the menu. This is accomplished by insisting that servers communicate with the kitchen staff at the start of each day. This rule is equally important with regard to the wine list, whose additions and deletions should be brought to the attention of the servers. Most servers only know three words about wine: Chablis, rosé, and Burgundy. And, most servers also fill wine glasses to the brim so that it's virtually impossible to drink out of them without bringing your mouth to the glass while it's on the table. The phrase "Have you decided on a wine with your dinner this evening?"

carries a powerful punch but it's so subtle the customer would never feel pressured. Try it, or something similar at every table and see how it brings in the order. It is preferable to the normal "Would you like a glass of wine?" The idea is to think positively about every order and every customer.

It is not imperative that servers, including bartenders, know everything there is to know about wines, but they *must* possess at least minimal knowledge of wine names, tastes, grape varieties, and the viticultural growing regions of the world. In addition, they must know the basics of wine service, and especially how to sell the wines on your list.

Service is important, but unfortunately there is usually little emphasis placed on training, discipline, pride, and caring. All too many of us look for the quick sale instead of cultivating new customers and finding new ways of keeping old ones.

Staff Training

Training is an extremely vital part of the service of alcoholic beverages. The correct wine served in the correct glass alone will not suffice. Your servers must be thoroughly trained in all aspects of beverage service. Perhaps the most important point of their training is to educate them about beverages and brand names so that they will be able to answer questions posed by customers.

Wine sales have as much to do with your servers as with your wine list. A server who is intimidated by and uncomfortable with wine will do a poor job selling it. Servers must know what they are selling, and this can be accomplished through mini-tastings. If there is no one on your staff qualified to conduct such tastings, contact a distributor for assistance. If servers find just one or two wines on the list that they really enjoy, those are the wines they will strive to sell.

Servers' enthusiastic descriptions of special drinks can result in an increase of orders and reorders. You might consider, as part of their training, giving them small samples of these drinks, thereby increasing their ability to sell through the first-hand knowledge they will have acquired. Then, offer appropriate incentives to reach high sales goals.

Customers cringe when wine is presented improperly or the server struggles to open a bottle. Avoid these problems by conducting wine service lessons. Most servers hate to appear inept in front of customers, so teach them proper wine service and have them practice until they feel comfortable.

Wine Service

The wine list should always be brought to the table with the food menu. This usually ensures that the customer is at least aware that wines are available before, during, and after dinner.

Some restaurants, for example The Cellar in the Sky, located in the World Trade Center in New York City, display their aperitifs by the use of a rolling beverage cart, which conveniently shows off a dozen or more possibilities.

After the customer has selected a wine, instruct your servers that they should present the bottle of wine *unopened* to the customer who ordered the wine for his or her approval. At no time should an opened bottle be brought to the table. The bottle should be opened at the table after the customer has approved it (see figure 14-2). If a bottle of white wine is selected and was not previously chilled, an ice bucket filled with ice and water should be brought to the table and the bottle immersed into the ice bath until properly chilled.

To open the bottle, first cut the lead foil or plastic seal (known as a capsule) at the middle of the bulge which appears near the bottle's neck. When removing the foil capsule from the neck of the bottle you must cut the foil in a neat, clean, and even manner. Remove the foil carefully using the edge of the knife blade to "peel" the cut edge of the foil upward to the top of the bottle. Do this in several motions to avoid peeling off little bits and pieces of foil; once the capsule is pulled back a bit, it should come off in one piece. After removing the capsule, wipe the bottle's top with a damp cloth prior to opening, which will remove any foreign particles or mold that may have gathered beneath the capsule. Using a corkscrew will simplify the uncorking process. Corkscrews should have a helical worm (like wire wrapped around a pencil) instead of a bore or screw, which "drills" a hole in the cork, rather than grasping it for extraction. Insert the point of the corkscrew's worm by lining it up perfectly straight over the cork. Beware of "centering" the end of the worm in the cork, for this will put the entire worm off center. With a gentle downward pressure, screw the worm clockwise until only two notches are showing, for most whites, and a bit further for reds. The goal is to insert the worm far enough to successfully extract the cork without breaking through the bottom end of the cork. Typically, white wine corks are from 1.5 to 2 inches long and red wine corks from 2 to 2.5 inches long. Then, attach the lever to the lip on top of the bottle, and while holding it firmly gently lift up in a straight motion the handle of the corkscrew until the cork comes completely out of the bottle. Do not bend

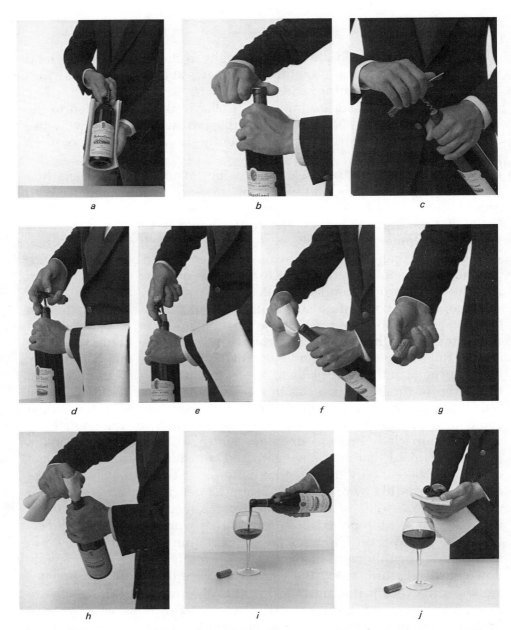

Figure 14-2a–j Step-by-step method of correctly presenting and opening a bottle of wine. (Courtesy Sebastiani Vineyards, Sonoma, California)

the cork. Immediately wipe the neck of the bottle. Take the cork and place it on the table to the right of the person who selected the wine.

The purpose of the presentation of the cork is not, contrary to popular belief, to determine if the cork smells of vinegar, but rather so that its physical condition can be checked. Corks, if stored properly, will maintain pliability, which is easily checked by gently pressing it between the thumb and index finger. While pressing the cork one should notice moisture at the end that faced the wine. This is the most important thing to check on wine corks. If the cork is not pliable there is a good chance that it is drying out, and the wine's storage conditions and thus its own condition might be suspect.

To serve the wine, pour an ounce of it into the host's glass (in a party of customers), and stand back and wait for approval. When approval has been given, gently pour the wine, first for the women, then for the men. Wine glasses should be filled no more than one-third for white wines and one-half to two-thirds for red wines.

When serving wine, the bottle should be held in the right hand in such a way that the person being served can easily see and read the label. Most people like to know what they are drinking. Therefore, do not wrap a napkin around a bottle of wine being served.

After gently pouring wine into a glass with one complete motion, gently twist the wrist with an inward movement, while at the same time tilting the neck of the bottle upward. This avoids dripping wine on the customer, the tablecloth, or the wine's label. It is a good idea to carry a towel in the opposite hand and gently wipe the bottle's neck after each and every pouring.

Serving temperatures for wine

Dry, full-bodied red wines	65°–68°F
Dry, light-bodied red wines	60°–65°F
Dry white wines	50°–55°F
Sparkling wines and champagne	42°–46°F
Sweet red and sweet white wines	42°–46°F

A very simple way to increase sales of white wine is to instruct your servers to *never* fill a glass (8 to 10 oz.) more than one-third full. Most people enjoy white wines because they are chilled. It takes fifteen to twenty minutes for a customer to finish four to five ounces of wine. If you fill the glass one-half to two-thirds full, the first, second, and perhaps the third mouthful will be refreshing, but not the fourth and fifth;

the wine will have become warm. But if the glass is only one-third filled, each and every mouthful will be chilled, and the customer might even order another bottle of white wine.

The proper order of serving wines. The selection of the wine served should be given the same care and consideration that is given to the choice of the food. If the dinner is a special event and more than one type of wine is to be served, these suggestions might be helpful:

Light wines should precede heavy or full-bodied wines.

Dry wines should precede sweet wines.

Dry white wines should precede dry red wines.

Dry red wines should precede sweet white wines.

Dry sparkling wines can be served either before or after dinner, while sweet sparkling wines are best after dinner.

The art of decanting wine. It is a normal and natural process for any long-lived wine (mostly red) to develop or "throw" sediment as it ages. In red wines, sedimentation is caused by slow reactions in and the eventual precipitation of fruits, tannins, tartrates, pigments, and other compounds as the wine matures in the bottle. A brown deposit settles on the side or bottom of the bottle, depending on how the bottle was stored. Sediment is quite harmless, although aesthetically unpleasant, and tastes like sand.

The purpose of decanting a wine is twofold. First, aeration during the decanting process allows the wine to "breathe," to gain in bouquet, and to dissipate any "off" odors or gasses that may have accumulated under the cork. Second, separating the wine from its sediment allows it to be served perfectly bright and clear, thus enhancing its appearance.

Decanting requires little preparation and is extremely simple. Before starting, prepare the following pieces of equipment: a candle holder and candle; a corkscrew; and a colorless glass decanter or carafe (33 oz. minimum). Be sure that it has been rinsed with a small amount of tepid water and is absolutely free of odor, for certain detergents, if incompletely rinsed away, can ruin a wine's bouquet. Do *not* store your decanters closed with their own stoppers, but instead stuff the necks gently with a bit of tissue paper.

Follow this simple step-by-step procedure:

1. Stand the bottle upright for at least twenty-four hours before decanting so that the sediment, which is lying along the side of the bottle, can drop gently to the bottle's bottom. If a twenty-four hour time period

is not possible because of immediate ordering, let the bottle rest horizontally for the time being. Decanting should not be done more than one hour before the wine is to be served because the wine may lose its bouquet. Very old wines should be decanted immediately before serving, as the wine fades and oxidizes rapidly. Bottles of vintage Port might have to be stood upright for longer than twenty-four hours to allow the crusted sediment, known as the dreggs, to settle to the bottom.

2. Gently uncork the bottle to avoid disturbing any sediment. If the bottle is lying horizontal, place it into a wicker basket and begin the uncorking process.

3. Light the candle and place the holder in front of a colorless carafe (between the wine and carafe). Then carefully tilt the wine bottle toward the open mouth of the carafe and allow its contents to trickle in slowly and smoothly. While you do this the flame of the candle should be directly underneath the neck of the wine bottle so that you can follow the movement of sediment from the bottom of the bottle to the neck, ensuring the decanted wine's clarity. When the sediment reaches the point where the neck and shoulders of the bottle meet, you should be able to see some of the sediment, which is cloudy or hazy, starting to appear. When this starts to happen, you should stop the decanting process. You will find that only one ounce or so of wine will remain in the bottle, and you will have a wine that is bright and clear in the decanter.

The remaining contents of the bottle should be discarded, and the customer should be asked if he would prefer to have the wine served from the decanter or replaced in the cleaned bottle.

Wine spills. If for any reason wine, especially red wine, is spilled on a customer's clothing or on the tablecloth, it can be removed by several easy methods.

If white wine is spilled, a little mild soap and water will remove it. If red wine has been spilled a bit more work is required. Rub some salt or seltzer on the stain, let it sit for a few minutes, and most of the stain should be removed. Or, immediately pour white wine over the red wine stain and rub it in until the red disappears. Then simply wash out the white wine with some mild soap and water.

Customers' Demand for Quality Products

Knowledgeable customers who are brand name conscious seek labels that they are not only familiar with but have loyalty toward. Stocking identifiable brands establishes a good image for your bar, which increases repeat patronage. This name brand identification is not only applicable to distilled spirits, but also to imported and American beers and wines.

When customers see a bar stocked with "off" brands or bar brands of spirits, the bar immediately gets a reputation for low quality (and high profits for the owner). Today's discriminating consumer demands high quality and is willing to pay for it, especially when it involves brand names and especially super-premium brands. When customers are served beverage brands with which they are familiar they feel that they are getting a certain perceived value for their dollar. With bar brands, the perceived value is low, and so *should* be the selling price, which unfortunately is usually the same as or only slightly lower than for brand name spirits.

Seagram's, the distilled spirits giant, recommends taking quality one step further—establishing a "premium well." Stocking your well with premium brands and serving them whether or not they are specified can actually increase profits. How? Through higher drink prices. Though a premium brand costs more per bottle than an unknown brand, studies show that people will pay more for a drink made with a brand of liquor they recognize.

Smart beverage managers will capitalize on the fact that people are drinking less alcohol, but are drinking better brands of beer, distilled spirits, and wines. This trend is not confined to the United States alone; the consumption of alcohol has also dropped off significantly in most European countries. If your customers drink better brands, it usually means increased profits for your business.

Liquor Liability

It is beyond the scope of this book to cover or discuss the laws relating to "liquor liability." Instead, we feel that both general and specific questions regarding sections of the law should be addressed to your state alcoholic beverage office or the regional offices of the Bureau of Alcohol, Tobacco and Firearms listed below.

Bureau of Alcohol, Tobacco
  and Firearms
Washington, D.C. 20226
202–566–7135

Midwest Regional Office
Room 1544
230 S. Dearborn Street
Chicago, Illinois 60604
312–353–3778

North-Atlantic Regional Office
Room 620H
6 World Trade Center
New York, New York 10048
212–264–2328

Southeast Regional Office
Room 200
3835 Northeast Expressway
Atlanta, Georgia 30340
404–455–2631

Southwest Regional Office
Room 709
1114 Commerce Street
Dallas, Texas 75242
214–767–2280

Western Regional Office
34th Floor
525 Market Street
San Francisco, California 94105
415–974–9616

Methods of Protection from Liquor Liability

Today's strict drunk driving laws, the new "liquor liability" laws, and the existence of neo-prohibitionist and other citizens' groups all attest to the fact that drunk driving is an extremely serious matter about which all owners of drinking establishments must concern themselves.

To avoid problems with the law, it is suggested that some or all of the following be reduced or eliminated:

Offering two-for-one drinks during "happy hours."

Giving more than two drinks to one person at a time.

Selling, offering, or delivering to any person an unlimited number of drinks during any set period of time for a fixed price.

Serving larger-than-normal drinks.

Increasing the size of a drink without raising its price.

Selling, offering, or delivering beer or mixed drinks by the pitcher.

Encouraging or permitting contests on the premises in which drinks are the prizes.

Giving free drinks to any person or groups of persons.

The following practices, instead, should be developed:

Instituting a designated driver program.

Serving free soda or "mocktails" to designated drivers.

Guaranteeing free cab rides home for intoxicated guests.

Recommending or requiring your bartenders/waiters to attend a server intervention course, which can be offered by the National Health Education Foundation.

Training your staff in intervention techniques and general awareness.

Serving foods that are high in protein and fat, which slows the absorption of alcohol into the bloodstream. Cheese and bread, for instance, could be served during "happy hours."

There are many inexpensive ways to take the focus off drinking and place it on fun. The National Restaurant Association has suggested several possible tactics.

Make your bartender a celebrity. Since a bartender is often considered the "personality" of a bar, send him out to make presentations for your establishment. Also, make your bartender your spokesperson against drunk driving. Promote guest bartender nights, using local celebrities or regular customers. Hire your staff members based on personality. Once they have been with you for a while, name a drink after them.

Serve dinner at the bar. The National Restaurant Association suggests that singles may be more apt to eat out alone if they are sitting at the bar rather than at a table. The price of the dinner will make up for revenues lost through lowered alcohol consumption; and providing food of any kind helps to ameliorate the effects of alcohol on drinkers.

Another idea is to sponsor contests. Americans love to compete; eating contests, from pretzels to oysters, are always popular.

Bartenders' Responsibilities

According to the National Restaurant Association, bartenders are shouldering more responsibility for patrons' alcohol consumption than ever before. Laws in at least thirty-five states hold establishments liable for accidents caused by intoxicated patrons they served. And, the number of lawsuits filed against bars and restaurants is increasing each year. You can control excessive drinking in your bar or restaurant by recognizing when a patron has had too much to drink and taking appropriate action.

Note how quickly a patron is drinking. Generally, a 150-pound person consuming four drinks (four ounces of alcohol) in an hour registers a 0.1 percent blood alcohol content and is legally intoxicated. Watch for progressive symptoms of intoxication: lack of inhibition, followed by loss of muscular control and impaired judgment.

If a patron seems to have reached his or her limit and asks for another cocktail, suggest a "mocktail" or something to eat instead. Encourage intoxicated patrons to let a friend drive them home, or offer to call a cab. If you are serving a large group, suggest that someone become the "designated driver." Provide the driver with complimentary "mocktails."

For further information about alcohol server education programs contact the National Restaurant Association in Washington, D.C. or Intermission, Ltd., a nonprofit "responsible beverage service organization" in Northampton, Massachusetts.

TIPS

Training for Intervention Procedures by Servers of Alcohol (TIPS) is a nationwide program to train servers of alcohol on ways to prevent alcohol abuse in taverns, restaurants, and other businesses where beverages containing alcohol are sold. Through written materials, videotapes, and "role playing" your bartenders, waitresses, and other employees will learn important information on the effects of alcohol; how to identify potentially troublesome drinkers or situations before they become a problem; and how they can deal with intoxicated customers or those who appear to be on the verge of overindulging without creating a scene.

TIPS is a practical, common-sense approach to helping prevent alcohol abuse while at the same time not damaging your business. It can be an important addition to the training your employees already receive in such areas as company procedures and product handling. The program was developed by Dr. Morris E. Chafetz, one of the world's leading authorities on alcohol and the founder and director of the National Institute on Alcohol Abuse and Alcoholism. He is also president of the Health Education Foundation in Washington, D.C., which administers the TIPS program. The basic training takes six hours; employees must pass a written test before they will be certified as having successfully completed the basic training.

Suggested Readings

Dahmer, Sondra J. and Kurt W. Kahl. *The Waiter and Waitress Training Manual*, 2d ed. New York: CBI, 1982.

Katsigris, Costas and Mary Porter. *The Bar and Beverage Book: Basics of Profitable Management*. New York: John Wiley, 1983.

Morgan, William J., Jr. *Food and Beverage Management and Service*. Lansing,

Mich.: Educational Institute of the American Hotel and Motel Association, 1981.

Ninemeier, Jack D. *Principles of Food and Beverage Operations*. Lansing, Mich.: Educational Institute of the American Hotel and Motel Associations, 1984.

Discussion Topics and Questions

1. What security equipment is available to monitor the activities of your head bartender?

2. What policy would you formulate for smoking and drinking behind the bar by your staff while on duty?

3. Should you allow bartenders to make an involved, time-consuming drink during peak times, or should they be instructed that only certain drinks be made? Why?

4. Does the glass determine the drink recipe, or does the recipe of the drink determine the glass used?

5. Should bartenders be included with servers and bus people in tip pools? Explain.

6. What alternatives, if any, are there to decanting an old bottle of red wine?

7. Can consumers really recognize the taste of certain brands of spirits? What about the brand's name, bottle shape, label, price, and advertising; what role do they play in forming consumer perceptions and preferences?

8. Should both owners and the bartenders be responsible for damages in drunk driving lawsuits? Why?

9. How far should training go relative to instructions in handling intoxicated customers?

10. What alternatives are there for making up for loss of revenues due to diminished drinking by your customers?

Glossary

The following abbreviations will be used to represent their respective countries: (AUS) Austria, (FR) France, (GERM) Germany, (HUN) Hungary, (ITAL) Italy, (SP) Spain, (PORTUG) Portugal.

A

Abboccato (ITAL) Semisweet wine. *See* Amabile.

Abfüllung (GERM) Bottling or bottler, must be listed on all quality wines.

Absolute Alcohol Clinically pure or 200 proof (100%), ethyl alcohol.

Abocado (SP) Semisweet wine.

Acescence A name given to the vinegar smell of a wine that has undergone aerobic bacterial spoilage. Equivalent to volatile acidity. In some wines, notably port and well wood-aged red table wines, a small amount of acescence is considered a desirable part of the wine's nose. However, when excessive, acescence will completely destroy the acceptability of any wine.

Acetic The vinegary smell of acetic acid.

Acidity Indicates the quality of tartness or sharpness to the taste due to the presence of agreeable fruit acids. An important constituent which contributes flavor and freshness to wine when it is in proper balance. Not to be confused with sourness, dryness, or astringency. The principle acids found in wine are tartaric, citric, malic, and lactic.

Adamado (PORTUG) Sweet. *See* Doce.

Adega (PORTUG) Wine cellar.

Aerobic Fermentation A fermentation conducted in the presence of oxygen.

Aftertaste What remains in the throat or on tongue after a wine is swallowed. Both the character and the length of the aftertaste may be described collectively as "finish."

Aging The process wherein wine, whiskey, or brandy is stored in oak barrels, stainless steel tanks, or glass so that complex changes that only time can implement take place. Aging smooths a rough, new wine, whiskey, or brandy and adds bouquet and character.

Agrafe, Agraffe A metal clip that holds the champagne cork in place during the secondary fermentation.

Aguardente (PORTUG) Brandy used to fortify port wines.

Aguardiente (SP) Distilled spirits.

Albariza (SP) A chalky-type of soil found in the finest growing areas of Jerez (sherry).

Alberello (ITAL) (little trees) A pruning method employed in Sicily, where the vines are grown close to the ground so that they are able to derive reflected heat from the ground onto the leaves.

Alcohol *Aqua ardens* was the Latin term for alcohol frequently used by writers of early treatises. The chemical formula of ethyl alcohol or ethanol is C_2H_5OH—the preservative and intoxicating constituent of wine.

Alambic, Alembic A large, onion-shaped copper pot still used for the double distillation of cognac and other brandies.

Alt (GERM) Old.

Amabile (ITAL) Semisweet wine. *See* Abboccato.

Amaro (ITAL) Bitter.

Amer (FR) Bitter.

Amontillado (SP) A type of sherry, usually semidry in taste.

Ampelography The descriptive study and identification of grape vines.

Ampelos Greek word for vine.

Amphora An ancient vessel often made of ceramic or earthenware, usually with two handles, which was used as a container for wine.

Amtliche Prüfungsnummer (GERM) The "A.P." number which appears on the bottom of some wine labels. It certifies that the wine met all legal requirements and has passed a rigid battery of laboratory and sensory tests.

Añada (SP) Wine obtained from the harvest of a certain year.

Anaerobic Fermentation Fermentation during which the atmosphere is oxygen-free.

Añejo or Añejado Por (SP) Aged by.

Angel's Share The portion of cognac or armagnac that evaporates while aging in the wooden casks.

Annata (ITAL) Vintage year or harvest. *See* Vendemmia.

Année (FR) Year.

Anreichern (GERM) *See* Chaptalization.

Anthocyanin The pigmentation or coloring matter contained in grapes, especially red.

Antioxidant Ascorbic acid (vitamin C) in tablets or crystals added to wine at the time of bottling to prevent excess oxidation or browning.

Aperitif (FR) From the Latin term *aperire*, which means "to open." A wine taken before meals to stimulate the appetite.

Appearance Refers to clarity, not color. Wines should be free of cloud and suspended particles when evaluated in a glass.

Appellation d'Origine Contrôlée (FR) Wine laws enacted in 1935.

Appellation of Origin Place name of geographic origin; e.g., area from which the wine came.

Aqua Ardens Latin term used by early manuscript writers to denote alcohol.

Aroma The particular smell, odor, or fragrance of a specific grape used to produce the wine. That is why white wines, which are usually produced by a single grape variety, are associated with aroma.

Aromatico (ITAL) Amply scented, aromatic.

Aromatized or Aromatic Wine A fortified wine which has "aromatics" infused into its bouquet. An example is vermouth.

Arpent During the eighteenth century in France, one "arpent" was translated to mean 1¼ acres of land.

Asciutto (ITAL) A wine that is extremely dry.

Assemblage (FR) Blending of various cuvées in the making of champagne.

Asti (ITAL) A town in southern Piedmont, famous for production of spumante.

Astringency Sensation which makes the mouth pucker. Combination of sourness and bitterness. Also denotes too much tannin, which is derived from the stems, skins, and pits.

Aszú (HUN) Overripe grapes used in the making of Tokay wine.

Aktien Gesellschaft (AUS) The "A.G." after the name of a firm on a wine label is the equivalent of *incorporated*.

Atmosphere In physics, a unit of pressure equal to 14.69 pounds per square inch, or the pressure exerted upon the human body at 30 feet under water.

Auslese (GERM) A pradikat wine made from particularly ripe, selected late harvested grapes; all unripe grapes from the bunches are discarded. Generally sweeter and more expensive than spätlese wines. *See* Szemelt.

Autoclave (ITAL) *See* Bulk-fermented, Charmat.

Autolysis Self-destruction of yeast cells, which release their different cell compounds into the surrounding medium. Often gives wine a toasty or "bad" aroma and flavor.

Azienda Agricola (ITAL) Under the new legislation, only companies that can prove that their wines have been made solely from grapes gathered in their own vineyards, and vinified in their own cellars, have the right to describe themselves as an *azienda agricola* or winery.

B

B.A.T.F. Bureau of Alcohol, Tobacco, and Firearms. This bureau of the U.S. Department of Treasury regulates the production, transportation, and sale of alcoholic beverages; enforces legal sale; and ensures the collection of federal excise taxes, which are sent to the Internal Revenue Service.

Bacchus The Roman god of wine.

Back Bar The cabinet or display area behind the bar; usually used for display, placement of cash register, and storage.

Balance A wine in which all the components, sugar, tannin, acid, alcohol, etc. are in harmony with the varietal fruit flavor.

Balling *See* Brix.

Bamboo Juice The name given to alcoholic beverages by members of the U.S. Air Force who were stationed in the South Pacific during the Korean War.

Bar Back A bartender's helper or an apprentice bartender.

Bar Brands *See* Well Brands or House Brands.

Barrel of Beer A large wooden or metal barrel containing 31 gallons; 13.8 cases of 12-ounce cans or bottles.

Barrique (FR) A barrel.

Barriquot (FR) An old term for a small barrel.

Bar Sugar Superfine sugar which quickly dissolves in mixed drinks.

Basket Press A type of press wherein grapes are put in a wooden tub with slotted sides. Pressure is applied by means of a large screw, which presses the grapes and allows the juice to run out through the slots.

Baster Small cylindrical plastic tube, useful for taking samples of wine or must to test specific gravity, clarity, or flavor.

Beechwood Aging As practiced by Anheuser-Busch, beechwood aging is quite different from aging wine in barrels at a winery. In beechwood aging, a number of short slats of beechwood are tied together and then immersed into a tank where the beer is undergoing a process known as "krausening." The beechwood doesn't impart any particular flavor to the beer, but it does increase the surface area for encouraged fermentation. After use, these slats are washed off and used over and over again.

Beerenauslese (GERM) "Berry selection" wines made from overripe grapes, picked individually and produced in very small quantities only in best vintages. These grapes must be affected by Botrytis cinerea.

Beeswing (PORTUG) The name of the light thin crust which resembles the transparent wing of a bee and often forms in some bottles of port. Also known as a crust or crusted ports.

Beloe Russian for white wine.

Bentonite An excellent fining agent first used in 1931 by Lothrop and Paine for fining honey. It is basically clay (which looks like grey crystalline powder) from the state of Wyoming consisting of "montmorillonite," a hydrated silicate of magnesium produced from decomposition under water of volcanic glass. Chemically it is hydrated aluminum silicate. Other fining agents are casein, charcoal, colloidal silica, egg whites, gelatin, isinglass, and Sparkolloid.

Bereich (GERM) District within a Gebiet (region).

Berg (GERM) Mountain.

Bergeron, Victor The originator of "Trader Vics."

Bianco (ITAL) White wine.

Bite Infers a substantial degree of acidity.

Bitter One of the four basic sensations recognized by the taste buds.

Black Rot A fungus disease which forms black speckled stains on the vines, causing the fruit to brown and shrivel.

Black Velvet A mixture of stout and champagne popular in England during the Edwardian days (nineteenth century). It was created when Prince Albert died, which sent Queen Victoria (mother of Edward VII, King of England 1901–1910), along with the entire country into shock. They shrouded everything in black, including champagne, which was mixed with stout.

The Black Velvet has had a resurgence in popularity; today, ginger ale is usually substituted because of the high cost of champagne.

Blanc (FR) White wine.

Blanc de Blancs (FR) White wine made entirely from white grapes. Champagnes or sparkling wines so labeled are usually "lighter" in body.

Blanc de Noirs (FR) White wine made entirely from black grapes. Champagnes or sparkling wines so labeled are usually "fuller" in body.

Blanco (SP) White wine.

Bleichert (GERM) Rosé wine.

Blush Wine A white wine made from red grapes whose juice and skins were left in contact long enough to produce a blush, or salmon-tinted, color.

Bocksbeutel, Boxbeutel An unusual "flask-shaped" bottle used in Franconia, Germany, parts of Chile, and Portugal.

Bodega (SP) Literally, a wine cellar, but used to designate the producer and shipper.

Bodeguero (SP) Winemaker.

Body The tactile impression of weight or fullness (roundness) on the palate. Light-bodied wines tend to be low in alcohol, tannin, and extract. Big, full-bodied wines tend to be alcoholic, tannic, and, if white, occasionally sweet.

Boilermaker A shot of whiskey drunk straight and immediately followed by a glass of beer.

Bonde (FR) A barrel stopper or bung.

Bonne-Chauffe (FR) The second distillation in the cognac process.

Bootlegger It was a practice of stagecoach travelers to conceal a pint-sized, thick-glass, flat bottle in their boot, to have refilled at taverns along their way.

Booze From E. G. Booz, a grocer in Philadelphia around 1840. He used to bottle and sell bourbon whiskey, which he bought in barrels.

Bor (HUNG) Wine.

Bore On a corkscrew, the piece that is inserted into the cork. *See* Worm.

Botrytis Cinerea A mold that grows on the surface of grapes under certain conditions. Called "noble rot," botrytis is highly prized for the richness it confers to certain wines, especially Johannisberg Riesling, Sauvignon Blanc, and Sémillon. The resulting wines are uniquely aromatic and intensely flavored, sweet and luscious, and usually become long-lived dessert wines. During growth, the mold shrivels the grapes, concentrating both sugar and flavor. Fermentation of botrytis-affected grapes is often slow and laborious. *See* Edelfäule, Muffa Nobile, and Pourriture Noble.

Botte (ITAL) Barrel.

Botte Madre (SP) "Mother-Cask," the solera system as used in the production of sherry wines.

Bottiglia (ITAL) Bottle.

Bottle Derived from the French *bouteille* which in turn was probably from *bautille*, the familiar wine flask. While early bottles had many names, such as flask, flagon, and carafe, only a vessel containing wine could correctly be called a bouteille.

Bottle Fermented On a sparkling wine label, means that secondary fermentation took place in the bottle or that transfer method was used.

Bottled Sunshine Slang term used by the British during World War II for a bottle or can of beer.

Bottlescrew The original name for a corkscrew used around 1750.

Bottom-Fermented Lager-style beers that ferment at cooler temperatures for a longer period of time than ales, which are top-fermented beers.

Bouchon (FR) Cork.

Bouillage (FR) In the production of champagne, the fermentation.

Bouquet The smell imparted to the wine from the fermentation and aging process.

Bowl That part of a goblet or glass which contains the wine.

Branch Water Southern term for cold water added to distilled spirits.

Branco (PORTUG) White wine.

Brandy Derivation of the word *brandewijn*, which is Dutch for burnt wine.

Brasserie (FR) A brewery.

Breathing Allowing air to reach wine by uncorking and pouring it. The wine breathes to shed any unpleasant odors and bring out its bouquet.

Breed A distinguishing and distinctive quality.

Brew A slang term or name for a beer, especially draught.

Brilliant The quality of a wine free from any visible solids and having a sparkling clarity.

Bristol Cream Specially blended sherries coming from Bristol, England. They are made by a secret blending of mostly amontillado and oloroso sherries, and additionally sweetened with P.X. grapes.

Brix A measure of total soluble solids in grape juice, more than 90% of which are fermentable sugars. The percentage of sugar in a solution (by weight) at a specified temperature, generally 20° C (68° F). *See* Balling.

Bronze The amber hue apparent around the rim of a glass of aged red or white wine.

Brouillis (FR) The heart of the first distillate in the making of cognac.

Brown Brandy During the second-half of the last century, there was a beverage made in France which consisted of brandy mixed with molasses.

Brut (FR) Very dry. The driest of French champagnes.

Bual, Boal (PORTUG) Semisweet Madeira wine.

Bucket Slang term for an oversized (double) "rocks" glass.

Bulk Containers with a capacity in excess of one wine gallon. In practice, shipments in bulk involve much larger containers.

Bulk-Fermented *See* Charmat.

Bumper A cup or glass filled to the brim with an alcoholic drink. An old English toast, "To Drink a Bumper."

Bung Cork or wooden plug which fits into the opening at the top of a barrel for a tight seal.

Butt A barrel, cask, or vat used to store or ship sherry wine, ale, or other wines. It varies in proportion to the area in which it is used.

Buttons Up An old Scandinavian custom at formal gatherings to drink as many toasts, often with Aquavit or Akvavit, as there were buttons on a man's dress coat.

C

Call Liquor Brand-named distilled spirits which have brand recognition. Brands for which the customer will "call" for by name. Also referred to as name brand.

Campden Tablet Seven-grain tablet of potassium metabisulfite. Dissolved in must of wine, it releases sulfur dioxide, which acts as a sterilant and antioxidant.

Canary Sack Originated in the sixteenth century and the favorite drink of the English dramatist William Shakespeare (1564–1616).

Cañas (SP) A small, stumpy, and cylindrical glass in which Manzanilla sherry is traditionally drunk.

Cantina Sociale (ITAL) Cooperative winery.

Cantine (ITAL) Winery or wine cellar.

Capsule Plastic, lead, or aluminum cover placed over the cork in a wine bottle to give a more secure closure and to improve the appearance of the bottle.

Carafe (FR) Decanter or glass bottle used in restaurants for serving "house wines."

Caramel Burnt sugar, slightly bitter but otherwise tasteless, used for coloring whiskey, brandy, etc.

Carbon Dioxide A naturally occurring odorless, colorless gas, which is a by-product of fermentation. It is allowed to dissipate into the atmosphere when making still wines. However, during the production of sparkling wines, the carbon dioxide gasses are trapped to retain the "bubble" in the wine.

Carbonic Maceration Grapes are held under carbon dioxide pressure while a complex fermentation takes place within the berries themselves. The juice is pressed and conventionally fermented; drinkable red wine is ready just a few weeks after fermentation. A process used to make the Beaujolais wines of France.

Carboy *See* Demi-John.

Casa Establecida (SP) Estate bottled.

Casa Vinicola (ITAL) Winery.

Casein *See* Bentonite.

Cask Oak barrel used for aging wines.

Catador (SP) A wine taster.

Cava (SP) Sparkling wine made by the méthode champenoise technique.

Cavatappi (ITAL) Corkscrew.

Cave (FR) A wine cellar.

Cavistes (FR) Cellarman.

Cepa (PORTUG or SP) Grape or grapevine.

Cépage (FR) Grape variety.

Chai (FR) An above-ground facility for the storage and aging of wines.

Champagne (FR) A sparkling wine produced only by the méthode champenoise in the Champagne region of France. In the United States, champagne is used as a generic name for sparkling wine.

Champagne The Russian term for a sparkling wine.

Champanski The Bulgarian term for a sparkling wine.

Chantepleure (FR) Glass, stainless-steel, or plastic tube or cylinder used to extract samples of wine from a barrel. Used in the Vouvray area of the Loire Valley. *See* Preuve, Saggiavino, and Wine Thief.

Chapeau (FR) The "hat" or thick layer of solids (skins) that rise to the top of the fermenting vats.

Chaptalization (FR) The addition of sugar to the "must" to make up for natural sugar deficiencies. The term is derived from the name of Dr. Jean-Antoine Chaptal de Chanteloup (1756–1832), the Minister of the Interior, Agriculture, and President of the Academy of Science under Napoleon I in 1800. *See* Anreichern.

Character Typical characteristics of a wine according to vintage, soil, climate, and treatment (aging in wood, steel, etc.).

Charcoal *See* Bentonite.

Charente (FR) The valley in southwest France which lies in the Cognac region.

Charmat (FR) Method of producing sparkling wine developed by Eugéne Charmat in 1910. Wine is fermented in glass-lined tanks, filtered, and bottled. Also called bulk-fermented or autoclave.

Château Bottled (FR) Wine bottled at an estate, château, or domaine by the same proprietor who owns the property and the grapes that are grown there.

Cheese Board A board that fits around the screw of an old-fashioned "basket wine-press" and rests directly on top of the grapes. It is shaped like boards used to press cheese.

Chiaretto (ITAL) A light-colored red wine.

Chiu, Chiew The Chinese word for wine. The original words used before Chiu were *Li* or *Chang*.

Church Key A slang term for a beer bottle opener.

Claret A British word derived from the Earl of Clare, who served under Henry II of England (1154–1189).

Clarete (SP) Light red-colored wine.

Classico (ITAL) A geographic term applied to DOC wines; refers to the central area of a production zone.

Clean Free from bacterial and processing defects. Absence of any unpleasant odors.

Clear No suspended solids in the wine, no cloudiness. A brilliant wine.

Climat (FR) Vineyard as used in Burgundy.

Clos (FR) An enclosure or field, similar to the word *château* and used in St. Émilion, France.

Cloudy Wines containing excess colloidal material or sediment in suspension.

Coarse Rough-textured wine lacking breeding.

Coarse Salt Salt used for drinks that call for their glass rims to be salted. Also called kosher salt.

Cobbler Tall wine drinks generally made with fruits, sugar, and plenty of ice.

Cobwebs Often found in old wine cellars, cobwebs are really fungi which have been nurtured by alcohol fumes.

Cold Stabilization A clarification technique which involves lowering the temperature to 25° to 30° F from one to three weeks. The cold encourages the tartrates and other insoluble solids to precipitate, rendering the wine clear. The tartrates cast by the wine are actually tasteless and harmless and are removed for appearance only. *See* Tartar, Tartaric Acid.

Colheita (PORTUG) Another name often used to denote a "Port of (year)."

Colloidal Silica *See* Bentonite.

Color Each wine has its own "right" color. Judge a wine against the color that's correct for each wine type. Golden or amber is right for many dessert wines, but not for white table wines. Rosés should be distinctly pink with only a suggestion of orange or red. Whites can be yellow, gold, or straw color, but are flawed if they're too dark or too "water white." Reds can have violet hints if young and amber tints if aged. Brown is a flaw, as is too little red color.

Commune (FR) Town or village.

Complexity The various elements which make up bouquet, aroma, and taste in a wine. When a wine is described as having the bouquet of fresh peaches or apples, it is distinguishing some of its complexities.

Compounder A machine which blends liqueurs and cordials.

Congeners Trace-flavoring constituents vaporized off with the alcohol in distillation above 190 proof and developed and expanded during the aging process.

These components contribute to palatability and create the characteristic appearance, aroma, and taste of a particular spirit. When the spirit is distilled at a lower proof, more congeners are present, and the spirit will possess more character.

Consortia Seal (ITAL) Label of Growers Consortium.

Consumo (PORTUG or SP) Ordinary wine, generally for local consumption.

Controllable Costs or Expenses A cost that is controlled by an individual (such as department head) in a company. In this case, the manager can exert some influence and act to lower the expense.

Cooper Experienced craftspeople who make wooden barrels by hand.

Cooperage All containers used for holding or aging wine, brandy, and spirits while in the cellar and prior to bottling.

Copa (SP) A long, "tulip-shaped" stem-glass which contains 6 ounces and is traditionally used for the service of sherry wine.

Copita (SP) A long, "tulip-shaped" stem-glass which holds 4 ounces and is traditionally used for the service of sherry wine.

Cordial Derived from the Latin word *cor* or *cordis*, meaning "heart," because the earliest cordials were administered to the sick to stimulate the heart and lighten the spirit. *See* Liqueur.

Corkage A fee charged by a restaurant for the opening and serving of a wine that a customer brought with him or her.

Corky Smell or taste of the cork, usually from a poor, soft, or disintegrating cork.

Cosecha (SP) Vintage or harvest. *See* Vendimia.

Cosecheros (SP) Growers with relatively small vineyard holdings.

Côte (FR) A hill or slope.

Côteau (FR) Hillside.

Côteaux Champenois (FR) "Still" wines produced in the region of Champagne.

Cotto (ITAL) A wine whose liquid content has been reduced by "cooking" over heat.

Coulure (FR) Term used to describe what occasionally happens in the springtime, when the flowers fall from the grapevines, with no fruit-bearing ability.

Coupage (FR) The blending of many cognacs or champagnes.

Coupé (FR) The familiar flat, saucer-shaped glass often incorrectly used for sparkling wines.

Courtier (FR) A wine broker.

Crackling Slightly sparkling wines produced in any manner which results in a carbonation of less than 2.7 atmospheres of pressure. *See* Frizzante, Pétillant, and Spritzig.

Crémant (FR) A champagne usually produced exclusively from Chardonnay grapes. Perhaps the biggest difference between Crémant and other champagnes lies in the fact that during the secondary fermentation, less sugar is added, which in turn produces less alcohol and less carbon dioxide. In fact, Crémant champagne usually contains 2.5 to 3.5 atmospheres of pressure, compared to the normal 5 to 6 atmospheres of pressure. It is appreciated for its lightness of flavor and less gassy taste.

Criado Por (SP) Produced by. *See* Elaborado Por.

Crianza (SP) Nursery; refers to the aging process in a sherry bodega.

Cru (FR) Literally, growth, but synonymous with vineyard.

Crushing The process whereby the skins of the grapes are cracked open by a machine, liberating the juice.

Crust (PORTUG) *See* Beeswing.

Cuba (SP) A fermenting tank.

Culaton (ITAL) The sediment contained in a bottle of wine.

Cuve (FR) Literally, the contents of a cask of wine.

Cuvée (FR) A blend of wines bottled as one lot. Any volume of wine produced and (in sparkling wine production) specially selected to be fermented a second time for sparkling wine.

Cyathi An ancient Roman cup which held the equivalent of the modern "quartino" or quarter of a liter.

D

Daisy A very large cocktail to which soda is added.

Dame-Jeanne (FR) A large glass bottle used for the transportation of wine. It holds anywhere from 1 to 10 gallons and is usually wrapped with wicker or straw.

Dash One-sixth teaspoon or ¼₈ fluid ounce.

Decant To pour wine from the bottle into a serving container so that any sediment remains in the bottle.

Dégorgement (FR) The process of freezing the neck of the bottle which contains champagne and a small amount of riddled sediment. This ice plug of sediment and champagne is then forced out by pressure within the bottle when the temporary cap is removed, leaving the remaining champagne crystal clear.

Dégustation An old word or term which described a wine tasting.

Demi-John A large glass (or plastic) container which usually holds 5 gallons of liquid and which often is used for the transportation or storage of wine or spring/mineral water. *See* Carboy.

Demi-Sec (FR) Semidry, used mostly in the Champagne region.

Denominacão de Origem (PORTUG) The equivalent of Italy's DOC wine laws.

Denominación de Origen (SP) The equivalent of Italy's DOC wine laws.

Denominazione di Origine Controllata (DOC) (ITAL) Italy's wine laws, enacted in 1963.

Depth Charge Take a shot glass full of whiskey and plunge it (glass and all) into a large glass of beer; then drink the beer.

Dessert Wine A still wine which naturally contains more than 14 percent alcohol. It can be dry or sweet.

Dionysus The Greek god of wine.

Doce (PORTUG) *See* Adamado.

Dock Glasses (PORTUG) Glasses which are elongated and tulip-shaped, used by professional port tasters for evaluation purposes.

Dolce (ITAL) Sweet.

Dom (GERM) Cathedral.

Domaine (FR) Wine estate.

Dosage (FR) The addition of sugar syrup to champagne before recorking and eventual shipping which establishes the level of sweetness in the finished champagne.

Doubling In whiskey production, it is the redistilling of a spirit to help improve its strength and flavor.

Doux (FR) The sweetest champagne produced which is *not* available in the United States and which is only produced in limited quantities for Eastern Europe.

Draft, Draught Beer According to the U.S. government, draft beer may be so labeled on cans or bottles if it is unpasteurized or if it has been bottled under sterile filtration methods. It may not be labeled "draft beer" if it has been pasteurized, but it may use the terminology "draft-brewed," "old time on tap taste," or "draft beer flavor."

Draw One Slang request for a draft beer.

Dregs (PORTUG) The sediment in a bottle of port wine.

Dripping Rod A graduated rod (sometimes glass) that measures the contents of a cask of wine.

Dry A wine with little or no residual sugar. On champagne and sparkling wines, only refers to faintly sweet—not as dry as brut.

Dry County County (or similar governmental jurisdiction) whose voters have not approved the sale of alcoholic beverages. Counties permitting sale only by private clubs are considered dry. *See* Wet County.

Dulce (SP) Sweet.

E

Edelfäule (GERM) The noble mold responsible for Eiswein, Beerenauslese, and Trockenbeerenauslese wines. *See* Botrytis Cinerea, Muffa Nobile, and Pourriture Noble.

Egg Whites *See* Bentonite.

Égrappage (FR) The separation of the grapes from the stalks before pressing.

Eiswein or Ice Wine (GERM) Wine literally made from grapes which have been allowed to freeze on the vines. Eiswein must be made from wines which have attained the minimum sugar level of Beerenauslese.

Elaborado Por (SP) Produced by. *See* Criado Por.

Elegant Refers to a complex wine with refinement and good balance; not a big robust wine.

Elongated Wine British term for wine that is stretched by the addition of water, often used to reduce the alcohol for purposes of excise duty.

Embotellado en la Bodega (SP) Bottled at the bodega.

Embotellado en Origen (SP) Estate bottled.

Embotellado Por (SP) Produced and bottled by.

Engarrafado na Origem (PORTUG) Estate bottled.

Enocianina (ITAL) A well-known concentrated, powdered pigment extract made from the coloring of black grapes. It is used in perfumes, and in its liquid form it is used by the Department of Agriculture when stamping and labeling various cuts and grades of meat.

Enology, Oenology The science or the study of winemaking; related to viticulture, which is the science of grape culture.

Enophile, Oenophile A person who loves wine and wine lore.

Enoteca (ITAL) A wine library or wine bottle collection used for display and reference.

Enotheque, Oenotheque (FR) A wine library or wine bottle collection used for display and reference.

Envejecido Por (SP) Aged by.

Erzeuger Abfüllung (GERM) Estate bottled by a producer, not a shipper.

Especial (SP) A specially selected vintage.

Espumante Term used in Brazil and Portugal for a sparkling wine.

Espumosa (SP) Sparkling wine.

Estate Bottling A term accepted by the federal government to designate only those wines that are produced from grapes grown on lands surrounding the family estate winery. This is the same designation as the château-bottled wines of Europe.

Esters Organic compounds which contribute fruity aromas to wine. Esters sometimes contribute rather solventlike smells, such as those of vinegar or nail-polish remover.

Estufa (PORTUG) Huge heating chambers or ovens used to make Madeira, a fortified wine.

Etampé (FR) A branded or stamped cork.

Ethyl Alcohol, Ethanol Principal alcohol found in all alcoholic beverages.

Etichetta (ITAL) Wine label.

Excise Tax Indirect tax levied by the U.S. government on the alcohol content by volume of distilled spirits and on malt beverages and the various categories of wine.

Extra Dry Term used for a champagne that is not as dry as brut, but drier than sec.

F

Fass (GERM) A barrel.

Fassle (GERM) Usually during a contest, people bet to see how far away wine can be poured (without splashing one's face, or spilling it) into one's mouth through a hand-held, long-spouted drinking vessel. The Spanish name is *porron*.

Fattoria (ITAL) Farm.

Federweisser (GERM) A new or freshly fermented wine similar to Beaujolais Nouveau of France. *See* Vino Novello.

Fehér Bór (HUN) White wine.

Fermentation The process of converting the natural sugars in grape juice into alcohol. Yeasts are introduced into tanks of must to start the process; fermentation stops when the sugars are depleted or when the alcohol level reaches about 14 percent and kills the yeast. Secondary fermentation takes place in sparkling wines to give them their distinctive carbonation.

Fiasco (ITAL) The name of the straw-covered bottle that houses an inexpensive red chianti wine from Tuscany.

Fillettes (FR) Half-bottles (375 milliliters) used in Bordeaux; also referred to as "little girls."

Filtering Clarification of wine by passing it through a material or device that removes suspended particles.

Fining Clarification of wine by passing a material through it that coagulates suspended particles and precipitates them out. *See* Bentonite.

Finish The sensual impression that lingers after the wine is swallowed. Some wines finish crisp and clean while others have a long, rich aftertaste.

Fino (SP) A pale, very dry sherry.

Fire-Brewed The brewing kettle is heated directly by fire, rather than by the more conventional high pressure, heated steam process. Contrary to some beliefs, the resulting beer does *not* taste any different.

Firing Glass A glass used for drinking toasts; firing glasses were banged down hard on the dining table simulating the sound of firing muskets, hence the need for a stout base and the name.

Firkin A beer barrel used in England which contains 41 liters or 10.8 gallons.

Flag A toothpick holding a cherry and orange slice as a garnish.

Flat A sparkling wine or beer which has lost its bubble. Also denotes wine which is lacking in natural acidity.

Flavor Those complex impressions originating on the palate when the wine is swirled in the mouth.

Flip A popular drink in the United States during the early 1700s. It was made by combining rum, beer, cream, beaten eggs, and various spices, which were then heated by plunging a hot loggerhead (a long-handled tool with a ball or bulb at the end) into the mixture.

Float Pouring a shot of spirits on top of a finished drink without stirring or mixing.

Flogging a Cork Home To drive the cork into the bottle by means of a wooden hammer—a practice no longer used today.

Floot A slang term meaning a full 8-ounce glass of whiskey.

Flor The heavy coating of yeast found floating on top of some sherry wine which gives it unique bouquet and flavor.

Floraison (FR) Flowering.

Flowery When the wine's aroma suggests the scent of flowers. A term usually applied to young wines.

Flute (FR) An elongated-shaped bottle used in Alsace and the Rhine in Germany.

Forbidden Fruit The name of a grape concentrate for home winemakers produced by the Louis M. Martini Winery of Napa Valley, California during Prohibition.

Foreshot In whiskey production, the first crude spirit to appear from the still.

Fortified Wine A table wine which has been strengthened by the addition of brandy or spirits and which has a higher alcoholic content. Examples are madeira, marsala, port, and sherry.

Forzato (ITAL) A wine, made from very overripe grapes, which contains a high degree of alcohol.

Foxiness The pronounced aroma of many native American grapes (*Vitis labrusca*).

Frappé (FR) A drink that is super-chilled by the addition of crushed or shaved ice, over which cordials are then poured.

Free-Pour Pouring distilled spirits from a bottle without the aid of a measuring device.

Free-run Juice The initial juice released by the grapes by the shear weight or pressure of the mass, before the press is used. The people of ancient Greece called it *Prodomos* or *Protopos*.

Frizzante (ITAL) Slightly effervescent. *See* Crackling, Pétillant, and Spritzig.

French Hybrids Grape varieties which are crosses of American species with European *Vitis vinifera*.

Fresco (ITAL) Fresh.

Frosting The chilling of a glass for beer and mixed drinks served "straight up."

Fruity Having a definite aroma and flavor of grapes or other fresh fruits. The fruitiness is never cloying; rather, it imparts a lively, refreshing quality to the wine.

Full-Bodied Pleasingly strong bouquet, flavor, and taste. Fills the mouth.

Fürst (GERM) Prince.

Fut (FR) A barrel, cask, or vat.

G

Gallon An old United States term for a glass container, holding 128 ounces.

Garnish A citrus fruit, vegetable, or item added to a drink (generally for eye appeal) prior to serving.

Garrafeira (PORTUG) The wine has been specially aged; similar to *reserve* or *special reserve*.

Gasificado, Granvas (SP) A sparkling wine which is not produced by the *méthode champenoise* (champagne method).

Gazéifié (FR) A sparkling wine which is artificially carbonated.

Gebiet (GERM) Wine-producing region.

Gelatin *See* Bentonite.

Generic Wine The name of a district, commune, or region from which the wine originates. A simpler definition would be "place-name"—wines that are named after European wine-producing districts such as Burgundy, Chablis, Champagne, Chianti, Port, Rhine, Sauternes, Sherry, etc.

Generoso (SP) An aperitif wine.

Gill An ancient drinking glass which held about ¼ pint (4 ounces).

Gin Mill Slang name given to a bar.

Glycerin, Glycerine Syrupy or mouth-coating by-product of fermentation.

Goblet (FR) A pruning method used in Beaujolais.

Gönci (HUNG) A small 35-gallon barrel in which Tokay wine is aged.

Governo (ITAL) A process occasionally used to produce Chianti wine, meant for early consumption. It consists of inducing a secondary fermentation by the addition of 5 to 10% must, pressed from selected grapes partly dried on wicker frames.

Graf (GERM) A count.

Grain Spirits Neutral spirits distilled from a fermented mash of grains and stored in oak containers. By recognizing the qualities developed by distillation, grain spirits are distinguished from grain neutral spirits.

Grand Cru (FR) A great growth which is a legal grade of quality.

Grande Champagne (FR) The premier vineyard area of the Cognac region.

Granite Shotting A procedure that hasn't been used in many years. It involves roughening up or "scoring" the inside of bottles by use of granite chips so that the crust formed by port wine, is provided with a grip, thus rendering decanting much easier.

Grape Brick During Prohibition you could buy a package containing dehydrated grape juice which had a warning label on its wrapper which stated, "Do Not Mix This Package with Warm Water, Yeast, and Keep in a Warm Location for Two Weeks, for This Will Make Wine, and That Is Illegal!"

Grappa (ITAL) A very strong distillate made from the skins, stems, and pits of grapes. *See* Marc.

Graves (FR) A wine district in Bordeaux which produces both red and white wines.

Green A very young wine which usually displays a high level of acidity.

Grog or Navy Grog A name for rum, derived from the nickname of Admiral Edward Vernon (1684–1757), the English naval officer for whom George Washington's estate was named. The admiral was known as "old grog" because he wore a shabby boat coat made out of grogram, a coarse fabric woven from silk and wool and often stiffened with gum. He ordered his men to take a daily drink of rum and water as a caution against scurvy, and until September 1, 1862, sea-going sailors from the United States were served grog.

Grog Blossom The British during World Wars I and II were said to occasionally have a Grog Blossom, which was a rosy nose, presumably from years of drinking.

Grosslage (GERM) A composite vineyard made up of a number of individual vineyards with subregions.

Growths (FR) A standard of quality, applied to wines of France; also referred to as *cru*.

Guyot (FR) A pruning method used in Beaujolais.

H

Habillage (FR) Bottle-dressing (combination of label and foil capsule).

Halbrot Swiss term for a rosé wine.

Halb-Trocken (GERM) Semidry wine.

Half-Bottle Usually contains 12.7 ounces or 375 milliliters.

Half & Half In England, a drink consisting of equal parts of stout and ale.

Hammondsport A wine-producing district in the Finger Lakes region of New York State.

Hard A wine with excessive tannin. Not necessarily a fault in a young wine because it may indicate a long maturity period.

Head Space In a barrel, tank, or cask, the space of air between the top of the wine and the top of the container. *See* Ullage.

Heads In distillation, elements that boil at low temperatures and vaporize first.

Hearts In distillation, elements that vaporize between the heads and tails.

Hectare A measurement of land: 1 hectare equals 2.471 acres.

Hectoliter A metric measurement equal to 26.418 gallons or 11.111 cases of twelve 750-milliliter bottles.

Hippocras An ancient "highly spiced" wine made with cinnamon and honey liqueur and popular until the time of Louis XV.

Hooch A home-concocted drink made of boiled ferns and flour by the Alaskan Indians of the Hutsnuwu tribe, who called it "Hoochino." Soldiers who were sent from the United States to Alaska after the territory was purchased from Russia in 1867, added molasses and distilled it, shortening the name to "Hooch." Hooch was the army's term for liquor during the first and second World Wars.

Hops An herblike plant (humulus lupulus) whose use is almost indispensable to the aroma, taste, and character of beer. Only flowers from the unfertilized female hop vine called "catkin" are used as the prime ingredient. The hops contain a naturally occurring amount of resin, plus various oils, which are the perfect "bittering" agents for beer. They provide the backbone of aroma and taste to most beers and ales alike. The taste of hops is generally characterized by a slight bitterness in some beers to a distinctive bitter, almost astringent taste in others.

Hospices de Beaune (FR) A charity hospital located in Burgundy which hosts an annual wine auction to raise money.

House Brands *See* Well Brands or Bar Brands.

Hudson River Valley The oldest wine-producing district in the United States, located in New York State.

Hue Usually the separation of colors of wine seen at the edge of the glass.

Hybrid Grapes The group of grape varieties referred to as hybrids, French-American hybrids, or French hybrids. They are crosses of some American grape species, such as *Vitis labrusca, Vitis riparia,* and *Vitis rupestris,* with *Vitis vinifera.*

Hydrometer A gauge used to measure the sugar content in the must prior to fermentation. Other hydrometers measure specific gravity and potential of alcohol.

I

Imbottigliato (ITAL) Bottled.

Imbottigliato all'origine (ITAL) Estate bottled.

Imbottigliato nella zona di Produzione (ITAL) Bottled in the production zone.

Import Duty Levy on distilled spirit products imported into the United States. Import duties are assessed on a proof gallon.

I.N.E. Seal (ITAL) A round red seal with the words "Marchio Nazionale" appears on the neck of every Italian wine bottle exported to North

America. It indicates compliance with governmental quality control procedures. The letters I.N.E. stand for Instituto Nazionale Esportazione (Institute National Exportation).

Inoculating The action of adding yeast or bacteria to a biological environment in order to trigger development or fermentation.

In Vino Veritas An expression that goes back to the roman scholar Gaius Plinius (better known as Pliny the Elder) in 33–79 A.D., and which means "In Wine There is Truth."

Isinglass *See* Bentonite.

J

Jerez de la Frontera (SP) The city in southern Spain where sherry wine is produced.

Jeroboam A large bottle that holds 104 ounces of champagne is named for the mighty man of valor, Jeroboam, who led the 10 northern tribes of ancient Israel in revolt against King Rehoboam, the son and successor to King Solomon.

Jigger A United States term for a shot-glass of alcohol usually measuring 1½ ounces.

Jug Wine A wine of no particular breed or quality which is usually sold in quantity.

K

Kabinett (GERM) The most basic of qualitätswein mit prädikat grade of wines, usually dry.

Keg A container generally holding less than 16 gallons of beer.

Keller (GERM) Cellar.

Kellergasse (AUS) Wine cellar.

Kir (FR) A popular aperitif drink made with creme de cassis and dry white wine.

Klapotetz A windmill with huge clappers which sounds like a carbine gun with a high-pitched whistle or shrill; used to frighten birds away.

Konsumwein (GERM) An ordinary wine; not be be confused with Tafelwein.

Kosher Salt *See* Coarse Salt.

Kräusening A fermentation process whereby new, actively fermenting beer is added to lager beer to encourage a complete fermentation and a natural carbonation.

L

Lagar (PORTUG) Large stone tanks into which boxes of grapes are dumped prior to crushing.

Lage (GERM) A small vineyard.

Lager Translated from the German word *lagern*, which means to store and is applied to bottom fermented beer in particular because it must be stored at low temperatures for prolonged periods of time.

Leaching Filtering of raw, newly distilled whiskey through a cistern or vat filled with finely ground and tamped-down charcoal.

Lees Dead yeast cells, pulp, skins, pits, and other solids that form on the bottom of a tank during fermentation.

Length Continuation of taste that lingers after swallowing.

Levure (FR) Wine yeast.

Light A pleasant, refreshing wine; opposite of full-bodied.

Likörwein (GERM) Dessert or sweet wine.

Limousin Oak (FR) Barrels which are made from wood grown in the Limousin forest and used for wine and cognac.

Liqueur Distilled spirits treated with fruits, aromatic herbs, flowers, juices, or other flavoring materials; contain at least 2½% sugar by weight. The words *cordial* and *liqueur* are interchangeable. *See* Cordial.

Liquor A word commonly used to mean distilled spirits.

Liquoroso (ITAL) A sweet wine that has been fortified by adding grape alcohol.

Liter A metric unit of liquid measurement equaling 1.0567 quarts or 33.814 ounces.

Loire Valley (FR) One of the six major wine-producing regions, located along the Loire River in north-central France.

Luscious Soft, sweet, fat, fruity. A word often used when referring to naturally sweet wines of extremely high sugar content, e.g., Sauternes, Trockenbeerenauslese.

M

Maderized A term applied to a wine that is past its prime, somewhat oxidized, and which has acquired a brownish tinge. Usually has a baked smell and flavor, reminiscent of Madeira wine.

Maduro (PORTUG) Old or matured.

Magnum A bottle size equivalent to 50.8 ounces of wine or champagne.

Make Love to a Blonde in a Black Skirt An expression used when drinking a pint of stout (a dark beer from Ireland). Using a stirrer, you carve the shape of a shamrock in the head of the stout. If the stout is fresh and you carve the figure correctly, you should be able to see the shamrock in the bottom of the glass in the remaining head when the stout is finished.

Malolactic Fermentation A bacteria fermentation which converts malic acid to lactic acid, thereby reducing the wine's acid level.

Malt Sprouted or germinated barley used in beer and spirit-making.

Manzanilla (SP) An extremely dry style of sherry wine.

Marc (FR) *See* Grappa.

Marie-Jeanne (FR) A bottle used in Bordeaux which contains approximately 84.53 ounces or about three regular-sized bottles.

Marque Déposée (FR) A registered trademark.

Mature A wine that has developed all of its characteristic qualities.

Mavro A Greek term for red wine.

May Wine A festive German wine which has woodruff herbs infused. *See* Waldmeister.

Mead A wine made from honey.

Medallions Tiny medallions embossed on necks of certain wine bottles or carafes. Originally Italian winemakers used lead medallions to certify the proper volume of a bottle. The glass version serves no official function today, except perhaps to provide a better grip.

Medio Seco (SP) Semidry.

Mellow A "soft" wine, often with some sweetness. Often used in reference to some red table wines from California.

Metabisulfite Sodium or potassium, used in wine making to produce sulfur dioxide, which is a sterilant and antioxidant.

Méthode Champenoise (FR) Fermented wine is bottled with yeast cells and sugar added to induce a secondary fermentation. When secondary fermentation is completed, wine is aged, and yeast sediment is removed by freezing the neck of the bottle thereby removing the crown cap and allowing internal pressure to force the sediment out. Additional champagne is added with some occasional sugar. The bottle is corked, aged, labeled, and sold.

Metodo Classico (ITAL) A sparkling wine that is made by the méthode champenoise method.

Mildew A serious fungal vine disease which must be treated with various fungicide sprays.

Millésime (FR) Harvest or vintage.

Milling The mechanical process by which whole grain is reduced to suitable size, with the outer cellulosic wall broken to expose more starch surface to the cooking and conversion of starch to sugars.

Mind Your P's and Q's In the old alehouses before cash registers were invented, there was a chalkboard where the barkeep would put chalk marks to keep track of how many "pints" (p's) and "quarts" (q's) you consumed. When you were ready to leave the pub, the barkeep would then add up the chalk marks and tell you how much you owed. To make sure that the barkeep remembered this task, the owner would often tell him to "Mind your p's and q's," then leave.

Mise en Bouteilles à la Propriété (FR) Bottled by the proprietor.

Mise en Bouteilles au Château (FR) Estate bottled.

Monopole (FR) A wine blended by a merchant-shipper and given a brand name.

Mousse (FR) The froth or foam on the surface of a glass of champagne or beer.

Moussec English term for a sparkling wine.

Mousseux (FR) A sparkling wine other than champagne.

Muddler A hardwood instrument, hand-held, which is used for crushing ice or fresh mint leaves.

Muffa Nobile (ITAL) *See* Botrytis Cinerea, Edelfäule, and Pourriture Noble.

Muscadine A native American grape variety indigenous to the south Atlantic states.

Muselet (FR) *See* Wire Hood.

Must, Mout, Moot, Mosto (ENG, FR, ITAL, SP) The unfermented grape juice, prior to fermentation. The term is derived from the Latin term mustum. *See* Stum Wine.

Musty An unpleasant odor or flavor. Similar to a mold smell, often due to an unclean cellar.

Mute (FR) Partially fermented wine in which fermentation has been halted, usually through the addition of brandy. Also a technique widely used in making aperitif wines.

Muté *See* Süssreserve.

N

Name Brand *See* Call Liquor.

Natural or Au Naturel Designation for bone dry; used on the labels of bottles of sparkling wine.

Naturrein, Naturwein (GERM) A natural wine, unsugared.

Négociant (FR) The individual or firm who produces and/or ships the wine.

Négociant-Éleveur (FR) A shipper who buys wine in barrels from growers, and then ages and bottles it in his or her own cellars.

Nero (ITAL) Black, as in a dark red wine.

Neutral Spirits Spirits, distilled from any material at or above 190 proof, which lack any distinctive taste, color, and odor—thus being neutral in character. These spirits are used for blending with straight whiskey and for making gin, vodka, and liqueurs.

Nip The British term for a quarter of a bottle; also the name of the smallest bottle in which champagne is sold (usually 6 ounces).

Noble Rot *See* Botrytis Cinerea.

Noggin An English measure equaling ¼ pint or 4 ounces.

Noncontrollable Costs or Expenses Costs or expenses that are generally fixed in nature in the short run, such as rent or interest. In this case, the manager cannot control them.

Nose The combination of aroma and bouquet.

Nouveau (FR) Literally, a new wine; used in conjunction with Beaujolais.

Nutty Term denoting the characteristic flavor of sherry.

N.V. The abbreviation for nonvintage dated wines.

O

Oaky The smell and/or taste of wines aged in small oak barrels. Delicate use of oak aging can add subtle complexity to full-bodied wines.

Ochoko Small porcelain cups traditionally used for serving sake. *See* Sakazuki.

Odor The odor of a wine; or simply, the way it smells.

Öechsle (GERM) A scale for measuring the sugar content of the grapes.

Oeil de Perdrix (FR) A wine that has a slight pinkish or copper tint in its color; translated, it means "eye of the partridge."

Öidium A grapevine disease characterized by a powdery film of spores that attacks and mildews the grapes.

Oily An attribute related to the presence of glycerine in a wine.

Oktoberfest (GERM) A beer festival held each year in Germany which begins at the end of September and lasts into the beginning of October. An estimated 1.2 million gallons of beer are consumed by 5 million visitors during this 16-day festival.

In 1810, when Prince Ludwig, the Crown Prince, married Theresia of Sachsen-Hildburghausen in Munich, his father Max Jospeh, the royal Wittelsbach of Bavaria, threw him a large and massive wedding. The party was so successful that the meadow where it was held was renamed "Theresia's Meadow." That tradition or party which actually started out as a wedding ceremony still continues to this day, and it is known as the Oktoberfest.

Oloroso (SP) A dark, semisweet, full-bodied sherry wine.

On the Rocks A mixed drink served over ice cubes.

On the Yeast The period during secondary fermentation when yeast cells are allowed to remain in contact with the wine, thereby contributing to the traditional "yeasty" nose of champagne. The process may last anywhere from three weeks to several years, depending on the producer.

Organoleptic The evaluation of wine by sight, smell, and taste.

Overproof A spirit whose alcoholic content is more than 100 proof.

Oxidation A chemical change in wine due to exposure of excessive oxygen which causes premature browning of the color and taste.

P

Par Stock The minimum/maximum amount of a product on hand to satisfy customers' needs for a specific period of time. Usually refers to the amount of alcoholic beverages needed during a shift or day at the bar.

Passé (FR) A wine which is past its prime of drinkability.

Passito (ITAL) A sweet wine made from grapes that have dried-up or shriveled from the sun, then pressed. *See* Roti.

Pasteurization The process in which wines are heated to sterilize them, thereby killing any organisms present.

Peg A small glass used for whiskey which holds the equivalent of about 1½ ounces. In England, it is a drink usually made with brandy and soda water.

Pelure d'Oignon (FR) A very light colored wine, similar to that of an onion skin.

Perlant (FR) Slightly sparkling wine, similar to pétillant.

Perlwein (GERM) *See* Sekt and Schaumwein.

Perry A sparkling wine, produced in England, which is made from pears.

Pétillant (FR) Slightly effervescent. *See* Crackling, Frizzante, and Spritzig.

Petit, Petite (FR) Small.

Pezsgo (HUN) Sparkling wine.

Phenolics *See* Tannin.

Phylloxera Vastatrix A root-louse pest which invaded and totally devastated Europe's vineyards during the 1870s.

Pichet (FR) Small, opaque decanter popular in restaurants.

Piece During the early 1800s, a term used to denote 250 bottles of wine.

Pinard (FR) Slang for an ordinary red wine.

Pinot The name of a great grape wine family. For example, Pinot Noir, Pinot Meunier, Pinot Bianco, Pinot Grigio, etc.

Pint A liquid measurement equal to 16 ounces.

Pith The bitter, white layer of a citrus fruit which lies directly beneath the outer skin.

Plonk A slang term for the lowest quality of wine.

Pomace The residual skins, stems, and pits remaining after the grapes have been pressed.

Pony Glass A small shot glass which holds approximately 1½ ounces.

Pot (FR) In Beaujolais, a bottle that contains approximately 16.90 ounces or a two-thirds bottle of wine.

Poteen, Potheen Illicit Irish whiskey, similar to moonshine.

pH Potential of hydrogen. A measurement of acid strength. The lower the pH, the stronger the acid. Premium wines usually register between 3.1 and 3.5 pH.

Pourriture Noble (FR) *See* Botrytis Cinerea, Edelfäule, and Muffa Nobile.

Powerful With a very strong bouquet and/or taste.

Pramnian An ancient Greek wine which was purportedly the favorite wine of Nestor.

Premier-Chauffe (FR) The first distillation in the making of cognac.

Premier Cru (FR) A first growth wine which refers specifically to the finest wines of Bordeaux and Burgundy.

Premium Brands Those brands of alcoholic beverages that are top quality, have brand recognition, are positioned well in a customer's mind, and generally command the highest prices. Also referred to as premium pour, super call, and top shelf.

Premium Pour *See* Premium Brands.

Press A machine by which direct pressure extracts the juice from the skins.

Preuve (FR) A small glass cup that is lowered into cognac barrels for a sample for evaluation and testing. *See* Chantepleure, Saggiavino, and Wine Thief.

Producido Por (SP) Produced and bottled by.

Produttori (ITAL) Producers.

Prohibition The Eighteenth Amendment went into effect January 16, 1920 (during the administration of President Woodrow Wilson, 1913–1921), and was repealed on December 5, 1933 (during the administration of President Franklin D. Roosevelt), by the Twenty-first Amendment. It was referred to by many as "The Noble Experiment."

From 1736 to 1742, the Gin Act, or Gin Prohibition was put into enforcement in England. From 1735 to 1742, in the state of Georgia, a prohibition against hard liquor was imposed. The heaviest drinking by Americans took place between 1790 and 1830, where the per capita consumption of absolute alcohol was 7.1 gallons per year. From 1908 to 1934 (26 years), there was a prohibition against drinking in Iceland, which is considered to be the longest in modern time. From 1914 to 1924, there was a prohibition against drinking in Russia.

Proof An old English term which was once called "gunpowder proof." To test the strength of the liquor, old-time distillers poured it on gunpowder or black powder and struck a match. If the liquor blazed up, it was too strong. Liquor at proper strength mixed with the powder would burn slowly in a blue flame. If it did not burn well, it was too high in water. Mixing 50% alcohol with 50% water gave a slow, steady flame. That strength was considered perfect and was called "100 proof." Today, the same scale is applied to the alcoholic content of spirits on the following basis: Pure 100% alcohol is 200 proof; 1 degree of proof is equal to ½% alcohol. Divide the proof by 2 and you get the percentage of alcohol in the bottle.

Proprietaire-Recoltant (FR) Owner or manager of a winery.

Proprietary Wine Wines carrying a made-up name originated by a specific winery or "proprietor." Essentially a brand name. For example, Blue Nun, Bell'Agio, Hearty Burgundy.

Pruning The removal of the excess portion of the vines to increase the vigor of the plant to produce finer quality grapes. It is generally performed during December through February.

Pubs English term for a bar where ale and lager are served.

Puckering A sensation noticed in the front of the mouth which is caused by an excess of tannin in a wine.

Pulcianelle (ITAL) *See* Toscanello.

Puncheon The name of the large barrel used in the West Indies which holds approximately 100 gallons of rum.

Punt The inverted bottom of a champagne bottle.

Pupîtres (FR) The name of the A-framed wooden racks that hold champagne bottles for "riddling," the shaking and turning of each bottle to move the sediment to the neck of the bottle.

Puttonyos (HUNG) Literally, the baskets which are used as a measurement to indicate the intensity and degree of sweetness of Tokay wine. It is on a 1 to 5 scale, with five Puttonyos being the sweetest.

Q

Quaff To drink beer or wine in large gulps.

Qualitätswein bestimmter Anbaugebiete (QbA) (GERM) Quality wine of designated areas of origin.

Qualitätswein mit Prädikat (GERM) The equivalent of France's Appellation Contrôlée wine laws, revised in 1971.

Quart A liquid measurement equal to 32 ounces.

Quinta (PORTUG) A wine estate or single vineyard designation.

R

Racking The process in which wine is carefully moved from one barrel to another in order to separate it from the lees or sediment. This helps to clarify the wine. *See* Soutirage.

Rancio (SP) A nutty flavor in a wine, often used to describe a sherrylike taste.

Rebêche (FR) The fourth pressing, which is not used for champagne making.

Recioto (ITAL) A special wine made from dried grapes. Unless accompanied by "Amarone," it will be semisweet to sweet.

Récolte (FR) Vintage or harvest.

Récolte Tardive (FR) Late-harvested, referring to the picking of the grapes in Alsace. *See* Vendange Tardive.

Remuage (FR) The process of removing the sediment by inverting and turning (riddling) champagne bottles for the eventual settling and collection of sediment in the bottle's neck. *See* Riddling.

Renault Wine Tonic During Prohibition, the Renault Winery of Egg Harbor City, New Jersey, produced a wine containing 22% alcohol and legally sold it in drug stores.

Reserva (PORTUG or SP) A wine which represents an exceptional harvest that has been set aside for extra long aging to develop a depth of character and delicacy of bouquet.

Reserve A term often found on wine labels which has no legal or real meaning.

Residual Sugar The measure of natural grape sugar left in the wine after fermentation. Sweetness is balanced by acidity creating a harmonious taste experience. Wines are often placed in three categories of sweetness: dry, medium-dry, and sweet. A wine below 0.8% is considered dry; between 0.8% and 2.2%, medium-dry; while wine with greater than 2.2% sugar is generally considered sweet. Sweetness is a function of style, not quality. Some rare and expensive sweet wines have sugar levels at high as 20, 25, and even 30%.

Retsina A Greek wine to which pine resin has been added for a unique flavor.

Riddling *See* Remuage.

Riserva (ITAL) A DOC wine with extra barrel aging at the winery.

Robust A full-bodied, mouth-filling wine.

Rosado (PORTUG or SP) Rosé wine.

Rosato (ITAL) Rosé wine.

Rosé Wine Wine, made from red grapes, which has a light pink color, acquired by only short contact with the skins.

Roseewein (GERM) Rosé wine.

Rosso (ITAL) Red wine.

Roti (FR) *See* Passito.

Rotwein (GERM) Red wine.

Rouge (FR) Red wine.

Rough A coarse or hard wine, immature, not well-balanced, or too as-tringent; usually of ordinary quality.

Rounded A taster's term meaning well-balanced with no major defects.

Rumbullion or Rumbustion A popular seventeenth-century term for rum, which originated either from the English or in the West Indies. A popular Colonial drink, called Rumfustian, was produced from rum, eggs, spices, and hot cider.

Rummy An old slang term used to describe a person that drank too much.

S

Saccharomyces The yeasts used in wine fermentation.

Sack An old English name, originating in Elizabethean England, to mean sherry wine of Spain.

Sacramental or Altar Wines Wines used during religious ceremonies of the mass and produced under the strictest regulations. These were per-mitted to be made during Prohibition.

Saggiavino (ITAL) Glass, stainless-steel, or plastic tube or cylinder used to extract samples of wine from a barrel. *See* Chantepleure, Preuve, and Wine Thief.

St. Bernard Those dogs which are usually identified with the carrying of a small keg of brandy or other spirits around their necks to give "relief and warmth" to stranded skiers in Scandinavian countries.

On the hit television show of the 1950s and 1960s, "Topper," which starred Leo G. Carroll, a St. Bernard dog named Neil was portrayed as a "martini-drinking" alcoholic, who often carried the small barrel of brandy around his neck.

Sake Colorless brewed alcoholic product made from rice and tradition-ally served warm in small cups. Sake is native to Japan, although it is produced in other parts of the world, including California.

Sakazuki *See* Ochoko.

Samogon Russian term for bootlegged vodka.

Sampanjac Yugoslavian term for sparkling wine.

Schaumwein (GERM) Sparkling wine. *See* Perlwein and Sekt.

Schloss (GERM) Equivalent for the French word *château*.

Schooner A tall drinking glass that holds about 15 ounces of beer.

Sec (FR) Dry, but when used on champagne or sparkling wine labels, indicates a semisweet sparkling wine.

Secco (ITAL) Dry.

Seco (PORTUG or SP) Dry.

Sediment The slow reaction and eventual precipitation of fruits, tannins, tartrates, pigments, and other compounds as the wine matures in the bottle. A brown deposit, known as sediment, settles on the side or bottom of the bottle.

Sekt (GERM) Latin from the word *siccus*, meaning dry. Used in Germany and Austria to denote a sparkling wine. *See* Perlwein and Schaumwein.

Set A term applied by viticulturists for the stage at which flowering is over and grape berries begin to form.

Sercial (PORTUG) The driest category of Madeira wine.

Shaft and Globe The name used by bottle collectors for long-necked wine bottles that were in existence in the early seventeenth century.

Shandy or Radlmass A drink in which beer is mixed with either lemonade or ginger beer. It is quite popular in England and Germany, where it is often consumed by cyclists.

Shooter Slang term for a shot of liquor.

Shot Glass A small glass holding approximately 1½ ounces of liquor.

Silky Wines that are significantly smooth and finely textured.

Simple Sugar or Syrup A syrup made by dissolving sugar into warm water.

Singlings Brandy after the first distillation and prior to the second distillation.

Sling A mixed drink for which a mug is filled with two-thirds strong beer and sweetened with sugar, molasses, or dried pumpkin. Rum is then added to this mixture and stirred with a loggerhead.

Slurry Mashed apples; used in the making of apple brandy.

Smash Short drink made from brandy, bourbon, or other distilled spirits, mixed with sugar and mint. Another name for a small mint julep.

Smell Olfactory sensation noticed directly by the nose; to be distinguished from aroma.

Soft Pleasant smoothness of wine with low astringency.

Solera Date (SP) The date which appears on the label of some sherries identifies the year the solera "was established" and has nothing to do with when the grapes were harvested or when the sherry was bottled. If, for example, a sherry from the firm of Pedro Domecq states on the label, Solera 1908, this means that the solera was established in 1908. And the chances of having any of the wine remaining in the current system is quite remote.

Sommelier (FR) A wine waiter who usually carries around his or her neck a cellar key and wine-tasting cup on a silver chain.

Sound A wine which is pleasant to look at, good smelling, and good tasting.

Sour A disagreeable tart sensation; acid and vinegary, indicating a spoiled, undrinkable wine.

Soutirage (FR) *See* Racking.

Sparkling wine Wine with effervescence exceeding 2.7 atmospheres of pressure; produced by a secondary fermentation in a closed container or stoppered bottle.

Spätlese (GERM) Late-picking or harvesting of the grapes. The date is not as important as the degree of ripeness of the berries.

Sparkolloid *See* Bentonite.

Speakeasy Applied to illicit saloons in New York City in 1899 (which pre-dated Prohibition). Speakeasies served alcoholic beverages only to persons who would appear at the door and softly speak the password in order to enter.

Speed Pour A pouring device inserted into the neck of a bottle of distilled spirits which aids in its dispensing.

Speed Rack or Rail A stainless steel rack directly in front of a bartender which contains bottles of distilled spirits or mixes which have the greatest consumer demand.

Splash A measurement containing a small amount of an ingredient added to a drink.

Splice the Main Brace An old navy term meaning to drink whiskey. The term often appears in Herman Melville's writings.

Split A small wine or champagne bottle containing about 6.4 ounces.

Spritzer A tall drink made with a base of wine (white, red or rosé) and filled with a carbonated mixer.

Spritzig (GERM) Slightly effervescent. *See* Crackling, Frizzante, and Pétillant.

Spumante (ITAL) Sparkling wine.

Staatsweingut (GERM) State wine estate.

Stable A wine is said to be stable if there is no chance of refermentation taking place.

Steely A tasting term used to describe wines that are hard and occasionally even tart, while displaying a good level of acidity. The wines of Chablis, France are often called steely.

Stemmy The flavor of those wines which have been fermented too long in the presence of stems.

Still Apparatus used to concentrate beverage spirits. Stills may be classified by method of introducing fermented mixture.

Stillage The residue in the still after distillation of the alcohol. It is drawn off for making distillers feed.

Still Wine Nonsparkling table wine.

Stravecchio (ITAL) A very old wine or brandy.

Stum Wine Unfermented grape juice. *See* Must.

Style Originates in the winemaker's vision of the grape's potential expression. Wine styles vary because of the diversity and intensity of aromas and flavors, the wine emphasis (fruit or wood predominating in the aroma or flavor), and balance (toward tannin, acidity, or sweetness). Winemakers affect style by their selection of grapes, vineyard management techniques and winemaking methods, and equipment.

Sugaring of Wine *See* Chaptalization.

Sulfur Dioxide A naturally appearing substance used worldwide as an antioxidant, which also kills bacteria. Often used as a sterilizing agent.

Super Call *See* Premium Brands.

Superiore (ITAL) A higher alcohol (therefore, superior quality) style of a DOC wine.

Supple Smoothness and softness on the palate; acidity and alcohol are balanced.

Süssreserve (GERM) Prior to fermentation, some of the unfermented juice, which is high in natural sugar, is filtered and held under refrigeration until after the fermentation is complete. At this point, a small amount of this sugar-rich juice, called "mute" (in California) is then added back to the wine to add a sweet flavor.

Sweet Presence of sugar to the taste in wines, cordials, etc.

Swizzle Stick Another name for a drink stirrer.

Symposium In ancient Greece (around 400 B.C.), a social-drinking gathering during which individuals expressed judgment and compared wines of similar origin, while simultaneously creating a glossary for the less knowledgeable.

Szemelt (HUN) *See* Auslese.

T

Table Wine A still wine which contains 7 to 14% alcohol.

Tafelwein (GERM) Table wine.

Taglio (ITAL) A blended wine.

Tailles (FR) The second and third pressing of the grapes used to make champagne.

Tails In brandy making, elements that have the highest boiling points and which vaporize last.

Tall A drink prepared in a larger-than-usual glass, which permits the addition of more mix.

Tankard A tall, one-handled drinking vessel with a lid used for serving beer; usually made of pewter or silver.

Tannin A group of bitter compounds better known as phenolics. The group consists of pits, stems, skins, and extracts from the wooden barrel. It is quite astringent and causes a puckering sensation in the front of your mouth.

Tart Sharp, astringent taste of fruit acid. When present in a moderate amount, tartness lends a pleasant freshness to a wine.

Tartar More precisely named "cream of tartar," tartar is a crystalline material which settles to the bottom of wine containers after a wine has been stored cold for several days. *See* Cold Stabilization, Tartaric Acid.

Tartaric Acid The principal natural acid found in grapes and wine. Tartaric acid often occurs in such high levels in wine grapes that it crystallizes out as cream of tartar when the wine is chilled.

Tastevin (FR) A small saucerlike silver cup used by a sommelier to examine wine prior to its being served.

Tawny Brownish colored. A term applied to ports and other red wines which have a brownish or golden tinge, instead of the customary ruby, which results from the loss of pigment by oxidation and during long aging, filtering, or fining.

Tenuta Vinicola (ITAL) A wine estate, similar to a château.

Terroir (FR) A wine that is earthy tasting or which has a taste of the earth.

Thin Lacking body; watery, light.

Tinto (PORTUG or SP) Red wine.

Tirage or Liqueur de Tirage (FR) The sugar or sweetener added to still wine to induce yeast cells to begin secondary fermentation, producing a sparkling wine.

Tischwein (GERM) A common or ordinary wine.

Tokkuri The name of the decanter that is traditionally used for the heating of sake.

Tonsil Paint In the old western movies, the name given to whiskey by cowboys.

Top Hat A slang term or phrase denoting a container of beer (usually made of white cardboard with a waxed inner lining) much like a take-out container which is taken out of a bar for future drinking.

Top Shelf *See* Premium Pour.

Toscanello (ITAL) A squat-shaped bottle, which is also called "pulcianelle," used for Orvieto wine from Umbria.

Trade Buyer Any wholesaler or retailer of distilled spirits, wine, or malt beverages.

Transfer Method or Transvasage To produce sparkling wine. After secondary fermentation is completed in the bottle, wine is passed through a filter to remove sediment and then transferred to another bottle, which saves having to manually remove sediment, as in méthode champenoise.

Tren (SP) A bottling line used in preparation for shipping.

Trocken (GERM) Dry.

Trockenbeerenauslese (GERM) Wine made from grapes that are raisin in shape and very high in sugar density. Extremely rich and luscious.

U

Ullage The space in a bottle between the top of the wine and bottom of the cork. Also used as a substitute word for head space.

Uva (ITAL & SP) Grape.

V

Vappa (ITAL) A wine that has turned to vinegar.

Varietal A wine made wholly or predominantly from a single grape variety, named on the label. For example, Cabernet Sauvignon, Chardonnay, Zinfandel.

Varietal Character The specific and unique combination of odor, taste, and sometimes tactile impression of a wine which is directly attributed to the source grape variety.

Vat English word for a tub or barrel.

Vecchio (ITAL) Old.

Veldt, Veltes (FR) A now extinct unit of measurement which was used in cognac, contained approximately 2 gallons (27 veldts equaled a cognac cask of 205 liters; 35 veldts equaled 72 U.S. gallons).

Velvety Related to silky and smooth, but connotes more opulence.

Vendange (FR) Vintage or harvest.

Vendange Tardive (FR) *See* Récolte Tardive.

Vendemmia (ITAL) Vintage or harvest. *See* Annata.

Vendimia (SP) Vintage or harvest. *See* Cosecha.

Venencia (SP) The name of the special cup that has a flexible whalebone handle with a silver cup at one end and a decorative hook, also of solid silver, at the other end. This cup is plunged into the barrel and immediately filled with sherry wine. It is then removed and poured into several glasses from a height of perhaps 12 to 18 inches.

Veraison (FR) The stage when the grape changes from green to its red color, but before it reaches final maturity.

Verdelho (PORTUG) Semidry Madeira wine.

Vid (SP) Grape or grapevine.

Vigneron (FR) A combination winemaker and grape grower.

Vignoble (FR) Vineyard.

Vin (FR) Wine.

Vin de Cuvée (FR) Wine made from the first pressing of the grapes in Champagne.

Vin de Pays (FR) Country wine; used to describe small wines of each region that are consumed locally.

Vin de Primeur (FR) Wines which mature and are drunk very young.

Vin Ordinaire (FR) An ordinary, everyday wine below the VDQS level of quality.

Vin Rosé (FR) Rosé wine.

Viña, Viñedo (SP) Vineyard.

Vinha (PORTUG) Vineyard.

Vinho (PORTUG) Wine.

Vinho de Consumo (PORTUG) Ordinary wine.

Vinho de Mesa (PORTUG) Table wine.

Vinho do Rodo (PORTUG) Sparkling wine.

Vinho Liquoroso (PORTUG) Fortified wine.

Viniculture The art and science of winemaking.

Vinification The entire process of turning grapes into wine, including crushing/destemming, fermenting, pressing, aging, bottling, etc.

Vino (ITAL) Wine.

Vino Corriente (SP) An ordinary wine.

Vino de Pasto (SP) An ordinary table wine.

Vino da Tavola (ITAL) Table wine.

Vino de Cosecha Propia (SP) Estate bottled.

Vino de Mesa (SP) Table wine.

Vino Novello (ITAL) A new or freshly fermented wine similar to Beaujolais Nouveau of France. *See* Federweisser.

Vino Tipico (ITAL) An emerging category of wines which will be one step below the DOC level.

Vinous Pertaining to wine.

Vins Délimités de Qualité Supérieure (VDQS) (FR) First used on December 18, 1949.

Vintage The harvesting of grapes and the making of wine; the wine produced in a given year, with the date of that year shown on the label. A season of unusually favorable growing conditions is called a "vintage year" and is said to produce "vintage wines" connotating a very good year.

Vintage Wine Wine from a single year named on the label, rather than a blend from several years.

Vintner A winemaker.

Virgin Any drink which is prepared without the addition of an alcoholic beverage.

Viticultural Area A delimited grape-growing region distinguished by geographic features and federally approved (United States).

Viticulture Cultivation of the vine; science or study of the production of the grapes. Also called viniculture when applied to the growing of grapes for wine.

Vitis Grapevine.

Vitis Labrusca A species of grapevines native to North America.

Vitis Riparia A species of grapevines native to North America.

Vitis Rotundifolia A species of grapevines native to North America and grown predominately in the south Atlantic states.

Vitis Rupestris A species of grapevines native to North America.

Vitis Vinifera European grapevine species considered by many to be the premium grapes in winemaking; e.g., Chardonnay, Cabernet Sauvignon, etc.

Vorosbor (HUN) Red wine.

W

Waldmeister or Woodruff (GERM) The very special wild herb used to make May wine; technically known as "Asperula Odorata," of the Madder family. May wine is quite enjoyable when slightly chilled or served from a punch bowl with fresh strawberries.

Weeper Describes a bottle of wine that shows leakage around the cork due to either poor storage or a faulty cork.

Wein (GERM) Wine.

Weinbau (GERM) Viticulture.

Weinberg (GERM) Vineyard.

Weingut (GERM) Wine estate.

Weingütesiegel Osterreich (AUS) The seal of quality which appears on labels of Austrian wines.

Weinkeller (GERM) Wine cellar.

Weinlese (GERM) Harvest or vintage.

Weinprobe (GERM) Wine tasting.

Weisswein (GERM) White wine.

Well-Balanced When the many odors, flavors, and tastes are in perfect harmony with each other.

Well Brands House brands with little name recognition; generally lower in quality and price. Used when customers ask for generic drinks. *See* House Brands or Bar Brands.

Wet County Counties permitting the sale of alcoholic beverages by the drink and "by package" (e.g., in liquor stores, convenience stores, etc.), or by package only. *See* Dry County.

Whistle-Belly Vengeance A drink made from sour beer, molasses, and crusts of brown bread. It was popular in the United States during the late 1600s and early 1700s.

Wine Thief Glass, stainless-steel, or plastic tube or cylinder used to extract samples of wine from a barrel. *See* Chantepleure, Preuve, and Saggiavino.

Wino A slang term used to describe a person who is addicted to cheap wine and is often an alcoholic.

Winzergenossenschaft (GERM) Co-op of wine grape growers.

Winzerverein (GERM) Producers co-op.

Wire Hood The wire which holds sparkling wine and champagne corks in place, which must be twisted counterclockwise to remove from the bottle. *See* Muselet.

Woody Characteristic odor of wine aged in wooden cooperage for an extended period. Smells somewhat like wet wood.

Worm On a corkscrew, the piece that is inserted into the cork. *See* Bore.

Wort The liquid that remains after grinding and mashing the malt and other cereals, which is then boiled with hops before being fermented into beer.

X

Xampan The Catalonian term for a sparkling wine.

Y

Yard of Ale An elongated drinking glass, measuring approximately 36 inches in length and containing 42 ounces of ale. It was used primarily in England during the seventeenth and eighteenth centuries in roadside taverns or pubs, where keepers kept them close to the door so that small "pint-sized" waitresses could easily pass up a cold ale to stagecoach drivers who were required to stay aboard to contain the horses.

Yard of Flannel A recipe which is a reputed remedy for colds. It is made by mixing ale with eggs, brown sugar, and nutmeg. It is then served at a rather warm temperature.

Yayin The biblical term related to "vinum" for wine.

Yeast A minute living organism which brings about fermentation in wine by converting the sugar to roughly equal parts of ethyl alcohol and carbon dioxide.

Z

Zest The outer layer of a citrus fruit which contains the coloring and essence of oils. Used in cooking and certain alcoholic drink recipes.

Zinfandel Club An informal wine club located in London, England, founded in October 1976.

Zwickel A device, similar to a spigot on a wine barrel, which enables the brewmaster to sample the aging beer for evaluation purposes.

Zwickle A bung tap used to loosen or tighten bungs on a barrel.

Zymase A by-product of yeast that is used to convert sugar into alcohol.

Suggested Reading

Pogash, Jeffrey M. *How to Read a Wine Label.* New York: Hawthorn Books, 1978.

Metric Conversions for Weights and Measures

LITERS TO GALLONS CONVERSION TABLE

Liters	Gallons	Liters	Gallons	Liters	Gallons
1	0.3	34	9.0	67	17.7
2	0.5	35	9.2	68	18.0
3	0.8	36	9.5	69	18.2
4	1.1	37	9.8	70	18.5
5	1.3	38	10.0	71	18.8
6	1.6	39	10.3	72	19.0
7	1.8	40	10.6	73	19.3
8	2.1	41	10.8	74	19.6
9	2.4	42	11.1	75	19.8
10	2.6	43	11.4	76	20.1
11	2.9	44	11.6	77	20.3
12	3.2	45	11.9	78	20.6
13	3.4	46	12.2	79	20.9
14	3.7	47	12.4	80	21.1
15	4.0	48	12.7	81	21.4
16	4.2	49	12.9	82	21.7
17	4.5	50	13.2	83	21.9
18	4.8	51	13.5	84	22.2
19	5.0	52	13.7	85	22.5
20	5.3	53	14.0	86	22.7
21	5.5	54	14.3	87	23.0
22	5.8	55	14.5	88	23.2
23	6.1	56	14.8	89	23.5
24	6.3	57	15.0	90	23.8
25	6.6	58	15.3	91	24.0
26	6.9	59	15.6	92	24.3
27	7.1	60	15.9	93	24.6
28	7.4	61	16.1	94	24.8

LITERS TO GALLONS CONVERSION TABLE (continued)

Liters	Gallons	Liters	Gallons	Liters	Gallons
29	7.7	62	16.4	95	25.1
30	7.9	63	16.6	96	25.4
31	8.2	64	16.9	97	25.6
32	8.5	65	17.2	98	25.9
33	8.7	66	17.4	99	26.1
				100	26.4

For a more precise conversion: 1 liter = 0.26418 gallons and 1 gallon = 3.7853 liters

CAPACITY MEASURE

1 milliliter	= 0.001 liters	=	0.0338 fluid ounces
10 milliliters	= 1 centiliter	=	0.3381 fluid ounces
50 milliliters		=	1.7 fluid ounces
100 milliliters	= 10 centiliters	=	3.3814 fluid ounces
10 centiliters	= 1 deciliter	=	3.3814 fluid ounces
167 milliliters		=	6.3 fluid ounces
187 milliliters		=	6.76 fluid ounces
200 milliliters		=	6.8 fluid ounces
375 milliliters		=	12.7 fluid ounces
750 milliliters		=	25.4 fluid ounces
1000 milliliters	= 100 centiliters*	=	33.814 fluid ounces
10 deciliters	= 1 liter	=	1.0567 liquid quarts
1.5 liters		=	50.7 fluid ounces
1.75 liters		=	59.2 fluid ounces
3 liters		=	101.4 fluid ounces
4 liters		=	135.2 fluid ounces
10 liters	= 1 decaliter	=	2.64 gallons
10 decaliters	= 1 hectoliter	=	26.418 gallons†
10 hectoliters	= 1 kiloliter	=	264.18 gallons

* Or 1 liter or 10 deciliters.

† Or 11.111 cases of twelve 750-milliliter bottles.

APPROXIMATE CONVERSION FACTORS

To change	To	Multiply by
Inches	Millimeters	25.0
Millimeters	Inches	0.04
Inches	Centimeters	2.540
Centimeters	Inches	0.394
Feet	Centimeters	30.0
Feet	Meters	0.305
Meters	Feet	3.280
Yards	Meters	0.914
Meters	Yards	1.094
Miles	Kilometers	1.609
Kilometers	Miles	0.621
Square inches	Square centimeters	6.451
Square centimeters	Square inches	0.155
Square feet	Square meters	0.093
Square meters	Square feet	10.764
Square yards	Square meters	0.836
Square meters	Square yards	1.196
Square miles	Square kilometers	2.590
Square kilometers	Square miles	0.386
Acres	Square hectometers	0.405
Square hectometers	Acres	2.471
Acres	Hectares	2.471
Hectares	Acres	0.405
Cubic feet	Cubic meters	0.028
Cubic meters	Cubic feet	35.315
Cubic yards	Cubic meters	0.765
Cubic meters	Cubic yards	1.308
Fluid ounces	Milliliters	29.573
Milliliters	Fluid ounces	0.034
Liters	Fluid ounces	33.81
Fluid ounces	Liters	0.0296
Pints	Liters	0.473
Liters	Pints	2.113
Quarts	Liters	0.846
Liters	Quarts	1.057
Gallons	Liters	3.785*
Liters	Gallons	0.26418
Ounces	Grams	28.349
Grams	Ounces	0.035
Pounds	Kilograms	0.454
Kilograms	Pounds	2.205
Miles per gallon	Kilometers per liter	0.425
Kilometers per liter	Miles per gallon	2.354

APPROXIMATE CONVERSION FACTORS (continued)

To change	To	Multiply by
Miles per hour	Kilometers per hour	1.609
Kilometers per hour	Miles per hour	0.621

* *Or* divide the number of gallons by 0.26418.

The two charts that follow give approximations of figures.

LIQUID CONVERSIONS

		Milliliter(s)	Ounce(s)	Pint(s)	Quart(s)	Liter(s)	Gallon(s)
1 Milliliter	=	1	29.6	473.2	946.3	1000	3785
1 Ounce	=	0.0338	1	16	32	33.81	128
1 Pint	=	0.0021	0.0625	1	2	2.1134	8
1 Quart	=	0.0011	0.0312	0.5000	1	1.0567	4
1 Liter	=	0.0010	0.0296	0.4732	0.9463	1	3.7853
1 Gallon	=	0.0003	0.0078	0.125	0.25	0.264	1

WEIGHT CONVERSIONS

		Grain(s)	Gram(s)	Ounce(s)*	Pound(s)*
1 Grain	=	1	15.43	437.5	7000
1 Gram	=	0.0648	1	28.35	453.6
1 Ounce*	=	0.0023	0.0353	1	16
1 Pound*	=	0.00014	0.0021	0.0625	1

* Avoirdupois weight.

WEIGHTS

1 grain	=	64.79 milligrams		
10 milligrams	=	1 centigram	=	0.1543 grains
10 centigrams	=	1 decigram	=	1.5432 grains
10 decigrams	=	1 gram	=	15.432 grains*
27.34 grains	=	1 dram	=	1.772 grams
16 drams	=	1 ounce	=	28.3495 grams†
10 grams	=	1 decagram	=	0.3527 ounces
10 decagrams	=	1 hectogram	=	3.5274 ounces
10 hectograms	=	1 kilogram	=	2.2046 pounds‡
1 pound	=	16 ounces	=	0.4536 kilograms§
10 kilograms	=	1 myriagram	=	22.046 pounds
10 myriagrams	=	1 quintal‖	=	220.46 pounds
10 quintals	=	1 metric ton	=	2,204.62 pounds#
1 piece	=	205 liters	=	55 gallons

* *Or 0.03527 ounces or 0.001 kilograms or 1000 milligrams.*

† *Or 437.5 grains.*

‡ *Or 35.3 ounces.*

§ *Or 7000 grains or 453.59 grams.*

‖ *Or 100 kilograms.*

Or 1000 kilograms.

LENGTH AND DISTANCE

1 inch	= 25.4 millimeters	= 2.54 centimeters	= 0.0254 meters
1 foot	= 304.9 millimeters	= 30.48 centimeters	= 0.3049 meters
1 yard	= 0.9144 meters		
1 millimeter	= 0.03937 inches		
1 centimeter	= 0.3937 inches		
1 meter	= 1.0936 yards	= 3.281 feet	= 39.37 inches
1 hectometer	= 328.0833 feet		
1 kilometer	= 0.62137 miles		
1 mile	= 5,280 feet	= 1,609 meters	= 1.6093 kilometers

OTHER MEASUREMENTS

1 barrel of beer	= 31 gallons	= 13.8 cases of 12-ounce cans or bottles
½ barrel of beer	= 15.5 gallons	= 1 keg
¼ barrel of beer	= 7.75 gallons	= ½ keg
⅛ barrel of beer	= 3.88 gallons	= ¼ keg
1 case of twelve 750-milliliter bottles	= 2.376 gallons *or* 9 liters	
1 dash	= ¹⁄₄₈ fluid ounces *or* ⅙ teaspoon	= 6 to 8 drops
20 dashes	= 1 fluid ounce	
1 orange	= 6 to 7 tablespoons of juice	
1 lemon	= 3 tablespoons of juice	
1 barrique*	= 59.4 gallons of wine	
1 tonneau	= 4 barriques	= 237.8 gallons of wine

* A very common barrel used in Bordeaux, France.

To convert wine grape acreage into potential cases of wine, use this formula:

Tons per acre $\times$ gallons per ton $\div$ by 2.3 = cases of 750-milliliter bottles per acre

For table wines, assume 160 to 165 gallons per ton; for dessert wines, 90.

TEMPERATURE

Celsius	Fahrenheit	Celsius	Fahrenheit
100.0	212.0	27.8	82.0
97.2	207.0	25.0	77.0
95.0	203.0	22.2	72.0
94.4	202.0	20.0	68.0
91.7	197.0	19.4	67.0
90.0	194.0	16.7	62.0
88.9	192.0	15.0	59.0
86.1	187.0	13.9	57.0
85.0	185.0	11.1	52.0
83.3	182.0	10.0	50.0
80.5	177.0	8.3	47.0
80.0	176.0	5.5	42.0
77.8	172.0	5.0	41.0
75.0	167.0	2.8	37.0
72.2	162.0	0.0	32.0
70.0	158.0	− 2.8	27.0
69.4	157.0	− 5.0	23.0
66.7	152.0	− 5.5	22.0
65.0	149.0	− 8.3	17.0

TEMPERATURE (continued)

Celsius	Fahrenheit	Celsius	Fahrenheit
63.9	147.0	−10.0	14.0
61.1	142.0	−11.1	12.0
60.0	140.0	−13.9	7.0
58.3	137.0	−15.0	5.0
55.5	132.0	−16.0	3.0
55.0	131.0	−17.0	2.0
52.8	127.0	−18.0	−1.0
50.0	122.0	−19.0	−3.0
47.2	117.0	−20.0	−4.0
45.0	113.0	−21.0	−6.0
44.4	112.0	−22.0	−8.0
41.7	107.0	−23.0	−10.0
40.0	104.0	−24.0	−12.0
38.9	102.0	−25.0	−15.0
36.1	97.0	−26.0	−16.0
35.0	95.0	−27.0	−17.0
33.3	92.0	−28.0	−19.0
30.5	87.0		
30.0	86.0		

To convert Fahrenheit into Celsius, subtract 32 from the Fahrenheit temperature, then divide by 1.8; *or* subtract 32 from Fahrenheit, then multiply by 0.55.

To convert Celsius into Fahrenheit, multiply the Celsius temperature by 1.8 and then add 32; *or* divide Celsius by 0.55, then add 32.

Note: 212° F is equivalent to 100° C.
90° F is equivalent to 32.2° C.
32° F is equivalent to 0° C.

CONVERSION TABLE FOR SUGARS

Baumé is the term used in France to measure the level of unfermented sugar present in the must. To determine Brix, take degrees Baumé and multiply by 1.8. To determine Baumé, take degrees Brix and divide by 1.8

Brix or *Balling* is the term used in the United States to measure the level of unfermented sugar present in the must.

Essenz is the term used in Hungary to measure the level of unfermented sugar present in the must.

Gluco-oenometer is the name of the device used to measure the unfermented sugar in the must for the production of Portuguese port wine.

Öechsle is a term derived from Ferdinand Öechsle (1774–1852), a chemist in the early nineteenth century, who lived in the town of Pforzheim in Baden, Germany. He devised the method used to measure the level of sugar present in the must.

Öechsle is a measurement of the specific gravity of must (it refers to the number of grams by which 1 liter of grape must is heavier than 1 liter of water). Each quality category of German wine (Spätlese, Auslese, etc.) has to have a certain minimum Öechsle level to justify its title. When you divide by 8, you get the future alcoholic content of the wine. You must remember, however, that it includes the sweetness of unfermented sugar of a Spätlese or Auslese wine. Therefore, the actual alcoholic strength is likely to be less, since part of the sugar remains in the wine as unfermented residual sugar. To determine *Brix*, take Öechsle, divide by 4 and subtract 1. To determine Öechsle, take *Brix*, add 1 and multiply by 4.

Klosterneuburg (KMW for Klosterneuburg Mostwaage Scale) is the term used in Austria to measure the level of unfermented sugar present in the must; the KMW was devised by Freiherr von Babo. One degree KMW = 5 degrees Öechsle. To determine *Brix*, multiply KMW degrees by 1.25. To determine KMW degrees, divide *Brix* by 1.25.

APPENDIX C

Vintage Charts

The purpose of vintage reports, charts, and guides is to give retailers, restaurateurs, and consumers an indication as to how a particular vintage or growing season progressed, and what the final outcome was relative to the quantity and quality of the grapes harvested.

Just saying that the "19—" vintage was very good, great, or poor is not enough and is a general blanket statement simply because questions that should follow would be, where and in which country?

As an example, let's pick France. The first logical question would be, in which region of France (there are six major ones)? The next question could be (if we selected the region of Bordeaux), in which district, the Medoc or St. Émilion? The following question would be, red or white, sweet or dry? As you can see in today's wine drinking society, we must be more specific when dealing with vintages.

Vintage charts are actually "generalizations" of a specific wine-growing region, and most charts don't take into consideration the region, when the grapes were harvested, climate (the combination of sunshine, temperature, and precipitation), various microclimates, or the expertise of the individual winemaker. Therefore, the numbers used on a vintage chart represent broad-range averages or estimations. Some mediocre wines have been made in great years and excellent wines produced in moderate to poor years.

Another problem inherent in vintage charts is that most of them list vintage years for wines which are well past their prime and even possibly completely undrinkable. The problem that arises when listing older vintages is the lack of availability at either the wholesale or retail level.

A vintage guide is just that—a guide—and should *not* be accepted as the final word or quoted with biblical authority regarding a particular vintage.

An excellent book on the subject of great wines, which also contains extensive tasting notes back to the 1700s, has been written by Michael Broadbent, a master of wine. Mr. Broadbent is perhaps the foremost authority in the world on old wines. The book, *Great Vintage Wine Book*, was published by Alfred Knopf in 1980.

The vintage ratings contained in this book are based on a scale of 1 to 10, with 10 being the highest rating.

10 = Very great	4–5 = Fair
9 = Great	3 = Poor
7–8 = Very good	1–2 = Very poor
6 = Good	0 = Useless

The symbol (—), when appearing in the tables that follow, indicates the wine is probably too old for consumption.

Major Wine-Producing Areas of the World

Austria

Only the white wines of Austria are rated in this chart. Vintages older than 1979 should be avoided with the possible exception of late-harvested grapes, which produce wines such as Spätlese, Auslese, Beerenauslese, Trockenbeerenauslese, and Eiswein.

Year	Rating
1985	8
1984	7
1983	8
1982	6
1981	6
1980	6
1979	8

France

Alsace. Most of the wine produced in Alsace is white (90 percent) and, with the exception of late-harvested Gewürztraminer or White Riesling, should be consumed within four years of the vintage date. The ratings are for white wines only.

Year	Rating
1986	8
1985	10
1984	5
1983	10
1982	7
1981	8
1980	4
1979	8

Great vintages: 1976, 1973, 1971, 1970, 1967, 1966, 1961, 1959, 1947, 1945.

Beaujolais. Beaujolais, which appears on the retail shelves some two months after the vintage, is known as "Beaujolais Nouveau." It is best enjoyed within one year after harvest.

Other types of Beaujolais, such as Beaujolais-Villages and the Grand Crus, can be aged for about five to seven years. Older than that, you are taking a chance that the wine is probably "over-the-hill."

Year	Rating
1986	7
1985	10
1984	6
1983	8
1982	6
1981	8
1980	5

Great vintages: 1976, 1971, 1969, 1961, 1959, 1949, 1945, 1929, 1928.

Bordeaux. Generally speaking, in good to great years, these are the red wines of France to lay away. Most of them generally last 7 to 10 years, and the very best will last 25 to 30 years and possibly longer, depending on the vintage.

The dry white wines produced today are for current consumption; many receive little or no barrel age. These are best consumed up to five years old.

Sauternes usually don't begin reaching maturity until they are at least 10 years old. The better quality Sauternes should easily last 15 to 20 years, and if produced in a great year, 30 to 40 years or more is possible.

Year	Red	White dry	White sweet (Sauternes)
1986	8	7	9
1985	9	8	7
1984	5	5	6
1983	9	8	10
1982	9	10	8
1981	8	8	9
1980	6	—	7
1979	6	—	8
1978	9	—	7
1977	6	—	6
1976	7	—	8
1975	9	—	9
1974	6	—	6
1973	6	—	6
1972	5	—	6
1971	8	—	9
1970	9	—	9
1969	5	—	7
1968	4	—	2
1967	7	—	9
1966	9	—	7
1965	3	—	3
1964	8	—	6
1963	3	—	3
1962	7	—	9
1961	10	—	9
1960	5	—	4
1959	9	—	9
1958	7	—	7
1957	7	—	5
1956	3	—	4
1955	9	—	9
1954	5	—	4
1953	8	—	7
1952	8	—	7
1951	1	—	4
1950	7	—	8

Great vintages (red wine): 1948, 1947, 1945, 1934, 1929, 1928.

(white dry wine): 1975, 1971, 1970, 1967, 1966, 1964, 1962, 1961, 1959, 1955, 1953, 1952, 1949, 1947, 1945, 1937, 1929, 1928.

(white sweet wine—Sauternes): 1947, 1945, 1937, 1929, 1928, 1926, 1921, 1919, 1908, 1904, 1901, 1900.

Burgundy. Most of the red burgundies produced today are not vinified for long aging; a smart consumer would be wise not to put away large stocks of these wines.

With the exception of very good to great vintages, don't purchase white burgundies prior to 1978 and red burgundies prior to 1976.

Year	Red Burgundy	White Burgundy	Chablis
1986	7	9	9
1985	9	9	9
1984	5	5	7
1983	9	8	10
1982	8	8	8
1981	7	7	7
1980	6	6	6
1979	6	6	8
1978	8	—	10
1977	5	—	—
1976	10	—	—
1975	5	—	—
1974	7	—	—
1973	7	—	—
1972	7	—	—
1971	10	—	—
1970	8	—	—
1969	10	—	—
1968	3	—	—
1967	5	—	—
1966	9	—	—
1965	3	—	—
1964	9	—	—
1963	4	—	—
1962	8	—	—
1961	9	—	—
1960	4	—	—
1959	10	—	—

Great vintages (red wines): 1949, 1947, 1945, 1937, 1934, 1929, 1928, 1926, 1923, 1921, 1900.

(white wines): 1976, 1971, 1969, 1967, 1966, 1962, 1955, 1953, 1952, 1949, 1947, 1928, 1921. White burgundies do last longer than other white wines because most of them are barrel fermented and aged.

Champagne. For years, champagne producers, importers, writers, and others have presented vintage charts for various vintages of champagne, informing you of such great vintages as 1921, 1943, 1955, 1965, 1969, etc. Unfortunately, you are not informed that champagne is at its best within 10 years of the vintage date. For example, a 1969 Dom Pérignon was at its best until 1979, then it started to slowly decline in quality. Exceptions do occur; however, as a general rule for both consuming and purchasing, stay away from vintage-dated sparkling wines and champagnes more than 10 years past their vintage date, and always try to purchase the newest vintage possible.

Loire Valley. The wines of the Loire Valley are predominantly white (75 percent), and with the exception of Pouilly Fume and some sweet Vouvray, should be consumed within four years of the vintage date. The ratings are for white wines only.

Year	Rating
1986	8
1985	10
1984	7
1983	9
1982	8
1981	8

Great vintages: 1978, 1976, 1975, 1973, 1971, 1970, 1969, 1964, 1955, 1953, 1947, 1945.

Rhône Valley. Although some excellent white wines are produced in the Rhône Valley, the majority of wine (95 percent) is red. White Rhône wines appear to have more longevity than whites of either Alsace or the Loire Valley. Your best bet is to avoid white Rhône wines more than seven years old.

The reds, on the other hand, will continue to improve for about 10 years past their vintage date. There are, of course, exceptions to the rule, and for that reason a vintage chart dating back to 1950, along with some older greats, is presented.

Year	Red wines	White wines
1986	8	8
1985	10	10
1984	6	6
1983	8	8
1982	8	8
1981	8	8
1980	7	7
1979	8	8
1978	9	—
1977	7	—
1976	8	—
1975	6	—
1974	6	—
1973	7	—
1972	8	—
1971	8	—
1970	8	—
1969	7	—
1968	6	—
1967	8	—
1966	8	—
1965	8	—
1964	8	—
1963	5	—
1962	8	—
1961	10	—
1960	8	—
1959	8	—
1958	6	—
1957	7	—
1956	4	—
1955	8	—
1954	4	—
1953	7	—
1952	7	—
1951	4	—
1950	8	—

Great vintages: 1949, 1945, 1929.

Germany

With the exception of the late-harvested wines (Auslese, Beerenauslese, Trockenbeerenauslese, and Eiswein), it is best to refrain from purchasing wines prior to 1976. The chart is for white wines only.

Year	Rhine	Mosel
1986	7	7
1985	8	9
1984	4	4
1983	9	9
1982	6	7
1981	8	7
1980	6	6
1979	8	8
1978	6	6

Great vintages (Rhine): 1976, 1971, 1967, 1964, 1959, 1953, 1949, 1945, 1937, 1934, 1921.

(Mosel): 1971, 1964, 1959, 1949, 1945, 1937, 1934, 1921.

Italy

Italy presents the most diversification and also problems in attempting to state the quality of each vintage. For starters, there are 20 wine-producing regions and each of them has grapes indigenous to its specific region in addition to grapes shared by a number of regions.

In an attempt to clarify and present a workable vintage chart, only the major red and white wine regions are presented.

With very few exceptions, it is best to consume Italian white wines within three years of their vintage and rarely past five years. During this time they are at their best: fresh, lively, and fruity.

Year	Piedmont		Tuscany		Veneto	
	Red	White	Red	White	Red	White
1986	9	9	9	9	8	8
1985	10	10	9	9	9	9
1984	4	5	4	4	4	5
1983	8	8	8	7	9	9

Year						
1982	9	8	9	8	8	8
1981	6	7	7	8	6	7
1980	7	—	7	—	7	—
1979	6	—	8	—	8	—
1978	10	—	9	—	6	—
1977	5	—	8	—	8	—
1976	6	—	6	—	6	—
1975	5	—	9	—	8	—
1974	9	—	9	—	8	—
1973	6	—	6	—	7	—
1972	3	—	5	—	6	—
1971	10	—	10	—	7	—
1970	9	—	9	—	6	—
1969	7	—	8	—	8	—
1968	7	—	9	—	7	—
1967	8	—	8	—	8	—
1966	3	—	6	—	8	—
1965	8	—	6	—	6	—
1964	10	—	9	—	10	—
1963	5	—	4	—	7	—
1962	8	—	6	—	8	—
1961	10	—	8	—	8	—
1960	4	—	5	—	4	—

Great vintages (Piedmont): 1958, 1952, 1947.
(Tuscany): 1949, 1947, 1945.
(Veneto): 1959, 1958.

The rating chart above represents the following regions and individuals wines from each.

Piedmont (red wines): Barbaresco, Barolo, Gattinara, Ghemme, Nebbiolo, Spanna, and other comparable, full-bodied wines. Other red wines, which include Barbera, Dolcetto, Freisa, and Grignolino, should be consumed within five years of the vintage date.
(white wines): Gavi, Moscato.

Tuscany (red wines): Brunello di Montalcino, Cabernet Sauvignon, Cabernet Sauvignon/Sangiovese Blends, Chianti, Vino Nobile di Montepulciano, and other comparable full-bodied wines.
(white wines): Galestro, Bianco Toscano, Chardonnay, Vernaccia di San Gimignano.

Veneto (red wines): Bardolino and Valpolicella should be consumed within five years of the vintage date. The only two wines that can be consumed older are Recioto della Valpolicella and Recioto della Valpolicella Amarone.
(white wines): Bianco di Custoza, Soave.

Port Wine

It may be interesting to list every single year declared, then assign it a numerical rating. However, it is probably better to list those years that in fact a majority of shippers declared a vintage: 1982, 1980*, 1977*, 1975, 1970*, 1967, 1966*, 1963*, 1960*, 1959, 1958, 1957, 1955, 1950, 1948, 1947, 1945, 1942, 1935, 1934, 1927. Years marked with an asterisk are best quality vintages.

Spain

Year	Rioja red	Rioja white
1986	6	6
1985	9	7
1984	5	5
1983	9	9
1982	8	8
1981	8	8
1980	9	—
1979	5	—
1978	8	—
1977	4	—
1976	7	—
1975	6	—
1974	6	—
1973	7	—
1972	2	—
1971	3	—
1970	10	—

Great vintages: 1968, 1966, 1964.

United States

California. California is an extremely large and diversified wine-producing area with many viticultural areas. It would be extremely difficult for anyone to compile a chart showing each viticultural area, then the multitude of grape varieties (both red and white) that grow in each area, and finally normal grape harvest time compared to late-harvested time.

The vintages listed below are for wines produced in Mendocino, Monterey, Napa, and Sonoma Valley.

The red wines are Cabernet Sauvignon, Merlot, Petite Sirah, Pinot Noir, and Zinfandel.

The white wines are Chardonnay, Chenin Blanc, Gewürztraminer, Sauvignon Blanc, and White Riesling.

Year	Red wine	White wine
1986	9	10
1985	10	10
1984	9	9
1983	8	8
1982	6	7
1981	5	6
1980	8	8
1979	7	8
1978	9	9
1977	7	—
1976	9	—
1975	7	—
1974	9	—
1973	6	—
1972	4	—
1971	7	—
1970	10	—
1969	6	—
1968	9	—
1967	4	—
1966	8	—
1965	6	—
1964	9	—

Great vintages: 1958, 1955, 1951, 1946, 1935.

New York State.

	Finger Lakes		Hudson Valley	
Year	Red	White	Red	White
1986	7	8	7	8
1985	9	10	9	9
1984	7	8	7	8
1983	9	9	8	8
1982	7	8	6	7
1981	6	6	7	7
1980	10	10	10	10
1979	8	—	8	—
1978	9	—	9	—
1977	8	—	7	—
1976	7	—	8	—

Washington State. This chart comprises the wines produced in the Columbia Valley of Washington State.

Year	Red and white wines
1985	9
1984	9
1983	8
1982	9
1981	8
1980	9
1979	6
1978	9
1977	8
1976	8
1975	9
1974	7
1973	7
1972	9
1971	6
1970	7
1969	7
1968	8
1967	7

Suggested Reading

Broadbent, Michael. *The Great Vintage Wine Book.* New York: Alfred A. Knopf, 1980.

d

Sensory Evaluation of Alcoholic Beverages

The Art of Wine Tasting

There is no mystery to wine tasting, but there is a technique and as is true in most things, "practice makes perfect." While professional tasters must treat wine objectively, for most people likes and dislikes of any particular wine are subjective. Moreover, everyone's tasting ability varies from day to day, even from morning to afternoon.

Wine appeals to three senses: sight, smell, and taste. While each is important, the overall impression of the wine is determined by a combination of all three. The sensation of taste involves smell, sight, and even touch, but the greatest proportion of what is normally considered to be taste, or flavor, is actually smell. This phenomenon is due to the fact that with the tongue we can distinguish only sweet, sour, salty, and bitter. The balance of "flavors" we perceive in wine or food actually is smell. When we sip wine, it is the olfactory, or odor-sensitive portion of the nose which transmits information to the brain. As the wine is warmed in the mouth, additional aromatic compounds are released which are then captured by the nose, adding to our sense of taste.

The actual wine-tasting technique, though it may seem awkward at first, is easy to master, and as more of the intricacies of wine unfold, you will find the effort worthwhile as well as exciting.

The first step in tasting wine is to examine it for color and clarity. This observation often gives clues about the wine even before it is tasted. A red or white wine held up to the light should appear clean and free from particles. Color is best judged by tilting the glass to one side and examining the rim of the liquid. If the rim of a red wine is a purple shade, the wine is young, or has a high pH. If it is slightly brown, the wine is older and more mature. Red wines range in color anywhere from light red to deep garnet and even inky black. White wines range from a hint of straw yellow with an occasional greenish cast, to medium yellow, and light-to-medium gold. As a white wine ages, the color eventually darkens and changes toward brown.

After examining the color and clarity, swirl the wine in the glass, which increases the surface area from which the volatile compounds can evaporate, releasing the aromatic qualities. Then put your nose into the glass and take a deep, sharp whiff. You will notice the "bouquet" which is the vinous or "winey" scent developed through the process of fermentation. The many acids present and the combination of organic acids with alcohol are vital contributions to the wine's bouquet. When you smell the wine you will also notice the "aroma." Although aroma is often confused with the term "bouquet," it is the particular scent of the grape varietal from which the wine is made. For example, Sauvignon Blanc has a "smoky" aroma and Cabernet has a "chocolatey" or "green pepper" aroma. The combination of the wine's aroma and bouquet is known as the "nose."

Now you are ready to taste the wine, and here is where you can apply the tricks used by all professionals. Take a moderate sip and swirl the wine around in your mouth making sure to fully contact all parts of your tongue. Next, part your lips slightly, draw air through them slurping the wine to agitate and aerate it, much like when you're eating hot soup. Then exhale gently through your nose and swallow the wine. Though this rather noisy, seemingly ungenteel technique (something your mother told you never to do) may gain the curious attention of others not as knowledgeable, it is necessary in order to achieve the full impact of the wine on your senses.

In addition to the vital role of the olfactory sense mentioned earlier, the tongue also plays an important part in the analysis of wine. True tastes are perceived at various points on the tongue, and recognizing them will help you separate different flavors. At the tip of the tongue we taste sweet and salty. Along the sides we taste salty, sweet, sour, and bitter (astringency), which is also experienced at the back of the tongue where some people are especially sensitive to bitterness. Because some of these areas are more sensitive than others, it is important that the wine reach all parts of the tongue to fully separate flavors.

Once the wine is tasted, you will immediately recognize if the wine is sweet or "dry." Wines are referred to as being dry if during the process of fermentation the yeast metabolizes all the available sugar and converts that sugar to roughly equal parts of carbon dioxide (CO_2) and alcohol. A dry wine (red or white) will taste crisp, clean, and almost sharp in acidity.

Residual sugar is a term associated with wines which are not quite dry and refers to the percentage of sugar purposely left in the wine by stopping the fermentation prior to the wine becoming dry. Residual sugar is most desirable in white wines and tends to make the wine more "round" and full-flavored. Most people do not detect any sweetness when the wine contains less than one percent residual sugar.

As mentioned earlier "touch" is one aspect of wine tasting. Touch is not referring to putting your fingers in the glass, but simply to the "feel" of the wine in your mouth. We are not only able to feel astringency, but most importantly, the body or viscosity of which alcohol is the major contributor. For example, a sweet wine will feel heavy to the palate and a dry wine much lighter.

Temperature plays yet another role in wine tasting. Red wines are best tasted at room temperature (65° to 68° F) to lessen astringency. But white wines, on the other hand, are best lightly chilled (50° to 55° F) to enhance the delicate flavors and nose.

When you finally swallow the wine, you will notice an aftertaste. This is called the "finish" and, in general, a longer finish is most desirable.

(Adapted from Papagni Press, Angelo Papagni Vineyards, Madera, California. Vol. VII, No. 2; Summer 1983.)

Grape Varieties of the World

Each of the over 8000 different grape varieties of the world has its own individual color, aroma, taste, and flavor—sort of a "fingerprint" which identifies it either by minute and subtle nuances, or by a wide and marked margin. The following grape varieties can be identified by the aroma or flavor they exhibit.

Barbera. Vinous, tart, fruity.

Cabernet Franc. Distinct aroma and taste of green olives: herbaceous, minty, weedy.

Cabernet Sauvignon. Black tea, herbs, black or green olives, cedar, bell pepper, blackberry, and black currants.

Chardonnay. Apples, figs, pineapples, green apple, peaches, or somewhat melonlike. If aged in wood, a certain butteryness.

Chenin Blanc. Pleasantly fruity, melonlike; resembles a fresh fruit salad.

Folle-Blanche. Mild apple-grape aromas.

French Colombard. Lively applelike flavors.

Gamay-Beaujolais. Extremely fruity, berrylike; resembles cherries, blackberries, raspberries.

Gewürztraminer. Floral, spicy, cinnamon, grapefruit.

Grenache. Hints of strawberries in the aroma.

Merlot. Green olives.

Muscat. Grapey, spicy, fruity; resembles a fruit salad.

Petite Sirah. Fruit flavors of wild blackberries, plums, and cassis.

Pinot Noir. Mint or black cherry.

Sauvignon Blanc. Grassy, herbaceous odor like new-mown hay, green olives.

Sémillon. Fresh figs, or the smell of freshly laundered bed sheets drying in the sun; a steely, spicy aroma, and crisp herbaceous flavor. Underlying hints of citrus.

White Riesling. Tropical fruits, peaches, apricots, floral aromas, with hints of muscat grapes when very-ripe grapes are used.

Zinfandel. Berrylike, sometimes resembling raspberries; briary; hints of spices.

Acidity in Wine

When the acid level is low in certain wines, they are "perceived" by the taster to be sweet. Yet, on the other hand, if the same wine has a high level of acidity, it would be perceived to be dry, since the impression of sweetness is in direct relationship to the amount of acidity present.

The human palate can more easily recognize fruity aroma when it is enhanced by sugar, and this can be demonstrated by the fact that strawberries will release more aroma and flavor if first treated with sugar.

The Art of Tasting Whiskey/Brandy

To properly sample whiskey, brandy, or even clear distillates (gin, rum, tequila, vodka), you should start with the proper atmosphere and tools.

The Atmosphere

Sampling should take place in a quiet, pleasant atmosphere, free from distraction and foreign odors. It should be conducted at your own pace and never under pressure for a quick judgment.

The Tools

- Good, clear, odorless, and taste-free water (bottled spring water—still or effervescent or distilled water is best).
- A clean goblet large enough in diameter to encompass your nose. The goblet should hold at least 100 milliliters (3⅓ ounces). Some professional tasters prefer the more traditional cognac snifters. Most any shape glass will do except for shot glasses, which in addition to being too small to appreciate the bouquet, can easily be knocked over.

  If you use ice and too wide a glass, you will find your nose hitting the ice before you reach the whiskey.
- If you plan to taste a large number of whiskies, do consider the use of spit buckets so that you don't become inebriated. You'll need something in which to spit since, when done properly, tasters never swallow the sample. (If you swallow two or three samples, it deadens your taste buds, and most likely your physical coordination and judgment will get a little out of balance.)
- A good comfortable chair helps, since the more relaxed you are, the better your sampling will be.
- Last, but most important, you need some various brands to sample.

Now that you have all the necessities, you need to know how to perform the sampling.

The Procedure

1. You must first cleanse the palate. To cleanse the palate, sip some chilled water and eat a piece of unsalted bread, cracker, or preferably matzos.
2. Break the seal, open the bottle, and pour about 20 milliliters of the whiskey into a glass. Never fill your goblet when sampling, unless you want to give your nose an alcohol bath. The reason for not filling the goblet is to allow you to raise the goblet so it

encompasses the nose, allowing you to get the full aroma from the whiskey. This helps eliminate any foreign odors. Higher-proof whiskies have a strong alcohol smell, which irritates the nose and tends to cover up other possible unfavorable characteristics in the spirit, since you only get the strong alcohol smell and taste.

3. If you are sampling brown whiskies, remember that no two brands look alike; observe it as you pour. Some whiskies are pale as wheat; others have a mellow tone of amber or burnished brass. The color of a brand of whiskey is not an indication of its age or quality. Color is derived mainly from the type and age of the oak cask and char in which the whiskey has matured, coupled with a slight amount of oxidation. In most cases, a little natural coloring in the form of caramel may be added to bring the color to a standard which can be always recognized to be the same. Therefore, a lighter-colored whiskey has nothing to do with being light in body.

4. As you look at the liquid, rock the glass a little and warm it with your hands to aid evaporation and release the bouquet. Now you are ready to sniff your sample. Simply take one short sniff, hold it in your nasal passage, then exhale. A second sniff might be necessary to reaffirm your first impression. Never take more than two sniffs, for your olfactory senses tire easily and you will be getting a false sensation. In addition, because of the high alcoholic level of distilled spirits, your nasal passages will become quite irritated, which will eventually deaden your sense of smell (figure D-1).

5. Now for the second part of the sniffing. Pour into the glass approximately 20 milliliters of warm water and mix. The reason for mixing equal parts of the whiskey and water is to reduce the proof and alcohol content of the whiskey. Again swirl the whiskey, then repeat the sniffing. This second and equally important step will change radically the smell of the whiskey. Through a chemical change, the trapped or subdued aromas will be volatilized by the act of adding water; the bouquet and taste will be changed dramatically.

   The whiskey should be mellow, yet potent, without any of the sharpness of raw spirit. Every whiskey drinker has his or her interpretation of aroma. Some whiskies, particularly those with a higher proportion of the heavier malt whiskies, will seem quite sweet. Others have a dry tang. Sometimes the scent of the peat

Figure D-1 Professional scotch taster evaluating samples of scotch for eventual blending. (Courtesy Scotch Whisky Information Bureau)

comes through. You should get a pleasant, full, rounded bouquet of caramel and alcohol which is not raw or medicinal.

6. Now you're ready to taste. Take a very small amount of the whiskey and let it lie on the front of the tongue (about a teaspoon full) and breathe very lightly and slowly in and out your nose, with your mouth closed. The breathing in and out of the nose enhances the taste buds. Then swish the whiskey around in your mouth for a couple of seconds and spit it out. Wash your mouth with a few ounces of water. (This procedure ensures that all foreign taste is removed from your mouth prior to actually tasting the whiskey.)

7. A smoky aroma may give way to a nutty flavor; a lemony bouquet can lead to an unexpected honied taste. Some whiskey flavors linger longer on the palate; others subtly appear and are gone. When sampling distilled spirits at a higher proof (100 proof as

against those in the 80s), the alcohol tends to burn your tongue and inside mouth a little, which deadens your taste.

The characteristic flavor should appear quickly, develop, then disappear rather rapidly after swallowing. To meet the required expectations, you will experience a slight caramel, semisweet alcohol taste which is pleasant, without any bite or bitter taste. Now, spit the spirit out, sort of forcing it through your lips. This allows the taste sensors in your lips to double check the taste buds in your mouth and tongue. Once you've spit out the spirit, the flavor should not rebound. You should not experience any lingering aftertaste or burning sensation. You should be finished.

8. As some tasters term it, aftertaste or finish can be quite different from the in-mouth flavor. But in whiskey it tends to disappear quickly, although brands vary greatly in the length and intensity of their aftertaste. Everyone, even the experts, has one or more aromas which appeal to him or her, and everyone will describe it in a unique way.

9. After each sampling, wash your mouth out with water before tasting another whiskey.

Tasting Beer

The art of tasting beer is not much different from the sensory evaluation of wine. Sight, aroma or bouquet, taste, flavor, balance, finish, and aftertaste are all assessed. The glass utilized for tasting must be crystal clear, contain a stem, and should hold 8 to 12 ounces. Unchilled and definitely not frozen glasses or mugs should be used. The glass should be held by the stem, because the fingers (which contain oils and considerable heat) will cause the beer to warm up too quickly and leave the glass, if held by the bowl, covered with unsightly fingerprints, distracting from the beer's natural beauty.

Actually speaking, a beer glass should be wet before pouring draft or bottle beer because it will maintain a better foam head. The most popular serving temperature for beer is 38° to 40° F. However, for evaluation purposes, beer should never be tasted while it is too chilled or cold. Allow the beer to come up to 50° to 55° F (wine cellar temperature), then begin.

Open the bottle or can, and pour the beer into a glass while slightly tilting the glass on a 45° angle and straightening it up as it fills. A "head" on a beer is desirable and generally should be about one inch in thickness. Beer, like wine, should be crystal clear and brilliant (light and dark beer alike) without a haze (which is usually caused by an excess of protein or occasionally because the beer wasn't allowed to completely settle-out its sediment prior to bottling). An exception to this clarity and brilliance are most of the Weisse beers (wheat beers, mostly from Germany), which are usually unfiltered with some yeast residue in the bottom and, therefore, which appear to be cloudy in appearance.

The next step employs the use of your "olfactory" senses. Swirl the beer once, then take one good "sniff" of it, allowing your senses to determine what was revealed in its aroma or bouquet while your nose recovers its acuity. Naturally, hops will be picked out, which fill the entire aroma gamut from a delicate light, somewhat spicy or herbal aroma, to a very pungent, cutting, forest or pinelike smell which has been known to snap back one's head with its intensity. Other aromas or smells present can be described as floral, fruity (apples, apricots, cantaloupe, melons, peaches, pears), custardlike, tealike, yeasty, sweet, roasty or toasty, woody, malty, beefy (which could be reminiscent of bouillon), and even charcoallike. If a different "off smell" is encountered, which is foreign to the senses, it should be assumed it is a negative aspect of the beer; e.g., the smells of a skunk, must (old rags), wet cardboard, wet dog's hair, something sour, cleaning fluid, medicine, metal, cabbage, or even hints of sulfur.

Now take a sip of the beer and gently roll it around in your mouth for a few seconds; allow your tongue to come in complete contact with its taste. Swallow gently and reflect on what you have just tasted. The flavor or taste of beer should contain some bitterness, crispiness, carbonation, hopiness, tartness, acidity, and maltiness. Dark beers will additionally have overtones of malt, bitterness, sweetness, and caramel. Beer should have a good "feel" in your mouth, followed by a clean finish and aftertaste when swallowing. The various flavor elements (including carbonation) should harmoniously balance out each other.

Suggested Readings

Amerine, Maynard A. and Edward B. Roessler. *Wines: Their Sensory Evaluation*. New York: W. H. Freeman, 2d ed., 1983.

Broadbent, Michael. *Wine Tasting: Enjoying Understanding*. London: Christie's Wine Publications, 5th ed., 1977.

Heath, Henry B. *Source Book of Flavors*. Westport, Connecticut: AVI Publishing Co., 1981.

Food Aspects of Alcoholic Beverages

Cooking Wines

There are some cardinal rules which must *never* be broken. Never cook with wines that are spoiled, or by putting it another way . . . if you wouldn't drink the wine by itself, then discard it. Using an inferior or spoiled wine is false economy since you run the risk of ruining your ingredients and you make good food taste bad with bad wine. Avoid using wines labeled "cooking wines," because they are usually heavily laden with salt and potassium. Also given today's sensible concerns about sodium, they're even more loathsome.

During Prohibition, wineries choosing to remain in business either sold bulk grapes, grape juice, wine tonics, produced sacramental wines, or completely circumvented the law by producing cooking wines (taking perfectly sound wines and judiciously adding salt and other seasonings, rendering them unfit for consumption). Since the repeal of Prohibition, cooking wines are still made and sold both to industry restaurants and supermarkets. Some restaurants actually made it a practice to add salt to wines designed to be used in cooking, to discourage the help from consuming them.

Cooking with Wine

More and more people are using wine in their cooking, and it can often mean the difference between ordinary and zestful dishes. The same factors causing wine to harmonize with foods—their ability to balance the sweetness, acidity, saltiness, and bitterness—hold true when wine is used in cooking.

The confident chef to whom wine is as essential as salt and pepper, is eager to experiment and often comes up with exciting new tastes by bending the rules.

Any of us who enjoys creating gourmet dinners and even those who take pride tinkering around the stove, can transform dishes into epicurean triumphs with wine. Chefs the world over know the value of wine and have been cooking with it daily, transforming the most bland of dishes into tasty treats. Like salt, you do not use too much for seasoning; but by replacing some of the water in the recipe with the proper wine, you add magic flavor. After all, wine is about 90 percent water anyway.

Alcohol vaporizes at 173°F, and if exposed for about three to five minutes to this heat, the alcohol present in the wine will vaporize. Wine changes character depending upon the amount of heat to which it is exposed and the length of cooking time. A wine that is simmered for a short time over low heat will have a different flavor than the same wine subjected to high heat over an extended period. Sweet wines with high residual sugar should be used sparingly, for after the alcohol vaporizes, the sugar in the wine tends to caramelize quickly. Young red wines with a high level of tannin tend to add bitterness to the food.

Meat recipes which call for liquid in the cooking process may be converted to a wine-flavored recipe by a simple substitution. For instance, replace ¼ cup of water for each pound of meat with an equal amount of red or white table wine; this will in turn actually tenderize the meat while adding to its flavor.

Wines destined to be used for marinating should be at room temperature, for cold wine actually toughens the fibers of the food, especially meats. A benefit of wine in cooking is that it tenderizes meats and some vegetables.

Marinating fish in a dry white wine before cooking or using the wine for basting during cooking will moderate the fish odor and add the fragrance of the wine to the finished dish. Fish, which contains high degrees of oil, merge gracefully with dry white wines, which are high in natural acidity.

For dieters and cholesterol watchers, substitute dry red or white wine in basting, instead of using the meat's fat.

Adding or changing a food's color is possible if a red sweet vermouth is used for the basting of meats, poultry, game, etc.

The old rule of "red wine with red meats" and "white wines with white meats," is simply that . . . old . . . and should not be followed.

Instead, serve light food with light-bodied wines, heavy foods with full-bodied wines, dry foods with dry wines, and sweet foods with sweet wines.

The bottom line is common sense and flavor. You can substitute wine for some of the liquid called for in any recipe. Don't add wine at the end of the cooking, as all the flavor you'll get will be wine. Always simmer, never boil wine—it simply scalds out the flavor. And nothing perks up pan juices (and makes an easier quick sauce) than a little wine.

Jill Davis, a winemaker at Buena Vista Winery in Sonoma, California, offers the following information on how to pair wine with food. You don't want to punish your tastebuds by jumping back and forth between bland and highly spiced foods or sweet and sour flavors. Nor do you want to pair a heavy cream soup with a tart, acidic wine. If you've ever had a sip of milk right after you've eaten a grapefruit you know what a terrible shock that is. However, to keep your tastebuds fresh and excited about what you're eating instead of fatigued from repetitious flavors and textures, you need to vary the foods you eat, while still remembering the basic rules of sequencing. Some food flavors linger in the mouth; and this, too, affects the taste of the wine. Here are some simple facts about wine and food tastes (sweet, sour, salty, and bitter):

Acidic wine will make seafood seem sweet.

A wine with residual sugar balances salt and sharp spices.

Protein balances tannin (in red wines).

Fat (cream) balances acid (in white wines).

Delicate foods need delicate wines.

More flavorful foods need heavier wines.

The sauce can change the character of the food which affects the choice of wine.

Sweet desserts need wines of similar sweetness.

The acidity of wine balances the alkalinity of cheese.

The Dos and Don'ts of Food and Wine

The dos. To make pairing more enjoyable and less traumatic, it is suggested that you adhere to a few basic concepts:

1. Try to strike a balance between the wine and food so that they each taste better when tasted together. To do this remember:

a. Stronger-flavored wines seem to taste better when balanced with stronger-flavored foods.

b. Conversely, more delicately flavored wines are better appreciated when served with foods that are more delicately seasoned or textured.

c. Wines with spicier aromas and flavors are often enhanced by similar spicy accents in foods; to carry this further, wines with bolder, coarser flavors are better matches for coarser, simpler fare.

2. When developing a recipe or deciding on a dish to pair with wine, it sometimes helps to think that most foods have little flavor of their own that enhances or competes with wine. Rather, foods serve as a base flavor or medium to carry other seasonings that can be matched to a wine variety or style. These seasonings can be the key to toying with wine and food flavors together.

3. Learn to use specific herbs, spices, and seasonings to enhance certain wine varieties or styles. For example, marjoram butter with fish and Fume Blanc; beef with tarragon sauce and Cabernet Sauvignon; lamb with rosemary and Petite Syrah.

4. Use wine as a cooking ingredient in sauces, etc. It really doesn't take much wine, and it reinforces the same flavors in the food that are in the wine. If this sounds too inconvenient or expensive, you can use a wine of similar flavor, structure, or style.

5. When serving more than one wine variety or style, it is suggested that you progress from cold to room temperature; dry to sweet; white to rosé, then to red; delicate to bold; old to young.

6. Serve more simple foods with older wine vintages to better appreciate their complexities and elegance.

The don'ts. To avoid being disappointed, here are a few words of caution when working with fine wines.

1. Wine that does not taste good enough to drink should *not* be considered good enough to cook with. The "off" flavors are often transferred to the dish.

2. Excessive use of some seasonings can overpower the taste and pleasure of wine. These include salt, garlic, vinegar, ginger, sugar, hot peppers, and cilantro. Don't avoid using them altogether, just use with some restraint. Or combine with milder ingredients to "cut" their strength.

3. **Vegetable acids can compete with wine.** Many vegetables have acids that compete with the pleasures of wine, particularly artichokes, asparagus, spinach, and sorrel. Diminish the competitive effect of their acids by using sweet spices or sauces containing cheese, cream, mayonnaise, or other dairy products.

4. **Cold temperatures subdue wine aromas and flavors.** Temperatures that are too cold (below 55°F) can subdue the aromas and flavors of more complex wines.

(Reprinted with permission of McDowell Valley Vineyards, 3811 Highway 175, P.O. Box 449, Hopland, California. Copyright 1987.)

Wine and Cheese

The happiest marriage in the world of gastronomy is the mating of cheese and wine. They complement each other; they agree with the stomach as eagerly as they agree with the palate and offer doubly delicious possibilities for guests.

According to history, the use of cheese was pictured on stone tablets in 4000 B.C. Legend has it that the first cheese was made accidentally by a shepherd who carried milk in a pouch made from a sheep's stomach. The rennet in the pouch lining, combined with the sun's heat, caused the milk to separate into curds and whey.

The making of cheese was a natural consequence of man's ability to procure more milk from his domestic animals than he could consume before it spoiled. For ages, he has produced cheese from the milk of cows, goats, sheep, mares, camels, yaks, lamas, and even reindeer.

When selecting wines to match the foods, consider the chemical makeup of both the food and wine. Wine is high in acidity, and cheese is naturally high in alkaline, so as to offer a balance to both.

A few hints on serving cheese might make the difference between a mediocre and a great wine-cheese event. Cheese should be stored cool at 35° to 38°F. Turn the cheese every couple of days so as to keep the natural oils distributed evenly. When ready to serve, cut off only as much as you plan to consume and replace the remaining in the refrigerator, tightly wrapped in clear plastic wrap. Avoid reusing the original plastic wrap it came in because the lack of a proper seal allows the entry of air. Don't be afraid of mold, for it is a naturally occurring phenomena. Simply cut or scrape away, and serve as usual. Before serving the cheese, allow it to sit for an hour or so at room temperature, which will soften the texture, release the aromas, and maximize the flavor.

Flambéing

The dictionary dryly defines the word *ritual* as a "ceremonial act" or "action." But to the connoisseur and gourmet, the rituals of food or wine service are an essential ingredient of a meal, adding pleasure to the moment, heightening the anticipation of the delicacy to come, and spurring conversation.

What is Irish coffee without a flaming glass of brandy? Or tequila without a knuckle of salt and a wedge of lemon to dash against the palate? And who would deny any patron (or maître d' for that matter) the tableside ritual of a finely prepared caesar salad or chateaubriand?

Figure E-1 Cognac Flambé: The ultimate way to end a gastronomic dinner. (Courtesy Cognac Information Bureau)

You can easily add an additional two to three dollars to the check if you can make the person feel as if they are the center of attention.

The Art of Flambéing

Very few of us can resist the spectacle of *flambé*. Flaming any course, dessert, cordial, brandy, or even coffee can end a most sumptuous meal in a blaze of glory (figure E-1). When you flame foods, you add new flavor and excitement that your customers will long remember.

Flaming is not a carnival sideshow; it is the secret of complete flavor release just at the moment of serving. It is an art easily learned.

When you flambé with spirits, you achieve much more than the drama of a blazing dish. Many spirits contain a treasury of subtle, complex tastes and aromas that are released as the spirit flames, adding unique flavor and distinction to your fare. Incidentally, most or all of the alcohol content is burned off during the process.

Some helpful hints.

Use a spirit that is at least 80 proof for a brighter, longer-lasting flame.

Gently warm the spirit before igniting. This causes the alcohol to begin vaporizing, and it's the vapors that ignite first.

To warm the spirit, pour it into a small metal container and set it over low heat (pilot light, candle), for five to seven seconds. Or pour it into a well-heated ladle for warming.

Hold a *long* wooden or fireplace match over the spirit to ignite the vapors of the alcohol; never use small book matches.

If possible, dim or lower the lights prior to bringing the flaming dish to the table so that you become the center of attention.

Caution.

Do not pour the spirit directly from the bottle into a hot pan or over already flaming food. This can cause a blaze to travel up the bottle.

If you flame at the table, protect surface with a heat-resistant tray.

Remember, a little caution goes a long way; stand back when flambéing. Keep clothing, long hair, and children away from flame.

Other helpful hints. To keep flames alive longer and burn off maximum amount of alcohol:

Use a shallow pan; it lets more oxygen reach the flame, helping to keep it going.

Sprinkle a little sugar (or salt) on dishes before flambéing.

Rock the pan gently while contents are flaming.

Spoon flaming liquid repeatedly over contents of pan.

Dishes to be flamed can be prepared in the kitchen, then transferred to a warmed, heat-proof serving platter, and carried to the table for flaming. Or the dish can be prepared at the table in a chafing dish or attractive skillet set over a tabletop burner.

Timing is important. Have all your ingredients and equipment ready to go before you start.

Practice makes perfect. Do rehearse your flambé technique before doing it for guests.

Flaming Drinks

Occasionally, dramatic rituals seem to emphasize the attractiveness of the scenario to follow, and one purely romantic ritual is flaming drinks. Properly executed by an experienced bartender (or host extraordinaire), it can set the mood for entire evening to follow, for it combines the seductive elements of sight and smell with a touch of the dramatic.

Pour several ounces of your favorite aperitif or liqueur into an ice-filled wine goblet or old-fashion glass.

Cut a slice of orange, lemon, or lime peel (about 2½ inches by 1½ inches) from a thick-skinned, room-temperature fruit. Be careful to cut away only the rind and zest of the fruit, not the pith or pulp. Pat the peel dry to make sure there's no moisture on it.

After lighting a match, hold the peel between your thumb and forefinger and bring it close to the flame (about a ½ inch).

Now quickly but gently squeeze the peel to release the citrus oils and vapors from the skin side while holding the flame in front of the spray. A brilliant burst of flame will flare from the peel.

Now drop the peel into the iced aperitif/liqueur, stir twice (you don't want to melt the ice too fast), and you're ready to enjoy your drink.

Suggested Reading

McGee, Harold. *On Food and Cooking: The Science and Lore of the Kitchen.* New York: Scribner's, 1984.

Mixology

Mixology is the art of following a recipe or formula to produce a standard and consistent drink according to specifications. An experienced mixologist can be compared to a chemist or a chef, producing perfect tasting and eye-appealing drinks every time. Unfortunately, mixology is slowly becoming a lost art, for most of the mixes are premixed, and the popularity of "standard drinks" are also fading.

One major problem with restaurant bars making their own mix from scratch is consistency of taste. This is why bottled mixes often replace old-fashioned hand mixed ingredients in popular drinks.

Mixing Methods

There are basically three methods of mixing drinks: shaking, blending, and stirring. The reason for these methods is simply to blend the ingredients and properly chill them.

Shaking

In making the shake drink, ice is placed in the shaker, the liquor is added, then the other ingredients (carbonated beverages are never shaken). The top is placed securely on the shaker and shaken vigorously for about 10 seconds. To serve the drink, the top of the shaker is removed and the drink is strained into a cocktail glass. The drink is then garnished and presented to the customer. If the customer has requested that his or her drink be served "on the rocks," a rocks glass is used instead of the customary cocktail glass, and fresh ice is placed in it prior to straining the cocktail. The customary garnish would then be used.

Blending

Blended drinks are made in the same way as shaken drinks, except that drinks containing frozen, partially frozen, or solid ingredients must be blended. Also by adding shaved ice to the blender, a "frozen" drink will be produced. As in the shaking process, carbonated beverages must *never* be used.

Stirring

The process for making and serving stirred drinks is exactly the same as for shaken drinks, except that they are stirred rather than shaken and carbonated beverages should be added prior to stirring.

Some customers will request their drink be served "neat." They are referring to the drink being served without ice, soda, water, etc.—just "straight."

Drinks and Name Origins

Next to the name of each drink, is the key method of mixing (shake, blend, or stir) which refers to the information provided above.

■
_____

Alexander   *(Shake/Blend)*

¾ oz. brandy or gin

½ oz. white crème de cacao

¾ oz. heavy cream

Garnish: Nutmeg for dusting

■
_____

Americano   *(Shake/Blend)*

1½ oz. Campari

1½ oz. sweet vermouth

Splash of seltzer

Garnish: Twist of lemon peel

■

Bacardi Cocktail   *(Shake/Blend)*

1½ oz. Bacardi Light Rum
½ tsp. grenadine syrup
Juice of ½ lime
½ tsp. sugar
Garnish: *Cherry*

■

Bee's Knee's   *(Shake/Blend)*

1 oz. gin
1 oz. lemon juice
1 oz. honey

Excellent for sore throats.

■

Bellini   *(Shake/Blend)*

This drink was created by Giuseppe Cipriani at Harry's Bar in Venice, Italy.

3 medium-sized fully ripened peaches
Juice of 1 lemon
1 chilled bottle of dry Italian Spumante
2–3 tsp. grenadine syrup (optional)
A carafe

Peel and cut peaches into cubes, then put into a blender, adding the lemon juice at the end (and optional grenadine syrup). Pour the pulp into the carafe, then add the entire bottle of Spumante. Stir gently and serve.

Serves: *6 persons.*

■

Black Russian   *(Shake/Blend)*

¾ oz. vodka
½ oz. Kahlua

Black Velvet

A mixture of stout and champagne, which was popular in England during the Edwardian days (nineteenth century). It was created when Prince Albert died, which sent Queen Victoria (mother of Edward VII, King of England, 1901–1910), along with the entire country into shock. They shrouded everything in black, including champagne, which was mixed with stout.

The Black Velvet has had a resurgence in popularity. Today, ginger ale is usually substituted because of the high cost of champagne.

Bloody Mary   (*Shake/Blend*)

The Bloody Mary created by Ferdinand Petiot, a bartender at Harry's Bar in Paris in the 1920s, was named after Queen Mary I of England who, because of her persecution of Protestants, attained the nickname Bloody Mary. It was later called a "Bucket of Blood," then "Red Snapper," and "Morning Glory." It was introduced into the United States in the 1930s.

1¼ oz. vodka

3–4 drops Tabasco sauce or other hot pepper sauce

½ tsp. Worcestershire sauce

6–8 oz. tomato juice

Juice of 1 lemon

Salt and pepper to taste

Garnish: *Stalk of celery*

Optional ingredients: celery stick, celery salt, horseradish, A-1 Steak Sauce.

Cape Codder   (*Stir*)

1 oz. vodka

Cranberry juice

Cobbler

Tall iced drinks with fruit juices, wines, or spirits decorated with pieces of fruit and laden generously with ice.

Cocktail

In 1776, Betsy Flanagan invented the American "cocktail." It was in her bar in Elmsford, New York, which was decorated with brightly colored tail feathers of cocks that she had the notion to add a cock's tail feather as a stirrer to each drink. During that time, cocktails were often referred to as "Roosters."

Collins—Tom/John   *(Stir)*

1¼ oz. gin (Tom) or vodka (John)
Juice of 1 lemon
½ tsp. sugar
2 tsp. grenadine syrup (optional)
Seltzer to fill

Copacabana   *(Shake/Blend)*

1 oz. coffee-flavored brandy
1 oz. light rum
Dash lemon juice
3 drops white crème de menthe
Dash of seltzer

Daiquiri   *(Shake/Blend)*

Named after the Daiquiri Iron Mines near Santiago, Cuba, where the drink originated around the turn of the century.

1½ oz. light rum
1 tsp. sugar
Juice of ½ lime

Fruit daiquiris can be made by cutting back on the amount of sugar, and then by adding the desired fresh fruit to a blender. Blend for about 30 seconds.

Depth Charge

A Depth Charge is made when you take a shot glass full of whiskey and plunge it (glass and all) into a large glass of beer, then drink the beer!

Frappé

Frappé is a French term for a drink that is super chilled by the addition of crushed or shaved ice, over which cordials are poured.

Gin or Vodka and Tonic   *(Stir)*

1¼ oz. gin or vodka

Tonic (quinine water) water

Garnish: Squeeze a wedge of lime into the drink and across the rim of the glass, then drop into the drink.

Gimlet   *(Shake/Blend)*

In the 1890s, a British naval surgeon, Sir T. O. Gimlette was concerned with the heavy drinking to which his men were accustomed. So he diluted the gin with lime juice, and although it didn't dissuade them, he unintentionally created a new drink.

3 parts gin

1 part Roses Lime Juice

Gin Rickey   *(Shake/Blend)*

Civil War Colonel Joe Rickey had this drink named after him at the St. James Hotel in New York City in 1895.

1 oz. gin

½ oz. lime juice

Glögg

A truly Scandinavian drink

1 bottle (750 ml.) Akvavit
¾ cup raisins
2 bottles (750 ml.) dry red wine
½ cup blanched almonds
1 tbsp. cardamon seeds peeled
½ tsp. whole cloves
½ cup sugar
3, ½-inch pieces cinnamon stick
1 small piece of a lemon and orange peel

Pour one-half of the Akvavit and all of the wine into a large saucepan. Add raisins, almonds, and sugar. Tie spices in a cheesecloth bag and drop into the mixture. Cover pan. Bring very slowly to the boiling point, but *do not let it boil;* add remaining Akvavit and let simmer 30 minutes. Remove from heat and let steep 2 hours. When ready to serve, remove the cheesecloth bag, slowly reheat liquid until thoroughly warmed, and then with a long-handled ladle, pour into punch glasses. Serve with raisins and almonds.

Godfather   *(Shake/Blend)*

¾ oz. amaretto
1½ oz. Scotch whisky

Godmother   *(Shake/Blend)*

1½ oz. vodka
1½ oz. amaretto

Golden Cadillac   *(Shake/Blend)*

1½ oz. heavy cream
1 oz. Galliano liqueur
¾ oz. white crème de cacao

Grasshopper *(Shake/Blend)*

¾ oz. green crème de menthe
¾ oz. white crème de cacao
¾ oz. heavy cream

Harvey Wallbanger *(Shake/Stir)*

It seems that in southern California (according to legend), Tom Harvey would arrive at his favorite pub after a day's surfing and order an "Italian Screwdriver"; then after consuming several of them, he would attempt to leave and start "banging" into walls! Hence the name.

6 oz. orange juice
1 oz. vodka
½ oz. Galliano liqueur

Highball

Originally in St. Louis in the 1880s, early railroaders used a ball on a high pole as a signal for railroad trains to go ahead or speed up. This signaling device was called a "highball."

Hence, when bartenders found that ice, whiskey, and water could be mixed speedily into a delightful drink, they called it a "highball."

1½ oz. blended whiskey
Ginger ale to fill

Irish Coffee

1 cube sugar
1½–2 oz. Irish whiskey
Strong coffee
Heaping tbsp. whipped heavy cream

To make Irish coffee, place into the bottom of a large stem-glass (12 ounces), one cube of sugar. Pour 1 ½–2 ounces of a good quality Irish whiskey over the cube. Then put a spoon into the glass and pour in very hot and extremely strong coffee (not espresso). The purpose of the spoon is to absorb the heat so that the glass does not break. Then stir gently and add a heaping tablespoon of freshly whipped heavy cream, not one of the dairy creamers or premixed cream from an aerosol can. Serve without stirring.

■
Jack Rose Cocktail   *(Shake/Blend)*
1½ oz. applejack (apple brandy)

2 oz. lemon juice

1 dash grenadine syrup

■
Jelly Bean   *(Shake/Blend)*
1½ oz. anisette

1½ oz. blackberry flavored brandy

■
Kir   *(Stir)*
1 oz. crème de cassis

4–5 oz. dry white wine

There are several variations of this drink: the Kir Royale listed below, the Kir Communiste (cassis and red wine), and the Kir Imperiale (raspberry liquer instead of cassis and champagne).

■
Kir Royale   *(Stir)*
1 oz. crème de cassis

4–5 oz. dry sparkling wine

■
Long Island Ice Tea   *(Shake/Blend/Stir)*
½ oz. gin

½ oz. rum

½ oz. tequila

½ oz. vodka

¼ oz. triple sec

3 oz. lemon juice

Splash of Coke or Pepsi

Put into blender for 30 seconds; then pour over ice, add a splash of Coke or Pepsi, and serve with lemon wedge.

Mai Tai   *(Shake/Blend)*

This world-famous drink (created in the early 1940s) called "Mai Tai" is translated from Polynesian to mean "the best, out of this world."

1¼ oz. light rum
1 oz. dark rum
¾ oz. orgeat syrup
¼ oz. triple sec
1 oz. pineapple juice
½ oz. grenadine syrup
½ oz. lime juice

Manhattan   *(Shake/Stir)*

The former Manhattan Club, a six-story building erected on Madison Avenue in 1859, was originally a residence for Leonard Jerome, the father of Jennie Jerome (1854–1921), a New Yorker (one-sixteenth Iroquois Indian). In 1874, she married Lord Randolph Churchill, and two years later she bore a son, Sir Winston, who would later figure quite heavily in English politics. It was this same Lady Churchill who first persuaded a reluctant bartender there to mix bourbon "with a lesser portion of sweet vermouth—and aromatic bitters" to please a guest of honor. As one of New York's leading socialites, she was giving a party in honor of Samuel J. Tilden's election as a reform governor. She named the drink a "Manhattan" after the club where the celebration was being held—and it is still one of the world's most popular cocktails.

1¼ oz. bourbon or blended whiskey
½ oz. sweet red vermouth
Dash of bitters
Garnish: *Cherry*

■

Margarita   *(Shake/Blend)*

Purportedly concocted by a Virginia City bartender in memory of his girlfriend, who was accidentally shot during a barroom brawl.

1½ oz. tequila

1 oz. triple sec liqueur (minimum 60 proof)

¾ oz. freshly squeezed lemon juice

Coarse salt for the rim of the glass

Lots and lots of shaved ice

■

Martini   *(Shake/Stir)*

"Martinez" was the original name of this popular drink, first introduced in 1860. The original recipe was considerably different from what we know today. It consisted of one jigger of gin; one wine glass of sweet vermouth; a dash of bitters; and two dashes maraschino liqueur. It was then shaken well and garnished with lemon slice.

2 oz. gin or vodka

Dash of white dry vermouth

Garnish: *Lemon peel or green olive*

Use a large stainless steel cocktail shaker. Add plenty of ice cubes, then add the gin or vodka and a dash of vermouth. Now, if you are serving James Bond, shake the ingredients until the shaker becomes coated with ice, or with a long metal stirrer, stir for several minutes. Either strain the martini into a cocktail glass or pour over ice in an old-fashioned glass. Garnish with lemon peel, green olive or pearl cocktail onion. (If a pearl cocktail onion is substituted for the lemon peel or green olive, the drink then becomes a "Gibson.")

Although the ingredients of today's "Silver Bullet" is considerably different from its original, it did consist of a very dry vodka martini served arctic cold.

The martini was really popularized by James Bond movies in which the super spy requested his "vodka martini" be served to him "shaken, not stirred." Before Bond movies became the "in-thing," television viewers might remember Neil, the alcoholic St. Bernard dog in the television show "Topper," starring Leo G. Carroll, during the 1950s and 1960s.

■ Mimosa   *(Stir)*

3 oz. dry sparkling wine
4 oz. orange juice

■ Mint Julep

There are probably as many different recipes for the preparation and serving of mint juleps as there are people who drink them on Kentucky Derby Day. To quote from R. B. Harwell in his 1975 drink book, "The julep is part ceremony, tradition, and regional nostalgia; part flavor, taste, and aroma; and only by definition liquor, simple syrup, mint, and ice."

History and folklore. Kentuckians were awarding silver julep cups at country fairs as long ago as 1816. The word *julep* itself can be traced back more than 600 years and stems from the Arabic *julab* or Persian *jul-ab*, meaning "rose water." The word is cited in English as early as the year 1400 and indicated "a syrup made only of water and sugar." In actuality, the mint and sugar were being blended with spirits before the birth of America. The true "Southern-style" mint julep coincided with the discovery of genuine Kentucky straight bourbon whiskey around the 1880s.

The receptacle, stirring instrument, quality of water and bourbon, method of crushing, bruising or muddling the mint, and the gentility of the hands preparing it, are among the subjects of lengthy advice to those who would create a perfect mint julep. For instance Irvin S. Cobb, Kentucky writer, called for crushing the mint with a wooden pestle and using a pewter tankard. He saluted his creation by proclaiming, "Who has not tasted one, has lived in vain."

Mint juleps and the Kentucky Derby. In 1982, at the Kentucky Derby, 80,000 mint juleps were served. The juleps needed the following ingredients: 150 bushels of fresh mint; 100,000 pounds of shaved ice, and 1,875 gallons of bourbon whiskey!

The mixologist. Following is a free-form combination of prose borrowed from three late but notable julep authorities: Henry Clay, famous

Kentucky politician; Judge Soule Smith, a Lexington attorney; and General Simon Bolivar Buckner, grandson of the great Confederate general.

A mint julep is not the product of a formula—it is ceremony and must be performed by a gentleman possessing a true sense of the artist, a deep reverence for the ingredients and a proper appreciation of the occasion. It is a rite that must not be entrusted to a novice, a statistician, nor a Yankee. It is a heritage of the Old South, an emblem of hospitality and a vehicle in which noble minds can travel together upon the flower strewn paths of a happy and congenial thought.

The ingredients.

Water. Limestone water, preferably hand-drawn from a spring where cool, crystal-clear water bubbles from under a bank of dew-washed ferns. In a consecrated vessel, dip up a little water at the source.

Spirits. Kentucky Bourbon distilled by a master hand, mellowed with age in oaken barrels yet still vigorous and inspiring.

Mint. Mint leaves, fresh and tender. Follow a stream through its banks of green moss and wild flowers until it broadens and trickles through beds of mint growing in aromatic profusion and waving softly in the wind. Gather the sweetest and tenderest shoots and gently carry them home.

Simple syrup. Take from the cold spring some water, pure as angels are; mix it with sugar from an ancestral bowl to make a silvery mixture as smooth as some rare Egyptian oil.

Ice. Into a canvas bag, pound twice as much ice as you think you will need. Make it fine as snow, keep it dry, and do not allow it to degenerate into slush. Gather together your finest silver cups and spoons, and you are ready to begin.

Combining. Take your glass and crush your mint within it, pressing the fresh mint against the goblet with the back of a silver spoon. Crush it around the borders of the glass and leave no place untouched. Then throw the mint away—it is a sacrifice. Fill the glass with cracked ice; pour in the quantity of bourbon which you want. It trickles slowly through the ice. Let it cool for a moment, then pour your sugared water over it. Let the cup stand until nature, wishing to take a further hand and add another of its beautiful phenomena, encrusts the whole in a glistening coat of white frost. Around the rim, place sprigs of mint so that the one who drinks may find a taste and odor at one draught.

Fulfillment. When all is ready, assemble your guests on the porch or in the garden where the aroma of the juleps will rise heavenward and make the birds sing. Propose a worthy toast, raise the goblet to your lips, bury your nose in the mint, inhale a deep breath of its fragrance, and sip the nectar of the gods. Sip it and dream.

Colonel Henry Watterson, for 50 years editor of the *Louisville Courier-Journal* had still another method of making mint juleps:

"Take a silver goblet, that holds one pint—and dissolve a lump of loaf sugar with not more than a tablespoon of water. Take one mint leaf, no more, and crush it gently between the thumb and forefinger before dropping it into the dissolved sugar. Then fill the goblet nearly full to the brim with shaved ice. Take a few sprigs of mint leaves and use for decorating the top of the mixture, after it has been frapped with a spoon. In a second silver goblet—pour in all the bourbon whiskey the goblet will hold. Drink the whiskey and throw away the other ingredients."

Making the mint julep. One of the unfortunate realities of mint juleps is no matter how hard you try, you really can't make a mint julep that tastes authentic, unless it is made in Kentucky. Kentucky is where the ingredients either grow naturally or are produced locally. One of the most important ingredients is delicately scented spearmint leaves (not the peppermint that grows like weeds in home gardens).

For individual mint juleps. Place 1 teaspoon of superfine sugar into a shallow dish and add three to four sprigs of mint, barely covering this with about ½ teaspoon cool water. Lightly bruise the mint leaves and rub them around the rim of a julep glass and discard. Fill the cup three-quarters full of crushed ice and add 3 to 4 ounces of bourbon. Then add the bruised mint, sugar and water mixture, and stir gently. On top of this, gently place several sprigs of mint, dusted with powdered sugar. Wait about 30 seconds and all at once the cup or glass will become encrusted with a layer of white frost. Gently sip and enjoy.

For larger batches, you should mull or crush 5 to 6 mint leaves in a glass bowl with the aid of a silver spoon until some of the juice is extracted. Then rub the leaves on the inside of the silver mint julep cup or glass before discarding. Add to the mint juice about 5 to 6 tablespoons of superfine sugar and just enough cool water to mix them thoroughly into a sort of slurry, which is known as a simple sugar or syrup. Then place them in the refrigerator. Fill the julep cup or glass with plenty of shaved or crushed ice. Add 1 to 2 tablespoons of the simple sugar mixture (according to the desired sweetness) to each cup or glass, then add 2 jiggers (3 to 4 ounces) bourbon. Stir well and wait for the cup or glass to become frosted. Then place several fresh sprigs of mint around the rim of the cup or glass, dusted lightly with powdered sugar so that one who drinks may find taste and odor at one draft. Place plastic straws into the cup so that they extend about 2 inches above the mint. You might have to cut them slightly to fit the size of the glass.

■
Mint Julep—Party Batches

58 full fresh mint leaves

1 cup of sugar

½ cup of hot water

48 jiggers (about 80 ounces) of bourbon

Plenty of shaved or crushed ice

In a separate bowl, muddle (bruise with forceful strokes) the mint with the sugar and hot water to make a mint syrup. Then strain mixture and refrigerate overnight. Fill 24 julep cups three-quarters full of shaved ice. Add 2 jiggers of bourbon and 1 teaspoon mint syrup per drink. Stir each drink gently and add additional ice to fill cups. Then garnish with mint sprigs.

Serves: *24 thirsty people.*

■
Negroni   *(Shake/Stir)*

1½ oz. Campari

1 oz. gin

1 oz. sweet vermouth

Splash of seltzer and twist of lemon (optional)

■
Old-Fashioned   *(Shake/Blend)*

1¼ oz. bourbon whiskey

2 dashes bitters

Splash of water

Simple sugar

■

Orgasm   *(Shake/Blend)*

1½ oz. Bailey's Irish Cream
1½ oz. Kahlua
Splash of cream

■

Piña Colada   *(Shake/Blend)*

1¼ oz. light rum
3 oz. pineapple juice
2 oz. coconut milk

Garnish: *Cherry, pineapple wedge, and lime*

■

Pink Squirrel   *(Shake/Blend)*

1½ oz. light cream
½ oz. white crème de cacao
½ oz. crème de almond or crème de noyaux

■

Planter's Punch   *(Shake/Blend)*

1 oz. light rum
2 oz. pineapple juice
1 oz. orange juice
1 oz. lemon or lime juice
¼ oz. grenadine syrup
Orange slice

Float ½ oz. Myers's Rum on top.

■

Presbyterian   *(Stir)*

1¼ oz. blended whiskey
Seltzer water
Ginger ale

After adding whiskey, fill remainder of glass half with seltzer water and half with ginger ale.

■
Ramos Gin Fizz   *(Shake/Blend)*

Supposedly named for Henry C. Ramos, who concocted it about 100 years ago at his famous Imperial Cabinet Bar and Saloon in New Orleans.

1¼ oz. gin
½ oz. lemon juice .
½ oz. lime juice
1 tsp. sugar
1 egg white
1 oz. cream
Soda water to fill

Blend or shake all ingredients, then top with soda water.

■
Rob Roy   *(Shake/Stir)*

Supposedly named after Rob Roy (Robert MacGregor), a famous Highland outlaw in Scotland.

1½ oz. Scotch whisky
¾ oz. sweet red vermouth
Dash of orange bitters

For a dry Rob Roy, substitute dry white vermouth.

■
Rum & Coca-Cola   *(Stir)*

The Andrews Sisters, a world-famous female singing group, made the song "Rum & Coca-Cola" famous.

1½ oz. rum
Coca-Cola

After adding rum, fill remainder of glass with Coca-Cola or other cola-based mixes.

Garnish: *Twist of lime or lemon*

Rusty Nail   *(Shake/Stir)*

¾ oz. Scotch whisky
½ oz. drambuie liqueur

Salty Dog   *(Shake/Blend)*

1½ oz. gin
4 oz. grapefruit juice
Salt for rim of glass

Screwdriver/Orange Blossom   *(Shake/Stir)*

This very popular drink was supposedly created by oilmen or oil riggers, who would use their tools to stir it.

1¼ oz. vodka (screwdriver)
or
1¼ oz. gin (orange blossom)
Orange juice to fill

Scotch and Soda   *(Stir)*

The Kingston Trio, world-famous singing group from the 1950s, recorded a song entitled, "Scotch N Soda."

1½ oz. Scotch whisky
Seltzer water to fill

Screaming Orgasm   *(Shake/Blend)*

1½ oz. Bailey's Irish Cream
1½ oz. Kahlua liqueur
1½ oz. vodka
Splash of cream

■

Seven & Seven   *(Stir)*

1½ oz. Seagram's 7 Crown whiskey

7-Up

■

Shooter

A straight shot of a liqueur called "peppermint schnapps."

■

Sidecar   *(Shake/Blend)*

¾ oz. brandy

½ oz. triple sec

½ oz. lemon juice

■

Singapore Gin Sling   *(Shake/Blend)*

This drink, originally called a "Straits Sling," was created in 1915 by Ngiam Tong Boon, a bartender of the Long Bar at the Raffles Hotel in Singapore.

1½ oz. gin

¾ oz. cherry-flavored brandy

1 oz. consisting of lemon and orange juice

Top with a squirt of seltzer

Garnish: Cherry, orange slice or sprig of mint

Pimm's Cup, a "gin sling" flavored with various herbs, spices, and sweeteners, was invented in 1841 by James Pimm, in London. Years back, Pimm's Cup was produced in six different versions, each with a different base ingredient, and identified by a number on the label. For instance: Pimm's Cup #1, #2, #3, #4, #5, #6. But because the gin version (number 1) comprised 99 percent of total sales, the other variations were dropped, along with the "No. 1" on the label.

■

Slippery Nipple   *(Shake/Blend)*

1½ oz. sambuca

1½ oz. Bailey's Irish Cream

■

Sloe Gin Fizz   *(Stir)*

1½ oz. sloe gin

¾ oz. lemon juice

1 tsp. sugar

Top with seltzer

■

Sloe and Comfortable Screw   *(Shake/Blend)*

1½ oz. vodka

1½ oz. Southern Comfort

¾ oz. sloe gin

Orange juice to fill

■

Sour   *(Shake/Blend)*

1¼ oz. bourbon, blended whiskey, or Scotch whisky

¾ oz. lemon juice

1 tsp. sugar

Garnish: *Cherry, orange slice*

Note: Instead of using whiskey, basically any other distilled spirit, along with liqueurs and fruit-flavored brandies may also be used.

■

Stinger   *(Shake/Blend)*

1¾ oz. brandy

¾ oz. white crème de menthe

■

Swampwater   *(Shake/Stir)*

1½ oz. green Chartreuse

Juice of ½ lime

6 oz. pineapple juice

Must be drunk from a mason jar.

■

Tequila

When drinking tequila straight, first wet the fleshy area between your thumb and index finger, sprinkle salt on the wet spot, and then "lick" the salt with your tongue. Immediately follow with a straight shot of tequila, downed in one gulp. Then put a lemon wedge into your mouth and suck deeply. This ritual is known in Mexico as *Los Tres Cuates*—"The Three Chums."

■

Tequila Sunrise *(Shake/Stir)*

1½ oz. tequila

6 oz. orange juice

Float ¼ oz. grenadine syrup on top

■

Tom and Jerry *(Shake/Blend)*

The "Tom and Jerry" was created from Edan's *Life in London*, also known as *Days and Nights of Jerry Hawthorne and his Elegant Friend, Corinthian Tom*, in 1928.

1 egg yolk beaten

1 egg white beaten

1 tsp. sugar

¼ tsp. allspice

1 oz. white rum

Milk

Dusting of nutmeg

Beat egg white until fluffy. Then beat egg yolk with sugar, allspice, and rum until smooth and thick. Add egg white and pour into heated mug. Fill with hot milk and dust with nutmeg.

■

White Russian *(Shake/Blend)*

¾ oz. vodka

½ oz. Kahlua

1 oz. cream

■

Zombie *(Shake/Blend)*

Another Don-the-Beachcomber drink which featured perhaps every type of rum he had on hand at his bar. This drink boasted a challenge that many simply could not pass up, "only one to a customer."

1 oz. light rum
1 oz. dark rum
¾ oz. gold rum
¾ oz. pineapple juice
¾ oz. papaya juice
¾ oz. lime juice
2 tsp. Falernum or simple sugar
½ oz. apricot-flavored brandy
½ oz. orange curacao or passion fruit syrup
½ oz. 151 proof Demeraran Rum

Shake all ingredients with cracked ice and either strain into a cocktail glass or pour over ice in an old-fashioned glass. Float 151-proof rum on top.

Garnish: *Orange wheels and several sprigs of mint*

World Drink Records

The world's record for the largest "drink" (liquor) is called a Golden Spiral Cocktail and is made by combining 480 pineapples, 300 coconuts, and 109 gallons of orange juice. Then stir in 14,000 ounces of Piña Colada mix, 12 bottles of Galliano, and 20 bottles of Jim Beam bourbon; top with 2½ tons of cracked ice. The end result—the largest mixed drink ever! The container for mixing is 11 feet tall, and 5 feet in diameter, with a capacity of 1500 gallons. (Record set in early 1982).

In 1985, at the Hyatt Regency/Chicago, the world's largest Bloody Mary—1200 gallons of Mr. & Mrs. "T" Bloody Mary mix was mixed with Smirnoff vodka.

The world's record for the "biggest round of drinks" ever bought by an individual was 5095 "C. C. Waterbacks" (Canadian Club whisky with a water chaser). They were for the patrons of Billy Bob's Texas, in Ft. Worth, which considers itself the largest honky tonk in the world. The purchaser of all the drinks (in 1974) is a world-famous country and western singer Merle Haggard, who also recorded the song "C. C. Waterbacks."

Suggested Readings

Braun, Lionel and Marion Gorman. *The Drink Directory*. New York: Bobbs-Merrill, 1982.

Duffy, Patrick Gavin. *The Official Mixers Manual for Home and Professional Use*. New York: Doubleday, 7th ed., 1983.

Mr. Boston Official Bartender's Guide. New York: Warner Books, 49th ed., 1984.

Index

531